# Amiga System
# Programmer's G

**Dittrich**
**Gelfand**
**Schemmel**

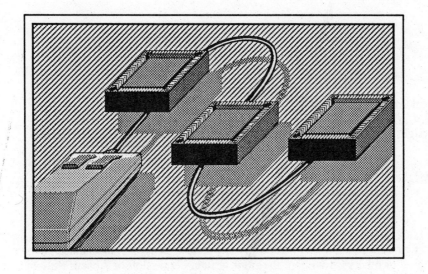

## Abacus
### A Data Becker Book

# Contents

# 1
# The Amiga
# Hardware

# 1.1     Introduction

The Commodore Amiga offers the user capabilities at a price which one would never have dreamed of a few years ago. To make these features possible, a powerful operating system and hardware work closely together.

A high level of user friendliness was one of the main goals the developers of this computer had. The intent was to use the mouse and the Workbench as a graphic user interface to make it easy to use the computer. But not only did they want to make it easy to use, they wanted to provide good support for programmers as well. For almost any conceivable task there is a routine in the operating system which makes direct programming of the hardware unnecessary.

But in spite of all of these system routines, for maximum speed you can't avoid direct machine language programming. The speed of the operating system routines are much slower than you would expect from a computer as advanced as the Amiga. The reason for this is that large parts of the Amiga's operating system were written in the C programming language. The C language produces portable, readable and quick running code, but programs developed in C are not as compact, efficient or as fast as programs developed completely in machine language.

If you want to write fast and efficient programs, or if you just want to learn more about your Amiga, you have to work directly with the hardware. The following chapter offers a description of the Amiga hardware and the programming of the individual components.

# 1.2    Amiga system components

Essentially the Amiga hardware consists of the following components, regardless of whether the system is an Amiga 500, 1000 or 2000:

- The Motorola MC68000 microprocessor
- Two serial interfaces, type 8250
- Three custom chips from Commodore, called Agnus, Denise and Paula

If you ignore the RAM and logic components for a moment, the six chips listed above are responsible for all the functions of the Amiga.

*Interfaces*       All of the necessary interfaces are also available on the Amiga:

- Parallel printer port
- Serial RS-232 interface
- RGB monitor connection
- Composite video connection (not on early Amiga 2000s)
- Stereo audio output
- Connector for an RF modulator (Amiga 1000 only)
- Keyboard
- Connector for an external disk drive (Shugart-bus compatible)
- Two identical connectors for various input devices like a mouse, joystick or paddle
- Connector for 256K RAM expansion (Amiga 1000 — This will not be discussed in this book because only the original expansion from 256K to 512K bytes can be connected here. On the Amiga 500 and 2000 these 256K bytes are already built in. The Amiga 500 has a connection for a 512K RAM expansion, but it's completely different from this connector)
- Expansion port to connect system expansions of all types (on the Amiga 500 and 1000 this connection is on the side of the case, while on the Amiga 2000 it is in the form of multiple card connector inside the housing)

In order to understand how all of these components work together, we must first explain the function of the individual chips.

## 1.2.1        The 68000 processor

The 68000 from Motorola is unquestionably one of the most powerful
16-bit processors available. Although it has been on the market since
1979, it has only recently found its way into computers in the price
range of the Amiga.

Naturally, we can't give you a detailed description of the 68000 here,
since this is beyond the scope of this book. Those who want to know
more about programming the 68000 should seek out the appropriate
technical literature. Mentioned is the pin layout and a brief description
of the individual signal groups, since many books about programming
the 68000 offer a good instruction to the software side, but have little
to say about the hardware. A basic knowledge of the signals available
from the 68000 is essential to understanding the Amiga hardware.

*Figure  1.2.1.1*

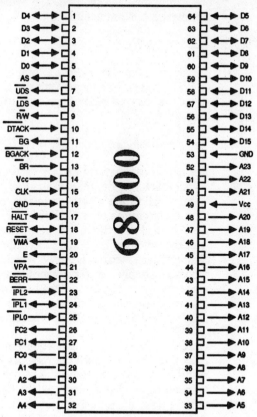

NOTE: The arrows indicate the direction of the signal. A line above a
signal name means that the signal is active when low (0=active).

The connections can be divided into the following function groups:

*Power supply: Vcc and GND*

The 68000 works with a simple power supply of 5 volts. There are two connections each for power (Vcc) and ground (GND) and are centrally located in order to keep voltage loss in the housing to a minimum.

*The clock input: CLK*

The 68000 needs only one clock. The frequency depends on the version of the processor. The clock frequency of the Amiga's processor is 7.16 MHz.

*The data bus: D0-D15*

The data bus is set up as a 16-bit bus and can therefore transfer one word (16 bits) at a time. When transferring a single byte (8 bits), only one half of the lines are used. The byte is read or written through either the lower 8 bits or the upper 8 bits.

*The address bus: A1-A23*

The address bus can address a total of 8 megawords with its 23 lines ($2^{23}$ corresponds to 8 megawords or 16 megabytes). The UDS and LDS signals (explained below) are used to make up for the lack of an A0 line.

*Bus control lines in the asynchronous mode: AS, R/W, UDS, LDS, DTACK*

The 68000 can perform memory access in two different modes. In the asynchronous mode, the processor signals with AS (Address Strobe/ address valid) that a valid address is on the address bus. At the same time it determines with the R/W line (Read/Write) whether a byte or word is read or written. The selection between byte or word is made with the two lines UDS and LDS (Upper Data Strobe and Lower Data Strobe). Since memory is always word-addressed by the address bus, the processor simply transfers either the upper half or lower half of a word when doing a byte access. This is signaled through UDS and LDS. For a word access, the 68000 sets both lines. To access a byte, it sets only one line or the other to 9 (the other line stays at 1).

Once the processor has signaled its request with the AS, R/W, UDS and LDS lines, it waits until the memory tells it that the desired data are ready. The DTACK line is used for this, which is set to 0 by the responding device as soon as the data is ready. If the processor is writing data, the recipient uses the DTACK line to tell the processor that it has received the data.

Thus in asychronous mode, the processor always adapts itself to the speed of memory.

The individual words and bytes lie in memory as follows:

|          |        | Data bus lines used | |
|          |        | D8-15   | D0-7    |
| Address: |        | UDS=0   | LDS =0  |
|----------|--------|---------|---------|
| 0        | Word 0 | Byte 0  | Byte 1  |
| 2        | Word 1 | Byte 2  | Byte 3  |
| 4        | Word 2 | Byte 4  | Byte 5  |
| 6        | Word 3 | Byte 6  | Byte 7  |
| ...      | ...    | ...     | ...     |

*Bus control signals in the synchronous mode: E, VPA, VMA*

To make better sense of these signals, you have to understand the technological situation when the 68000 was introduced onto the market. At the time there were no peripheral chips available specifically for the 68000. The chips available from Motorola for the 68000 series (a precursor of the 6502) could not be used with the asynchronous bus control without additional hardware. Thus the 68000 was given a synchronous bus mode, such as that found on eight-bit processors like the 6800 or 6502.

The E line constantly outputs a clock which is a factor of ten less in frequency than the processor clock, or 716KHz on the Amiga, which is used as the clock for the peripheral chips. The switch from asynchronous to synchronous mode is made with the input VPA (Valid Peripheral Address). This input must be set to 0 by an external address decoder as soon as the address of a peripheral chip is recognized. The processor answers this by bringing the VMA line (Valid Memory Address) to 0. The appropriate peripheral chip must then receive or prepare the data within one clock cycle of E. After that the 68000 automatically leaves the synchronous mode until the next VPA signal occurs.

*The system control signals: RESET, HALT, BERR*

The most important task of a reset signal is to reset the system so that all system components are placed in some known initial state and program execution can begin at a set address.

To generate such a system reset on the 68000, both the HALT and RESET lines must be set to 0. As soon as these lines go to 1 again, the 68000 starts execution at the address found in location 4.

The RESET line can also be pulled to 0 by the 68000 in order to initialize the system without changing the processor state.

With the BERR (Bus ERRor) line an external circuit can inform the processor that something is not in order. A reason for a bus error can be a hardware error or an attempt to access something at a nonexistent address.

When a BERR signal occurs, the 68000 jumps to a special operating system routine which then handles the error (e.g., Guru Meditation?). If another bus error occurs during this error handling routine, the 68000 stops all processing and sets HALT low. This double bus error is, by the way, the only situation in which the 68000 actually crashes and refuses to execute anything. For all other errors it jumps through special vectors to program routines which can then handle the error and allow the system to continue operating. The Amiga's error handling is not as friendly as it could be! (On the early Amiga's the frequency of Guru Meditations, kept the Amiga true to Murphy's Law: A computer always crashes whenever it is processing important data which has not been saved yet).

Once the processor halts as a result of a double bus error, it can only be restarted with a reset (HALT and RESET low).

Another function of the HALT line is to temporarily stop the processor. If you bring HALT low, the 68000 finishes the current memory access and waits until HALT goes high again.

There are other details concerning the interplay of BERR and HALT, but they do not concern the operation of the Amiga.

*The operating state of the processor: FC0, FC1, FC2*

The lines FC0-FC2 signal the operating state of the processor. The following states are possible:

| FC2 | FC1 | FC0 | State |
|-----|-----|-----|-------|
| 0 | 0 | 1 | Accessing user data |
| 0 | 1 | 0 | Accessing user program |
| 1 | 0 | 1 | Accessing supervisor data |
| 1 | 1 | 0 | Accessing supervisor program |
| 1 | 1 | 1 | Signals a valid interrupt |

The processor can be run in two different modes: the user mode and the supervisor mode. A program which runs in supervisor mode has unrestricted access to all processor registers. The operating system, for example, always runs in supervisor mode.

In the user mode, certain processor registers cannot be used. More about this can be found in 68000 literature.

The three FCx lines allow system hardware to recognize the current state of the processor and react to it. For example, access to the operating system while in user mode can be made to cause a bus error (BERR=0).

*The interrupt inputs: IPL0, IPL1, IPL2*

The signals at the three interrupt inputs (IPL=Interrupt Pending Level) are interpreted by the 68000 as a 3-bit binary number. The 68000 can therefore distinguish different interrupt signals, called interrupt levels, whereby 0 means that no interrupt is present, while 7 signals an interrupt of the highest priority. Each of the seven interrupt levels has its own interrupt vector which contains the address of the routine executed when that interrupt occurs.

If an interrupt of the corresponding level is allowed, the processor places a 1 on all FCx lines, signaling that it recognizes the interrupt and that it is waiting for confirmation on the side of the interrupt. This can be done with either VPA or DTACK. If the interrupt is confirmed with VPA, an autovector interrupt is performed. The processor branches to the address it finds in the vector assigned to the given interrupt level. This means that it can jump to seven different addresses (level 0 indicates that no interrupt is present).

If there are only seven interrupt sources in the system, then the software doesn't have to try to figure out which device caused a given interrupt. You simply assign an interrupt level to each interrupt source and the processor jumps to the appropriate routine. The Amiga only uses these autovector interrupts.

More options for hardware recognition of various interrupt sources are offered by the class of non-autovector interrupts. Since these are not used in the Amiga, we will not discuss them any further here. We'll only say that for non-autovector interrupts the interrupt is confirmed with DTACK and the component which generated the interrupt can place an interrupt vector on the data bus which then selects from up to 192 different interrupt vectors.

*Bus control signals: BR, BG, BGACK*

These three signals allow another chip to take control of the bus. This might be the case for a hard disk controller, for example, which then writes the data from the hard disk directly into memory (called DMA = Direct Memory Access).

These three signals are also unused in the Amiga, since DMA is realized in a different manner. This is explained at the end of this chapter.

## 1.2.2     The 8520 CIA

*Figure 1.2.2.1*

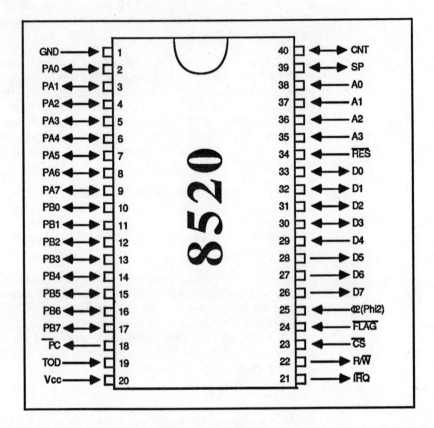

NOTE: The arrows indicate the direction of the signal. A line above a signal name means that the signal is active when low (0=active).

*Figure   1.2.2.2*

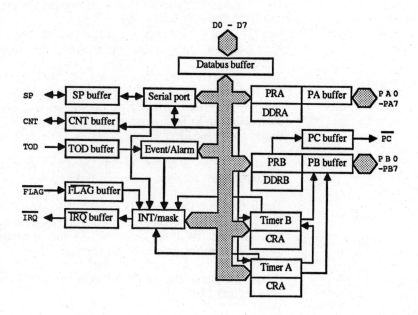

**8520 - block diagram**

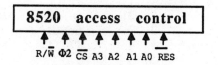

**8520   access   control**

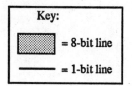

Key:

= 8-bit line

— = 1-bit line

*The 8520*

The 8520 is a peripheral of the Complex Interface Adapter (CIA) class, which basically means that the developers of the 8520 tried to put as many functions into one chip as possible. If you look at the 8520 more closely, you'll see that it bears a strong resemblance to the 6526 used in the C64. Only the operation of registers 8 to 11 ($8 to $B) is somewhat changed. This should be good news for those who have programmed a 6526 before.

The 8520 has the following features: two programmable 8-bit parallel ports (PA and PB), two 16-bit timers (A and B), a bidirectional serial port (SP) and a 24-bit counter (event counter) with an alarm function upon reaching a programmed value. All of the functions can generate interrupts.

The functions of the 8520 are organized in 16 registers. To the processor they look like ordinary memory locations, since all peripheral components in a 68000 system are memory mapped. The registers of a chip are accessed like memory locations.

Since the 8520 was originally developed for use with 8-bit processors, the 68000 must access it in the synchronous mode (see Section 1.2.1).

The E clock on the 68000 is connected to the φ2 input of the 8520. The 16 internal registers are selected with the four address inputs A0-A3. More details about how the CIA are integrated in the Amiga system are given at the end of this chapter.

Here is an explanation of the 16 registers (actually only 15 registers, since register 11 ($B) is unused):

*8520 registers*

| Register | | Name | Function |
|---|---|---|---|
| 0 | 0 | PRA | Port A data register |
| 1 | 1 | PRB | Port B data register |
| 2 | 2 | DDRA | Port A data direction register |
| 3 | 3 | DDRB | Port B data direction register |
| 4 | 4 | TALO | Timer A lower 8 bits |
| 5 | 5 | TAHI | Timer A upper 8 bits |
| 6 | 6 | TBLO | Timer B lower 8 bits |
| 7 | 7 | TBHI | Timer B upper 8 bits |
| 8 | 8 | Event low | Counter bits 0-7 |
| 9 | 9 | Event med. | Counter bits 8-15 |
| 10 | A | Event high | Counter bits 16-23 |
| 11 | B | — | Unused |
| 12 | C | SP | Serial port data register |
| 13 | D | ICR | Interrupt control register |
| 14 | E | CRA | Control register A |
| 15 | F | CRB | Control register B |

*The parallel*
*ports*

| Reg. | Name | D7 | D6 | D5 | D4 | D3 | D2 | D1 | D0 |
|------|------|-----|-----|-----|-----|-----|-----|-----|-----|
| 0 | PRA | PA7 | PA6 | PA5 | PA4 | PA3 | PA2 | PA1 | PA0 |
| 1 | PRB | PB7 | PB6 | PB5 | PB4 | PB3 | PB2 | PB1 | PB0 |
| 2 | DDRA | DPA7 | DPA6 | DPA5 | DPA4 | DPA3 | DPA2 | DPA1 | DPA0 |
| 3 | DDRB | DPB7 | DPB6 | DPB5 | DPB4 | DPB3 | DPB2 | DPB1 | DPB0 |

The 8520 has two 8-bit parallel ports, PA and PB, each of which is assigned a data register, PRA (Port Register A) and PRB (Port Register B). The chip has 16 port lines, PA0-PA7 and PB0-PB7. Each port line can be used as either an input or an output. The input or output of a port line is called the data direction. The 8520 allows the data direction of each line to be controlled individually. Each port has data direction registers, DDRA and DDRB. If a bit in the data direction register is 0, the corresponding line is an input. The state of the port lines can be determined by reading the appropriate bits of the data direction register.

If a bit in the DDR is set to 1, then the corresponding port line becomes an output. The signal on the port line then corresponds directly to the value of the corresponding bit in the data register for that port.

In general, writing to a data register always stores the value in it, while reading always returns the states of the port lines. The bits in the data direction register determines whether the value of the data register is placed on the port lines. Therefore when reading the port which is configured as an output, the contents of the data register are returned, while when writing to an input port, the value is stored in the data register, but doesn't appear on the port lines until the port is configured as output.

To simplify the data transfer through the parallel ports, the 8520 has two handshake lines, PC and FLAG.

The PC output goes low for one clock period on each access to data register B (PRB, reg. 1). The FLAG input responds to such downward transitions. Every time the state of the FLAG line changes from 1 to 0, the FLAG bit is set in the interrupt control register (ICR, reg. $D). These two lines allow a simple form of handshaking in which the FLAG and PC lines of two CIAs are cross-connected.

The sender need only write its data to the port register and then wait for a FLAG signal before sending each additional byte. Since FLAG can generate an interrupt, the sender can even perform other tasks while it is waiting. The same applies to the receiver, except that it reads the data from the port instead of writing it.

*The timers:*

*Read access*

| Reg. | Name | D7 | D6 | D5 | D4 | D3 | D2 | D1 | D0 |
|------|------|-----|-----|-----|-----|-----|-----|-----|-----|
| 0 | TALO | TAL7 | TAL6 | TAL5 | TAL4 | TAL3 | TAL2 | TAL1 | TAL0 |
| 1 | TAHI | TAH7 | TAH6 | TAH5 | TAH4 | TAH3 | TAH2 | TAH1 | TAH0 |
| 2 | TBLO | TBL7 | TBL6 | TBL5 | TBL4 | TBL3 | TBL2 | TBL1 | TBL0 |
| 3 | TBHI | TBH7 | TBH6 | TBH5 | TBH4 | TBH3 | TBH2 | TBH1 | TBH0 |

*Write access*

| Reg. Name | D7 | D6 | D5 | D4 | D3 | D2 | D1 | D0 |
|-----------|-----|-----|-----|-----|-----|-----|-----|-----|
| 0   PALO  | PAL7 | PAL6 | PAL5 | PAL4 | PAL3 | PAL2 | PAL1 | PAL0 |
| 1   PAHI  | PAH7 | PAH6 | PAH5 | PAH4 | PAH3 | PAH2 | PAH1 | PAH0 |
| 2   PBLO  | PBL7 | PBL6 | PBL5 | PBL4 | PBL3 | PBL2 | BL1 | PBIO |
| 3   PBHI  | PBH7 | PBH6 | PBH5 | PBH4 | PBH3 | PBH2 | PBH1 | PBH0 |

The 8520 has two 16-bit timers. These timers can count from a preset value down to zero. A number of modes are possible and can be selected through a control register, one for each timer.

Each timer consists internally of four registers (timer A: TALO+TAHI and PALO+ PAHI), or two register pairs, since each low and high register pair forms the 16-bit timer value. On each write access to one of the timer registers the value is stored in a latch. This value is loaded into the count register and decremented until the timer reaches zero. Then the value is loaded from the latch back into the timer register.

When a timer register is read, it returns the current state of the timer. To get a correct value, the timer must be stopped. The following example shows why:

- Timer state: $0100. A read access to register 5 returns the high byte of the current state: $01

- Before the low byte (reg. 4) can be read, the timer is decremented again and the timer count is now at $00FF.

- The low byte is read: $FF.

- Resulting timer state: $01FF.

Instead of stopping the timer, which also causes problems since timer pulses are ignored, a more elegant method can be used: Read the high byte, then the low byte and then the high byte again. If the two high byte values match, then the value read is correct. If not, the procedure must be repeated.

Bits 5 and 6 of the control register determine what signals decrement the timers.

*Timer A*

Only two sources are possible for timer A:

1. Timer A is decremented each clock cycle (since the CIAs in the Amiga are connected to the E clock of the processor, the count frequency is 716KHz). (INMODE=0)

2. Each high pulse on the CNT line decrements the timer. (INMODE=1)

*Timer B*

Timer B has four input modes:

1.    Clock cycles (INMODE bits = 00 (binary—the first digit stands for bit 6, the second for bit 5).

2.    CNT pulses (INMODE bits = 01)

3.    Timer A timeouts (allows two timers to form a 32-bit timer). (INMODE bits = 10)

4.    Timer A timeouts when the CNT line is high (allows the length of a pulse on the CNT line to be measured). (INMODE bits =11)

The timeouts of a timer are registered in the Interrupt Control Register (ICR). When timer A timeouts, the TA bit (no. 0) is set, while when timer B timeouts the TB bit is set (no. 1). These bits, like all of the bits in the ICR, remain set until the ICR is read. In addition, it is also possible to output the timeouts to parallel port B. If the PBon bit is set in the control register for the given timer (CRA or CRB), then each timeout appears on the appropriate port line (PB6 for timer A and PB7 for timer B).

Two output modes can be selected with the OUTMODE bit:

OUTMODE = 0  Pulse mode     Each timeout appears as a positive pulse one clock period long on the corresponding port line.

OUTMODE = 1  Toggle mode    Each timeout causes the corresponding port line to change value from high to low or low to high. Each time the timer is started the output starts at high.

The timers are started and stopped with the START bit in the control registers. START = 0 stops the timer, START = 1 starts it.

The RUNMODE bit selects between the one-shot mode and the continuous mode. In the one-shot mode the timer stops after each timeout and sets the START bit back to 0. In the continuous mode the timer restarts after each timeout.

As mentioned before, writing to a timer register doesn't write the value directly to the count register, but to a latch (also called the prescaler, since the number of timeouts per second is equal to the clock frequency divided by the value in the prescaler).

There are several ways to transfer the value from the latch to the timer:

1. Set the LOAD bit in the control register. This causes a forced load, that is, the value in the latch is transferred to the timer registers regardless of the timer state. The LOAD bit is called a strobe bit, which means that it causes a one-time operation instead of the value being stored. To cause another forced load, a 1 must be written in the LOAD bit.

2. Each time the timer runs out, the latch is automatically transferred to the counter.

3. After a write access to the timer high register, the timer is stopped (stop = 0), it is automatically loaded with the value in the latch. Therefore the low byte of the timer should always be initialized first.

Assignment of the bits in control register A:

*Register No. 14 / $E Name: CRA*

| D7 | D6 | D5 | D4 | D3 | D2 | D1 | D0 |
|---|---|---|---|---|---|---|---|
| not used | SPMOD | INMODE | LOAD | RUNMODE | OUTMODE | PBon | START |
| | 0=input | 0=clock | 1=force | 0=cont. | 0=pulse | 0=PB6off | 0=off |
| | 1=output | 1=CNT | load | 1=one- | 1=toggle | 1=PB6on | 1=on |
| | | | (strobe) | shot | | | |

Assignment of the bits in control register B:

*Register No. 15 / $F Name: CRB*

| D7 | D6+D5 | D4 | D3 | D2 | D1 | D0 |
|---|---|---|---|---|---|---|
| ALARM | INMODE | LOAD | RUNMODE | OUTMODE | PBon | START |
| 0=TOD | 00=clock | 1=force | 0=cont. | 0=pulse | 0=PB7off | 0=off |
| 1=Alarm | 01=CNT | load | 1=one- | 1=toggle | 1=PB7on | 1=on |
| | | | (strobe) | shot | | |
| | 10=timer A | | | | | |
| | 11=timer A+ | | | | | |
| | CNT | | | | | |

*The event counter*

| Reg. | Name | D7 | D6 | D5 | D4 | D3 | D2 | D1 | D0 |
|---|---|---|---|---|---|---|---|---|---|
| 8 $8 | LSB event | E7 | E6 | E5 | E4 | E3 | E2 | E1 | E0 |
| 9 $9 | Event 8-15 | E15 | E14 | E13 | E12 | E11 | E10 | E9 | E8 |
| 10 $A | MSB event | E23 | E22 | E21 | E20 | E19 | E18 | E17 | E16 |

As mentioned before, there are only minor differences between the 8250 and 6526. All of these differences concern the function of registers 8-11. The 6526 has a real-time clock which returns the time of day in hours, minutes, and seconds in the individual registers. On the 8250 this clock is replaced by a simple 24-bit counter, called an event counter. This can lead to some confusion, because Commodore often uses the old designation TOD (Time-Of-Day) in their literature when referring to the 8250.

The operation of the event counter is simple. It is a 24-bit counter, meaning that it can count from 0 to 16777215 ($FFFFFF). With each rising edge (transition from low to high) on the TOD line, the counter value is incremented by one. When the counter has reached $FFFFFF, it starts over at 0 on the next count pulse. The counter can be set to a defined state by writing the desired value into the counter register. Register 8 contains bits 0-7 of the counter, the least significant byte (LSB), in register 9 are bits 8-16, and in register 10 are bits 16-23, the Most-Significant Byte (MSB) of the counter value.

The counter stops on each write access so that no errors result from a sudden carry from one register to another. The counter starts running again when a value is written into the LSB (reg. 8). Normally the counter is written in the order: register 10 (MSB), then register 9, and finally register 8 (MSB).

To prevent carry errors when the counter is read, the counter value is written into a latch when the MSB (reg. 10) is read. Each additional access to a count register now returns the value of the latch, which can be read in peace while the counter continues to run internally. The latch is turned off again when the LSB is read. The counter should be read in the same order as it is written (see previous paragraph).

An alarm function is also built into the event counter. If the alarm bit (bit 7) is set to 1 in control register B, an alarm value can be set by writing registers 8-10. As soon as the value of the counter matches this alarm value, the alarm bit in the interrupt control register is set. The alarm value can only be set—a read access to registers 8-10 always returns the current counter state, regardless of whether the alarm bit is set in control register B or not.

*The serial port*

| Register | Name | D7 | D6 | D5 | D4 | D3 | D2 | D1 | D0 |
|----------|------|----|----|----|----|----|----|----|----|
| 12 $C | SDR | S7 | S6 | S5 | S4 | S3 | S2 | S1 | S0 |

The serial port consists of the serial data register and an 8-bit shift register which cannot be accessed directly. The port can be configured as input (SPMODE = 0) or output (SPMODE=1) with the SPMODE bit in control register A. In the input mode the serial data on the SP line are shifted into the shift register on each rising edge on the CNT line. After eight CNT pulses the shift register is full and its contents are transferred to the serial data register. At the same time, the SP bit in the interrupt control register is set. If more CNT pulses occur, the data continues to shift into the shift register until it is full again. If the user has read the Serial Data Register (SDR) in the mean time, the new value is copied into the SDR and the transfer continues in this manner.

To use the serial port as output, set SPMODE to 1. The timeout rate of timer A, which must be operated in continuous mode, determines the baud rate (number of bits per second). The data are always shifted out of the shift register at half the timeout rate of timer A, whereby the maximum output rate is one quarter of the clock-frequency of the 8520.

The transfer begins after the first data byte is transferred into the SDR. The CIA transfers the data byte into the shift register. The individual data bits now appear at half the timeout rate of timer A on the SP line and the clock signal from timer A appears on the CNT line (it changes value on each timeout so that the next bit appears on the SP line on each negative transition [high to low]). The transfer begins with the MSB of the data byte. Once all eight bits have been output, CNT remains high and the SP line retains the value of the last bit sent. In addition, the SP bit in the interrupt control register is set to show that the shift register can be supplied with new data. If the next data byte was loaded into the data register before the output of the last bit, the data output continues without interruption.

To keep the transfer continuous, the serial data register must be supplied with new data at the proper time.

The SP and CNT lines are open-collector outputs so that CNT and SP lines of multiple 8520's can be connected together.

*The interrupt control register:*

Read access = data register

| Register | Name | D7 | D6 | D5 | D4 | D3 | D2 | D1 | D0 |
|----------|------|----|----|----|------|----|-------|----|----|
| 13 $D | ICR | IR | 0 | 0 | FLAG | SP | Alarm | TB | TA |

Write access = mask register

| Register | Name | D7 | D6 | D5 | D4 | D3 | D2 | D1 | D0 |
|----------|------|-----|----|----|------|----|-------|----|----|
| 13 $D | ICR | S/C | x | x | FLAG | SP | Alarm | TB | TA |

The ICR consists of a data register and a mask register. Each of the five interrupt sources can set its corresponding bit in the data register. Here again are all five possible interrupt sources:

1.    Timeout of timer A (TA, bit 0)

2.    Timeout of timer B (TB, bit 1)

3.    Match of the event counter value and alarm value (Alarm, bit 2)

4.    The shift register of the serial port is full (input) or empty (output) (SP, bit 3)

5.    Negative transition on the FLAG input (FLAG, bit 4)

If the ICR register is read, it always returns the value of the data register, which is cleared after it is read (all set bits, including the IR bit are cleared). If this value is needed later, it must be stored somewhere else.

The mask register can only be written. Its value determines whether a set bit in the data register can generate an interrupt. To make an interrupt possible, the corresponding bit in the mask register must be set to 1. The 8520 pulls the IRQ line low (it is active low) whenever a bit is set in both the mask register and the data register and sets the IR bit (bit 7) in the data register so that an interrupt is also signalled in software. The IRQ line does not return to 1 until the ICR is read and thus cleared.

The mask register cannot be written like a normal memory location. To set a bit in the mask register, the desired bit must be set and the S/C bit (Set/Clear, bit # 7) must also be set. All other bits remain unchanged. To clear a bit, the desired bit must again be set, but this time the S/C bit is cleared. The S/C bit determines whether the set bits are set (S/C = 1) or clear (S/C = 0) the corresponding bits in the mask register. All cleared bits in the byte written to the ICR have no effect on it. Here is an example:

We want to allow an interrupt through the FLAG line. The current value of the mask register is 00000011 binary, meaning that timer interrupts are allowed. The following value must be written into the mask register: 10010000 binary (S/C=1). The mask register then has the following contents: 00010011. If you now want to turn the two timer interrupts off, write the following value: 00000011 (S/C=0). Now the mask register contains 00010000, and only the FLAG interrupt is allowed.

*Integration of CIAs into the Amiga system*

As already mentioned, the Amiga has two CIAs of the type 8520. The base address of the first 8520, which we call 8520-A, is $BFE001. The registers are not at contiguous memory addresses, however, but at 256 byte intervals. This means that all of the 8520-A registers are at odd addresses because the 8520-A is connected to the lower 8-bits of the processor data bus (D0-7). The following table lists the addresses of the individual registers with their uses in the Amiga (see the chapter on interfaces for more information on the individual port bits):

*CIA-A: Register addresses*

| Address | Name | D7 | D6 | D5 | D4 | D3 | D2 | D1 | D0 |
|---|---|---|---|---|---|---|---|---|---|
| $BFE001 | PRA /LED | /FIR1 OVL | | /FIR0 | /RDY | /TK0 | /WPR0 | /CHNG | |
| $BFE101 | PRB | Centronics parallel port | | | | | | | |
| $BFE201 | DDRA | 0 | 0 | 0 | 0 | 0 | 0 | 1 | 1 |
| $BFE301 | DDRB | input or output depending on the application | | | | | | | |
| $BFE401 | TALO | timer A is used by the operating system for communication | | | | | | | |
| $BFE501 | TAHI | with the keyboard | | | | | | | |
| $BFE601 | TBLO | timer B is used by the OS for various tasks | | | | | | | |
| $BFE701 | TBHI | | | | | | | | |
| $BFE801 | E. LSB | The event counter in the CIA-A counts 60Hz pulses | | | | | | | |
| $BFE901 | E. 8-15 | from the power supply (called ticks) | | | | | | | |
| $BFEA01 | E. MSB | which are taken from the power-line frequency | | | | | | | |
| $BFEB01 | SP | Input for key codes from the keyboard | | | | | | | |
| $BFEC01 | ICR | Interrupt control register | | | | | | | |
| $BFEE01 | CRA | Control register A | | | | | | | |
| $BFEF01 | CRB | Control register B | | | | | | | |

The second CIA, CIA-B, is addressed at address $BFD000. Its registers lie at even addresses because the data bus of CIA-B is connected to the upper half of the processor data bus.

*CIA-B:*
*Register*
*addresses*

| Address | Name | D7 | D6 | D5 | D4 | D3 | D2 | D1 | D0 |
|---------|------|-----|------|------|------|------|------|------|------|
| $BFD000 | PRA | /DTR | /RTS | /CD | /CTS | /DSR | /SEL | POUT | BUSY |
| $BFD100 | PRB | /MTR | /SEL3 | /SEL2 | /SEL1 | /SEL0 | /SIDE | DIR | /STEP |
| $BFD200 | DDRA | 1 | 1 | 0 | 0 | 0 | 0 | 0 | 0 |
| $BFD300 | DDRB | 1 | 1 | 1 | 1 | 1 | 1 | 1 | 1 |
| $BFD400 | TALO | Timer A is used only for serial transfers. | | | | | | | |
| $BFD500 | TAHI | Otherwise it is free. | | | | | | | |
| $BFD600 | TBLO | Timer B is used to synchronize the blitter with the screen | | | | | | | |
| $BFD700 | TBHI | Otherwise it is free. | | | | | | | |
| $BFD800 | E. LSB | The event counter in CIA-B counts the horizontal | | | | | | | |
| $BFD900 | E. 8-15 | sync pulses. | | | | | | | |
| $BFDA00 | E. MSB | | | | | | | | |
| $BFDB00 | SP | unused | | | | | | | |
| $BFDC00 | ICR | Interrupt control register | | | | | | | |
| $BFDE00 | CRA | Control register A | | | | | | | |
| $BFDF00 | CRB | Control register B | | | | | | | |

The addresses $BFD000 for CIA-B and $BFE001 for CIA-A are the base addresses of the CIAs specified by Commodore. A closer look at the schematic reveals that the two CIAs are addressed in the entire range from A0xxxx to BFxxxx. The selection between the two CIAs is made with address lines A12 and A13. CIA-A is selected when A12=0 and CIA-B is selected when A13=0, assuming that the addresses are between A0xxxx and BFxxxx. Since the data bus of CIA-A is connected to processor data lines D0-7 (odd addresses) and CIA-B to D8-15 (even addresses), the two can be accessed together in one word access if A12 and A13 are both 0.

MOVE.W $BF0000,D0 moves the PA registers of both CIAs into D0 such that the lower 8 bits of D0 contain the data from the PA of CIA-A and bits 9-15 contain the contents of PA from CIA-B.

The addressing scheme for the CIAs can be summarized as follows. CIA-A is selected by the following addresses (binary):

    101x xxxx xxx0 rrrr xxxx xxx1

and CIA-B by:

    101x xxxx xx0x rrrr xxxx xxx0

The four bits designated rrrr select the corresponding registers.

This information completely applies only to the Amiga 1000 only. It is possible that this has changed in the newer Amiga models. To be certain, use only the addresses specified by Commodore (CIA-A at $BFE001 and CIA-B at $BFD000).

The following list shows the various signal lines of the Amiga's CIAs:

## CIA-A:

| | | |
|---|---|---|
| /IRQ | /INT2 input from Paula | |
| /RES | System reset line | |
| D0-D7 | Processor data bus bits 0-7 | |
| D0-A3 | Processor address bus bits 8-11 | |
| f2 | Processor E clock | |
| R/W | Processor R/W | |
| PA7 | Game port 1 pin 6 (fire button) | |
| PA6 | Game port 0 pin 6 (fire button) | |
| PA5 | /RDY | "disk ready" signal from disk drive |
| PA4 | /TK0 | "disk track 00" signal from disk drive |
| PA3 | /WPRO | "write protect" signal from the disk drive |
| PA2 | /CHNG | "disk change" signal from disk drive |
| PA1 | LED | Control over the power LED (0=on, 1=off) |
| PA0 | OVL | memory overlay bit (do not change!) |
| SP | KDAT | Serial keyboard data |
| CNT | KCLK | Clock for keyboard data |
| PB0-PB7 | | Centronics port data lines |
| PC | /DRDY | Centronics handshake signal: data ready |
| FLAG | /ACK | Centronics handshake signal: data acknowledge |

## CIA-B:

| | | |
|---|---|---|
| /IRQ | /INT6 input from Paula | |
| /RES | System reset line | |
| D0-D7 | Processor data bus lines 8-15 | |
| A0-A3 | Processor address bus lines 8-11 | |
| f2 | Processor E clock | |
| R/W | Processor R/W | |
| PA7 | /DTR | serial interface, /DTR signal |
| PA6 | /RTS | serial interface, /RTS signal |
| PA5 | /CD | serial interface, /CD signal |
| PA4 | /CTS | serial interface, /CTS signal |
| PA3 | /DSR | serial interface, /DSR signal |
| PA2 | SEL | "select" signal for Centronics interface |
| PA1 | POUT | "paper out" signal from Centronics interface |
| PA0 | BUSY | "busy" signal from Centronics interface |
| SP | BUSY | connected directly to PA0 |
| CNT | POUT | connected directly to PA1 |
| PB7 | /MTR | "motor" signal to disk drive |
| PB6 | /SEL3 | "drive select" for drive 3 |
| PB5 | /SEL2 | "drive select" for drive 2 |
| PB4 | /SEL1 | "drive select" for drive 1 |
| PB3 | /SEL0 | "drive select" for drive 0 (internal) |
| PB2 | /SIDE | "side select" signal to disk drive |
| PB1 | DIR | "direction" signal to disk drive |
| PB0 | /STEP | "step" signal to disk drive |
| FLAG | /INDEX | "index" signal from disk drive |
| PC | not used | |

# 1.2.3        The custom chips

The chips that we have discussed so far are rather boring in comparison to what's coming up. Even the 68000, in spite of its power, is pretty much a standard part these days available at most electronics stores. Although the capabilities of the Amiga finally depend on the speed of the processor, other things are more apparent to someone meeting the Amiga for the first time. When broadcast quality computer graphics appear on the screen and digitized orchestral music comes out of the speakers, that's when the curiosity is aroused. Whether the computer can also calculate so many prime numbers in fractions of a second or whether it is scarcely faster than the old pocket calculator is something that doesn't matter that much to the purchaser of a computer like the Amiga.

The developers of the Amiga were aware of this and equipped it with previously unheard of graphic and sound capabilities for a computer of its price class. The goal of this section is to explain the hardware responsible for the fantastic sound and graphics capabilities of the Amiga and to give the reader a basis for programming these features of the Amiga.

*Agnus, Denise and Paula*   The foundation of all of the features mentioned is a set of three chips developed specifically for the Amiga. Their part numbers are 8361, 8362 and 8364, but these numbers didn't have enough personality for the Amiga developers, so they gave the chips the names Agnus (8361), Denise (8362) and Paula (8364).

These custom chips take care of the sound generation, screen display, processor-independent diskette access and much more. These tasks are not strictly divided up among the chips so that one is in charge of sound generation, one of graphics and another of diskette operation, as is the case with most concurrent devices. Instead, the tasks are divided up among all three chips so that graphic display is handled by two chips.

The three chips could have been combined into one, but the manufacture of such a complex circuit would have been more expensive than making the three separate chips.

Before we get into the details of how Agnus, Denise and Paula work, we have a short introduction to the structure of the Amiga.

## 1.2.3.1 Basic structure of the Amiga

*Figure*
*1.2.3.1.1*

| Amiga - basic block diagram |

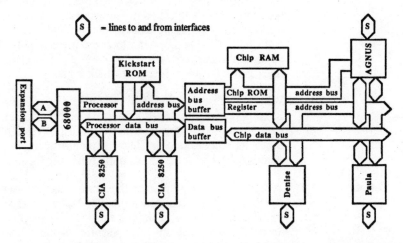

A simple computer system normally consists of a processor, the ROM with the operating system, a certain amount of RAM, and at least one peripheral component for data input and output. All components are connected to the address and data bus. The processor controls the system and only it can place addresses on the bus and thus write or read data to or from various system components, such as RAM. It also controls bus control signals like the R/W line (for the sake of simplicity these are not drawn on Figure 1.2.3.1.1; the individual 68000 bus control signals are explained in Section 1.2.1).

Every computer system also contains control circuits like an address decoder, which activates certain components based on values on the address bus.

But back to the Amiga. As you can see from Figure 1.2.3.1.1, the structure of the Amiga deviates somewhat from what we described. On the left side, you see the 68000 microprocessor whose data and address lines are connected directly to the two 8250 CIA's and the Kickstart ROM. This part of the Amiga is conventional—only the processor has access to the two CIA's and the ROM. What does the right side look like? Here we find the three custom chips Agnus, Denise and Paula, and the chip RAM, which are all connected to a common data bus. However, this data bus is separated from the processor data bus by a buffer which can either connect the processor data bus to the data bus or can separate the two. The three custom chips are connected to each other through the register address bus, which can be connected to the processor address bus or not.

*Multiplexed addresses*

Since the chip RAM has a much larger address range than custom chips and also requires multiplexed addresses, there is a separate chip RAM address bus. *Multiplexed addresses* implies that the RAM chips in the Amiga 1000 have an address range of 216 addresses (65536) and in order to access all of the addresses of a chip, 16 address lines are needed. But since the actual chips are very small, such a large number of address lines would have lead to a very large enclosure. To get around this problem, something called multiplexed addressing was introduced. The package has only eight address lines which are first applied the upper eight bits of the address and then the lower eight. The chip stores the upper eight and then, when the lower eight are applied to the address lines, it has the 16 address bits which it needs.

Why are these two buses separated? The reason is that the various input/output devices need a constant supply of data. For example, the data for individual dots on the screen must be read from the RAM thirty times per second, since a television picture according to the NTSC standard is refreshed at the rate of thirty times per second.

*DMA*

A high-resolution graphic on the Amiga can require more than 64KB of screen memory. This means that per second 30x64KB access must be applied to memory. This is nearly 2 million memory accesses per second! If the processor must perform this task, it would be hopelessly overloaded. Even a 68000 cannot produce such a high data rate. And in addition to this the Amiga can perform digital sound output and diskette accesses in addition to the graphics, all without using the 68000. The solution lies in a second processor which performs all of these memory accesses itself. Such a processor is also called a DMA controller (Direct Memory Access). On the Amiga this is contained in Agnus. This is why Agnus is also connected to the chip RAM address bus.

The other two chips, Denise and Paula, and also the remainder of Agnus, are constructed like standard peripheral chips. They have a certain number of registers which can be read or written by the processor (or the DMA controller). The individual registers are selected through the register address bus. It has eight lines, so 256 different states are possible. There is no special chip selection. If the address bus has the value 255 or $FF, so that all lines are high, no registers are selected. If a valid register number is on these lines, then the chip containing the selected register recognizes this and activates it. This task is performed in the individual chips by the register address decoders. The fact that the selection of a register depends only on its register address and not on the chip in which it is located means that two registers in two different chips can be written with the same value if they have the same register address. This capability is used for some of the registers which contain data which is needed by more than one chip.

***Read and***
***Write register***

Each chip register can be either a read register or a write register. Switching between read and write is accomplished with a special R/W line, something the 8250 doesn't have. The register address also determines whether a read or write access is taking place. Registers which can be read as well as written are realized such that the write access goes to one register address and the read access goes to another. This property is clearly shown in the list of the chip registers (see Section 1.5.1).

Since Agnus contains the DMA controller, it can access the custom chip registers itself. It can output an address on the register address bus.

***Bus***
***contention***

One obvious problem is still unresolved. There is only one data bus and one address bus which both the processor and the DMA controller wants to access. A bus can be controlled by one bus controller at a time. If two chips try to place an address on the bus simultaneously, there would be a problem known as *bus contention*, leading to a system crash. Therefore the bus accesses must take turns and access the bus alternately, whereby each access wants to have the bus for itself as often as possible. This problem is elegantly solved on the Amiga in three levels:

First, the normally continuous buses on the Amiga are divided into two parts. One (on the left in the figure) connects all of the components which can be accessed only by the processor. When the 68000 accesses one of these components, the two buffers (in the middle of the figure), break the connection between the processor data and processor address buses and the chip data and chip address buses. This way the processor can access things on its side undisturbed and Agnus can access the bus on its side. The processor thus has undisturbed access to the operating system and RAM expansions connected to the expansion port. This expansion is also called fast RAM because the processor can always access it without loss of speed. (The RAM expansions which are inserted on the front of the Amiga 1000 and on the underside of the Amiga 500 belong to the chip RAM.)

Second, bus accesses from the processor and from Agnus are nested so that normally even accesses to the chip RAM or the chip registers of the 68000 are not slower. For such an access the buffers connect the two systems again.

Third, the processor can wait until Agnus has finished its DMA accesses and the bus is free again. This case occurs only when either very high graphic resolutions are used or when the blitter is being used. More about this later. Now we'll discuss the internal structure of the three custom chips.

## 1.2.3.2    The structure of Agnus

*Figure*
*1.2.3.2.1*

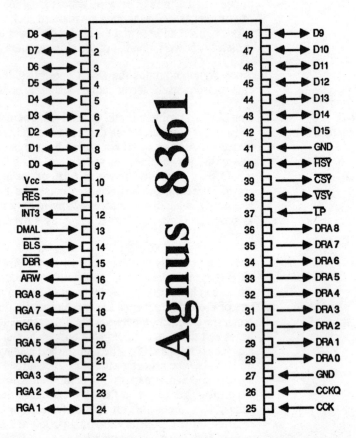

NOTE: The arrows indicate the direction of the signal. A line above a signal name means that the signal is active when low (0=active).

*Figure*
*1.2.3.2.2*

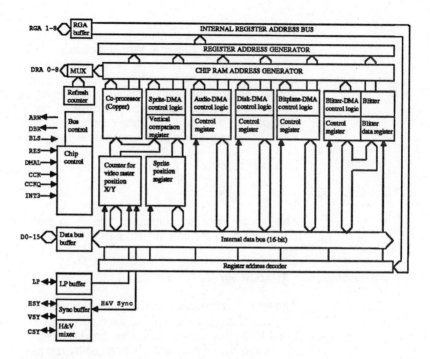

As we mentioned before, Agnus contains all of the DMA circuitry. Each of the six possible DMA sources has its own control logic. They are all connected to the chip RAM address generator as well as the register address generator. These address generators create the RAM address of the desired chip RAM location and the register address of the destination register. In this manner the DMA logic units supply the appropriate chip registers with data from the RAM or write the contents of a given register into RAM.

Also connected to the chip RAM address generator is the refresh counter which creates the refresh signals necessary for the dynamic RAM chips.

Agnus also controls the regular operation of the individual DMA accesses. The basis of these is a screen line. In each screen line 225 memory accesses take place, which are divided by Agnus among the individual DMA channels and the 68000. Since Agnus always needs the current row and column positions, it also contains the raster and column counters. These counters for the beam position also create the horizontal and vertical synchronization signals which signal the start of a new line (H-sync) and that of a new picture (V-sync). The horizontal and vertical synchronization signals can also be fed in from outside Agnus and then control the internal raster line and column counters. This allows the video picture of the Amiga to be synchronized to that of another source, such as a video recorder. This genlock can thus be easily performed on the Amiga. Simply put, synchonizing two video pictures means that the individual raster lines and the individual pictures of the two signals start at the same time.

Two other important elements in Agnus are the blitter and the Copper co-processor. The blitter is a special circuit which can manipulate or move areas of memory. It can be used to relieve the 68000 of some work, since it can perform these operations faster than the processor can. In addition, the blitter is capable of drawing lines and filling surfaces. The Copper is a simple co-processor. Its programs, called Copper lists, contain only three different commands. The Copper can change various chip registers at predetermined points in time.

Here are descriptions of the individual pins:

*Data bus: D0-D15*

The 16 data lines are connected directly to the chip RAM data bus. Internally all of the chip registers are connected through buffers to the bus.

*Register address bus: RGA0-RGA8 (ReGister Address)*

Agnus' register address bus is bidirectional. For a DMA access the register address generator places the desired register address on these bus lines. If the processor is accessing the chip registers, these lines act as inputs and the register address selected by the processor is sent to the register address decoder inside Agnus. In general, if a value of $FF is on the register address bus (all lines are high), no registers are selected.

*The address lines for the dynamic RAM: DRA0-DRA8 (Dynamic RAM Address)*

These address lines are connected to the chip RAM address bus. They are pure outputs and are always activated by Agnus when it wants to perform a DMA access to the chip RAM. The addresses on these pins are already multiplexed and can be connected directly to the address lines of dynamic 32KB RAMs (type 41256). This is the case in the Amiga 500 and 2000. On the old Amiga 1000 the RAMs have only eight address lines. The ninth DRA line is again demultiplexed and used to switch between various RAM banks.

*The clock lines CCK and CCKQ: (Color Clock and Color Clock delay)*

These two lines are the only clock lines in the Amiga. The frequency of both signals is 3.58MHz, which is half of the processor frequency. The CCKQ signal is delayed one quarter cycle (90 degrees) from the CCK signal. All of Agnus' timing is set according to these two signals.

*The bus control lines: BLS, ARW, DBR*

These three lines are connected to control logic of the Amiga. Agnus uses the DBR line (Data Bus Request) to tell this control logic that it wants control of the bus in the next bus cycle. This line always has precedence over a bus request from the processor. If Agnus needs the bus for several successive bus cycles, the 68000 must wait.

The ARW line (Agnus RAM Write) signals the control logic that Agnus wants to make a write access to the chip RAM.

The BLS signal (BLitter Slow down) signals Agnus that the processor has already waited three bus cycles for an access. Depending on its internal state, Agnus turns the bus over to the processor for one cycle.

### The control signals: RES, INT3, DMAL

The RES signal (RESet) is connected directly to the processor reset line and returns Agnus to a predefined start-up state.

The INT3 line (INTerrupt at level 3) is an output and is connected directly to the Paula line with the same name. Agnus uses this line to signal the interrupt logic in Paula that a component in Agnus has generated an interrupt.

The DMAL line (DMA request Line) also connects Agnus to Paula, only this time in the opposite direction. Paula uses this line to tell Agnus to perform a DMA transfer.

### The lines: HSY, VSY, CSY and LP

Normally the synchronization signals for the monitor to appear on the HSY (Horizontal SYnc) and VSY (Vertical SYnc) lines. The signal on the CSY (Composite SYnc) line is the sum of HSY and VSY and is used to connect to monitors which need a combined signal, as well as the circuit which creates the video signal, the video mixer.

The LP line (Light Pen) is an input and allows a light pen to be connected. The contents of the raster counter register is stored when a negative transition occurs on this pin (see Section 1.5.2).

The HSY and VSY lines can also be used as inputs and thus allow Agnus to be externally synchronized (genlock).

## 1.2.3.4     The structure of Denise

*Figure*
*1.2.3.4.1*

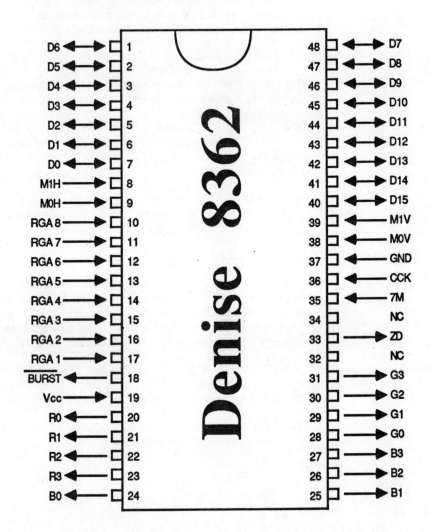

NOTE: The arrows indicate the direction of the signal. A line above a signal name means that the signal is active when low (0=active).

*Figure*
*1.2.3.4.2*

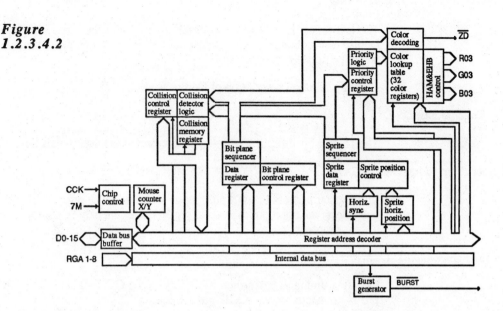

In general, the function of Denise can be described as graph generation. The first part of this task is already accomplished by Agnus. Agnus fetches the current graphic data from the chip RAM and writes them in the register responsible for the bit levels in Denise. It does the same for the sprite data. Denise always contains all graphic and sprite data for 15 pixels, since a bit always corresponds to one pixel on the screen and the data registers all have a width of one word, or 16 bits. These data must be converted into the appropriate RGB representation by Denise. First the graphic data are converted from a parallel 16-bit representation to a serial data stream by means of the bit-level sequencer. Since a maximum of six bit levels are possible, this function block is repeated six times. The serial data streams from the individual bit-level sequencers are now combined into a maximum 6-bit wide data stream.

The priority control logic selects the valid data for the current pixel based on its priority from among the graphic data from the bit-level sequencers and the sprite data from the sprite sequencers. According to this data the color decoder selects one of the 32 color registers. The value of this color register is then output as a digital RGB signal. If the Hold-And-Modify (HAM) or Extra-Half-Bright (EHB) mode is selected, the data from the color register are modified correspondingly before it leaves the chip.

The data from the sequencers is also fed into the collision control logic which, as the name implies, checks the data for a collision between the bit levels and the sprites and places the result of this test in the collision register.

The last function of Denise has nothing to do with the screen display. Denise also contains the mouse counter, which contains the current X and Y positions of the mice.

Here is a function description of Denise's pins:

*The data bus: D0-D15*

The 16 data bus lines are, like Agnus, connected to the chip data bus.

*Register address bus: RGA1-RGA8*

The register address bus is a pure input on Denise. The register address bus selects the appropriate internal register with the help of the register address decoder.

*The clock inputs: CCK and 7M*

Denise's timing is performed according to the CCK signal. The CCK pin is connected to the CCK pin on Agnus. The clock signal on the 7M line (7 Megahertz) has a frequency of 7.15909 MHz. The Denise chip needs this additional frequency to output the individual pixels because the pixel frequency is greater than the 3.58MHz of the CCK signal. A pixel at the lowest resolution has exactly the duration of a 7M clock cycle. In high-resolution mode (640 pixels/line) two pixels are output per 7M clock, one per edge of 7M. The 7M clock is also the 68000's clock and is connected to the processor's clock input.

*The output signals: R0-3, G0-3, B0-3, ZD and BURST*

The lines R0-3, G0-3 and B0-3 represent the RGB outputs of Denise. Denise outputs the corresponding RGB values digitally. Each of the three color components is represented by four bits. This allows 16 values per component and 16x16x16 (4096) total colors. After they leave Denise, the three color signals run through a buffer and then through three digital-to-analog converters to transform them into an analog RGB signal, which is then fed to the RGB port.

An additional video mixer turns this RGB signal into the video signal for the video connector. To do this it also needs the BURST signal from Denise. The BURST signal is a oscillator with the same frequency as CCK (3.58MHz). More about the function of the color burst can be found in a book on television technology.

The last output signal is the ZD signal (Zero Detect or background indicator). It is always low when a pixel in the background is being displayed, that is, when the color comes from color register number zero. This signal is used in the genlock adapter and is used to switch between the external video signal, when ZD=0, and the Amiga's video signal, when ZD=1. The ZD signal is also available on the RGB port. More about this in the section on interfaces.

*The mouse/joystck inputs: M0H, M1H, M0V, M1V*

These four inputs correspond directly to the mouse inputs of the two game ports (or joystick connectors). Since the Amiga has two game ports, it must actually have eight inputs. Apparently only four pins were free on Denise so Commodore used the following method to read all of the inputs: The eight input lines from the two game ports go to a switch which connects either the four lines from the front or back port to the four inputs on Denise. This switching is performed in synchonization with Denise's clock so that Denise can divide these four lines into two registers internally, one for each game port. More about the game ports can be found in the section on interfaces.

## 1.2.3.6    The structure of Paula

***Figure
1.2.3.6.1***

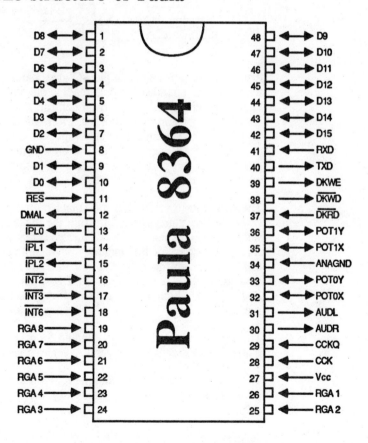

NOTE: The arrows indicate the direction of the signal. A line above a signal name means that the signal is active when low (0=active).

*Figure*
*1.2.3.6.2*

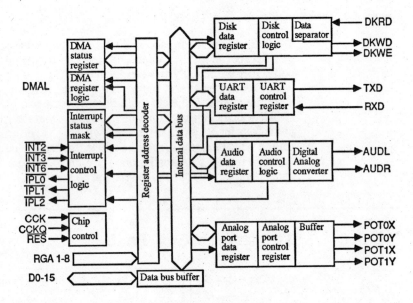

Paula's tasks fall mainly in the I/O area, namely the diskette I/O, the serial I/O, the sound output and reading the analog inputs. In addition, Paula is in charge of all interrupt control. All of the interrupts which occur in the system run through it. From these fourteen possible interrupt sources Paula creates the interrupt signals for the 68000. Interrupts on levels 1-6 are created on the IPL lines of the 68000. Paula gives the programmer the possibility to allow or prohibit each of the fourteen interrupt sources.

The disk data transfer and the sound output are performed through DMA. When transferring data from the diskette it is not always possible to predict when the next data word is ready for a DMA transfer by Agnus. Reasons for this include unavoidable speed variations of the disk drive. Even for the sound output, Agnus does not know when the data are needed. To make a smooth DMA transfer possible, Paula has a DMAL line which it can use to tell Agnus when a DMA access is needed.

The serial communication is handled by a UART component inside Paula. UART stands for Univeral Asynchronous Receive Transmit.

The function of the UART and the four audio channels and the analog ports are described later in the section on programming the custom chips.

As previously, here is the description of the pin functions:

*Data bus: D0-15*

As with the other chips, connected to the chip data bus.

*Register address bus: RGA 1-8*

>   As with Denise.

*The clock signals and reset: CCK, CCKQ, and RES*

>   Paula contains the same clock signals as Agnus. The reset line RES
>   returns the chip to a defined start-up state.

*DMA request: DMAL*

>   With this line Paula signals Agnus that a DMA transfer is needed.

*Audio outputs: AUDL and AUDR*

>   The outputs AUDL and AUDR (Left AUDio and Right AUDio) are
>   analog outputs on which Paula places the sound signals it generates.
>   AUDL carries the internal sound channels 0 and 3, and AUDR the
>   channels 1 and 2.

*The serial interface lines: TXD and RXD*

>   RXD (Receive Data) is the serial input to the UART and TXD (Trans-
>   mit Data) is the serial output. These lines have TTL levels, which
>   means that their input/output voltages range from 0 to 5 volts. An
>   additional level converter creates the +12/-5 volts for the RS-232 inter-
>   face standard.

*The analog inputs: POT0X, POT0Y, POT1X, POT1Y*

>   The inputs POT0X and POT0Y are connected to the corresponding lines
>   from game port 0, and POT1X and POT1Y are connected to port 1.
>   Paddles or analog joysticks can be connected to these inputs. These
>   input devices contain changeable resistances, called potentiometers,
>   which lie between +5 volts and the POT inputs. Paula can read the
>   value of these resistances and place this value in internal registers. The
>   POT inputs can also be configured as outputs through software.

*The disk lines: DKRD, DRWD, DKWE*

>   Through the DKRD line (DisKette ReaD) Paula receives the read data
>   from the diskette. The DKWD line (DisKette Write) is the output for
>   data to the disk drive. The DKWE line (DisKette Write Enable) serves
>   to switch the drive from read to write.

*The interrupt lines: INT2, INT3, INT6 and IPL0, IPL1, IPL2*

>   Paula receives instructions through the three INT lines to create an
>   interrupt on the appropriate level. The INT2 line is normally the one
>   connected to the CIA-A 8250. This line is also connected to the expan-
>   sion port and the serial interface. If it is low, Paula creates an interrupt
>   on level 2 provided that an interrupt at this level is allowed. The INT3

line is connected to the corresponding output from Agnus and the INT6 line to CIA-B and the expansion port. All other interrupts occur within the I/O components in Paula.

The IPL0-IPL2 lines (Interrupt Pending Level of the 68000, see Section 1.2.1) are connected directly to the corresponding processor lines. Paula uses these to create a processor interrupt at a given level.

## 1.2.3.7     Features of the Amiga 500

The descriptions of the Amiga hardware in this section originally came from the Amiga 1000. By large they also apply to the Amiga 500. None of the fundamental structure is changed in the Amiga 500, but an attempt was made to produce a less expensive version of the computer. The biggest differences between the two models lie in the division of the various hardware elements among the individual chips.

On the Amiga 1000, the custom chips require a large number of simple logic circuits to create the clock signals and serve for bus control and address decoding. On the Amiga 500, almost all of these logic functions are combined into larger chips. A new section was added to the Agnus chip and the new chip was given the name Fat Agnus (part number 8370).

*Figure 1.2.3.7.1*

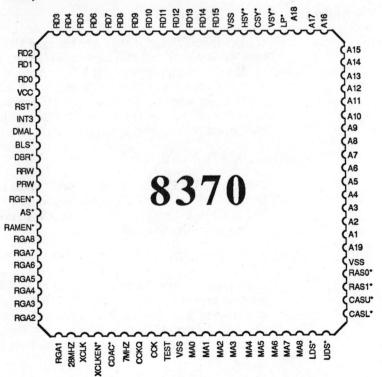

Figure 1.2.3.7.1 shows the pin layout for Fat Agnus. If some of the normal Agnus pins do not show up, it is because they were connected to circuits which are now inside Fat Agnus. These are the new functions integrated into Agnus:

*Clock generation*

All clock generation for the Amiga system is now integrated into Fat Agnus. Only the 28MHz main clock is needed. The lines belonging to this function block are:

28MHz, XCLK, XCLKEN, 7MHz, CCKQ, CCK and CDAC

*The address buffers*

In Figure 1.2.3.1 we showed a buffer which connects the address bus of the Amiga to the chip RAM address bus and multiplexed the register address bus and the processor address correspondingly. This buffer is completely integrated into Agnus. The processor address bus can now be connected directly to the lines A1 to A18 of Fat Agnus. The address decoder uses the two signals RAMEN (RAM ENable) and RGEN (ReGister ENable) to signal that the processor wants to access RAM or the register area. In addition, Agnus is now connected to the processor signals UDS, LDS and PR/W (Processor Read/Write).

*Control of the chip RAM*

The control of the chip RAM is now handled entirely by Agnus. Agnus creates the necessary RAS and CAS signals together with the multiplexed RAM addresses. In addition, Agnus has the ability to manage an additional 512KB RAM, for a total of 1 megabyte. The two banks are selected by means of the RAM control signals RAS0 and CAS0 for the chip RAM and RAS1 and CAS1 for the RAM expansion.

None of the principle functions of Agnus as described in Section 1.2.3.1 have changed.

In addition to Fat Agnus, a fourth custom chip was added. This chip is called Gary and takes over the functions of the address decoder and bus controller. It creates the control signals for all the chips in the Amiga, as well as VPA and DTACK for the processor.

Also, Gary contains the reset logic and the motor flip-flop for the disk drive (see Section 1.3.5).

# 1.3  The Amiga interfaces

*Figure 1.3.1*

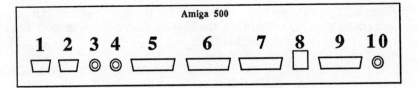

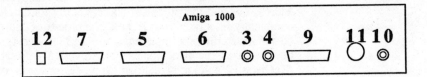

1  gameport 0
2  gameport 1
3  right audio channel
4  left audio channel
5  external disk drive interface
6  serial (RS232C) interface
7  Centronics printer interface
8  power connection (Amiga 500 only)
9  RGB connector
10 composite video jack
11 TV modulator jack (Amiga 1000 only)
12 Keyboard connection

## 1.3.1      The audio/video interfaces

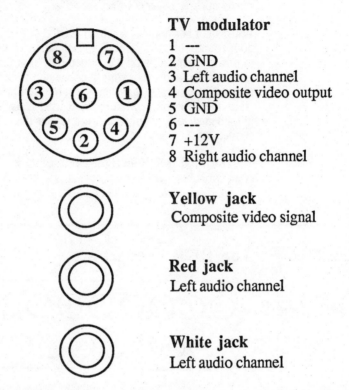

*Figure 1.3.1.1*

**TV modulator**
1 ---
2 GND
3 Left audio channel
4 Composite video output
5 GND
6 ---
7 +12V
8 Right audio channel

**Yellow jack**
Composite video signal

**Red jack**
Left audio channel

**White jack**
Left audio channel

The video connectors are quite different from one Amiga model to another. The most sparse of these is the early Amiga 2000, which had no composite video connectors. It has a connector to add a video modulator or a genlock interface available internally on the board. The Amiga 500, the Amiga 1000 and later Amiga 2000s have a video output in the form of a RCA jack phono connector. The video signal on this connector is a standard NTSC signal and can be connected to any standard monitor. The video signal travels through a transistor buffer with an output resistance of 75 Ohms, making it short-circuit proof.

On all Amiga models the audio signal is available through two phono connectors on the rear of the case. The right stereo channel is the red connector and the left is the white. A standard stereo phono cable can be used to connect these jacks to a stereo (AUX, TAPE or CD input). The output resistance of each channel is 1 KOhm (1000 Ohms). The outputs are protected against short circuit and have 360 Ohms inpedance.

The Amiga 1000 has another audio/video connector. The TV Mod connector was originally intended for connection of an RF modulator which would allow an ordinary television to be used with the Amiga. This RF modulator was never constructed.

What's left is a connector which carried both the video signal as well as both sound channels. This also includes a 12 volt connection intended to power the modulator. The video output at this jack has its own transistor buffer, and is not simply connected to the video phono jack. The two audio pins also have their own 1KOhm output resistances. But since they do not have an internal load resistance, their signals in an unloaded state is about four times higher than those at the audio phono connectors.

The TV Mod jack is an eight-pin connector. Suitable plugs for such connectors are hard to come by. It is useful to note, however, that the TV Mod connector is the same as the C64 video connector.

## 1.3.2    The RGB connector

*Figure 1.3.2.1*

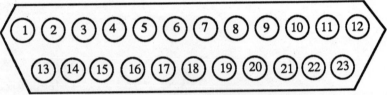

```
INPUT    1   XCLK    External clock frequency
INPUT    2   XCLKEN  Switch for external clock
OUTPUT   3   R       Analog red signal
OUTPUT   4   G       Analog green signal
OUTPUT   5   B       Analog blue signal
OUTPUT   6   DI      Digital brightness signal
OUTPUT   7   DB      Digital blue signal
OUTPUT   8   DG      Digital green signal
OUTPUT   9   DR      Digital red signal
OUTPUT  10   QCSY    Buffered composite sync signal
IN/OUT  11   HSY     Horizontal synchronization signal
IN/OUT  12   VSY     Vertical synchronization signal
        13   GND
OUTPUT  14   ZD      Background indicator signal
OUTPUT  15   C1U     Amiga C1U timer (3.58 MHz)
        16   GND
        17   GND
        18   GND
        19   GND
        20   GND
        21   -5 volts
        22   +12 volts
        23   +5 volts
```

*The RGB
Connector*

The RGB connector is the same on all three Amiga models. It allows various RGB monitors to be connected as well as special expansions such as a genlock adapter. To connect an analog RGB monitor like the Amiga monitor, all three analog RGB outputs and the Composite Sync output are used. The RGB signal on these three lines comes from the conversion of the buffered digital RGB signals from Denise into suitable analog signals by means of three 4-bit digital-to-analog converters. The composite sync signal comes from Agnus and is formed by mixing the horizontal and vertical sync signals. All of these four lines are provided with transistor buffers and 75 Ohm output resistances.

The lines DI, DB, DG and DR are provided for connecting a digital RGB monitor. The source of the digital RGB signals is the digital RGB output from Denise (Fig. 1.2.3.4.1). The three color lines are connected to the most signficant color line of Denise (for example, DB to B3 from Denise). A 74HC244 buffer lies between Denise and these outputs. Interestingly, the intensity or brightness line DI is connected to the B0 line. The four lines have 47 Ohm output resistances and have TTL levels, since they come from the 74HC244.

The HSY and VSY connections on the RGB connector are provided for monitors which require separate synchronization signals. Caution should be exercised with these lines since they are connected through 47 Ohm resistors directly to the HSY and VSY pins of Agnus. They also have TTL levels.

If the genlock bit in Agnus is set (see the section on programming the hardware), then these two lines become inputs. The Amiga then synchronizes its own video signal to the synchronization signals on the HSY and VSY lines. These lines also require TTL levels when they're input. As usual, the synchronization signals are active low, meaning that they are normally at 5 volts. Only during the active synchronization pulse is the line at 0 volts.

Another signal, related to genlock, is the ZD signal (Zero Detect). The Amiga places this signal low whenever the pixel currently being displayed is in the background, in other words, whenever its color comes from color register 0.

During the vertical blanking gaps, when VSY=0, the function of the ZD line changes. Then it reflects the state of the GAUD (Genlock AUDio enable) bit from Agnus register $100 (BPLCON0). This signal is used by the genlock interface to switch the sound signal.

Normally the ZD line is not of interest to the normal user since it is used only by the genlock interface. The ZD signal from Denise pin 33 is buffered with a 74HC244 driver, so that the signal has TTL levels.

The remaining lines of the RGB connector have nothing to do with the RGB signal.

The C1U signal is a 3.58MHz clock line and corresponds to the inverted clock signal of the custom chip.

The XCLK (eXternal CLocK) and XCLKEN (eXternal CLocK ENable) lines are used to feed an external clock frequency into the Amiga. All clock signals in the Amiga are derived from a single 28MHz clock. This 28MHz master clock can be replaced by another clock frequency on the XCLK input by pulling the XCLKEN low. This allows the Amiga to be accelerated, for example, by placing a 32MHz or higher clock on XCLK. How long the Amiga hardware continues to function at higher speeds must be determined experimentally. The ground pin 13 should be used when using the XCLK and XCLKEN lines. It is connected directly to the ground line of the clock generation circuit.

## 1.3.3     The Centronics interface

*Figure 1.3.3.1*

### Amiga 1000

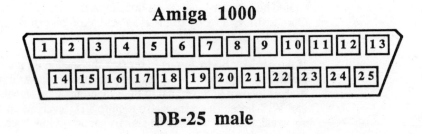

DB-25 male

### Amiga 500/Amiga 2000

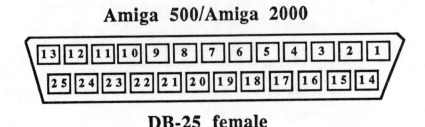

DB-25 female

| Output | 1 | /Strobe – data ready |
|---|---|---|
| I/O | 2 | Data bit 0 |
| I/O | 3 | Data bit 1 |
| I/O | 4 | Data bit 2 |
| I/O | 5 | Data bit 3 |
| I/O | 6 | Data bit 4 |
| I/O | 7 | Data bit 5 |
| I/O | 8 | Data bit 6 |
| I/O | 9 | Data bit 7 |
| | | |
| Input | 10 | /Acknowledge – data received |
| I/O | 11 | BUSY – printer busy |
| I/O | 12 | Paper Out |
| I/O | 13 | Select – printer ONLINE |
| | 14 | +5 volts |
| | 15 | unused |
| | | |
| Output | 16 | Reset / buffered reset line from the Amiga |
| | 17-25 | GND |

On the Amiga 1000 some lines are used differently:

| | 14-22 | GND |
|---|---|---|
| | 23 | +5 volts |
| | 24 | unused |
| Output | 25 | Reset / buffered reset line from the Amiga |

*Centronics interface*

The Centronics interface on the Amiga should bring joy to any hacker's heart. It is completely PC compatible. Any IBM-compatible printer can be connected directly to it. This gives the Amiga a large supply of printers ready to be connected to it. Unfortunately, this applies only to the Amiga 500 and Amiga 2000. The Amiga 1000 Centronics port does not conform to the PC standard. First, a female connector was used instead of the usual male DB-25 connector, and second pin 23 is +5 volts instead of ground as it is usually on most printer cables. If such a cable is used with the Amiga 1000, a short occurs and the Amiga can be damaged. As a result, you are generally forced to make custom cables for the Amiga 1000.

Internally all of the Centronics port lines (except for 5 volts and Reset) are connected directly to the port lines of the individual CIA's. The exact assignment is as follows:

| Centronics pin No. | Function | CIA | Pin | Pin designation |
|---|---|---|---|---|
| 1 | Strobe | A | 18 | PC |
| 2 | Data bit 0 | A | 10 | PB0 |
| 3 | Data bit 1 | A | 11 | PB1 |
| 4 | Data bit 2 | A | 12 | PB2 |
| 5 | Data bit 3 | A | 13 | PB3 |
| 6 | Data bit 4 | A | 14 | PB4 |
| 7 | Data bit 5 | A | 15 | PB5 |
| 8 | Data bit 6 | A | 16 | PB6 |
| 9 | Data bit 7 | A | 17 | PB7 |
| 10 | Acknowledge | A | 24 | PB8 |
| 11 | Busy | B | 2 | PA0 |
| | | | and 39 | SP |
| 12 | Paper Out | B | 3 | PA1 |
| | | | and 40 | CNT |
| 13 | Select | B | 4 | PA2 |

The Centronics interface is a parallel interface. The data byte lies on the eight data lines. When the computer has placed a valid byte on the data lines it clears the STROBE line to 0 for 1.4 microseconds, signalling the printer that a valid byte is read for it. The printer must then acknowledge this by pulling the Acknowledge line low for at least one microsecond. The computer can then place the next byte on the bus.

The printer uses the BUSY line to indicate that it is occupied and can not accept any more data at the moment. This occurs when the printer buffer is full, for example. The computer then waits until BUSY goes high again before it continues sending data. With the Paper Out line the printer tells the computer that it is out of paper. The Select line is also controlled by the printer and indicates whether it is ONLINE (selected, SEL high) or OFFLINE (unselected, SEL low).

The Centronics port is well suited as a universal interface for connecting home-built expansions or an audio digitizer or an EPROM burner, since almost all of its lines can be programmed to be either inputs or outputs.

## 1.3.4 The serial interface

*Figure
1.3.4.1*

### Amiga 500/Amiga 2000

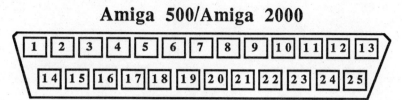

### DB-25 male

### Amiga 1000

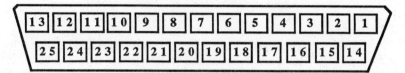

### DB-25 female

| | | |
|---|---|---|
| | 1 | GND (chassis ground) |
| Output | 2 | TXD Transmit Data |
| Input | 3 | RXD Receive Data |
| Output | 4 | RTS Request To Send |
| Input | 5 | CTS Clear To Send |
| Input | 6 | DSR Data Set Ready |
| | 7 | GND (signal ground) |
| Input | 8 | CD Carrier Detect |
| | 9 | +12 volts |
| | 10 | -12 volts |
| Output | 11 | AUDOUT left sound channel output |
| | 12 | unused |
| | 13 | unused |
| | 14 | unused |
| | 15 | unused |
| | 16 | unused |
| | 17 | unused |
| Input | 18 | AUDIN input to right sound channel |
| | 19 | unused |
| Output | 20 | DTR Data Terminal Ready |
| | 21 | unused |
| Input | 22 | RI Ring Indicator |
| | 23 | unused |
| | 24 | unused |
| | 25 | unused |

On the Amiga 1000 some lines are assigned differently:

| | | |
|---|---|---|
| | 9 | unused |
| | 10 | unused |
| | 11 | unused |
| | 12 | unused |
| | 13 | unused |
| | 14 | -5 volts |
| Output | 15 | AUDOUT left sound channel output |
| Input | 16 | AUDIN input to right sound channel |
| Output | 17 | E Buffered E clock (716KHz) |
| Input | 18 | /INT2 Interrupt on level 2 through Paula |
| | 19 | unused |
| Output | 20 | DTR Data Terminal Ready |
| | 21 | +5 volts |
| | 22 | unused |
| | 23 | +12 volts |
| Output | 24 | MCLK Clock output 2.58MHz |
| Output | 25 | /MRES Buffered reset output |

The serial interface has all of the usual RS-232 signal lines. In addition, there are many signals on this connector which have nothing to do with serial communications. Unfortunately, the assignment of the pins again differs on the Amiga 500 and 1000.

*Serial data lines*

The lines TXD, RXD, DSR, CTS, DTR, RTS and CD belong to the RS-232 interface. The TXD and RXD lines are the actual serial data lines. The TXD line is the serial output from the Amiga and RXD is the input. They are connected to the corresponding lines of Paula. The DTR line tells the peripheral device that the Amiga's serial interface is in operation. The RTS line tells the peripheral that the Amiga wants to send data over the serial line. The peripheral uses the CTS line to tell the Amiga that it is ready to receive it. The CD signal is usually used only with a modem and indicates that a carrier is being received.

These five RS-232 control lines are connected to CIA-B, PA3-PA7 as follows: DSR-PA3, CTS-PA4, CD-PA5, RTS-PA6 and DTR-PA7. The RI line is connected through a transistor to the SEL line of the Centronics interface.

To bring the signals up to RS-232 standards, the CIA lines are routed to the connector through RS-232 drivers. Inverting signal converters of the 1488 type are used for the output drivers. They require a power supply of +12 and -5 volts. The output voltage is also in this range. Chips of the type 1489A are used for the input buffers. These accept voltages between -12 and +0.5 volts as low and the range +3 to +25 volts as high.

The conventions for RS-232 interfaces dictate that the control lines be active high, while on the data lines TXD and RXD a logical 1 be represented as a low signal. Since the drivers invert, the corresponding port bits in CIA-B are also active low, so that a 0 value from CIA-B is used to set the corresponding RS-232 control line to high. The same also applies to the inputs, of course.

The remaining lines on the RS-232 connector have nothing to do with RS-232. The AUDOUT line is connected to the left audio channel and provided with its own 1 KOhm output resistance. The AUDIN line is connected directly to the AUDR pin of Paula through a 47 Ohm resistor. Audio signals fed into the AUDIN line on the Amiga are sent along with the right sound channel from Paula to the low-pass filter (see audio programming) to the right audio output. Nothing else is done to the signal. The INT2 input is directly connected to the INT2 input to Paula and can generate a processor interrupt of level 2 if the corresponding mask bit is set in Paula (see the section on interrupts). The E line is connected through a buffer to the processor E clock (see Section 1.2.1). A frequency of 3.58 MHz is available on the MCLK line. This clock is not in phase with either the RGB clock or the 3.58 MHz clocks for the custom chips. Finally, the reset signal is also available on this connector, naturally buffered.

# 1.3.5    External drive connector

*Figure 1.3.5.1*

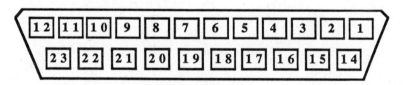

## DB-23 female

| | | |
|---|---|---|
| Input | 1 | /RDY Disk ready signal |
| Input | 2 | /DKRD Read data from disk |
| | 3 | GND |
| | 4 | GND |
| | 5 | GND |
| | 6 | GND |
| | 7 | GND |
| Output | 8 | /MTRX Motor on/off |
| Output | 9 | /SEL2 Select drive 2 |
| Output | 10 | /DRES Disk reset (turn motors off) |
| Input | 11 | /CHNG Disk change |
| | 12 | +5 volts |

| | | |
|---|---|---|
| Output | 13 | /SIDE Side selection |
| Input | 14 | /WPRO Write protect |
| Output | 15 | /TK0 Track 0 indicator |
| Output | 16 | /DKWE Switch to write |
| Output | 17 | /DKWD Write data to disk |
| Output | 18 | /STEP Move the read/write head |
| Output | 19 | /DIR Direction of head movement |
| Output | 20 | /SEL3 Select drive 3 |
| Output | 21 | /SEL1 Select drive 1 |
| Input | 22 | /INDEX Index signal from drive |
| | 23 | +12 volts |

*Figure 1.3.5.2*

2-row, 34-pin plug

All odd pins are grounded.

| | | | |
|---|---|---|---|
| 2 | /CHNG | 4 | /INUSE (connected to /MTR0D) |
| 6 | unused | 8 | /INDEX |
| 10 | /SEL0 | 12 | unused |
| 14 | unused | 16 | /MTR0 |
| 18 | DIR | 20 | /STEP |
| 22 | /DKWD | 24 | /DKWE |
| 26 | /TK0 | 28 | /WPRO |
| 30 | /DKRD | 32 | /SIDE |
| 34 | /RDY | | |

Power connector for the internal drive:

| | |
|---|---|
| 1 | +5 volts |
| 2 | GND |
| 3 | GND |
| 4 | +12 volts |

The disk drive connection on the Amiga is compatible with the Shugart bus. It allows up to four Shugart-compatible disk drives to be connected. The four drives are selected with the four drive selection SELx signals, where x is the number of the drive to select. Since the Amiga already has a built-in disk drive, only the SEL1, SEL2 and SEL3 lines are available on the external drive connector. The SEL0 line is connected to the internal connector to which the built-in drive is connected. Following is a description of the Shugart bus signals on the Amiga:

*Shugart bus*    SELX    The Amiga uses the SELX line to select one of the four
*signals*                drives. Except for the MTRX and DRES lines, all other
signals are active only when the corresponding SELX line is
activated.

MTRX    Normally this line causes all connected drives to turn their
motors on. With a maximum of up to four drives, this is
not an acceptable solution. Therefore the Amiga has a flip-
flop for each drive which takes on the value of the MTRX
line whenever the SEL line for the given drive goes low.
The output of the flip-flop is connected to the MTR line of
the drive. This allows the drive motors to be turned on and
off independently. For example, if the SEL0 line is placed
low while the MTRX line is at 0, the motor on the internal
floppy turns on. For the internal drive this flip-flop is on
the motherboard. For each additional drive, an additional one
is needed. On the 1010 disk drive Commodore placed this
flip-flop on a small adapter board.

RDY    When the MTR line of the corresponding drive goes to 0,
the RDY line (ready) signals the Amiga that the drive motor
has reached its optimum speed and the drive is now ready for
read or write accesses. If the MTR line is 1, so that the drive
motor is turned off, it is used for a special identification
mode (see below).

DRES    The DRES line (Drive RESet) is connected to the standard
Amiga reset and is used only to reset the motor flip-flop so
that all motors are turned off.

DKRD    The data from the drive selected by SELX travels to the
Amiga through the DKRD line (DisK Read Data) to the
DKRD line on Paula.

DKWD    Data from Paula's DKWD pin to the current drive, which
then writes it to the diskette.

DKWE    The DKWE line (DisK Write Enable) switches the drive
from read to write. If the line is high, the data are read from
diskette, while if it is low, data can be written to diskette.

SIDE    The SIDE line selects which side of the diskette the data are
read from or written to. If it is high, side 0 (the lower read/
write head) is active. If it is low, side 1 is selected.

WPRO    The WPRO line (Write PROtect) tells the Amiga that the
inserted disk is write-protected. If a write-protected disk is in
the drive, the WPRO line is 0.

STEP     A positive transition on the STEP line moves the read/write head of the drive one track in or out, depending on the state of the DIR line. The STEP signal should be at 1 when the SEL line of the activated drive if set back to high or there may be problems with the diskette-change detection.

DIR     The DIR line (DIRection) sets the direction in which the head moves when a pulse is sent on the STEP line. Low means that the head moves in toward the center of the disk and high indicates out toward the edge of the disk. Track 0 is the outermost track on the disk.

TK0     The TK0 (TracK 0) line is low whenever the read/write head of the selected drive is on track 0. This allows the head to be brought to a defined position.

INDEX     The INDEX signal is a short pulse which the drive delivers once per revolution of the diskette, between the start and end of a track.

CHNG     With the CHNG (CHaNGe) line the drive signals the Amiga that the diskette has been changed. As soon as the diskette has been removed from the drive, the CHNG line goes low. The line stays low until the computer issues a STEP pulse. If there is a diskette in the drive again by this time, CHNG goes back to 1. Otherwise it stays at 0 and the computer must issue STEP pulses at regular intervals in order to detect when a diskette has been inserted in the drive. These regular STEP pulses are the cause of the clacking noises that an Amiga drive makes when no diskette is inserted.

INUSE     The INUSE line exists only on the external floppy connector. If this line is placed low, the drive turns its LED on. Normally this line is connected to the MTR line.

To recognize when a drive has been connected to the bus, there is a special drive identification mode. A 32-bit word is read serially from the drive. To start this identification, the MTR line of the drive in question must be turned on and then off again (The description of the MTRX line tells how this is done). This resets the serial shift register in the drive. The individual data bits can then be read by placing the SELX line low and reading the value of the RDY as a data bit and then placing the SELX line high again. This process is repeated 32 times. The bit first received is the MSB (Most-Significant Bit) of the data word. Since the RDY line is active low, the data bits must be inverted.

The following are standard definitions for external drives:

        $0000 0000    No drive connected (00)
        $FFFF FFFF    Standard Amiga 3 1/2" drive (11)
        $5555 5555    Amiga 5 1/4" drive, 2x40 tracks (01)

As you can see, there are currently so few different identifications that it suffices to read just the first two bits. The values in parentheses are the combinations of these two bits.

As mentioned before, all of the lines except DRES affect only the drive selected. Originally the MTRX line was also independent of SELX, but the Amiga developers changed this by adding the motor flip-flop.

All lines on the Shugart bus are active low because the outputs in the Amiga as well as the drives themselves are provided with open-collector drives. In the Amiga these drives are 7407's.

The four inputs CHNG, WPRO, TK0 and RDY are connected in this order directly to PA4-PA7 of CIA-A. The eight outputs STEP, DIR, SIDE, SEL0, SEL1, SEL2, SEL3 and MTR come from CIA-B, PB0-7 and are connected through the 7407 drivers to the internal and external drive connectors. Since these drivers are non-inverting, the bits from the CIA's are inverted. The DKRD, DKWD and DKWE line come from Paula. Except for the MTRX line and the SEL signals, the connections to the internal and external floppies are the same. The internal drive is connected to SEL0. Its MTR line is derived from the flip-flop on the motherboard.

*Connecting an external drive to the Amiga*

It's pretty hard to get by with just one drive on the Amiga. But when the desire for a second drive becomes overpowering, the question arises: Should I buy one or build it myself? Since normal two-sided 3 1/2" drives, as used in the Amiga, have recently become available for a fraction of the price of the original Amiga second drive A1010, homebrew is a good alternative. What has to be done?

The connector for a 3 1/2" drive like the NEC FD1035 or FD 1036 is identical to the 34-pin connector used for the internal drive on the Amiga, as is the power connector. To connect a drive like the FD1035, all you have to do is add the motor flip-flop. Figure 1.3.5.3 shows the corresponding circuit.

*Figure   1.3.5.3*

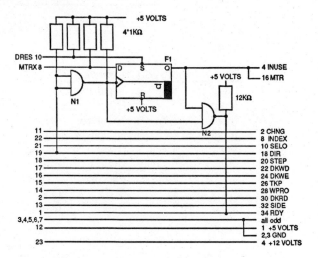

As you can see, the F1 flip-flop stores the signal on the MTRX line when the SEL1 line goes from high to low. Since the flip-flop stores the value on its data input on the leading edge of the clock, SEL1 must be inverted. This is accomplished by the NAND gate N1. The Q output is connected directly to the MTR input of the second drive.

The N2 NAND gate has nothing to do with motor control. It is used for the identification mode mentioned earlier, which most standard drives do not support. Whenever the motor is turned off and the SEL1 line is active (0), this gate pulls the RDY line low. Thus the Amiga recognizes this drive as a standard 3 1/2" drive with the number DF1:.

Since only half of the two IC's required are actually used, they can also be used to add a second additional drive. The inputs of N1 must then be connected to SEL2 (pin 9 on the external drive connector).

Some jumpers have to be added to most drives so that the CHNG line works properly. The best source for this information is the manual for the drive in question. As an example, jumper J1 has to be shorted on an NEC FC1035.

## 1.3.6     The game ports

*Figure 1.3.6.1*

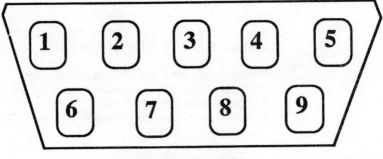

## 9-pin female

Use as:

|  | Mouse port | Joystick | Paddle | Lightpen |
|---|---|---|---|---|
| Input | 1 | V-pulse | Up | unused |
| Input | 2 | H-pulse | Down | unused |
| Input | 3 | VQ-pulse | Left | Left button unused |
| Input | 4 | HQ-pulse | Right | Right button unused |
| I/O | 5 | (Button 3) | unused | Right port button |
| I/O | 6 | Button 1 | Fire button | unused LP signal |
|  | 7 | +5 volts | +5 volts | +5 volts |
|  | 8 | GND | GND | GND |
| I/O | 9 | Button 2 | unused | Left port unused |

The game ports are inputs for input devices other than the keyboard, such as a mouse, joystick, trackball, paddle or lightpen. There are two game ports. The left one is numbered game port 0 and the right game port 1. The pin assignment of both ports is identical, except that the LP line is present only on game port 0. Internally the game ports are connected to CIA-A, Agnus, Denise and Paula.

*Game port 0:*

| Pin no. | Chip | Pin |
|---------|------|-----|
| 1 | Denise | M0V (via multiplexer) |
| 2 | Denise | M0H (via multiplexer) |
| 3 | Denise | M1V (via multiplexer) |
| 4 | Denise | M1H (via multiplexer) |
| 5 | Paula | P0Y |
| 6 | CIA-A | PA6 |
|  | as well as Agnus | LP |
| 9 | Paula | P0X |

*Game port 1:*

| Pin no. | Chip | Pin |
|---------|------|-----|
| 1 | Denise | M0V (via multiplexer) |
| 2 | Denise | M0H (via multiplexer) |
| 3 | Denise | M1V (via multiplexer) |
| 4 | Denise | M1H (via multiplexer) |
| 5 | Paula | P1Y |
| 6 | CIA-A | PA7 |
| 9 | Paula | P1X |

The function of the multiplexer is explained in Section 1.2.3.2.

The pin assignments for the various input devices were chosen so that almost all standard joysticks, mice, paddles and lightpens can be used. It is possible to use lightpens intended for the C64, for example. The button line is usually connected to a switch which is pressed when the lightpen touches the screen. The LP line is the actual lightpen signal, which is generated by the electronics in the pen when the electron beam passes its tip.

All of the lines labelled button and the four directions for the joystick are active low. In the various input devices are switches which are connected between the input and ground (GND). A high signal on the input means an open switch, while a closed switch generates a low.

Paddles (varying resistances potentiometers) can be connected to the P0X, P0Y, P1X and P1Y analog inputs. Their value should be 470 KOhms and they should be connected between the corresponding input and +5 volts.

The two fire-button lines connected to CIA-A can naturally be programmed as outputs. Some care must be exercised not to overwrite the lowest bit of the port register, or the system crashes (PA0:OVL).

The section on programming the custom chips explains how the game port lines are read.

The +5 volt line on the two game ports is not connected directly to the Amiga power supply. A current-protection circuit is inserted in these lines which limits the short-term peak current to 700 mA and the operating current to 400 mA. This makes these outputs short-circuit proof. To prevent the voltage on these two +5 volt pins from falling off too much, the current draw on the two ports should not exceed a total of 250 mA.

Unfortunately, this protection measure has been omitted from the Amiga 500 and 2000.

---

## 1.3.7        The expansion port

*Figure 1.3.7.1*

### 86-pin printed circuit connector
### (Amiga 500/Amiga 1000)

| | | | |
|---|---|---|---|
| 1 | GND | 2 | GND |
| 3 | GND | 4 | GND |
| 5 | +5 volts | 6 | +5 volts |
| 7 | Expansion | 8 | -5 volts |
| 9 | Exp. (28M on A2000) | 10 | +12 volts |
| 11 | Expansion | 12 | GND |
| 13 | GND | 14 | /C3 |
| 15 | CDAC | 16 | /C1 |
| 17 | /OVR | 18 | XRDY |
| 19 | /INT2 | 20 | /PALOPE (unsed on A2000) |
| 21 | A5 | 22 | /INT6 |
| 23 | A6 | 24 | A4 |
| 25 | GND | 26 | A3 |
| 27 | A2 | 28 | A7 |
| 29 | A1 | 30 | A8 |
| 31 | FC0 | 32 | A9 |
| 33 | FC1 | 34 | A10 |
| 35 | FC2 | 36 | A11 |
| 37 | GND | 38 | A12 |

| 39 | A13 | 40 | /IPL0 |
|----|-----|----|-------|
| 41 | A14 | 42 | /IPL1 |
| 43 | A15 | 44 | /IPL2 |
| 45 | A16 | 46 | /BERR |
| 47 | A17 | 48 | /VPA |
| 49 | GND | 50 | E |
| 51 | /VMA | 52 | A18 |
| 53 | /RES | 54 | A19 |
| 55 | /HLT | 56 | A20 |
| 57 | A22 | 58 | A21 |
| 59 | A23 | 60 | /BR |
| 61 | GND | 62 | /BGACK |
| 63 | PD15 | 64 | /BG |
| 65 | PD14 | 66 | /DTACK |
| 67 | PD13 | 68 | /PRW |
| 69 | PD12 | 70 | /LDS |
| 71 | PD11 | 72 | /UDS |
| 73 | GND | 74 | /AS |
| 75 | PD0 | 76 | PD10 |
| 77 | PD1 | 78 | PD9 |
| 79 | PD2 | 80 | PD8 |
| 81 | PD3 | 82 | PD7 |
| 83 | PD4 | 84 | PD6 |
| 85 | GND | 86 | PD5 |

*The expansion port*

The expansion port makes available virtually all of the important control lines and bus signals present in the Amiga system. It can be used to connect RAM expansions, new processors, hard disk controllers, etc. On the Amiga 1000 this port is located near the two game ports behind an easily removable plastic panel. On the Amiga 500 it is placed on the left side of the case, as seen from the front. It takes the form of an 86-pin edge connector. The distance between the pins is 1/10 inch. Suitable sockets for this connector are not easy to find at this time.

On the Amiga 2000 there are two different connections. One is the MMU connector which corresponds closely to that listed above (note parentheses), and the other is the five 100-pin Amiga connectors (also called the Zorro bus). On the Amiga 2000 these six connectors are found on the motherboard inside the case. They are sockets for 86- or 100-pin edges card. The distance between contacts is again 1/10 inch.

Most of the signals on the expansion port are connected directly to the corresponding lines of the 68000. The exact functions of these lines is discussed in Section 1.2.1. These are the following signals:

A0-A23: Address bus
PD0-PD15: Processor data bus
IPL0-IPL2: Processor interrupt lines
FC0-FC2: Function code lines from the 68000
AS, UDS, LDS, PRW, DTACK, VMA, VPA: Bus control lines
RES, HLT, BERR, BG, BGACK, BR, E: Miscellaneous control
signals from the 68000

The remaining signals have the following functions:

*INT2 and INT6*

These two lines are connected to the Paula pins with the same names.
They are used to generate a level 2 or level 6 interrupt.

*CDAC, C1, C3, and 28M on the Amiga 2000*

*Figure   1.3.7.2*

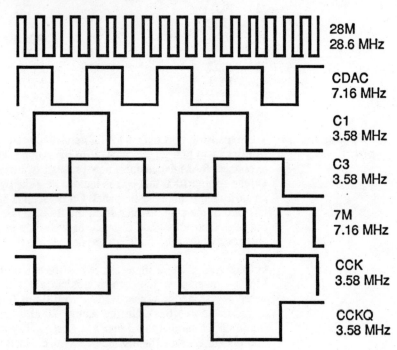

28M
28.6 MHz

CDAC
7.16 MHz

C1
3.58 MHz

C3
3.58 MHz

7M
7.16 MHz

CCK
3.58 MHz

CCKQ
3.58 MHz

These are the various Amiga clock signals. Their frequency and phase
can best be gathered from the figure above. On the Amiga 2000 the
28.64 MHz master clock of the Amiga is also available on the expansion port. The clock signals 7M, CCK and CCKQ shown above are not
on the expansion port. 7M is the 68000 clock and CCK and CCKQ are
connected to the custom chips.

*XRDY, OVR*      These signals are used to automatically configure an expansion board.
*and PALOPE*     Unfortunately, their exact function is still unknown.

The lines labelled "Expansion" are not used. They are reserved for future
expansions to the Amiga hardware. On the Amiga 2000 they are already
used to a degree. One of the expansion lines is used to supply the 28M
clock signal.

## 1.3.8      Supplying power from the interfaces

All of the interface connectors carry one or more of the three power
supply voltages present in the Amiga. This makes it possible to supply
peripheral devices with power through the given interface. You must
take into account the maximum load capability of these connections.
The following table shows the maximum loads recommended by Commodore on the Amiga 1000:

| Interface | +5 volts | +12 volts | -12 volts |
|---|---|---|---|
| TV Mod | - | 60 mA | - |
| RGB | 300 mA | 175 mA | 50 mA |
| RS232 | 100 mA | 50 mA | 50 mA |
| External disk | 270 mA | 160 mA | - |
| Centronics | 100 mA | - | - |
| Expansion port | 1000 mA | 50 mA | 50 mA |
| Game port 0 | 125 mA | - | - |
| Game port 1 | 125 mA | - | - |

This table should only be used as a rough guideline. First of all, the
values given apply only when all of the ports are actually loaded at the
same time. For example, if the expansion port is not used, then an
extra 1000 mA is available at the other +5 volt connections. If it is
certain that some ports remain free in a given system configuration,
then more power remains for the other outputs. Of course, you can
always use the brute force method and continue connecting expansions
until the power supply shuts down. As (generally accidental) short
circuits have shown, this does not seem to hurt it. The reader must,
however, take responsibility himself for such experiments. Caution is
recommended especially for the +5 volt supply. A short circuit can
cause currents as high as 8 mA to flow.

Second, the table above applies only to the Amiga 1000. It cannot be
used for the Amiga 500 or 2000 since the power supplies for these
computers have been designed differently. On the Amiga 500 the power
capability of the supply is more limited. Expansions with heavy current
draws should be given their own power supplies.

The power supply on the Amiga 2000 is clearly stronger than that on the Amiga 1000. It must be able to power entire additional Amigas and IBM cards.

*Note:*          Another difference between the Amiga 500 power supply verses the Amiga 1000 is the negative power supply. It is -12 volts instead of the -5 volts found on the Amiga 1000. This means that wherever -5 volts appears in this book, the Amiga 500 owner must allow for -12 volts instead.

# 1.4    The keyboard

*Figure 1.4.1*                    ## American keyboard

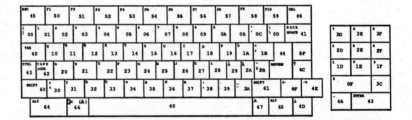

## German keyboard

The Amiga keyboard is an intelligent keyboard. It has its own micro-processor which handles the time-consuming job of reading the keys and return complete key codes to the Amiga. There have been many versions of the Amiga keyboard, but they differ only in new keys added to them and therefore new key codes as well. The figure shows the layout of the keys and their codes for the German and American versions of the keyboard. As you can see, the codes do **not** correspond to the ASCII standard. The keyboard only returns raw key codes, which are converted to ASCII by the operating system.

There is, however, a system to the key codes:

$00-$3F    These are the codes for the letters, digits and punctuation. Their assignments correspond to the arrangement on the keyboard.

$40-$4F    The codes for the standard special keys like SPACE, RETURN, TAB, etc.

$50-$5F    The function keys like HELP.

$60-$67    Keys for selecting different control levels (Shift, Amiga, Alternate and Control)

**KEYup/down**    The keyboard processor can do even more. It can distinguish between when a key is pressed and when it is released. As you can see, all keyboard codes are only 7 bits wide (values range from $00-$7F). The eight bit is the KEYup/down flag. It is used by the keyboard to tell the computer whether the key was just pressed or released. If the eighth bit is zero, this means that the key was just pressed (KEYdown). If it is 1, then the key was just released (KEYup). This way the Amiga always knows which keys are currently pressed. The keyboard can thus be used for other purposes which require various keys to be held simultaneously. This includes music programs, for example, which use the keyboard for playing polyphonically.

**CAPS LOCK**    One exception is the CAPS LOCK key. The keyboard simulates a push-button switch with this key. When it's pressed the first time, it engages and the LED goes on. It does not disengage until it is pressed again. The LED then turns off. This behavior is also reflected in the KEYup/down flag. If CAPS LOCK is pressed, the LED turns on and the key code for CAPS LOCK is sent to the computer along with a cleared 8th bit to show that a key was just pressed. When the key is released, no KEYup code is sent and the LED stays on. Not until CAPS LOCK is pressed again is a KEYup code sent (with a set 8th bit) and the LED turns off.

---

## 1.4.1    The keyboard circuit

**Figure 1.4.1.1**

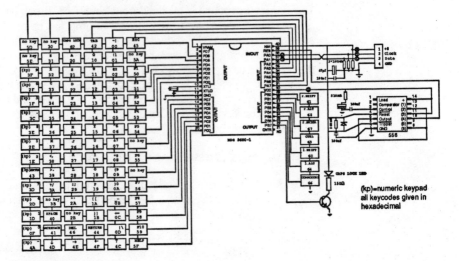

(kp)=numeric keypad
all keycodes given in hexadecimal

*6500/1 micro processor*

The heart of the keyboard circuit is the 6500/1 microprocessor. The 6500/1 is what is called a single-chip microcomputer. It contains all of the components necessary for a simple computer system to work. The heart of 6500/1 is a 6502 microprocessor. In addition, it contains 2KB ROM with the control program, 64 bytes of static RAM, 4 bidirectional 8-bit ports, a 16-bit counter with its own control input, and a clock generator.

All the 6500/1 needs for operation is a supply voltage of 5 volts and a crystal for the clock generation. The 6500/1 is operated with a 3MHz crystal in the Amiga keyboard. Since this frequency is divided by two internally, the clock frequency is 1.5MHz.

The second chip on the keyboard is a 556 precision timer. Actually, there are two of these precision timers in the package. The 556 and a few other components are used to provide the reset signal for the 6500/1.

The keys are combined into two groups. The seven special-function keys (Shift right, ALT right, Control, Amiga left, ALT left and Shift left) are connected directly to the first seven port lines of the PB port.

All remaining keys are set up in a matrix of six rows by 15 columns. The rows are connected to lines PA2 to PA7 of port A. These six lines are configured as inputs. The 15 columns are controlled by ports C and D. The 16th column, connected to PD7 is not used in the current version of the keyboard.

When the 6500/1 reads the keyboard, it pulls each of the individual columns low in turn. Since the outputs of ports C and D are open-collector outputs without internal pull-up resistors, they are completely in active when the output is set to 1. After the processor has pulled a line low, it reads the six rows. The six rows are provided with internal pull-up resistors so that all unpressed keys are interpreted as high. Each pressed key connects one column with one row. If keys are pressed in the column currently activated by the 6500/1, the corresponding row inputs are low. After all of the columns have been activated and the corresponding rows have been read, the processor knows the state of all the keys.

If this has changed since the last time the keys were read, it sends the appropriate key codes to the computer.

## 1.4.2    Data transfer

*Figure 1.4.2.1*

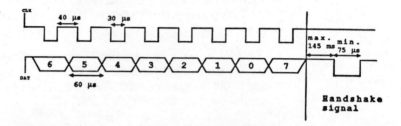

The keyboard is connected to the Amiga through a four-line coiled cable. Two of the lines are used to supply power to the keyboard electronics (5 volts). The entire data transfer takes place on the remaining two lines. One of the lines is used for data, KDAT, and the other is the clock line, KLCK. Inside the Amiga, KDAT is connected to the serial input SP and KCLK is connected to the CNT pin of CIA-A (see Section 1.2.2).

The data transfer is unidirectional. It always runs from the keyboard to the computer. The 6500/1 places the individual data bits on the data line (KDAT), accompanied by 20 microsecond-long low pulses on the clock line (KCLK). 40-microsecond pauses are placed between the individual clock pulses. This means that the transfer time for each bit is 60 microseconds. This yields a 480-microsecond transfer time for one byte, or a transfer rate of 16666 baud (bits/second).

After the last bit has been sent, the keyboard waits for a handshake pulse from the computer. The Amiga sends this signal by pulling the KDAT line low for at least 75 microseconds. The exact process can be seen in the figure.

The bits are not sent in the usual order 7-6-5-4-3-2-1-0, but rotated one bit position to the left: 6-5-4-3-2-1-0-7. For example, the key code for J with the eight bit set = 10100110 and after rotation it is 01001101. The KEYup/down flag is always the last bit sent.

The data line is active low. This means that a 0 is represented by a high signal and a 1 by a low.

The CIA shift register in the Amiga reads the current bit on the SP line at each clock pulse. After eight clock pulses the CIA has received a complete data byte. The CIA normally generates a level-2 interrupt, which causes the operating system to do the following:

- Read the serial data register in the CIA
- Invert and right-rotate the byte to get the original key code back
- Output the handshake pulse
- Process the received code

*Synchroniza-*
*tion*

In order to have an error-free data transfer, the timing of the sender and receiver must match. The bit position for the serial transfer must be identical for both. Otherwise the keyboard may have sent all eight bits, while the serial port of the CIA is still somewhere in the middle of the byte. Such a loss of synchronization occurs whenever the Amiga is turned on or the keyboard is plugged into a running Amiga. The computer has no way of recognizing improper synchronization. This task is handled by the keyboard.

After each byte is sent, the keyboard waits a maximum of 145 milliseconds for the handshake signal. If it does not occur in this time, the keyboard processor assumes that a transfer error occurred and enters a special mode in which it tries to restore the lost synchronization. It sends a 1 on the KDAT line together with a clock pulse and waits another 145ms for the synchronization signal. It repeats this until it receives a handshake signal from the Amiga. Synchronization is now restored.

The data byte received by the Amiga is incorrect, however. The state of the first seven bits is uncertain. Only the last bit received is definitely a 1, because the keyboard processor only outputs 1's during the procedure described above. Since this last bit is the KEYup/down flag, the incorrect code is always a KEYup code, or a released key. This makes program disturbances fewer than if an incorrect KEYdown code had been sent. This is why each byte is rotated one bit to the left before it is sent, so that the KEYup/down flag is always the last bit sent.

*Special Codes*

There are some special cases in the transmission, which the keyboard tells the Amiga through special key codes. The following table contains all possible special codes:

| Code | Meaning |
| --- | --- |
| $F9 | Last key code was incorrect |
| $FA | Keyboard buffer is full |
| $FC | Error in keyboard self test |
| $FD | Start of the keys held down on power up |
| $FE | End of the keys held on power up |
| $F9 | The $F9 code is always sent by the keyboard after a loss of synchronization and subsequent resynchronization. This is how the Amiga knows that the last key code was incorrect. After this code the keyboard retransmits the lost key code. |
| $FA | The keyboard has an internal buffer of 10 characters. When this buffer is full, it sends an $FA to the computer to signal that it must empty the buffer or lose characters. |

$FC          After it is turned on, the keyboard processor performs a self-test. This can be seen by the brief lighting of the CAPS LOCK LED. If it discovers an error, it sends an $FC to the Amiga and then goes into an endless loop in which it flashes the LED.

$FD & $FE
             If the self-test was successful, the keyboard transmits all of the keys which were held when the computer was turned on. To tell the computer this, it starts the transmission with the $FD code. Following this it sends the codes for the keys which were held down while the computer was turned on, and then an $FE. Then the normal transfer starts.

             If no keys were pressed, $FD and $FE are sent in succession.

*Reset through*   The keyboard can also generate a reset on the Amiga. If the two Amiga
*the keyboard*    keys and the Ctrl key are pressed simultaneously, the keyboard processor pulls the KCLK line low for about 0.5 seconds. This tells the reset circuit of the Amiga to generate a processor reset. After at least one of these keys has been released, the keyboard also resets itself. This can be seen by the flashing of the CAPS LOCK LED. (It is interesting that this reset is triggered by the KCLK line, which is connected internally to the CNT line of CIA-A. Apparently, you can cause a hardware reset through appropriate programming of this CIA).

---

# 1.4.3       Keyboard bugs

Finally, we should mention something about the weaknesses of this keyboard. If you have an Amiga 1000, try a little experiment: Press the three keys A, Q and TAB at the same time. Don't worry, your Amiga isn't broken. But it still is surprising that the CAPS LOCK LED lights up without having pressed this key. The same thing works for all other keys. For example, if you press S, W and D together, an E always appears on the screen.

**Figure   1.4.3.1**

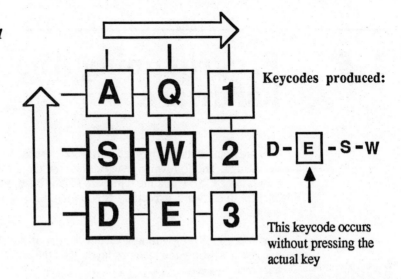

Keycodes produced:

D - E - S - W

This keycode occurs
without pressing the
actual key

The above figure illustrates this phenomenon. Each pressed key represents a short space between a row and a column. The keyboard processor controls a column and then reads the individual rows. The arrows show the direction of this reading. It determines the order in which the pressed keys are recognized, if more than one is held down. When the column belonging to E is selected and the processor reads the corresponding row while D, W and S are pressed, it recognizes a short between the row and column, which it naturally takes for a pressed E. Actually, this short is caused by the other three keys, but the keyboard processor has no way of recognizing this. It gets even more interesting if you hold down five keys at once. With the combination D, S, A, Q, 1, four additional codes are generated: W, 2, E and 3.

This effect can be seen in many inexpensive matrix keyboards; it isn't limited to just the Amiga.

The moral is that you shouldn't develop programs in which such key combinations are required. This is also why the Amiga, Shift, Alternate, Commodore and Control keys, which are generally used in combination with other keys, are left out of the normal key matrix.

# 1.5    Programming the hardware

The previous sections involved closer looks at the hardware structure of the Amiga. The following pages show how the three custom chips are programmed. Now that the hardware side is clear, we'll begin an introduction to software, especially concerning the creation of graphics and sound.

For successful programming of the Amiga at the machine level, it is necessary to know the memory layout and the addresses of the individual chip registers.

## 1.5.1    The memory layout

*Figure 1.5.1.1*

**Normal configuration**

|  | | |
|---|---|---|
| $000000 | 512K chip RAM | Copy of memory range $FC0000 - $FFFFFF |
| $080000 | copy of chip RAM | |
| $100000 | copy of chip RAM | |
| $180000 | copy of chip RAM | |
| $200000 | 8MB fast RAM area | |
| $A00000 | CIAs | Starting address of CIA B   Starting address of CIA A |
| $C00000 | 512K expansion (Amiga 500/2000) | |
| $C80000 | Unused | |
| $DC0000 | Realtime clock (Amiga 500/2000) | Base address - realtime clock |
| $DF0000 | Custom chips | Base address - custom chips |
| $E00000 | Unused | |
| $E80000 | Expansion slot area | |
| $F00000 | ROM module | |
| $F80000 | 256K copy of KickStart ROM | |
| $FC0000 | 256K KickStart ROM | |

The first figure shows the normal memory configuration of the Amiga as it appears after booting. The entire address range of the 68000 comprises 16 megabytes (addresses from 0 to $FFFFFF). Given its size, it's no wonder that large areas are unused or that some chips appear at several different addresses. There is no reason to be stingy with memory. The days of memory bank switching are fortunately over thanks to the 68000.

*RAM*

The RAM area designated as chip RAM contains the normal memory of the Amiga. If the memory expansion is not added to the Amiga 1000, it extends only to $3FFFF. This 512K is called the chip RAM because the three custom chips can access only this area of memory.

It is possible that processor accesses to the chip RAM can be slowed down by the activities of the custom chips. To prevent this, the Amiga can be expanded with what is called *fast RAM*. This lies at address $200000 in memory and can accommodate up to eight megabytes. Since the custom chips have no access to this memory, the 68000 can operate at full speed in this area. This is the origin of the term fast RAM. In the basic configuration, the Amiga does not have any fast RAM.

The 512K expansion card for the Amiga 500 or 2000 lies at $C00000 to $C7FFFF. It has a special status and is neither true chip RAM nor fast RAM. On one hand, the custom chips have no access to it, but on the other hand, the processor can be slowed down by the custom chips when it accesses this memory. This RAM expansion combines the bad properties of both chip RAM and fast RAM without having any of their positive qualities. The reason is not malice on the part of the Amiga developers, just the simplicity of this RAM expansion, and therefore its low manufacturing cost.

*CIAs*

The various registers of the CIAs appear multiple times in the range from $A00000 to $BFFFFF. More about the addressing of the CIAs can be obtained from Section 1.2. Here are the addresses of the individual registers at their normal positions:

| CIA-A | CIA-B | Name | Function |
|---|---|---|---|
| $BFE001 | $BFD000 | PA | Port register A |
| $BFE101 | $BFD100 | PB | Port register B |
| $BFE201 | $BFD200 | DDRA | Data direction register A |
| $BFE301 | $BFD300 | DDRB | Data direction register B |
| $BFE401 | $BFD400 | TALO | Timer A low byte |
| $BFE501 | $BFD500 | TAHI | Timer A high byte |
| $BFE601 | $BFD600 | TBLO | Timer B low byte |
| $BFE701 | $BFD700 | TBHI | Timer B high byte |
| $BFE801 | $BFD800 | E. LSB | Event counter bits 0-7 |
| $BFE901 | $BFD900 | E. MID | Event counter bits 8-15 |
| $BFEA01 | $BFDA00 | E. MSB | Event counter 16-23 |
| $BFEB01 | $BFDB00 | — | Unused |
| $BFEC01 | $BFDC00 | SP | Serial port register |
| $BFED01 | $BFDD00 | IRC | Interrupt control register |
| $BFEE01 | $BFDE00 | CRA | Control register A |
| $BFEF01 | $BFDE00 | CRB | Control register B |

*Custom chips*    The various custom chip registers occupy a 512-byte area. Each register is 2 bytes (one word) wide. All registers are on even addresses.

The base address of the register area is at $DFF00. The effective address is then $DFF000 + register address. The following list shows the names and functions of the individual chip registers. Most of the register descriptions are unfamiliar now since we haven't discussed the function of the registers, but this list will give you an overview and will later serve as a reference.

There are four types of registers:

r (Read)     This register can only be read.

w (Write)    This register can only be written.

s (Strobe)   An access to a register of this type causes a one-time action to occur in the chip. The value of the data bus, that is, the word which is written into the register, is irrelevant. These registers are usually only accessed by Agnus.

er (Early Read)
             A register designated as *early read* is a DMA output register. It contains the data to be written into the chip RAM through DMA. There are two such registers (DSKDATR and BLTDDAT—output registers for the disk and the blitter). They are accessed only by the DMA controller in Agnus, when their contents are written into the chip RAM. The processor cannot access these registers.

A, D, P      These three letters stand for the three chips Agnus, Denise and Paula. They indicate in which chip the given register is found. It is also possible for a register to be located in more than one chip. On such a write access, the value is then written into two or even all chips. This is the case when the contents of a given register are needed by more than one chip.

             For the programmer it is unimportant where the registers are located. The entire area can be treated as one custom chip. The programmer needs to know only the address and function of the desired register.

p, d         A lowercase d means that this register is accessible only by the DMA controller. Registers with a small p in front of them can be used only by the processor or the Copper. If both letters are in front of a register, it means that it is usually accessed by the DMA, but also by the processor from time to time.

Number of registers: 197

Registers which are normally accessed only by the DMA controller: 54

Base address of the register area: $DFF00

*Register table*

| Name | Reg. addr. | Chip | R/W | p/d | Function |
|------|-----------|------|-----|-----|----------|
| BLTDDAT | 000 | A | er | d | Blitter output data (from blitter to RAM) |
| DMACONR | 002 | AP | r | p | Read DMA controller register |
| VPOSR | 004 | A | r | p | MSB of the vertical position |
| VHPOSR | 006 | A | r | p | Vertical and horizontal beam position |
| DSKDATR | 008 | P | er | d | Disk read data (from disk to RAM) |
| JOY0DAT | 00A | D | r | p | Joystick/mouse position game port 0 |
| JOY1DAT | 00C | D | r | p | Joystick/mouse position game port 1 |
| CLXDAT | 00E | D | r | p | Collision register |
| ADKCONR | 010 | P | r | p | Read audio/disk control register |
| POT0DAT | 012 | P | r | p | Read potentiometer on game port 0 |
| POT1DAT | 014 | P | r | p | Read potentiometer on game port 1 |
| POTGOR | 016 | P | r | p | Read pot. port data |
| SERDATR | 018 | P | r | p | Read serial port and status |
| DSKBYTR | 01A | P | r | p | Read disk data byte and status |
| INTENAR | 01C | P | r | p | Read interrupt enable |
| INTREQR | 01E | P | r | p | Read interrupt request |
| DSKPTH | 020 | A | w | p | Disk DMA address bits 16-18 |
| DSKPTL | 022 | A | w | p | Disk DMA address bits 1-15 |
| DSKLEN | 024 | P | w | p | Disk DMA block length |
| DSKDAT | 026 | P | w | d | Disk write data (from RAM to disk) |
| REFPTR | 028 | A | w | d | Refresh counter |
| VPOSW | 02A | A | w | p | Write MSB of the vertical beam position |
| VHPOSW | 02C | A | w | p | Write vertical and horizontal beam position |
| COPCON | 02E | A | w | p | Copper control register |
| SERDAT | 030 | P | w | p | Write serial data and stop bits |
| SERPER | 032 | P | w | p | Serial port control register and baud rate |
| POTGO | 034 | P | w | p | Write pot. port data and start bit |
| JOYTEST | 036 | D | w, | p | Write in both mouse counters |
| STREQU | 038 | D | s | d | Horizontal sync with VB and equal frame |
| STRVBL | 03A | D | s | d | Horizontal sync with vertical blank |
| STRHOR | 03C | DP | s | d | Horizontal sync signal |
| STRLONG | 03E | D | s | d | Long horizontal line marker |

*Copper Registers*

The following registers can be accessed by Copper when COPCON=1.

| Name | Reg addr | Chip | R/W | p/d | Function |
|------|----------|------|-----|-----|----------|
| BLTCON0 | 040 | A | w | p | Blitter control register 0 |
| BLTCON1 | 042 | A | w | p | Blitter control register 1 |
| BLTAFWM | 044 | A | w | p | Mask for the first data word from A |
| BLTALWM | 046 | A | w | p | Mask for the last data word from A |
| BLTCPTH | 048 | A | w | p | Address of the source data C bits 16-18 |
| BLTCPTL | 04A | A | w | p | Address of the source data C bits 1-15 |
| BLTBPTH | 04C | A | w | p | Address of the source data B bits 16-18 |
| BLTBPTL | 04E | A | w | p | Address of the source data B bits 1-15 |
| BLTAPTH | 050 | A | w | p | Address of the source data A bits 16-18 |
| BLTAPTL | 052 | A | w | p | Address of the source data A bits 1-15 |
| BLTDPTH | 054 | A | w | p | Address of the destination data D bits 16-18 |
| BLTDPTL | 056 | A | w | p | Address of the destination data D bits 1-15 |
| BLTSIZE | 058 | A | w | p | Start bit and size of the blitter window |
| — | 05A | | | | unused |
| — | 05C | | | | unused |
| — | 05E | | | | unused |
| BLTCMOD | 060 | A | w | p | Blitter module for source data C |
| BLTBMOD | 062 | A | w | p | Blitter module for source data B |
| BLTAMOD | 064 | A | w | p | Blitter module for source data A |
| BLTDMOD | 066 | A | w | p | Blitter module for destination data D |
| — | 068 | | | | unused |
| — | 06A | | | | unused |
| — | 06C | | | | unused |
| — | 06E | | | | unused |
| BLTCDAT | 070 | A | w | d | Blitter source data register C |
| BLTBDAT | 072 | A | w | d | Blitter source data register B |
| BLTADAT | 074 | A | w | d | Blitter source data register A |
| — | 076 | | | | unused |
| — | 078 | | | | unused |
| — | 07A | | | | unused |
| — | 07C | | | | unused |
| DSKSYNC | 07E | P | w | p | Disk sync pattern |

*Copper Registers*

The following registers can always by written by the Copper:

| Name | Reg addr | Chip | R/W | p/d | Function |
|------|----------|------|-----|-----|----------|
| COP1LCH | 080 | A | w | p | Address of the 1st Copper list bits 16-18 |
| COP1LCL | 082 | A | w | p | Address of the 1st Copper list bits 1-15 |
| COP2LCH | 084 | A | w | p | Address of 2nd Copper list bits 16-18 |
| COP2LCL | 086 | A | w | p | Address of the 2nd Copper list bits 1-15 |
| COPJMP1 | 088 | A | s | p | Jump to the start of the 1st Copper list |
| COPJMP2 | 08A | A | s | p | Jump to the start of the 2nd Copper list |
| COPINS | 08C | A | w | d | Copper command register |
| DIWSTRT | 08E | A | w | p | Upper left corner of the display window |
| DIWSTOP | 090 | A | w | p | Lower right corner of the display window |
| DDFSTRT | 092 | A | w | p | Start of the bit plane DMA (horiz. pos.) |
| DDFSTOP | 094 | A | w | p | End of the bit plane DMA (horiz. pos.) |
| DMACON | 096 | ADP | w | p | Write DMA control register |
| CLXCON | 098 | D | w | p | Write collision control register |
| INTENA | 09A | P | w | p | Write interrupt enable |

| | Name | Reg addr | Chip | R/W | p/d | Function |
|---|---|---|---|---|---|---|
| *Copper* | | | | | | |
| *Registers* | INTREQ | 09C | P | w | p | Write interrupt request |
| | ADKCON | 09E | P | w | p | Audio, disk, and UART control register |
| | AUD0LCH | 0A0 | A | w | p | Address of the audio data bits 16-18 |
| | AUD0LCL | 0A2 | A | w | p | On sound channel 0, bits 1-15 |
| | AUD0LEN | 0A4 | P | w | p | Channel 0 length of audio data |
| | AUD0PER | 0A6 | P | w | p | Channel 0 period duration |
| | AUD0VOL | 0A8 | P | w | p | Channel 0 volume |
| | AUD0DAT | 0AA | P | w | d | Channel 0 audio data (to the D/A converter) |
| | — | 0AC | | | | unused |
| | — | 0AE | | | | unused |
| | AUD1LCH | 0B0 | A | w | p | Address of the audio data bits 16-18 |
| | AUD1LCL | 0B2 | A | w | p | On sound channel 1, bits 1-15 |
| | AUD1LEN | 0B4 | P | w | p | Channel 1 length of audio data |
| | AUD1PER | 0B6 | P | w | p | Channel 1 period duration |
| | AUD1VOL | 0B8 | P | w | p | Channel 1 volume |
| | AUD1DAT | 0BA | P | w | d | Channel 1 audio data (to the D/A converter) |
| | — | 0BC | | | | unused |
| | — | 0BE | | | | unused |
| | AUD2LCH | 0C0 | A | w | p | Address of the audio data bits 16-18 |
| | AUD2LCL | 0C2 | A | w | p | On sound channel 2, bits 1-15 |
| | AUD2LEN | 0C4 | P | w | p | Channel 2 length of audio data |
| | AUD2PER | 0C6 | P | w | p | Channel 2 period duration |
| | AUD2VOL | 0C8 | P | w | p | Channel 2 volume |
| | AUD2DAT | 0CA | P | w | d | Channel 2 audio data (to the D/A converter) |
| | — | 0CC | | | | unused |
| | — | 0CE | | | | unused |
| | AUD3LCH | 0D0 | A | w | p | Address of the audio data bits 16-18 |
| | AUD3LCL | 0D2 | A | w | p | On sound channel 3, bits 1-15 |
| | AUD3LEN | 0D4 | P | w | p | Channel 3 length of audio data |
| | AUD3PER | 0D6 | P | w | p | Channel 3 period duration |
| | AUD3VOL | 0D8 | P | w | p | Channel 3 volume |
| | AUD3DAT | 0DA | P | w | d | Channel 3 audio data (to the D/A converter) |
| | — | 0DC | | | | unused |
| | — | 0DE | | | | unused |
| | BPL1PTH | 0E0 | A | w | p | Address of bit plane 1, bits 16-18 |
| | BPL1PTL | 0E2 | A | w | p | Address of bit plane 1, bits 1-15 |
| | BPL2PTH | 0E4 | A | w | p | Address of bit plane 2, bits 16-18 |
| | BPL2PTL | 0E6 | A | w | p | Address of bit plane 2, bits 1-15 |
| | BPL3PTH | 0E8 | A | w | p | Address of bit plane 3, bits 16-18 |
| | BPL3PTL | 0EA | A | w | p | Address of bit plane 3, bits 1-15 |
| | BPL4PTH | 0EC | A | w | p | Address of bit plane 4, bits 16-18 |
| | BPL4PTL | 0EE | A | w | p | Address of bit plane 4, bits 1-15 |
| | BPL5PTH | 0F0 | A | w | p | Address of bit plane 5, bits 16-18 |
| | BPL5PTL | 0F2 | A | w | p | Address of bit plane 5, bits 1-15 |
| | BPL6PTH | 0F4 | A | w | p | Address of bit plane 6, bits 16-18 |
| | BPL6PTL | 0F6 | A | w | p | Address of bit plane 6, bits 1-15 |
| | — | 0F8 | | | | unused |
| | — | 0FA | | | | unused |
| | — | 0FC | | | | unused |
| | — | 0FE | | | | unused |
| | BPLCON0 | 100 | AD | w | p | Bit plane control register 0 |

*Copper*
*Registers*

| Name | Reg addr | Chip | R/W | p/d | Function |
|------|----------|------|-----|-----|----------|
| BPLCON1 | 102 | D | w | p | Control register 1 (scroll values) |
| BPLCON2 | 104 | D | w | p | Control register 2 (priority control) |
| — | 106 | | | | unused |
| BPL1MOD | 108 | A | w | p | Bit plane module for odd planes |
| BPL2MOD | 10A | A | w | p | Bit plane module for even planes |
| — | 10C | | | | unused |
| — | 10E | | | | unused |
| BPL1DAT | 110 | D | w | d | Bit plane 1 data (to RGB output) |
| BPL2DAT | 112 | D | w | d | Bit plane 2 data (to RGB output) |
| BPL3DAT | 114 | D | w | d | Bit plane 3 data (to RGB output) |
| BPL4DAT | 116 | D | w | d | Bit plane 4 data (to RGB output) |
| BPL5DAT | 118 | D | w | d | Bit plane 5 data (to RGB output) |
| BPL6DAT | 11A | D | w | d | Bit plane 6 data (to RGB output) |
| — | 11C | | | | unused |
| — | 11E | | | | unused |
| SPR0PTH | 120 | A | w | p | Sprite data 0, bits 16-18 |
| SPR0PTL | 122 | A | w | p | Sprite data 0, bits 1-15 |
| SPR1PTH | 124 | A | w | p | Sprite data 1, bits 16-18 |
| SPR1PTL | 126 | A | w | p | Sprite data 1, bits 1-15 |
| SPR2PTH | 128 | A | w | p | Sprite data 2, bits 16-18 |
| SPR2PTL | 12A | A | w | p | Sprite data 2, bits 1-15 |
| SPR3PTH | 12C | A | w | p | Sprite data 3, bits 16-18 |
| SPR3PTL | 12E | A | w | p | Sprite data 3, bits 1-15 |
| SPR4PTH | 130 | A | w | p | Sprite data 4, bits 16-18 |
| SPR4PTL | 132 | A | w | p | Sprite data 4, bits 1-15 |
| SPR5PTH | 134 | A | w | p | Sprite data 5, bits 16-18 |
| SPR5PTL | 136 | A | w | p | Sprite data 5, bits 1-15 |
| SPR6PTH | 138 | A | w | p | Sprite data 6, bits 16-18 |
| SPR6PTL | 13A | A | w | p | Sprite data 6, bits 1-15 |
| SPR7PTH | 13C | A | w | p | Sprite data 7, bits 16-18 |
| SPR7PTL | 13E | A | w | p | Sprite data 7, bits 1-15 |
| SPR0POS | 140 | AD | w | dp | Sprite 0 start position (vert. and horiz.) |
| SPR0CTL | 142 | AD | w | dp | Sprite 0 control reg. and vertical stop |
| SPR0DATA | 144 | D | w | dp | Sprite 0 data register A (to RGB output) |
| SPR0DATB | 146 | D | w | dp | Sprite 0 data register B (to RGB output) |
| SPR1POS | 148 | AD | w | dp | Sprite 1 start position (vert. and horiz.) |
| SPR1CTL | 14A | AD | w | dp | Sprite 1 control reg. and vertical stop |
| SPR1DATA | 14C | D | w | dp | Sprite 1 data register A (to RGB output) |
| SPR1DATB | 14E | D | w | dp | Sprite 1 data register B (to RGB output) |
| SPR2POS | 150 | AD | w | dp | Sprite 2 start position (vert. and horiz.) |
| SPR2CTL | 152 | AD | w | dp | Sprite 2 control reg. and vertical stop |
| SPR2DATA | 154 | D | w | dp | Sprite 2 data register A (to RGB output) |
| SPR2DATB | 156 | D | w | dp | Sprite 2 data register B (to RGB output) |
| SPR3POS | 158 | AD | w | dp | Sprite 3 start position (vert. and horiz.) |
| SPR3CTL | 15A | AD | w | dp | Sprite 3 control reg. and vertical stop |
| SPR3DATA | 15C | D | w | dp | Sprite 3 data register A (to RGB output) |
| SPR3DATB | 15E | D | w | dp | Sprite 3 data register B (to RGB output) |
| SPR4POS | 160 | AD | w | dp | Sprite 4 start position (vert. and horiz.) |
| SPR4CTL | 162 | AD | w | dp | Sprite 4 control reg. and vertical stop |
| SPR4DATA | 164 | D | w | dp | Sprite 4 data register A (to RGB output) |
| SPR4DATB | 166 | D | w | dp | Sprite 4 data register B (to RGB output) |
| SPR5POS | 168 | AD | w | dp | Sprite 5 start position (vert. and horiz.) |
| SPR5CTL | 16A | AD | w | dp | Sprite 5 control reg. and vertical stop |
| SPR5DATA | 16C | D | w | dp | Sprite 5 data register A (to RGB output) |
| SPR5DATB | 16E | D | w | dp | Sprite 5 data register B (to RGB output) |

*Copper Registers*

| Name | Reg addr | Chip | R/W | p/d | Function |
|------|----------|------|-----|-----|----------|
| SPR6POS | 170 | AD | w | dp | Sprite 6 start position (vert. and horiz.) |
| SPR6CTL | 172 | AD | w | dp | Sprite 6 control reg. and vertical stop |
| SPR6DATA | 174 | D | w | dp | Sprite 6 data register A (to RGB output) |
| SPR6DATB | 176 | D | w | dp | Sprite 6 data register B (to RGB output) |
| SPR7POS | 178 | AD | w | dp | Sprite 7 start position (vert. and horiz.) |
| SPR7CTL | 17A | AD | w | dp | Sprite 7 control reg. and vertical stop |
| SPR7DATA | 17C | D | w | dp | Sprite 7 data register A (to RGB output) |
| SPR7DATB | 17E | D | w | dp | Sprite 7 data register B (to RGB output) |
| COLOR00 | 180 | D | w | p | Color palette register 0 (color table) |
| COLOR01 | 182 | D | w | p | Color palette register 1 (color table) |
| COLOR02 | 184 | D | w | p | Color palette register 2 (color table) |
| COLOR03 | 186 | D | w | p | Color palette register 3 (color table) |
| COLOR04 | 188 | D | w | p | Color palette register 4 (color table) |
| COLOR05 | 18A | D | w | p | Color palette register 5 (color table) |
| COLOR06 | 18C | D | w | p | Color palette register 6 (color table) |
| COLOR07 | 18E | D | w | p | Color palette register 7 (color table) |
| COLOR08 | 190 | D | w | p | Color palette register 8 (color table) |
| COLOR09 | 192 | D | w | p | Color palette register 9 (color table) |
| COLOR10 | 194 | D | w | p | Color palette register 10 (color table) |
| COLOR11 | 196 | D | w | p | Color palette register 11 (color table) |
| COLOR12 | 198 | D | w | p | Color palette register 12 (color table) |
| COLOR13 | 19A | D | w | p | Color palette register 13 (color table) |
| COLOR14 | 19C | D | w | p | Color palette register 14 (color table) |
| COLOR15 | 19E | D | w | p | Color palette register 15 (color table) |
| COLOR16 | 1A0 | D | w | p | Color palette register 16 (color table) |
| COLOR17 | 1A2 | D | w | p | Color palette register 17 (color table) |
| COLOR18 | 1A4 | D | w | p | Color palette register 18 (color table) |
| COLOR19 | 1A6 | D | w | p | Color palette register 19 (color table) |
| COLOR20 | 1A8 | D | w | p | Color palette register 20 (color table) |
| COLOR21 | 1AA | D | w | p | Color palette register 21 (color table) |
| COLOR22 | 1AC | D | w | p | Color palette register 22 (color table) |
| COLOR23 | 1AE | D | w | p | Color palette register 23 (color table) |
| COLOR24 | 1B0 | D | w | p | Color palette register 24 (color table) |
| COLOR25 | 1B2 | D | w | p | Color palette register 25 (color table) |
| COLOR26 | 1B4 | D | w | p | Color palette register 26 (color table) |
| COLOR27 | 1B6 | D | w | p | Color palette register 27 (color table) |
| COLOR28 | 1B8 | D | w | p | Color palette register 28 (color table) |
| COLOR29 | 1BA | D | w | p | Color palette register 29 (color table) |
| COLOR30 | 1BC | D | w | p | Color palette register 30 (color table) |
| COLOR31 | 1BE | D | w | p | Color palette register 31 (color table) |

The registers from 1C0 to 1FC are unoccupied.

Accessing register address 1FE has no effect. The chips are not accessed (see Section 1.2.3).

*ROM*

Figure 1.5.1.1 shows the ROM area as its looks after booting. The 256KB of ROM at $FC0000 contains the Amiga Kickstart. The range from $F80000 to $FBFFFF is identical to the range from $FC0000 to $FFFFFF. This is a mirror of the Kickstart ROM. This configuration can change. After a reset, the 68000 fetches the address of the first command from location 4, called the reset vector. Since the contents of this location are undefined on power-up, the processor would jump to some random address and the system would crash. The solution to this is as follows: The chip which is responsible for the memory configuration has an input which is connected to the lowest port line of CIA-A (PA0). This OVL line is normally at 0 and the memory configuration corresponds to the figure. After a reset, the port line automatically goes high, causing the ROM area at $F80000 to $FFFFFF to be mapped into the range from 0 to $7FFFF. This means that address 4 (the reset vector) corresponds to address $F80004. Here the 68000 finds a valid reset address which tells it to jump to the Kickstart program. In the course of this reset routine the OVL line is set to 0 and the normal memory configuration returns.

You must be very careful when experimenting with this line. If the program that tries to set the OVL line is running in chip RAM, the result can be catastrophic, because the program more or less switches itself out of the memory range and the processor lands somewhere in the Kickstart, which takes the place of the chip RAM after the switch.

*Amiga 1000 WOM*

The Amiga 1000 models have additional special features. Owners of these machines may be surprised that we keep talking about a Kickstart ROM, even though the Amiga 1000 loads the Kickstart from disk when it's turned on. The situation with the Amiga 1000 was the following: The hardware was done, the machines were ready to be sold, but the software in the form of the Kickstart operating system wasn't complete and still had some bugs in it. A decision was made to provide the Amiga with special RAM which would be loaded with the operating system when the computer was turned on. After this, the Amiga would prevent write accesses to this RAM, making it behave like a 256K ROM. Commodore called the WOM, or Write-Once Memory. Now the first Amigas could be delivered with the incomplete Kickstart 1.0. After the new Kickstart versions were complete (1.1 and 1.2), the Amiga owner simply had to insert new Kickstart disks.

Since this WOM is naturally more expensive than a simple ROM, the Amiga 500 and 2000 are not equipped with it, since by then the final Kickstart (V1.2) was finished.

The WOM raises some questions, however: Where is the program which loads Kickstart? How can Kickstart be changed, since it is RAM?

Normally, the Amiga 1000 operates just like the newer models, with Kickstart at $FC0000 to $FFFFFF with a mirror at $F80000. If you try to write into Kickstart, nothing happens. Write access is not possible. The boot ROM which loads Kickstart is also nowhere to be found in memory.

The whole process is controlled by the reset line. After a reset, whether by turning the computer on, by pressing the Amiga, Commodore and Control keys or by executing a 68000 reset command, the memory configuration changes.

*Reset*         Immediately after a reset, the boot ROM is at $F80000 (since on a reset the OVL line is set, the reset vector also comes from boot ROM) and it is possible to write into Kickstart. It can be changed as desired! This condition holds only until you try to write something in the boot ROM range from $F8000 to $FBFFFF. Then the boot ROM is masked out again and the Kickstart memory is write-protected. In short:

Reset keeps the Kickstart WOM in memory and enables the boot ROM.

A write access to an address between $F80000 and $FBFFFF disables the write protection and the boot ROM.

## 1.5.2      Fundamentals

As mentioned in the previous section, there are some registers which are accessed by the processor and some which are read and written through DMA. We'll cover the first case first.

*Programming the chip registers*
The chip registers can be addressed directly. Example: Changing the value of the background color register. Looking in the register table in Section 1.5.1, you see that it has a register address of $180. To this we must add the base address of the register area, that is, the address of the first register in the address range which the 68000 accesses. This is $DFF000. This plus the register address of COLOR00 yields $DFF180. A simple MOVE.W command can be used to initialize the register:

```
MOVE.W #value,$DFF180     ;value in COLOR00
```

If more than one register is accessed, it is a good idea to store the base address in an address register and use indirect addressing with an offset. Here is an example:

```
LEA $DFF000,A5            ;store base address in A5
MOVE.W #value1,$180(A5)   ;value 1 in COLOR00
MOVE.W #value2,$182(A5)   ;value 2 in COLOR01
MOVE.W ... etc.
```

Normally the chip registers are accessed as shown above. The registers can also be accessed as a long word, however. In this case two registers are always written at once. This makes sense for the address registers, which consist of a pair of registers holding a single 19-bit address, with which the entire 512KB chip RAM area can be accessed. All of the data for the custom chips must be in the chip RAM. Since the chips always access the memory word-wise, the lowest bit (bit 0) is irrelevant. The address registers point only to even addresses. Since a chip register is only one word (16 bits) wide, two successive registers are used to store a 19-bit address. The first register contains the upper three bits (bits 16 to 18) and the second contains the lower 16 (bits 0-15). This makes it possible to initialize both registers with a single long-word access. Example: Setting the pointer for the first bit plane to address $40000. BPL1PTH is the name of the first register (bits 16-18) and BPL1PTL (bits 0-15) is the name of the second. Register address of BPL1PTH: $0E0, BPL1PTL = $0E2.

A5 contains the base address $DFF000.

```
MOVE.L #$40000,$0E0(A5)   ;initializes BPL1PTH and BPL1PTL
                         ;with the correct values
```

It should be noted that any given register address can never be both read from and written to. Most registers are write-only registers and cannot be read. This also includes the registers mentioned above. Others can only be read. Only a few can be both read and written, but these then have two different register addresses, one for reading and one for writing. The DMA control register, which is discussed in more detail shortly, is such a register. It can be written through the register address $096 (DMACON), while address $002 is used for reading (DMACONR).

*DMA access*  DMA, as described in Section 1.2.3, involves the direct access of a peripheral chip, called the DMA controller, to the system memory. In the case of the Amiga, the DMA controller is housed in Agnus. It represents the connection between the various input/output components of the custom chips and the chip RAM. A given I/O component, such as the disk controller, needs new data or has data which it wants to store in memory. The DMA controller waits until the memory for this DMA channel is free (not being accessed by another DMA channel or the processor) and then transfers the data to or from RAM itself. For the sake of simplicity there is no special transfer from the I/O device to the DMA controller. It always takes place through registers. Each of these I/O components has two different types of registers. One type is the normal registers which are accessed by the processor and in which the various operating parameters are stored. The second is the data registers which contain the data for the DMA controller. For a DMA transfer this involves simply the corresponding data register and a RAM location. Depending on the direction of the transfer, either a read register is selected and the chip RAM is set for write, or a write register is used and the chip RAM is set for read. Since the two can be connected through the data bus, the data are automatically routed to their destination. Data are not stored in any temporary registers.

The DMA transfer adds a third type of register: the DMA address register which holds the address or addresses of the data in RAM, depending on the needs of the I/O device.

There are many central control registers which are not assigned to a special I/O device, but have higher-level control functions. The DMACON register is one in this category.

The data registers can also be written by the processor, since they are realized in the form of normal registers. This is not generally useful, however, since the DMA controller can accomplish this faster and more elegantly.

Some I/O components do not have DMA channels. The 68000 must read and write their data itself. This group includes only those devices which by their nature do not deal in large quantities of data, so that DMA is not needed, such as the joystick and mouse inputs.

*Present DMA channels:*

| | | |
|---|---|---|
| Bit plane DMA | Through this DMA channel the screen data are read from memory and written into the data registers of the individual bit planes, from where they go to the bit plane sequences which convert the data for output to the screen. |
| Sprite DMA | Transfers the sprite data from the RAM to the sprite data register. |
| Disk DMA | Data from the disk to RAM or from RAM to the disk. |
| Audio DMA | Reads the digital tone data from the RAM and writes it to the appropriate audio data registers. |
| Copper DMA | The coprocessor (Copper) receives its command words through this channel. |
| Blitter DMA | Data to and from the blitter. |

There are a total of six DMA channels which all want to access the memory, plus the processor which naturally wants to have the chip RAM for itself as often as possible. To solve the problems that result from this, a complex system of time multiplexing was devised in which the individual channels have defined positions. Since this is oriented to the video picture, we must first go into its construction. This section has been kept as untechnical as possible since this section involves programming the custom chips, not the hardware.

*Construction
of the video
picture*

*Figure 1.5.2.2*

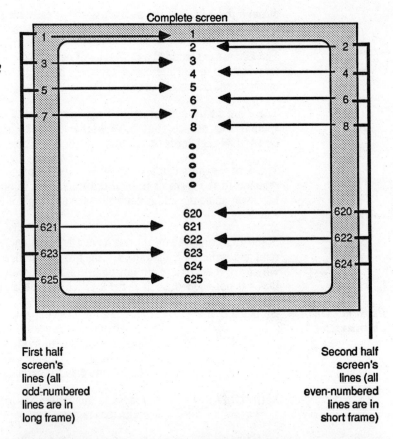

First half
screen's
lines (all
odd-numbered
lines are in
long frame)

Second half
screen's
lines (all
even-numbered
lines are in
short frame)

The illustration in Figure 1.5.2.2 displays the average screen design of an Amiga model in Europe. European video equipment uses the PAL standard, while the US relies on the NTSC standard.

The timing of the Amiga screen output corresponds exactly to the television standard of the country where the Amiga is sold, PAL for Europe and NTSC for the US. The 8361 Agnus chip is available in a NTSC US version and a PAL version for Europe. A PAL video picture consists of 625 horizontal rows an NTSC system of 525 horizontal rows. Each of these rows is constructed from left to right. After each line follows a pause, called the horizontal blanking gap, in which the electron that draws the picture has time to go back from right to left. During this blanking gap the electron beam is dark so that it cannot be seen tracing back to the left side. Then the process starts from the beginning and the next line results.

To keep the picture free of flickering, it must be continually redrawn. Since your eyes cannot respond to changes above a certain frequency, the number of pictures per second is placed above this limit. With the PAL standard, the number of individual pictures is set to 50 per second (30 per second for NTSC). But now we face a circumstance which complicates the whole matter. If all 625 lines where drawn 50 times per second, the result would be 31250 lines per second. If monitors and televisions were built to these specifications, they would not be affordably priced, so a trick is used.

*Flickering*

On one hand, the number of pictures should not be less than 50 per second or the screen begins to flicker, while on the other hand there must be enough lines per picture. The solution is as follows: 50 pictures are displayed per second, but the 625 lines are divided into two pictures. The first picture contains all of the odd lines (lines 1, 3, 5, ..., 625) while the second contains all of the even lines (2, 4, 6, ..., 624). Two of these half-pictures (called frames) are combined to form the entire picture, which contains 625 lines. Naturally, the number of complete pictures per second is only half as large as the number of half-pictures, or 25 per second. The line frequency for this technique is only 15625 Hz (25x625 or 50x312.5).

In spite of the high resolution of 625 lines, flickering occurs when a contour is restricted to only one line. Then it is displayed only every 25th of a second, which is perceived by the eye as a visible flickering. This effect can be seen on televisions especially on the horizontal edges of surfaces, since these consist of only a single horizontal line.

*Interlacing*

The term for this technique of alternating display of even and odd lines is called *interlacing*. Two additional terms are used to distinguish the difference between the two types of half-pictures. A long frame is the one in which the odd lines are displayed, and a short frame is the name for the picture which displays just the even lines. They are called long and short frame because there is one more odd line than even and it therefore takes slightly longer to display the frame containing the odd lines (from 1 to 625 there are 313 odd and 312 even numbers). After each frame there is a pause before the next frame begins. This blank space between frames is called the vertical blanking gap.

The picture created by the Amiga also follows this scheme, although with some deviations.

Normally the second half-picture (short frame) is somewhat delayed so that the even lines appear exactly between the odd lines.

On the Amiga, both frames are identical, so that the picture frequency is actually 50Hz. As a result, the number of lines is limited to 313. This can be clearly seen by the vertical distance between two lines on the screen, since the frames are no longer displaced, but drawn on top of each other.

To increase the number of lines, the Amiga can also create its picture in interlace mode. Then a full 625 lines are possible, but the disadvantages of interlace operation must be taken into account. More about this later.

*Construction
of the Amiga
screen output*

*Figure 1.5.2.3*

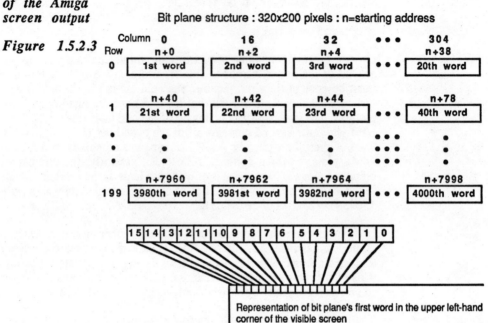

Bit plane structure : 320x200 pixels : n=starting address

Representation of bit plane's first word in the upper left-hand corner of the visible screen

*Bit planes*     The Amiga always displays its picture in a sort of graphic mode, that is, each point on the screen has a corresponding representation in memory. In the simplest case a set bit in RAM corresponds to a point on the screen. This way of using screen memory is called a bit plane. It is the basic element of each screen display on the Amiga. It consists of a contiguous block of memory. There are certain number of words per screen line, depending on the width of the screen. A word corresponds to 16 dots, since each bit represents a pixel. For a screen display with 320 pixels per line, 320/16 = 20 words are needed. Since only two states are possible in a bit plane, namely the point is set or it is not, it is possible to combine several bit planes. Bits at the same position in all planes are logically associated. The first point on the screen results from a combination of the first bit in the first word from all of the bit planes. The value resulting from these bits then determines the color of pixel on the screen. There are various ways to get from the bit combination of a pixel to its color on the screen, as explained later in Section 1.5.5.

*Different*
*graphic*
*resolutions*

The Amiga has two different horizontal resolutions. The high-resolution mode normally has 640 pixels per line, the lowest has 320 pixels. The "normally" used in the last sentence means that this value can change. It's better to define the two different resolutions in terms of the time per pixel. One pixel in the high-resolution mode is displayed for 70 nanoseconds, or 140 nanoseconds in low-resolution mode. In the doubled time the electron continues to trace on the screen, so the pixel appears twice as wide in the lowest resolution.

It is more important for the programmer to know that in the high-resolution mode only four bit planes can be active at a time, while in low-resolution mode, up to six planes are allowed.

*Construction*
*of a horizon-*
*tal raster line*

A raster line is a complete horizontal line, that is, the horizontal blanking gaps and their visible area. This raster line is used as the time measure for all DMA processes, particularly for the screen DMA's. To understand the division of the raster line, you must know how the memory accesses to the chip RAM and the custom chip registers are divided between the DMA controller and the processor. The accesses to these two memory ranges must conform to what are called *bus cycles*. The bus cycles determine the timing of the chip RAM. One memory access takes place in each bus cycle. It doesn't matter whether the data are read or written. If the processor wants to access the bus, it gets control of the bus for one bus cycle. The DMA controller is not able to access the RAM until the following cycle. A bus cycle lasts 280 nanoseconds. Almost four memory accesses are possible in one microsecond.

The 68000 cannot access the memory this often, however. It is simply not fast enough. With the clock frequency which the Amiga is driven, it accesses memory at a maximum rate of once every 560 nanoseconds. During this time, two bus cycles elapse. The 68000 can use only every other bus cycle. These cycles are called even cycles. The remaining cycles, the odd cycles, are reserved exclusively for the DMA controller.

*Figure 1.5.2.4*

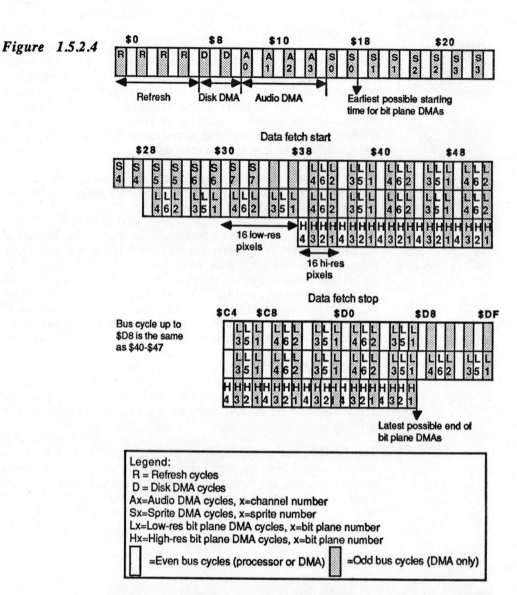

Figure 1.5.2.4 shows the development of a raster line over time. It takes 63.5 microseconds. This yields 227.5 bus cycles per line. Of these the first 225 can be taken by the DMA controller. The figure shows how this is done: The letters within the individual cycles stand for the corresponding DMA channel. While only the DMA controller uses the odd cycles, it must share the odd cycles with the processor. The DMA accesses always have priority. The blitter DMA and Copper DMA take place only during even cycles, although there is no defined timed for these two. The Copper DMA takes all even memory cycles until it has finished its task. It has precedence over the blitter. The blitter also takes all of the even cycles until it is finished, although it is possible to leave some cycles free for the 68000.

As you can see, disk, audio and sprite DMA accesses take only odd bus cycles and therefore do not affect the speed of the processor. The bus cycles designated with R are the refresh cycles. They are used to refresh the contents of the chip RAM (see the end of this section).

*DMA*

Somewhat more complicated is the distribution of the bit plane DMA. In order to be able to display the first 16 pixels on the screen, all bit planes must be read. While these 16 pixels appear on the screen, all of the bit planes for the next 16 pixels must be read. If the lowest resolution is enabled, 2 pixels are output during each bus cycle. This means that the bit planes must be read every eight bus cycles. So long as no more than four bit planes are active, the odd cycles suffice. If five or six planes are used, two even cycles must also be used so that all of the data can be read in eight bus cycles. It's even tighter in high-resolution mode. Here four pixels are displayed per memory cycle. If only the odd cycles are used, no more than two bit planes can be used. With the maximum number of four hi-res bit planes, all bus cycles are taken. As a result, the processor loses more than half of its free bus cycles! Its speed also decreases by the same amount, assuming that the current program is in the chip RAM, since the processor still has full-speed access to the fast RAM and Kickstart ROM.

The times labelled as data fetch start and data fetch stop designate the start and stop of the DMA accesses for the bit planes. They thereby determine the width and horizontal position of the visible picture. If the bit plane DMA starts early and ends late, more data words are read and more pixels are displayed. The normal resolution of 640 or 320 points per line can thus be changed by varying these values. If the data fetch start is set below $30, the bit plane DMA uses the cycles normally reserved for the sprite DMA. Depending on the exact value, up to seven sprites are lost this way. Only sprite 0, which is generally used for the mouse pointer, cannot be turned off in this manner.

The top line in the figure represents the division of the DMA cycles for a normal 320-point low-resolution picture. The start of the bit plane DMA, data fetch start, is at $38, and the end, data fetch stop is $D0. The data from bit plane number 1 is read in the cycles designated L1, the bit plane 2 data in L2, and so on. If the corresponding bit planes are not enabled, their DMA cycles are also omitted.

The second line represents the course of a raster line over time in which the data fetch points are moved outward. Up to the data fetch start everything is the same as the top line, but at $28 the bit plane DMA starts. As a result, sprites 5 to 7 are lost. The data fetch stop position is moved right to the maximum value of $D8.

The third line shows the distribution of the DMA cycles in a high-resolution screen, whereby the data fetch values match those of the first line.

No bit plane DMA accesses occur during the vertical blanking gaps.

*The DMA control register*

The individual DMA channels are enabled and disabled through a central DMA control register, DMACON.

DMACON Register addresses $096 (write) and $02 (read)

| Bit | Name | Function (when set) |
|---|---|---|
| 15 | SET/CLR | Set/clear bits |
| 14 | BBUSY | Blitter busy (read only) |
| 13 | BZERO | Result of all blitter operations is 0 (read only) |
| 12 and 11 | | Unused |
| 10 | BLTPRI | Blitter DMA has priority over processor |
| 9 | DMAEN | Enable all DMA (for bits 0 to 8) |
| 8 | BPLEN | Enable bit plane DMA |
| 7 | COPEN | Enable Copper DMA |
| 6 | BLTEN | Enable blitter DMA |
| 5 | SPREN | Enable sprite DMA |
| 4 | DSKEN | Enable disk DMA |
| 3-0 | AUDxEN | Enable audio DMA for sound channel x (the bit number corresponds to the number of the sound channel). |

The DMACON register is not written like a normal register. Bits can only be set or cleared. This is determined by bit 15 in the data word written to DMACON. If this bit is 1, all set bits of the data word are also set in DMACON. If bit 15 is 0, all set bits are cleared in the DMACON register. The remaining bits in DMACON are not affected.

Bit 9, designated as DMAEN is something of a main switch. If it is 0, all DMA channels are inactive, regardless of bits 0 to 8. If DMA is enabled, the bit for the appropriate DMA channel must be set and the DMAEN bit must be set. Here is an example:

Only the bit plane DMA is enabled (BPLEN=1), but without the DMAEN bit. The value of the DMACON register is thus $0100. Now you want to enable the disk DMA. DSKEN and DMAEN must be set and BPLEN cleared.

```
MOVE.W #$0100,$DFF096 ; clears the BPLEN bit (SET/CLR = 0)
MOVE.W #$8210,$DFF096 ; set DSKEN and DMAEN (SET/CLR = 1)
```

The DMACON register now contains the desired value of $0210.

Bits 13 and 14 can only be read. They supply information about the various states of the blitter, these are covered in the blitter section.

Bit 10 controls the priority of the blitter over the processor. If it is set, the blitter has absolute priority over the 68000. This can go so far that the processor may have no access at all to the chip registers or to the chip RAM during the blitter operation. If it is cleared, the processor gets every fourth even bus cycle from the blitter. This prevents the processor from being held up when it is executing an operating system routine or a program in the fast RAM which wants to access the chip RAM.

*Reading the*
*current beam*
*position*

Since all DMA timing is oriented according to the position within a raster line, it is sometimes useful to know where the electron beam is currently located. Agnus has an internal counter which contains the horizontal and vertical screen position. Two registers allow the processor access to this counter:

VHPOS $006 (read VHPOSR) and $02C (write VHPOSW)

| Bit no.:  | 15 | 14 | 13 | 12 | 11 | 10 | 9  | 8  | 7  | 6  | 5  | 4  | 3  | 2  | 1  | 0  |
|-----------|----|----|----|----|----|----|----|----|----|----|----|----|----|----|----|----|
| Function: | V7 | V6 | V5 | V4 | V3 | V2 | V1 | V0 | H8 | H7 | H6 | H5 | H4 | H3 | H2 | H1 |

VPOS $004 (read VPOSR) and $02A (write VPOSW)

| Bit no.:  | 15  | 14 | 13 | 12 | 11 | 10 | 9  | 8  | 7  | 6  | 5  | 4  | 3  | 2  | 1  | 0  |
|-----------|-----|----|----|----|----|----|----|----|----|----|----|----|----|----|----|----|
| Function: | LOF | -- | -- | -- | -- | -- | -- | -- | -- | -- | -- | -- | -- | -- | -- | V8 |

The bits designated H1 to H8 represent the horizontal beam position and they correspond directly to the numbers for the individual bus cycles in Figure 1.5.2.4 and thus have an accuracy or two low-resolution pixels or four high-resolution pixels. The value for the horizontal position can vary between $0 and $E3 (0 to 227). The horizontal blanking gap falls in the range from $F to $35.

The bits for the vertical position, the current screen line, are divided between two registers. The lower bits V0 to V7 are in VHPOS, while the uppermost bit, V8, is in VPOS. Together they yield the number of the current screen.

Lines from 0 to 312 are possible. The vertical blanking gap (the screen is always dark in this range) run from line 0 to 25.

The LOF bit (LOng Frame) indicates whether the current picture is a long or short frame. This bit is needed only in the interlace mode. Normally it is 1.

The beam position can also be set, but this capability is rarely needed.

The POS registers have another function in combination with a lightpen. When the lightpen input of Agnus is activated (see Section 1.5.5) and the lightpen is held against the screen, they store its position. This means that their contents are frozen as soon as the lightpen detects the electron beam moving past its tip. The counters are released again at the end of the vertical blanking gap, line 26. The following procedure must be used to read the lightpen position:

•       Wait for line 0 (start of the vertical blanking gap). This can be easily done by means of the vertical blanking interrupt.

•       Read the two registers.

If the vertical position is between 0 and 25 (within the vertical blanking gap), no lightpen signal was received. If the value is outside this range, it represents the position of the lightpen.

At the conclusion of this section there is some information concerning the refresh cycles:

Agnus possesses an integrated 8-bit refresh counter. It can be written through register $28 (Careful! The memory contents can be lost this way!). At the start of each raster line, Agnus places four refresh addresses on the chip RAM address bus. This means the contents of each memory row are refreshed every four milliseconds.

While the row address is being output on the chip RAM address bus, Agnus places the addresses of certain strobe registers on the register address bus. These strobe signals are used to inform the other chips, Denise and Paula, the start of a raster line or a picture. This is necessary because the counter for the screen position is inside Agnus. There are no lines for transmitting the synchronization signals to the other chips. There are four strobe addresses:

*Strobe addresses:*

| Addr | Chip | Function |
|------|------|----------|
| $38 | D | Vertical blanking gap of a short frame |
| $3A | D | Vertical blanking gap |
| $3C | D P | This strobe address is created in each raster line outside the vertical blanking gap |
| $3E | D | Marker for a long raster line (228 cycles) |

During the first refresh cycle, one of the three strobe addresses above is always addressed. Normally this is $3C, and $38 or $3A within the vertical blanking gap, depending on whether it is a short or long frame.

The situation is as follows with the fourth address: A raster line has a purely computational length of 227.5 bus cycles. But since there are no half-cycles, lines alternate between 227 and 228 bus cycles. The strobe address $3E signals the 228-cycle-long lines and is created during the second refresh cycle.

## 1.5.3     Interrupts

Almost all I/O components of the custom chips and the two CIA's can generate an interrupt. A special circuit in Paula manages the individual interrupt sources and creates the interrupt signals for the 68000. The processor's autovectors are used, levels 0 to 6. The non-maskable interrupt (NMI) level 7 isn't used. The two registers are the interrupt request register (INTREQ) and the interrupt mask register (INTENA, INTerrupt ENAble). The assignment of the bits in the two registers is identical.

*Interrupt*        Register addresses:  INTREQ    = $09C (write)
*register  layout*                      INTREQR   = $01E (read)
                                        INTENA    = $09A (write)
                                        INTENAR   = $01C (read)

| Bit | Name | IL | Function |
|-----|------|-----|----------|
| 15 | SET/CLR | | Write/read (see DMACON register) |
| 14 | INTEN | (6) | Enable interrupts |
| 13 | EXTER | 6 | Interrupt from CIA-B or expansion port |
| 12 | DSKSYN | 5 | Disk sync value recognized |
| 11 | RBF | 5 | Serial receive buffer full |
| 10 | AUD3 | 4 | Output audio data channel 3 |
| 9 | AUD2 | 4 | Output audio data channel 2 |
| 8 | AUD1 | 4 | Output audio data channel 1 |
| 7 | AUD0 | 4 | Output audio data channel 0 |
| 6 | BLIT | 3 | Blitter ready |
| 5 | VERTB | 3 | Start of the vertical blanking gap reached |
| 4 | COPER | 3 | Reserved for the Copper interrupt |
| 3 | PORTS | 2 | Interrupt from CIA-A or the expansion port |
| 2 | SOFT | 1 | Reserved for software interrupts |
| 1 | DSKBLK | 1 | Disk DMA transfer done |
| 0 | TBE | 1 | Serial transmit buffer empty |

The lower thirteen bits stand for the individual interrupt sources. The
CIA interrupts are combined into a single interrupt. The bits in the
DMAREQ register indicate which interrupts have occurred. A bit is set
if the corresponding interrupt has occurred. In order to generate a
processor interrupt, the corresponding bit must be set in the DMAENA
register and the INTEN bit must also be set. The INTEN bit thus acts
as the main switch for the remaining 14 interrupt sources which can be
turned on or off with the individual bits of the INTENA register. Only
when INTEN is 1 can any interrupts be generated.

If both the INTEN bit and the two corresponding bits in the INTENA
and INTREQ registers are set, a processor interrupt is generated. The
corresponding autovector numbers are listed in the IL (Interrupt Level)
column in the table. Here are the addresses of the seven interrupt
autovectors:

| Vector no. | Address (Dec/hex) | Autovector level |
|-----------|-------------------|------------------|
| 25 | 100 / $64 | Autovector level 1 |
| 26 | 104 / $68 | Autovector level 2 |
| 27 | 108 / $6C | Autovector level 3 |
| 28 | 112 / $70 | Autovector level 4 |
| 29 | 116 / $74 | Autovector level 5 |
| 30 | 120 / $78 | Autovector level 6 |
| (31 | 124 / $7C | Autovector level 7) |

As you can see, the interrupts which require faster processing are given
higher interrupt levels.

In order to change the bits in the two registers, you must use the same procedure described for the DMACON registers with a SET/CLR bit.

*INTREQ*
*register*

After processing an interrupt the bit which generated it must be reset in the INTREQ register. In contrast to the CIA interrupt control registers, the bits in the INTREQ register aren't automatically cleared on reading.

Setting a bit in the INTREQ register with a MOVE command has the same effect as if the corresponding interrupt had occurred. This is how a software interrupt is created, for example. The Copper can also create its own interrupt only by writing into INTREQ.

One peculiarity is bit 14 in the INTREQ register which has no specific function there as it does in INTENA. But when it is set by writing to INTREQ and INTEN in the INTENA register is high, a level 6 interrupt is generated.

On each interrupt from CIA-A, bit 3 in the DMAREQ register is set. For CIA-B this is bit 13. The interrupt source in the corresponding CIA must be determined by reading the interrupt control register of the CIA.

The interrupts no. 3 and 13 can also be generated by expansion cards on the expansion port.

Interrupt bit 5 indicates the vertical blanking interrupt. This occurs at the start of each video frame at the start of the vertical blanking gap (line 0), and thus 50 times per second.

The remaining interrupts are handled in the appropriate sections.

---

## 1.5.4      The Copper coprocessor

The Copper is a simple coprocessor. It has the task of writing certain values into various registers of the custom chips. These are defined points in time. More accurately, the Copper can change the contents of some registers at certain screen positions. It can thus divide the screen into different regions which can then have different colors and resolutions. This capability is used to implement multiple screens, for example.

The Copper is designated a coprocessor because it, like a real processor, has a program which is stored in memory and it executes this program command by command. The Copper recognizes only three different commands, but they are quite versatile:

*MOVE*

The MOVE command writes an immediate value into a custom-chip register.

*WAIT*            The WAIT command waits until the electron beam has reached a certain screen position.

*SKIP*            The SKIP command skips the next command if the electron beam has already reached a certain screen position. This allows conditional branches to be built into the program.

A Copper program is called a Copper list. In it the commands come one after ther other, whereby each command always consists of two words. Example:

```
Wait (X1,Y1)  ; waits until the screen position X1,Y1 is
              ; reached
Move #0,$180  ; writes the value 0 into the background
              ; register
Move #9,$181  ; writes the value 1 into color register 1
Wait (X2,Y2)  ; waits until the screen position X2,Y2 is
              ; reached
 ...               etc.
```

The Copper list alone is not sufficient to operate the Copper. Some registers are necessary, which contain the necessary parameters for the Copper.

*The Copper*
*registers:*

| Reg. | Name | Function |
|------|------|----------|
| $080 | COP1LCH | These two registers together contain the |
| $082 | COP1LCL | 18-bit address of the first Copper list |
| $084 | COP2LCH | These two registers together contain the |
| $086 | COP2LCL | 18-bit address of the second Copper list |
| $088 | COPJMP1 | Loads the address of the first Copper list into the Copper program counter |
| $08A | COPJMP2 | Loads the address of the second Copper list into the Copper program counter |
| $02E | COPCON | This register contains only one bit (bit 0). If it is set, the Copper can also access the registers from $040 to $07E (these registers belong to the blitter). |

*Copper*
*registers are*
*write-only*
*registers*

The two COPxLC registers contain the address of a Copper list. Since this list is 19 bits long, two registers are needed per address. As described in Section 1.5.2, they can be written together with one MOVE.L command. The Copper lists must, like all other data for the custom chips, lie within the 512KB RAM chip.

The Copper uses an internal program counter as a pointer to the current command. It is incremented by two each time a command is processed. To make the Copper start at a given address, the start address of the Copper list must be transferred to the program counter. The COPJMPx registers are used for this. They are strobe registers, meaning that a write access to one of them triggers an action in the Copper—they are not used to store actual values. Thus the value written to them is completely irrelevant.

On the Copper these two registers cause the contents of the corresponding COPxLC registers to be copied into the program counter. If a write access is made to COPJMP1, the address in COP1LC is copied into the program counter, which causes the Copper to execute the program at that address. The same holds for COPJMP2 and COP2LC.

At the start of the vertical blanking gap, line 0, the program counter is automatically loaded with the value COP1LC. This causes the Copper to execute the same program for every picture.

*The commands structure:*

| Bit | MOVE BW1 | MOVE BW2 | WAIT BW1 | WAIT BW2 | SKIP BW1 | SKIP BW2 |
|-----|-----|-----|-----|-----|-----|-----|
| 15 | x | DW15 | VP7 | BFD | VP7 | BFD |
| 14 | x | DW14 | VP6 | VM6 | VP6 | VM6 |
| 13 | x | DW13 | VP5 | VM5 | VP5 | VM5 |
| 12 | x | DW12 | VP4 | VM4 | VP4 | VM4 |
| 11 | x | DW11 | VP3 | VM3 | VP3 | VM3 |
| 10 | x | DW10 | VP2 | VM2 | VP2 | VM2 |
| 9 | x | DW9 | VP1 | VM1 | VP1 | VM1 |
| 8 | RA8 | DW8 | VP0 | VM0 | VP0 | VM0 |
| 7 | RA7 | DW7 | HP8 | HM8 | HP8 | HM8 |
| 6 | RA6 | DW6 | HP7 | HM7 | HP7 | HM7 |
| 5 | RA5 | DW5 | HP6 | HM6 | HP6 | HM6 |
| 4 | RA4 | DW4 | HP5 | HM5 | HP5 | HM5 |
| 3 | RA3 | DW3 | HP4 | HM4 | HP4 | HM4 |
| 2 | RA2 | DW2 | HP3 | HM3 | HP3 | HM3 |
| 1 | RA1 | DW1 | HP2 | HM2 | HP2 | HM2 |
| 0 | 0 | DW0 | 1 | 0 | 1 | 1 |

Legend:
| | |
|---|---|
| x | This bit is unsed. Should be initialized to 0. |
| RA | Register address |
| DW | Data word |
| VP | Vertical beam position |
| VM | Vertical mask bits |
| HP | Horizontal beam position |
| HM | Horizontal mask bits |
| BFD | Blitter finish disable |

*The MOVE command*

The MOVE command is indicated by a 0 in bit 0 of the first command word. With this command it is possible to write an immediate value to a custom-chip register. The register address of the desired register comes from the lower 9 bits of the first data word. Bit 0 must always be 0 (is already 0 for the register addresses because the registers lie only on even addresses). The second command word contains the data byte to be written to the register.

There are some limitations regarding the register address. Normally the Copper cannot affect the registers in the range from $000 to $07F. If the lowest (and only) bit in the COPCON register is set, then the Copper can access the registers in the range from $040 to $07F. This allows the Copper to influence the blitter. Access to the lowest registers ($000 to $03F) is never allowed.

*The WAIT command*

The WAIT command is indicated by a 1 in bit 0 of the first command word and a 0 in bit 0 of the second. It instructs the Copper to hold further execution until the desired beam position is reached. If it is already greater than that specified by the WAIT command when the command is executed so that the beam is already past the specified position, the Copper continues with the next instruction immediately.

This position can be set separately for the vertical lines and horizontal rows. Vertically the resolution is one raster line. But since there are only eight bits for the vertical position and there are 313 lines, the WAIT command cannot distinguish between the first 256 and the remaining 57 lines. The lowest 8 bits are the same for both line 0 and line 256. To wait for a line in the lower range, two WAIT commands must be used.

1.    WAIT for line 255

2.    WAIT for the desired line, ignoring the ninth bit

Horizontally there are 112 possible positions, since the two lower bits of the horizontal position, HP0 and HP1, cannot be specified. The command word of the WAIT command contains only the bits HP2 to HP8. This means that the horizontal coordinate of a WAIT command can only be specified in steps of four low-resolution pixels.

The second command word contains mask bits. These can be used to determine which bits of the horizontal and vertical position are actually taken into account in the comparison. Only the position bits whose mask bits are set are regarded. This opens up many possibilities:

```
Wait for vertical position $0F and vertical mask $0F
```

causes the WAIT condition to be fulfilled every 16 lines, namely whenever the lower four bits are all 1, since bits 4 to 6 are not taken into account in the comparison (mask bits 4 to 6 are at 0). The seventh bit of the vertical position cannot be masked. Thus the example above works only in the range of lines from 0 to 127 and 256 to 313.

The BFD (Blitter Finish Disable) bit has the following function: If the Copper is used to start a blitter operation, it must know when the blitter finishes this operation. If the BFD is cleared, the Copper waits at any WAIT command until the blitter is done. Then the wait condition is checked. This can be disabled by setting the BFD bit, causing the Copper to ignore the blitter status. If the Copper does not affect any of the blitter registers, this bit is set to 1.

*The SKIP command*

The SKIP command is identical in construction to the WAIT command. Bit 0 of the second command word is set in order to distinguish it from the WAIT command. The SKIP command checks to see if the actual beam position is greater than or equal to that given in the command word. If this comparison is positive, the Copper skips the next command. Otherwise it continues execution of the program with the next command. The SKIP command allows conditional branches to be constructed. The command following SKIP can be a MOVE into one of the COPJMP registers, causing a jump to be made based on the beam position.

*Construction of a Copper list*

A simple Copper list consists of a sequence of WAIT and MOVE commands, and a few SKIP commands. Its start address is found in COPLC1. A trick must be used to end the Copper list. After the last instruction comes a WAIT command with an impossible beam position. This effectively ends the processing of the Copper list until it is restarted at the start of a new picture. WAIT ($0,$FE) fulfills this condition, because a horizontal position greater than $E4 isn't possible.

*The Copper interrupt*

As you know, there is a special bit in the interrupt registers for the Copper interrupt. This interrupt can be generated with a MOVE command to the INTREQ register:

```
MOVE #$8010,INTREQ ; set SET/CLR and COPPER
```

Any other bit in this register can be affected the same way, but bit 4 is provided especially for the Copper.

A Copper interrupt can be used to tell the processor that a certain screen position has been reached. This allows what are called raster interrupts to be programmed, that is, the interruption of the processor in a certain screen line (and column).

*The Copper DMA*

The Copper fetches its commands from memory through its own DMA channel. It uses the even bus cycles and has precedence over the blitter and the 68000. Each command requires two cycles since two command words must be read. The WAIT command requires an additional cycle when the desired beam position is reached. The Copper leaves the bus free during the wait phase of a WAIT command.

The COPEN bit in the DMACON register is used to turn the Copper DMA on and off. If this bit is cleared, the Copper releases the bus and does not execute any more commands. If it is set, it starts its program execution at the address in its program counter. It is therefore absolutely necessary to supply this with a valid address before starting the Copper DMA. A Copper running in an unknown area of memory can crash the system. The usual initialization sequence for the Copper looks like this:

```
LEA $DFF000,A5                    ; load base address into
                                 ;register A5
MOVE.W #$0080,DMACON(A5)          ; copper DMA off
MOVE.L #copperlist,COP1LCH(A5)    ; set address of the copper
                                 ;list
MOVE.W #0,COPJMP1(A5)             ;transfer this address into
                                 ;the copper's program
                                 ;counter
MOVE.W #$8080,DMACON(A5)          ; enable copper DMA
```

Finally, here is an example program. It uses two WAIT commands and three MOVE commands to display black, red and yellow bars on the screen. It can be created with a simple Copper list and is a good example. Enter the program with a standard assembler for the Amiga (such as AssemPro).

```
;*** Example for a simple Copperlist ***

;CustomChip-Register

INTENA   = $9A           ;Interrupt-Enable-Register (write)
DMACON   = $96           ;DMA-control register (write)
COLOR00  = $180          ;Color palette register 0

;Copper Register

COP1LC   = $80           ;Address of 1. Copper list
COP2LC   = $84           ;Address of 2. Copper list
COPJMP1  = $88           ;Jump to Copper list 1
COPJMP2  = $8a           ;Jump to Copper list 2

;CIA-A Port register A (Mouse key)

CIAAPRA  = $BFE001

;Exec Library Base Offsets

OpenLibrary = -30-522    ;LibName,Version/a1,d0
Forbid      = -30-102
Permit      = -30-108
AllocMem    = -30-168    ;Byte Size, Requirements/d0,d1
FreeMem     = -30-180    ;Memory Block, Byte Size/a1,d0

;graphics base

StartList = 38

;other Labels

Execbase = 4
Chip = 2                 ;request Chip-RAM

;*** Initialize-programm ***

;Request memory for Copperlist
```

```
Start:
 move.l Execbase,a6
 moveq  #Clsize,d0          ;Set Parameter for AllocMem
 moveq  #chip,d1            ;ask for Chip-RAM
 jsr    AllocMem(a6)        ;request memory
 move.l d0,CLadr            ;Address of the RAM-area memory
 beq.s  Ende                ;Error! -> End

;copy Copperlist to CLadr

 lea    CLstart,a0
 move.l CLadr,a1
 moveq  #CLsize-1,d0        ;set loop value
CLcopy:
 move.b (a0)+,(a1)+         ;copy Copperlist Byte for Byte
 dbf    d0,CLcopy

;*** Main programm ***

 jsr    forbid(a6)          ;Task Switching off
 lea    $dff000,a5          ;Basic address of the Register
                            ;to A5
 move.w #$03a0,dmacon(a5)   ;DMA offn
 move.l CLadr,cop1lc(a5)    ;Address of the  Copperlist to
                            ;COP1LC
 clr.w  copjmp1(a5)         ;Load copperlist in program
                            ;counter

;Switch Copper DMA

 move.w #$8280,dmacon(a5)

;wait for left mouse key

Wait: btst #6,ciaapra       ;Bit test
 bne.s Wait                 ;done? else continue.

;*** End programm ***

;Restore old Copper list

 move.l #GRname,a1          ;Set parameter for OpenLibrary
 clr.l  d0
 jsr    OpenLibrary(a6)     ;Graphics Library open
 move.l d0,a4               ;Address of GraphicsBase to a4
 move.l StartList(a4),cop1lc(a5) ;load address of
                            ;Startlist
 clr.w  copjmp1(a5)
 move.w #$83e0,dmacon(a5)   ;all  DMA on
 jsr    permit(a6)          ;Task-Switching on

;Free memory of Copperlist

 move.l CLadr,a1            ;Set parameter for FreeMem
 moveq #CLsize,d0
```

```
      jsr   FreeMem(a6)           ;memory freed
Ende: clr.l d0                    ;error flag erased
      rts                         ;end program

;Variables

CLadr: dc.l 0

;Constants

GRname: dc.b "graphics.library",0
  align                          ;even for other assemblers

;Copperlist

CLstart:
  dc.w color00,$0000            ;Background color black
  dc.w $640f,$fffe              ;On line 100 change to
  dc.w color00,$0f00            ;Red. Switch
  dc.w $BE0f,$fffe              ;Line 190 to
  dc.w color00,$0fb0            ;Gold
  dc.w $ffff,$fffe              ;Impossible Position: End of
                                ;the Copperlist
CLend:

CLsize = CLend - CLstart

  end
;End of program
```

This program installs the Copper list and then waits until the left mouse button is pressed. Unfortunately, it isn't as easy to do as it sounds.

First, you need memory in which to store the Copper list. Like all data for the custom chips, it must be in the chip RAM. Since you can't be sure whether the program is actually in the chip RAM, it is necessary to copy the Copper list into the chip RAM. In a multi-tasking operating system like that of the Amiga, you can't just write something into memory anywhere you feel like it, you have to request the memory. This is done in the program with the AllocMem routine. This returns the address of the requested chip RAM in D0. The Copper list is then copied into memory at this address.

Next, the task switching is disabled by a call to Forbid so that the Amiga processes only your program. This prevents your program from being disturbed by another.

Finally, the Copper is initialized and started.

After this, the program tests for the left mouse button by reading the appropriate bit of CIA-A (see Section 1.2.2).

If the mouse button is pressed, the processor exits the wait loop.

To get back to the old display, a special Copper list is loaded into the Copper and started. This Copper list is called the startup Copper list and it initializes the screen. Its address is found in the variable area for the part of the operating system responsible for the graphics functions. At the end, multi-tasking is re-enabled with Permit and the occupied memory is released again with FreeMem.

This program contains a number of operating system functions which you are probably not familiar with yet. Unfortunately this cannot be avoided if you want to make the program work correctly. But it doesn't matter if you don't understand everything yet. We are discussing the Copper in this section, and this part of the program should be understandable. In the later sections of this book you'll discover the secrets of the operating system and its routines. Enter this example and experiment with the Copper list. Change the WAIT command or add new ones. Those who are interested can also experiment with a SKIP command.

One more thing about the Copper list: The two WAIT commands contain $E as the horizontal position. This is the start of the horizontal blanking gap. This way the Copper performs the color switch outside the visible area. If 0 is used as the horizontal position, the color switching can be seen at the extreme right edge of the screen.

*Figure 1.5.4.1*

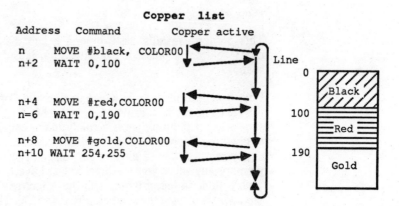

## 1.5.5     Playfields

The screen output of the Amiga consists of two basic elements: sprites and playfields. In this section we'll discuss the structure and programming of all types of playfields. The sprites are handled in Section 1.5.6.

The playfield is the basis of the normal screen display. It consists of at least one and a maximum of six bit planes. (The construction of a bit plane was explained in Section 1.5.2.) A playfield is something like a graphic screen which is composed of a variable number of individual memory blocks, the bit planes. The Amiga offers a large number of different possibilities for displaying playfields:

- Between 2 and 4096 simultaneous colors in one picture
- Resolutions of 16 by 1 to 704 to 625 pixels
- Two completely independent playfields are possible
- Smooth scrolling in both directions

All of these capabilities can be grouped into two groups.

1.    The combination of bit planes to achieve the color of a single pixel (the display of the bit pattern from the bit plane on the screen).

2.    Determining the form, size and position structure of the playfield(s).

*The various display options*

By using 1 to 6 bit planes, each point can be represented by as many bits as you like. This value must then be converted into one of 4096 colors since each pixel on the screen can naturally have only one color.

The Amiga creates its colors by mixing the three component colors red, green and blue. Each of these three components can have 16 different intensity levels. This results in 4096 color shades (16x16x16 = 4096). Four bits are needed per component to store the color values, or 12 bits per color.

If you wanted to assign each pixel one of 4096 colors, you would need 12 bits per pixel. But a maximum of 6 bits is possible. Therefore the six bits must be converted into one of the 4096 possible colors for the visible point.

*Figure 1.5.5.1*

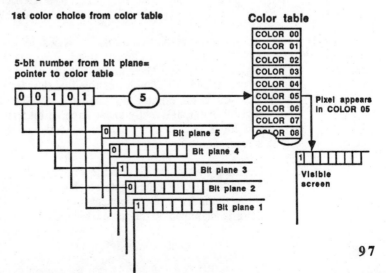

97

A color palette or color table is used to do this. On the Amiga this contains 32 entries, each of which can hold a 12-bit color value. The value of the first color register COLOR00 is used for both the background color and the border color. The color palette registers 0 to 32 (COLOR00 to COLOR31) are write-only:

| Register addr. | Color palette register |
|----------------|------------------------|
| $180           | COLOR00                |
| $182           | COLOR01                |
| ...            | etc.                   |
| $1BE           | COLOR31                |

*Structure of a table element:*

```
Bit:      15 14 13 12 11 10 9  8  7  6  5  4  3  2  1  0
COLORxx:  x  x  x  x  R3 R2 R1 R0 G3 G2 G1 G0 B3 B2 B1 B0
```

R0-R3    Four-bit value for the red component
G0-G3    Four-bit value for the green component
B0-B3    Four-bit value for the blue component

The value obtained from the bit planes is used as a pointer to a table element. Since there are only these 32 color table registers, a maximum of 5 bit planes can be combined in this mode. The bit from the bit plane with the lowest number supplies the LSB of this entry, and the bit plane with the highest number supplies the MSB.

This method of obtaining the color from a table allows a maximum of 32 colors in a picture, but these colors can be selected from a total of 4096. In high-resolution mode only 4 planes can be active at one time. Here 16 colors is the limit. In this display mode it doesn't matter how many planes are combined together. Some color registers remain unused:

| # of bit planes | Colors | Color registers used |
|-----------------|--------|----------------------|
| 1               | 2      | COLOR00 - COLOR01    |
| 2               | 4      | COLOR00 - COLOR03    |
| 3               | 8      | COLOR00 - COLOR07    |
| 4               | 16     | COLOR00 - COLOR15    |
| 5               | 32     | COLOR00 - COLOR31    |

*The extra half-bright mode*

In the lowest resolution a maximum of 6 bit planes can be used. This yields a value range of 26 or 0 to 63. There are, however, only 32 color registers available. The extra half-bright mode uses a special technique to get around this. The lower five bits (bits 0 to 4 from planes 1 to 5) are used as the pointer to a color register. The contents of this color register is output directly to the screen if bit 5 (from bit plane 6) is 0. If this bit is 1, the color value is divided by 2 before it is sent to the screen.

Dividing by two means that the values of the three color components are shifted 1 bit to the right, which corresponds to a division by two. Since the individual components are thus only half as large, the same color is displayed on the screen, but only half as bright (thus the name).

Example:

Bit no.                          5 4 3 2 1 0
Value from the bit planes:    1 0 0 1 0 0
yields table entry no. 8 (binary 00100 is 8)
COLOR08 contains the following value (color: orange):

| R3 | R2 | R1 | R0 | G3 | G2 | G1 | G0 | B3 | B2 | B1 | B0 |
|----|----|----|----|----|----|----|----|----|----|----|----|
| 1  | 1  | 1  | 0  | 0  | 1  | 1  | 0  | 0  | 0  | 0  | 1  |

Since bit 5 = 1, the values are shifted by 1 bit:

| R3 | R2 | R1 | R0 | G3 | G2 | G1 | G0 | B3 | B2 | B1 | B0 |
|----|----|----|----|----|----|----|----|----|----|----|----|
| 0  | 1  | 1  | 1  | 0  | 0  | 1  | 1  | 0  | 0  | 0  | 0  |

This value still corresponds to orange, but now it's only half as bright.

By selecting appropriate color values for the 32 registers, it is possible for each pixel to take on one of 64 possible colors on the extra half-bright mode. The color registers store the bright colors, which can then be dimmed by setting bit 5.

This mode allows all 4096 colors to be used in a picture. Like the extra half-bright mode, it can only be used in low-resolution mode since it requires all 6 bit planes. In this mode we make use of the fact that the colors in a normal picture seldom make radical changes from pixel to pixel. Usually smooth transitions from bright to dark colors or vice versa are needed.

*The hold-and-modify mode*

In the hold-and-modify mode, called HAM for short, the color of the previous pixels is modified by the one which follows it. This makes the fine color levels desired possible, for example by incrementing the blue component by one step with each successive pixel. The limitation is that only one component can be affected so that from one pixel to the next, either the red, green or blue value can change, but never more than one at a time. But to get a smooth transfer from dark to light, all three color components must change for many color mixes. In the HAM mode this can be accomplished only by setting one of the components to the desired value at each pixel. This requires three pixels.

By comparison, the color of a pixel can also be changed directly by fetching one of 16 colors from the color table.

How is the value from the bit planes interpreted in the HAM mode?

The upper two bits (bits 4 and 5 from bit planes 5 and 6) determine the use of the lower four bits (bit planes 1 to 4). If bits 4 and 5 are 0, the remaining four bits are used as a pointer into the color palette registers as usual. This allows 16 colors to be selected directly. With a combination of bits 4 and 5 which are not 0, the color value of the last pixel is used (to the left of the current pixel), two of the three color components remains the same, while the third is replaced by the lower four bits of the current pixel. The top two bits determine the selection of the three color components.

This all sounds more complicated than it is. The following table explains the use of the various bit combinations:

Bit no:

| 5 | 4 | 3 | 2 | 1 | 0 | Function |
|---|---|---|---|---|---|----------|
| 0 | 0 | C3 | C2 | C1 | C0 | Bits C0 to C3 are used as a pointer to one of the color registers in the range COLOR00 to COLOR15. This is identical to the normal color selection. |
| 0 | 1 | B3 | B2 | B1 | B0 | The red and green values of the last (left) pixel are used for the current pixel. The old blue value is replaced by the value in B0 to B3. |
| 1 | 0 | R3 | R2 | R1 | R0 | The blue and green values of the last (left) pixel are used for the current pixel. The old red value is replaced by the value in B0 to B3. |
| 1 | 1 | G3 | G2 | G1 | G0 | The blue and red values of the last (left) pixel are used for the current pixel. The old green value is replaced by the value in B0 to B3. |

The border color (COLOR00) is used as the color of the previous pixel for the first pixel on a line.

*The dual playfield mode*

*Figure 1.5.5.2*

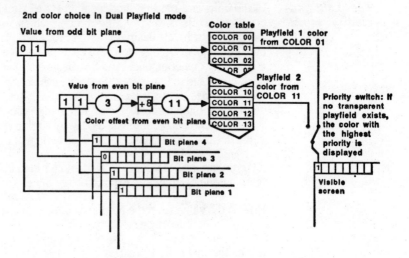

The previously described modes use only one playfield. The dual play-field mode allows two completely independent playfields to be displayed simultaneously. It's like there are two screens, superimposed on each other on the same monitor. They can (almost) be used completely inde-pendent of one another.

This is especially interesting for games. For example, a telescope effect can be produced very easily. The front playfield is filled with black points, all except for a hole in the middle through which a section of the second playfield can be seen.

Each of the two playfields gets half of the active bit planes. Playfield 1 is formed from the odd planes, and playfield 2 from the even ones. If an odd number of bit planes is being used, playfield 1 has one more bit plane available to it than playfield 2.

The color selection in the dual playfield mode is performed as usual: The value belonging to a pixel from all of the odd bit planes (playfield 1) or the even planes (playfield 2) is used as a pointer to an entry in the color table. Since each playfield can consist of a maximum of three planes, a maximum of eight colors are possible. For playfield 1, the lower eight entries of the color table are used (COLOR00 to COLOR07). For playfield 2, an offset of 8 is added to the value from the bit planes, which puts its colors in positions 8 to 15 (COLOR08 to COLOR15).

If the pixel has a value of 0, its color is not fetched from COLOR00 (or COLOR08) as usual, it is made transparent. This means that screen elements lying behind it can be seen. This can be the other playfield, sprites or simply the background (COLOR00).

The dual playfield mode can also be used in the high-resolution mode. Each playfield has only four colors in this mode. The division of the color registers doesn't change, but the upper four color registers of each playfield are unused (playfield 1: COLOR04 to 07, playfield 2: COLOR12 to 15).

*Division of*
*the bit planes*

| Bit planes | Planes in playfield 1 | Planes in playfield 2 |
|------------|----------------------|----------------------|
| 1 | Plane 1 | none |
| 2 | Plane 2 | Plane 2 |
| 3 | Planes 1 and 3 | Plane 2 |
| 4 | Planes 1 and 3 | Planes 2 and 4 |
| 5 | Planes 1, 3 and 5 | Planes 2 and 4 |
| 6 | Planes 1, 3 and 5 | Planes 2, 4 and 6 |

Color selection in the dual playfield mode:

| Playfield 1 | | Playfield 2 | |
|---|---|---|---|
| Planes 5, 3, 1 | Color reg. | Planes 6, 4, 2 | Color reg. |
| 0 0 0 | Transparent | 0 0 0 | Transparent |
| 0 0 1 | COLOR01 | 0 0 1 | COLOR09 |
| 0 1 0 | COLOR02 | 0 1 0 | COLOR10 |
| 0 1 1 | COLOR03 | 0 1 1 | COLOR11 |
| 1 0 0 | COLOR04 | 1 0 0 | COLOR12 |
| 1 0 1 | COLOR05 | 1 0 1 | COLOR13 |
| 1 1 0 | COLOR06 | 1 1 0 | COLOR14 |
| 1 1 1 | COLOR07 | 1 1 1 | COLOR15 |

*Construction of the playfields*

As mentioned, a playfield consists of a given number of bit planes. What do these bit planes look like? In Section 1.5.2 we said that they were conceived as continuous areas of memory, whereby a screen line was represented by a number of words depending on the screen width. In a normal case this is 20 words in the lowest resolution (320 pixels divided by 16 pixels per word) and 40 (640/16) in the high resolution.

The following steps are needed to determine the exact construction of the playfield:

- Define the desired screen size
- Set the bit plane size
- Select the number of bit planes
- Initialize the color table
- Set the desired mode (hi-res, lo-res, HAM, etc.)
- Construct the Copper list
- Initialize the Copper
- Activate the bit plane and Copper DMA

*Setting the screen size*

The Amiga allows the upper left corner and the lower right corner of the visible area of the playfield to be set anywhere. This allows both the picture position and size to be varied. The resolution is one raster line vertically and one low resolution pixel horizontally. Two registers contain the values. DIWSTRT (DIsplay Window STaRT) sets the horizontal and vertical start positions of the screen window, that is, the line and column where the display of the playfield begins.

DIWSTOP (DIsplay Window STOP) contains the end position +1. This refers to the line/column after the playfield. If the playfield extends up to line 250, 251 must be given as the DISTOP value.

The border color is displayed outside the visible area (this corresponds to the background color and comes from the COLOR00 register).

*DIWSTRT $08E (write-only)*

| Bit no.: | 15 | 14 | 13 | 12 | 11 | 10 | 9 | 8 | 7 | 6 | 5 | 4 | 3 | 2 | 1 | 0 |
|---|---|---|---|---|---|---|---|---|---|---|---|---|---|---|---|---|
| | V7 | V6 | V5 | V4 | V3 | V2 | V1 | V0 | H7 | H6 | H5 | H4 | H3 | H2 | H1 | H0 |

*DIWSTOP $090 (write-only)*

| Bit no.: | 15 | 14 | 13 | 12 | 11 | 10 | 9 | 8 | 7 | 6 | 5 | 4 | 3 | 2 | 1 | 0 |
|---|---|---|---|---|---|---|---|---|---|---|---|---|---|---|---|---|
| | V7 | V6 | V5 | V4 | V3 | V2 | V1 | V0 | H7 | H6 | H5 | H4 | H3 | H2 | H1 | H0 |

The start position stored in DIWSTRT is limited to the upper left quadrant of the screen, lines and columns 0 to 255, since the missing MSB's, V8 and H8, are assumed to be 0. The same applies to the horizontal end position, except that here H8 is assumed to 1, so that the horizontal position lies in the range 256 to 458. A different method is used for the vertical end position. Positions both less and greater than 256 should be possible. Thus the MSB of the vertical position, V8, is created by inverting the V7 bit. This makes an end position in the range of lines 128 to 312 possible. For end positions from 256 to 312, one sets V7 and this V8 to 1. If V7 is 1 and thus V8 0, a position between 128 and 255 is achieved.

**DIWSTOP and DISTRT**   The normal screen window has an upper left corner position of horizontal 129 and vertical 41. The lower right corner lies at 448, 296, so that DIWSTOP must be set to 449, 297. The corresponding DISTRT and DIWSTOP values are $2981 and $29C1. With these values the normal PAL Amiga screen of 640 by 256 pixels (or 320 by 256) is centered in the middle of the screen.

Why isn't the whole screen area used? There are several reasons for this. First, a normal monitor does not display the entire picture. Its visible range normally begins a few columns or lines after the blanking gap. In addition, a picture tube is not rectangular. If the screen window was set as high and wide as the monitor tube, the corners would hide part of the picture.

Another limitation on the DIWSTRT and DIWSTOP values is imposed by the blanking gaps. Vertically this is in the range from lines 0 to 25. This limits the visible vertical area to lines 26 to 312 ($1A to $138). The horizontal blanking gap lies between columns 30 and 106 ($1E $6A). Horizontal positions from 107 ($6B) on are possible.

After the position of the screen window has been set, the start and end of the bit plane DMA must be set. The data must be read from the bit planes at the right times so that the pixels appear on the screen at the desired time. Vertically this is no problem. The screen DMA starts and ends in the same line as the screen window set with DIWSTRT and DIWSTOP.

Horizontally it is somewhat more complicated. To display a pixel on the screen, the electronics need the current word from each bit plane. For six bit planes in the lowest resolution, eight bus cycles are necessary to read all of the bit planes. In high resolution there are only four

(Reminder: In one bus cycle, 2 low resolution or 4 high resolution pixels are displayed).

In addition, the hardware needs a half bus cycle before the data can appear on the screen. The bit plane DMA must therefore start exactly 8.5 cycles (17 pixels) before the start of the screen window (4.5 cycles or 9 pixels in high-resolution mode, see Figure 1.5.2.3).

The bus cycle of the first bit plane DMA in the line is stored in the DDFSTRT register (Display Data Fetch STaRT), and that of the last in DDFTSTOP (Display Data FeTch STOP):

*DDFSTRT $092 (write-only)*
*DDFSTOP $094 (write-only)*

```
Bit no.:   15  14  13  12  11  10 9  8   7   6   5   4   3   2   1  0
Function:  x   x   x   x   x   x  x  x   H8  H7  H6  H5  H4  H3  x  x
```

*DDFSTRT and DDFSTOP*

The resolution is eight bus cycles in low-resolution mode, whereby H3 is always 0, and four in high-resolution mode. Here H3 serves as the lowest bit. The reason for the limited resolution lies in the division of the bit plane DMA. In low-res mode each bit plane is read once every eight bus cycles. For this reason, the DDFSTRT value must be an integer multiple of eight (H1 to H3 = 0). The same applies to the high-res mode, except that the bit planes are read every four bus cycles (H1 and H2 = 0). Regardless of the resolution, the difference between DIWSTRT and DIWSTOP must always be divisible by eight, since the hardware always divides the lines into sections of 8 bus cycles. Even in high-res mode the bit plane DMA is performed for 8 bus cycles beyond DIWSTOP, so that 32 points are always read.

The correct values for DIWSTRT and DIWSTIO are calculated as follows:

Calculation of DDFSTRT and DDFSTOP in the low-res mode:

```
HStart = horizontal start of the screen window
DDFSTRT = (HStart/2 - 8.5) AND $FFF8
DDFSTOP = DDFSTRT + (pixels per line/2 - 8)
```

This yields $81 for HStart and 320 pixels per line:

```
DDFSTRT = ($81/2 - 8.5) AND $FFF8 = $38
DDFSTOP = $38 + (320/2 - 8) = $D0
```

Calculation of DDFSTRT and DDFSTOP in the high-res mode:

```
DDFSTRT = (HStart/2 - 4.5) AND $FFFC
DDFSTOP = DDFSTRT + (pixels per line/4 - 8)
```

This yields $81 for HStart and 640 pixels per line:

```
DDFSTRT = ($81/2 - 4.5) AND $FFFC = $3C
DDFSTOP = $3C + (640/4 - 8) = $D4
```

DDFSTRT cannot be less than $18. DDFSTOP is limited to a maximum of $D8. The reasons for this are explained in Section 1.5.2. A DDFSTRT value less than $28 has no purpose, since the pixels must then be displayed during the horizontal blanking gap, which is not possible (exception: scrolling). Since the DMA cycles of the bit planes and the sprites overlap with DDFSTRT positions less than $34, some sprites may not be visible, depending on the value of DDFSTRT.

*Moving the screen window*

If you want to move the screen window horizontally by means of DIWSTRT and DDFSTOP, it may occur that the difference between DIWSTRT and DDFSTRT is not exactly 8.5 bus cycles (17 pixels), since DDFSTRT can only be set in steps of eight bus cycles. In such a case a part of the first data word in the invisible area to the left of the screen window limit disappears. To prevent this, it is possible to shift the data read before outputting it to the screen so that it matches the start of the screen window. The section on scrolling explains how this is done.

*Setting bit map addresses*

The values in DDFSTRT and DDFSTOP determine how many data words are displayed per line. The start address must now be set for each bit map so that the DMA controller can find the data. 12 registers contain these addresses. A pair of registers, BPLxPTH and BPLxPTL is used for each bit plane. Together they are referred to simply as BPLxPT (Bit PLane x PoinTer).

| Addr. | Name | Function | |
|-------|------|----------|--|
| $0E0 | BPL1PTH | Start address of | Bits 16-18 |
| $0E2 | BPL1PTL | bit plane 1 | Bits 0-15 |
| $0E4 | BPL2PTH | Start address of | Bits 16-18 |
| $0E6 | BPL2PTL | bit plane 2 | Bits 0-15 |
| $0E8 | BPL3PTH | Start address of | Bits 16-18 |
| $0EA | BPL3PTL | bit plane 3 | Bits 0-15 |
| $0EC | BPL4PTH | Start address of | Bits 16-18 |
| $0EE | BPL4PTL | bit plane 4 | Bits 0-15 |
| $0F0 | BPL5PTH | Start address of | Bits 16-18 |
| $0F2 | BPL5PTL | bit plane 5 | Bits 0-15 |
| $0F4 | BPL6PTH | Start address of | Bits 16-18 |
| $0F6 | BPL6PTL | bit plane 6 | Bits 0-15 |

The DMA controller does the following when displaying a bit plane: The bit plane DMA remains inactive until the first line of the screen window is reached (DIWSTRT). Now it gets the data words from the various bit planes at the column stored in DFFSTRT, keeping to the timing in Figure 1.5.2.3. It uses BPLxPT as a pointer to the data in the chip RAM. After each data word is read BPLxPT is incremented by one word. The words read go to the BPLxDAT registers. These registers are used only by the DMA channel. When all six BPLxDAT registers have been provided with the corresponding data words from the bit planes, the data goes bit by bit to the video logic in Denise, which selects one of the 4096 colors depending on the mode and then outputs this to the screen.

When DFFSTOP is reached, the bit plane DMA pauses until DFFSTRT is on the next line, it repeats the process until the end of the last line of the screen window (DIWSTOP) is displayed.

The BPLxPT now points to the first word after the bit plane. But since BPLxPT should point to the first word in the bit plane by the next picture, it must be set back to this value. The Copper takes care of this quickly and easily. A Copper list for a playfield with 4 bit planes looks like this:

```
AddrPlanexH = address of bit plane x, bits 16-18
AddrPlanexL = address of bit plane x, bits 0-15

MOVE #AddrPlane1H,BPL1PTH ;initialize pointer to bit plane 1
MOVE #AddrPlane1L,BPL1PTL
MOVE #AddrPlane2H,BPL1PTH ;initialize pointer to bit plane 2
MOVE #AddrPlane2L,BPL1PTL
MOVE #AddrPlane3H,BPL1PTH ;initialize pointer to bit plane 3
MOVE #AddrPlane3L,BPL1PTL
MOVE #AddrPlane4H,BPL1PTH ;initialize pointer to bit plane 4
MOVE #AddrPlane4L,BPL1PTL
WAIT ($FF,$FE)            ;end of the Copper list (wait for an
                         ;impossible screen position)
```

Resetting the BPLxPT is absolutely necessary. If you don't use a Copper list, this must be done by the processor in the vertical blanking interrupt.

*Scrolling and extra-large playfields*

The previous playfields were always the same size as the screen. However, it would often be useful to have a large playfield in memory, not all of which is visible on the screen at one time, but which can be smoothly scrolled in all directions. This is easily done on the Amiga. The following sections illustrate this in both the X and Y directions.

*Figure 1.5.5.3*

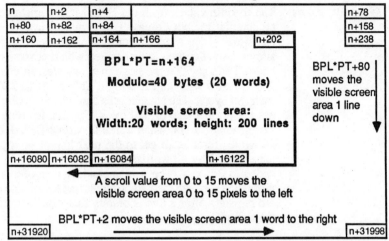

Bit plane - Width:40 words; height: 400 lines

n=Starting address of the bit plane       Total size of bit plane: 32,000 bytes

*Extra-tall playfields and vertical scrolling*

This can be done very easily vertically. The necessary bit planes are placed in memory as usual, but this time they contain more lines than the screen. In order to move the screen window smoothly of this tall playfield, the values of BPLxPT are changed. For example, if you want to display the areas from line 100 to 356, the BPLxPT must be set to the first word of the 100th line. With a screen width of 320 pixels each line occupies 20 words (40 bytes). Multiplies by 100 lines yields an address of 4000. Add this to the start address of the playfield, and you have the desired value for BPLxPT. To scroll the playfield in the screen window, simply change this value by one or more lines with each picture, depending on the scroll speed desired. Since the BPLxPT can only be changed outside the visible area, a Copper list is used. You can then change the values in the Copper list and the Copper automatically writes them into the BPLxPT registers at the right time. You have to be careful not to change the Copper list while the Copper is accessing its commands. Otherwise the processor may change one word of the address while the Copper is reading it and the Copper gets the wrong address.

*Extra-wide playfields and horizontal scrolling*

Special registers are present for horizontal scrolling and extra-wide playfields (all write-only):

$108 BPL1MOD Modulo value for the odd bit planes
$10A BPL2MOD Modulo value for the even bit planes

*BPLCON $102*

| Bit no.: | 15-8 | 7 | 6 | 5 | 4 | 3 | 2 | 1 | 0 |
|---|---|---|---|---|---|---|---|---|---|
| Function: | unused | P2H3 | P2H2 | P2H1 | P2H0 | P1H3 | P1H2 | P1H1 | P1H0 |

P1H0-P1H3     Position of the even planes (four bits)
P2H0-P2H3     Position of the odd planes (four bits)

*Memory areas*     The modulo values from the BPLxMOD registers allow (so to speak) rectangular memory areas. This principle is used often in the Amiga hardware. Inside a large memory area divided into rows and columns it allows a smaller area to be defined which possess a certain height and width. Let's say that the large memory area, in this case our playfield, is 640 pixels wide and 256 high. This gives us 256 lines of 40 words each (80 bytes). The smaller area corresponds to the screen window and has the normal size of 320 by 200 pixels, for only 20 words per line. The problem is that when a line is output, BPLxPT is incremented by 20 words. In order to get to the next line of your playfield, it must be incremented by 40 words. After each line, another 20 words must be added to BPLxPT. The Amiga can take care of this automatically. The difference between the two different line lengths is written into the modulo register. After a line is output, this value is automatically added to the BPLxPT.

Width of the playfield: 80 bytes (40 words)

Width of the screen window: 40 bytes (20 words)

Modulo value needed: 40 bytes (The modulo value must always be an even number of bytes).

Start: start address of the first line of the playfield

Output of the 1st line:

```
Word:      0         1         2         3        ...   19
BPLxPT:    Start     Start+2   Start+4   Start+6  ...   Start+38
```

After the last word is output, BPLxPT is incremented by 1 word:

```
BPLxPT = Start+40.
```

After the end of the line, the modulo value is added to BPLxPT:

```
BPLxPT = BPLxPT + modulo BPLxPT = Start+40 + 40 = Start+80
```

Output of the 2nd line:

```
Word:      0         1         2         3         ...   19
BPLxPT:    Start+80  Start+82  Start+84  Start+86  ...   Start+118
```

etc. This example shows the left half of the large bit map being displayed in the large screen window. To start at a different horizontal position, simply add the desired number of words to the start value of BPLxPT, whereby the modulo value remains the same.

The start values are as above. The only difference is that BPLxPT is not at Start, but at Start+40 so that the right half of the large playfield is displayed.

```
Word:      0         1         2         3         ...   19
BPLxPT:    Start+40  Start+42  Start+44  Start+46  ...   Start+78
```

After outputting the last word:

```
BPLxPT = Start+80
```

Now the modulo value is added to BPLxPT:

```
BPLxPT = BPLxPT + modulo BPLxPT = Start+80 + 40 = Start+120
```

Output of the 2nd line:

```
Word:      0          1          2          3       ...   19
BPLxPT:  Start+120  Start+122  Start+124  Start+126  ...  Start+158
```

etc. Separate modulo values can be set for the even and odd bit planes. This allows two different-sized playfields in the dual playfield mode. If this mode is not being used, set both BPLxMOD registers to the same modulo value.

*Scrolling*

The screen can be moved horizontally in steps of 16 pixels with the help of the BPLxPT and BPLxMOD registers. Fine scrolling in single pixel steps is possible with the BPLCON1 register. The lower four bits contain the scroll value for the even planes, bits 4 to 7 are that of the odd planes. This scroll value delays the output of the pixel data read for the corresponding planes. If it is zero, the data are output exactly 8.5 bus cycles (4.5 in high-res) after the DDFSTRT position, otherwise they appear up to 15 pixels later, depending on the scroll value. That is, the picture is shifted to the right within the screen window by the value in BPLCON1.

Smooth scrolling of the screen contents to the right can be accomplished by incrementing the value of BPLCON1 from 0 to 15 and then setting it back to 0 while decrementing the BPLxPT by one word as described above.

Left scrolling can be accomplished by decrementing the scroll value from 15 to 0 and then incrementing BPLxPT by one word. BPLCON1 should be changed only outside the visible area. This can be done either during the vertical blanking interrupt, or the Copper can be used. The values in the Copper list can be changed as desired and they are written into the BPLCON1 register during the vertical blanking gap.

But if the picture is shifted to the right by means of the BPLCON1 value, the excess points on the left are chopped off correctly. New pixels don't appear on the right since a new pixel data hasn't been read there. To prevent this, the DDFSTRT value must be set ahead of its normal start by 8 bus cycles (high-res: 4 bus cycles). The DDFSTRT value is calculated as usual from the desired screen window and it is decremented by 8 (or 4). This extra word is normally not visible. Only when the scroll value is non-zero its pixels appear in the free positions at the left of the screen window. If this is 320 pixels wide, 21 data words instead of the usual 20 are read per line. This must be taken into account when calculating the bit planes and the modulo values.

The screen window can also be positioned as desired by means of the scroll value. If the difference between DIWSTRT and DIWSTOO is more than 17 pixels, you simply shift the read data to the right by the amount over 17.

*The interlace mode*

Although the interlace mode doubles the number of lines which can be displayed, it differs only by a different modulo value and a new Copper list from the normal display mode. As described in Section 1.5.2, the odd and even lines are displayed alternately in each picture. To allow an interlace playfield to be represented normally in memory, the modulo value is set equal to the number of words per line. After a line is output, the length of the line is added again to BPLxPT, which amounts to skipping over the next line. In each picture only every other line is displayed. Now the BPLxPT must be set to the first or second line of the playfield, depending on the frame type, so that either the even or the odd lines are displayed. In a long frame BPLxPT is set to line 1 (odd lines only), and in a short frame it is set to line 2 (even lines only). The Copper list for an interlace playfield is somewhat more complicated because two lists are needed for the two frame types:

*Copper list for an interlace playfield:*

Line1 = address of the first line of the bit plane
Line2 = address of the second line of the bit plane

Copper1:

```
MOVE #Line1Hi,BPLxPTH      ;set pointer for BPLxPT to
MOVE #Line1Lo,BPLxPTL      ;the address of the first line
...                        ;other Copper commands
MOVE #Copper2Hi,COP1LCH    ;set address of Copper list
MOVE #Copper2Lo,COP1LCL    ;to Copper2
WAIT ($FF,$FE)             ;end of the 1st Copper list
```

Copper2:

```
MOVE #Line2Hi,BPLxPTH      ;set pointer for BPLxPT to
MOVE #Line2Lo,BPLxPTL      ;the address of the first line
...                        ;other Copper commands
MOVE #Copper1Hi,COP1LCH    ;set address of Copper list
MOVE #Copper1Lo,COP1LCL    ;to Copper1
WAIT ($FF,$FE)             ;end of the 1st Copper list
```

The Copper continually alternates its Copper list after each frame by loading the address of the other list into COP1LC at the end of a command list. This address is automatically loaded into the program counter of the Copper at the start of the next frame. The interlace mode should be initialized carefully, so that the Copper list for odd lines is actually processed within a long frame:

- • Set COP1LC to Copper1

- • Set the LOF bit (bit 15) in the VPOS register ($2A) to 0. This makes sure that the first frame after the interlace mode is enabled in a long frame and is therefore suited to Copper1. The LOF bit is inverted after each frame in the interlace mode. If it is set to 0, it changes to 1 at the start of the next frame. This makes this frame a long frame.

- • Interlace mode on

- • Wait until the first line of the next picture (line 0)

- • Copper DMA on

All other register functions are unchanged in the interlace mode. All line specifications (such as DIWSTRT) always refer to the line number within the current frame (0-311 for a short frame and 0-312 for a long frame). If the interlace mode is enabled without changing other registers, a faint flickering is noticeable because the lines of the frames are now displaced from each other, even though both frames contain the same graphics data. When doubly-large bit planes and the appropriate modulo values are set up with suitable Copper lists so that different data are displayed in each frame, then the desired increase in the number of lines is noticed.

The interlace mode results in a strong flickering since each line is displayed only once every two frames and is thus refreshed 25 times per second. This flickering can be reduced to a minimum by selecting the lowest possible contrast between colors displayed (lowest intensity differences).

*The control registers*

There are three control registers for activating the various modes: BPLCON0 to BPLCON2. BPLCON1 contains the scroll values. The other two are constructed as follows:

*BPLCON0 $100*

| Bit no. | Name | Function |
|---------|------|----------|
| 15 | HIRES | High-resolution mode on (HIRES=1) |
| 14 | BPU2 | The three BPUx bits comprise a three-bit number |
| 13 | BPU1 | which contains the number |
| 12 | BPU0 | of bit planes used (0 to 6). |
| 11 | HOMOD | Hold-and-modify on (HOMOD=1) |
| 10 | DBPLF | Dual playfield on (DBPLF=1) |
| 9 | COLOR | Video output color (COLOR=1) |
| 8 | GAUD | Genlock audio on (GAUD=1) |
| 7-4 | --- | unused |
| 3 | LPEN | Lightpen input active (LPEN=1) |
| 2 | LACE | Interlace mode on (LACE=1) |
| 1 | ERSY | External synchronization on (ERSY=1) |
| 0 | --- | unused |

HIRES   The HIRES bit enables the high-resolution display mode (640 pixels /line).

BPL0-BPL2

These three bits form a 3-bit number which selects the number of active bit planes. Values between 0 and 6 are allowed.

HOMOD and DBPLF

These two bits select the appropriate mode. They cannot both be active at the same time. The extra-half-bright mode is automatically activated when all six bit planes are enabled and neither HOMOD or DBPLF is selected.

LACE    When the LACE bit is set, the LFO frame bit in the VPOS register is inverted at the start of each frame, causing the desired alternation between long and short frames.

COLOR   The color bit turns the color burst output of Agnus on. Only when Agnus delivers this color burst signal can the video mixer create a color video signal. Otherwise it is black and white. The RGB is not affected by this.

ERSY    The ERSY bit switches the connections for the vertical and horizontal synchronization signals from output to input. This allows the Amiga to be synchronized by external signals. The genlock interface uses this bit to be able to mix the Amiga's picture with another video picture. The GAUD bit is also provided for the genlock interface (see Section 1.3.2).

*BPLCON2 $104*

| Bit no.: | 15-7 | 6 | 5 | 4 | 3 | 2 | 1 | 0 |
|----------|------|------|------|------|------|------|------|------|
| Function: | unused | PF2PRI | PF2P2 | PF2P1 | PF2P0 | PF1P2 | PF1P1 | PF1P0 |

PF2P0-PF2P2 and PF1P0-PF1P2 determine the priority of the sprites in relationship to the playfields (see the next section).

PF2PRI: If this bit is set, the even planes have priority over the odd planes, meaning that they appear in front of the odd planes. This bit has visible effect only in the dual playfield mode.

*Activating the screen display*  After all of the registers described thus far have been loaded with the desired values, the DMA channel for the bit planes must be enabled, and, if the Copper is used (which is normally the case), its DMA channel must also be enabled. The following MOVE command accomplishes this by setting the DMAEN, BPLEN and COPEN bits in the DMA control register DMACON:

```
MOVE.W #$8310,$DFF096
```

*Example*
*programs*

<u>Program 1: Extra-half-bright demo</u>

This program creates a playfield with the standard dimensions 320 by
200 pixels in the low-res mode. Six bit planes are used, so the extra-
half-bright mode is automatically enabled. At the beginning, the program allocates the memory needed. Since the addresses of the individual
bit planes are not known until this time, the Copper list is not copied
from the program, but created directly in the chip RAM. It contains
only commands to set the BPLxPT registers.

To show you something of the 64 possible colors, the program draws
16x16-pixel-large blocks in all colors at random positions. The
VHPOS register is used as a random-number generator.

```
;*** Demo for the Extra-Halfbright-Mode ***

;CustomChip-Register

INTENA   = $9A   ;Interrupt-Enable-Register (write)
DMACON   = $96   ;DMA-Control register (write)
COLOR00  = $180  ;Color palette register 0
VHPOSR   = $6    ;Ray position (read)

;Copper Register

COP1LC   = $80 ;Address of 1. Copperlist
COP2LC   = $84 ;Address of 2. Copperlist
COPJMP1  = $88 ;Jump to Copperlist 1
COPJMP2  = $8a ;Jump to Copperlist 2

;Bitplane Register

BPLCON0 = $100 ;Bitplane Control register 0
BPLCON1 = $102 ;1 (Scroll value)
BPLCON2 = $104 ;2 (Sprite<>Playfield Priority)
BPL1PTH = $0E0 ;Number of  1. Bitplane
BPL1PTL = $0E2 ;
BPL1MOD = $108 ;Modulo-Value for odd Bit-Planes
BPL2MOD = $10A ;Modulo-Value for even Bit-Planes
DIWSTRT = $08E ;Start of the screen windows
DIWSTOP = $090 ;End of the screen windows
DDFSTRT = $092 ;Bit-Plane DMA Start
DDFSTOP = $094 ;Bit-Plane DMA Stop

;CIA-A Port register A (Mouse key)

CIAAPRA = $bfe001

;Exec Library Base Offsets

OpenLibrary = -30-522        ;LibName,Version/a1,d0
Forbid      = -30-102
Permit      = -30-108
AllocMem    = -30-168        ;ByteSize,Requirements/d0,d1
FreeMem     = -30-180        ;MemoryBlock,ByteSize/a1,d0
```

```
;graphics base

StartList    = 38

;other Labels

Execbase    = 4
Planesize   = 40*200         ;Size of Bitplane: 40 Bytes by
                             ;200 lines
CLsize      = 13*4           ;The Copperlist with 13 commands
Chip        = 2              ;Chip-RAM request
Clear       = Chip+$10000    ;clear previous Chip-RAM

;*** Initialize program ***

Start:

;Request memory for the  Bitplanes

 move.l Execbase,a6
 move.l #Planesize*6,d0      ;Memory size of all Planes
 move.l #clear,d1            ;Memory to be with filled with
                             ;nulls
 jsr    AllocMem(a6)         ;Request memory
 move.l d0,Planeadr          ;Address of the first memory
                             ;Plane
 beq    End ;Error! -> End

;Request memory for  Copperlist

 moveq  #Clsize,d0           ;Size of the Copperlist
 moveq  #chip,d1
 jsr    AllocMem(a6)
 move.l d0,CLadr
 beq    FreePlane            ;Error! -> Free RAM for Bit
                             ;planes

;Build Copperlist

 moveq  #5,d4                ;6 Planes = 6 loops to run
                             ;through
 move.l d0,a0                ;Address of the Copperlist to
                             ;a0
 move.l Planeadr,d1
 move.w #bpl1pth,d3          ;first Register to d3

MakeCL: move.w d3,(a0)+      ;BPLxPTH ins RAM
 addq.w #2,d3                ;next Register
 swap   d1
 move.w d1,(a0)+             ;Hi-word of the Plane address
                             ;in RAM
 move.w d3,(a0)+             ;BPLxPTL ins RAM
 addq.w #2,d3                ;next Register
 swap   d1
 move.w d1,(a0)+            ;Lo-word of the  Plane address in RAM
```

```
        add.l   #planesize,d1   ;Address of the next Plane calculated

        dbf     d4,MakeCL

        move.l #$fffffffe,(a0)    ;End of Copperlist

;*** Main program ***

;DMA and Task switching off

        jsr     forbid(a6)
        lea     $dff000,a5
        move.w #$03e0,dmacon(a5)

;Copper initialization

        move.l CLadr,cop1lc(a5)
        clr.w   copjmp1(a5)

;Color table with different color fills

        moveq   #31,d0           ;Value for color register
        lea     color00(a5),a1
        moveq   #1,d1            ;first color
SetTab:
        move.w d1,(a1)+          ;Color in color register
        mulu    #3,d1           ;calculate next color
        dbf     d0,SetTab

;Playfield initialization

        move.w #$3081,diwstrt(a5)    ;Standard value for
        move.w #$30c1,diwstop(a5)    ;screen window
        move.w #$0038,ddfstrt(a5)    ;and BitplaneDMA
        move.w #$00d0,ddfstop(a5)
        move.w #%0110001000000000,bplcon0(a5) ;6 Bitplanes
        clr.w   bplcon1(a5)          ;no Scrolling
        clr.w   bplcon2(a5)          ;Priority makes no difference
        clr.w   bpl1mod(a5)          ;Modulo for all Planes equals
                                     ;Null
        clr.w   bpl2mod(a5)

;DMA on
        move.w #$8380,dmacon(a5)

;Bitplane modification

        moveq   #40,d5           ;Bytes per line
        clr.l   d2               ;Begin with color 0

Loop:   clr.l d0
        move.w vhposr(a5),d0     ;Random value to  d0
        and.w   #$3ffe,d0        ;Unnecessary  Bits masked out
        cmp.w   #$2580,d0        ;Large as Plane?
        bcs     Continue         ;When not, then continue
        and.w   #$1ffe,d0        ;else erase upper bit
```

```
          Continue: move.l Planeadr,a4 ;Address of the  1.Bitplane to
                                        ;a4
          add.l   d0,a4                 ;Calculate address of the Blocks
          moveq   #5,d4                 ;Number for Bitplanes
          move.l  d2,d3                 ;Color in work register

          Block:
          clr.l   d1
          lsr     #1,d3                 ;one Bit of color number in X-Flag
          negx.w  d1                    ;use d1 to adjust X-Flag
          moveq   #15,d0                ;16 lines per Block
          move.l  a4,a3                 ;Block address in working register

          Fill:
          move.w  d1,(a3)               ;Word in Bitplane
          add.l   d5,a3                 ;compute next line
          dbf     d0,Fill

          add.l   #Planesize,a4         ;next Bitplane
          dbf     d4,Block

          addq.b  #1,d2                 ;next color
          btst    #6,ciaapra            ;mouse key pressed?
          bne     Loop                  ;no  -> then continue

;*** End program ***

;Activate old  Copperlist

          move.l  #GRname,a1            ;Set parameter for OpenLibrary
          clr.l   d0
          jsr     OpenLibrary(a6)       ;Graphics Library open
          move.l  d0,a4
          move.l  StartList(a4),cop1lc(a5) ;Address of Startlist
          clr.w   copjmp1(a5)
          move.w  #$8060,dmacon(a5)     ;reenable  DMA
          jsr     permit(a6)            ;Task-Switching on

;Free memory for Copperlist

          move.l  CLadr,a1              ;Set parameter for FreeMem
          moveq   #CLsize,d0
          jsr     FreeMem(a6)           ;Free memory

;Free memory for Bitplanes
FreePlane:
          move.l  Planeadr,a1
          move.l  #Planesize*6,d0
          jsr     FreeMem(a6)

Ende:
          clr.l   d0
          rts                           ;Program end

;Variables
```

```
CLadr:     dc.l 0
Planeadr: dc.l 0

;Constants

GRname: dc.b "graphics.library",0


;Program end
 end
```

*Program 2:*      <u>Dual playfield and smooth scrolling</u>

This program uses several effects at once: First, it creates a dual playfield screen with one low-res bit plane per playfield. Then it enlarges
the normal screen window so that no borders can be seen, and finally, it
scrolls playfield 1 horizontally and playfield 2 vertically.

The usual routines for memory allocation, etc. are used at the start and
end.

Both playfields are filled with a checkerboard pattern of 16x16 point
blocks.

The main loop of the program, which performs the scrolling, first waits
for a line in the vertical blanking gap, in which the operating system
processes all of the interrupt routines and the Copper sets BPLxPT.
After this it increments the vertical scroll counter, calculates the new
BPLxPT for playfield 2, and writes it into the Copper list.

The horizontal scroll position results from separating the lower four
bits of the scroll counter from the rest. The lower four bits are written
into the BPLCON1 register as the scroll value for playfield 1, and the
5th bit is used to calculate the new BPLxPT, which is copied into the
Copper list.

Both the horizontal and vertical scroll counters are incremented from 0
to 31 and then reset to 0. This is sufficient for the scrolling effect since
the pattern used for the playfields repeats every 32 pixels.

```
*** Dual-Playfield & Scroll Demo ***
;CustomChip-Register

INTENA   = $9A ;Interrupt-Enable-Register (write)
INTREQR  = $1e ;Interrupt-Request-Register (read)
DMACON   = $96 ;DMA-Control register (write)
COLOR00  = $180 ;Color palette register 0
VPOSR    = $4   ;half line position (read)

;Copper Register

COP1LC  = $80 ;Address of 1. Copperlist
COP2LC  = $84 ;Address of 2. Copperlist
```

```
COPJMP1 = $88 ;Jump to Copperlist 1
COPJMP2 = $8a ;Jump to Copperlist 2

;Bitplane Register

BPLCON0 = $100 ;Bitplane control register 0
BPLCON1 = $102 ;1 (Scroll value)
BPLCON2 = $104 ;2 (Sprite<>Playfield Priority)
BPL1PTH = $0E0 ;Pointer to 1. Bitplane
BPL1PTL = $0E2 ;
BPL1MOD = $108 ;Modulo-Value for odd Bit-Planes
BPL2MOD = $10A ;Module-value for even Bit-Planes
DIWSTRT = $08E ;Start of screen windows
DIWSTOP = $090 ;End of screen windows
DDFSTRT = $092 ;Bit-Plane DMA Start
DDFSTOP = $094 ;Bit-Plane DMA Stop

;CIA-A Port register A (Mouse key)
CIAAPRA = $bfe001

;Exec Library Base Offsets

OpenLibrary = -30-522 ;LibName,Version/a1,d0
Forbid      = -30-102
Permit      = -30-108
AllocMem    = -30-168 ;ByteSize,Requirements/d0,d1
FreeMem     = -30-180 ;MemoryBlock,ByteSize/a1,d0

;graphics base

StartList   = 38

;Misc Labels

Execbase    = 4
Planesize   = 52*345      ;Size of the Bitplane
Planewidth  = 52
CLsize      = 5*4         ;The Copperlist contains 5 commands
Chip        = 2           ;request Chip-RAM
Clear       = Chip+$10000 ;clear previous Chip-RAM

;*** Pre-program ***

Start:

;Request memory for Bitplanes

 move.l Execbase,a6
 move.l #Planesize*2,d0      ;memory size of the Planes
 move.l #clear,d1
 jsr    AllocMem(a6)         ;Request memory
 move.l d0,Planeadr
 beq    Ende                 ;Error! -> End

;Request memory for the Copperlist
 moveq  #Clsize,d0
```

```
       moveq   #chip,d1
       jsr     AllocMem(a6)
       move.l  d0,CLadr
       beq     FreePlane           ;Error! -> Free memory for the Planes

;Build Copperlist

       moveq   #1,d4               ;two Bitplanes
       move.l  d0,a0
       move.l  Planeadr,d1
       move.w  #bpl1pth,d3

MakeCL: move.w d3,(a0)+
       addq.w  #2,d3
       swap    d1
       move.w  d1,(a0)+
       move.w  d3,(a0)+
       addq.w  #2,d3
       swap    d1
       move.w  d1,(a0)+
       add.l   #planesize,d1       ;Address of the next Plane

       dbf     d4,MakeCL
       move.l  #$fffffffe,(a0)     ;End of the Copperlist

;*** Main program ***

;DMA and Task switching off

       jsr     forbid(a6)
       lea     $dff000,a5
       move.w  #$01e0,dmacon(a5)

;Copper initialization

       move.l  CLadr,cop1lc(a5)
       clr.w   copjmp1(a5)

;Playfield initialization

       move.w  #0,color00(a5)
       move.w  #$0f00,color00+2(a5)
       move.w  #$000f,color00+18(a5)
       move.w  #$1a64,diwstrt(a5)    ;26,100
       move.w  #$39d1,diwstop(a5)    ;313,465
       move.w  #$0020,ddfstrt(a5)    ;read one extra word
       move.w  #$00d8,ddfstop(a5)
       move.w  #%0010011000000000,bplcon0(a5) ;Dual-Playfield
       clr.w   bplcon1(a5)           ;and scroll to start on 0
       clr.w   bplcon2(a5)           ;Playfield 1 or Playfield 2
       move.w  #4,bpl1mod(a5)        ;Modulo on 2 Words
       move.w  #4,bpl2mod(a5)

;DMA on
       move.w  #$8180,dmacon(a5)
```

```
;Bitplanes filled with checker pattern

  move.l  planeadr,a0
  move.w  #planesize/2-1,d0      ;loop value
  move.w  #13*16,d1              ;Height = 16 Lines
  move.l  #$ffff0000,d2          ;checker pattern
  move.w  d1,d3

fill:   move.l d2,(a0)+
  subq.w  #1,d3
  bne.s   continue
  swap    d2                     ;pattern change
  move.w  d1,d3
continue: dbf d0,fill

;Playfields scroll

  clr.l   d0                     ;vertical Scroll position
  clr.l   d1                     ;horizontal Scroll position
  move.l  CLadr,a1               ;Address of the Copperlist
  move.l  Planeadr,a0            ;Address of first Bitplane

;Wait on Raster line 16 (for the Exec-Interrupts)

wait:   move.l vposr(a5),d2      ;read Position
  and.l   #$0001FF00,d2          ;horizontal Bits masked
  cmp.l   #$00001000,d2          ;wait on line 16
  bne.s   wait

;Playfield 1 vertical scroll

  addq.b  #2,d0                  ;raise vertical Scroll value
  cmp.w   #$80,d0                ;already 128 (4*32)?
  bne.S   novover
  clr.l   d0                     ;Then back to 0
novover:
  move.l  d0,d2                  ;copy scroll value
  lsr.w   #2,d2                  ;copy divided by 4 s
  mulu    #52,d2                 ;Number Bytes per line * Scroll
                                 ;position
  add.l   a0,d2                  ;plus Address of first Plane
  add.l   #Planesize,d2          ;plus Plane size
  move.w  d2,14(a1)              ;give End address for Copperlist
  swap    d2
  move.w  d2,10(a1)

;Playfield 2 horizontal scroll

  addq.b  #1,d1                  ;raise horizontal Scroll value
  cmp.w   #$80,d1                ;already 128 (4*32)
  bne.S   nohover
  clr.l   d1                     ;then back to 0
nohover:
  move.l  d1,d2                  ;copy scroll value
  lsr.w   #2,d2                  ;copy divided by 4
  move.l  d2,d3                  ;copy Scroll position
```

```
        and.w   #$FFF0,d2           ;lower  4 Bit masked
        sub.w   d2,d3              ;lower 4 Bit in d3 isolated
        move.w  d4,bplcon1(a5)     ;last Value in BPLCON1
        move.w  d3,d4              ;new scroll value to  d4
        lsr.w   #3,d2              ;new Address for Copperlist
        add.l   a0,d2              ;calculate
        move.w  d2,6(a1)           ;and write in Copperlist
        swap    d2
        move.w  d2,2(a1)


        btst    #6,ciaapra         ;Mouse key pressed?
        bne.s   wait               ;NO -> continue

;*** End program ***

;Activate old Copperlist

        move.l  #GRname,a1         ;Set parameter for OpenLibrary
        clr.l   d0
        jsr     OpenLibrary(a6)    ;Graphics Library open
        move.l  d0,a4
        move.l  StartList(a4),cop1lc(a5)
        clr.w   copjmp1(a5)
        move.w  #$83e0,dmacon(a5)
        jsr     permit(a6)         ;Task-Switching permitted

;Free memory used by Copperlist

        move.l  CLadr,a1           ;Set parameter for FreeMem
        moveq   #CLsize,d0
        jsr     FreeMem(a6)        ;Free memory

;Free memory used by Bit planes
FreePlane:
        move.l  Planeadr,a1
        move.l  #Planesize*2,d0
        jsr     FreeMem(a6)


Ende:
        clr.l   d0
        rts                        ;Program ends

;Variables

CLadr:      dc.l 0
Planeadr:   dc.l 0
test:       dc.l 0

;Constants

GRname:  dc.b "graphics.library",0

        end
;Program end
```

# 1.5.6 Sprites

*Construction of the sprites*

Sprites are small graphic elements which can be used completely independent of the playfields. Each sprite is 16 pixels wide and can have a maximum height of the entire screen window. It can be displayed anywhere on the screen. Normally a sprite is in front of the playfield(s). Its pixels therefore cover the graphic behind it. The mouse pointer, for example, is implemented as a sprite. Up to eight sprites are possible on the Amiga. A sprite normally has three colors, but it is possible to combine two sprites into one to get a fifteen-color sprite.

*Color selection*

The color selection for sprites is very similar to that of a dual-playfield screen. A sprite is sixteen pixels wide, represented by two data words which are used as sort of "mini bit planes." Like the bit planes, the color of a pixel is formed from the corresponding bits in each of the bit planes. With a sprite, the color of the first pixel (this is the leftmost point of the sprite) is selected by the two highest-order bits (bit 15) of the two data words. The two lowest-order bits (bit 0) determine the color of the last pixel. Each pixel is thus represented by two bits, which means it can have one of four different colors. The color table is used to determine the actual color from this value. There are no special color registers for the sprites. The sprite colors are obtained from the upper half of the table, color registers 16-31. This means that sprite and playfield colors do not come in conflict unless playfield with more than 16 colors are created.

The following table shows the assignment of color registers and sprites:

*Color registers and Sprites*

| Sprite no. | Sprite data | Color register |
|------------|-------------|----------------|
| 0 & 1 | 0 0 | transparent |
|  | 0 1 | COLOR17 |
|  | 1 0 | COLOR18 |
|  | 1 1 | COLOR19 |
| 2 & 3 | 0 0 | transparent |
|  | 0 1 | COLOR21 |
|  | 1 0 | COLOR22 |
|  | 1 1 | COLOR23 |
| 4 & 5 | 0 0 | transparent |
|  | 0 1 | COLOR25 |
|  | 1 0 | COLOR26 |
|  | 1 1 | COLOR27 |
| 6 & 7 | 0 0 | transparent |
|  | 0 1 | COLOR29 |
|  | 1 0 | COLOR30 |
|  | 1 1 | COLOR31 |

Each two successive sprites have the same color registers.

As in the dual-playfield mode, the bit combination of two zeros does not represent a color, it causes the pixel to be transparent. This means that the color of anything below this pixel is visible in its place, whether this is another sprite, a playfield or just the background.

If three colors are not enough, two sprites can be combined with each other. The two-bit combinations of the sprites then make up a four-bit number. Sprites can only be combined in successive even-odd pairs, i.e. no. 0 with no. 1, no. 2 with no. 3, etc. The two data words from the sprite with the higher number are used as the two high-order bits of the total 4-bit value. This is then used as a pointer to one of fifteen color registers, whereby the value zero is again used as transparent. The color registers are the same for all four possible sprite combinations: COLOR16 to COLOR31.

| Sprite data | Color register | Sprite data | Color register |
|---|---|---|---|
| 0 0 0 0 | transparent | 1 0 0 0 | COLOR24 |
| 0 0 0 1 | COLOR17 | 1 0 0 1 | COLOR25 |
| 0 0 1 0 | COLOR18 | 1 0 1 0 | COLOR26 |
| 0 0 1 1 | COLOR19 | 1 0 1 1 | COLOR27 |
| 0 1 0 0 | COLOR20 | 1 1 0 0 | COLOR28 |
| 0 1 0 1 | COLOR21 | 1 1 0 1 | COLOR29 |
| 0 1 1 0 | COLOR22 | 1 1 1 0 | COLOR30 |
| 0 1 1 1 | COLOT23 | 1 1 1 1 | COLOR31 |

*The sprite DMA*

The Amiga sprites can be programmed very easily. Almost all of the work is handled by the sprite DMA channels. The only thing needed to display a sprite on the screen is a special sprite data list in memory. This contains almost all of the data needed for the sprite. The DMA controller must still be told the address of this list in order for the sprite to appear.

The DMA controller has a DMA channel for each sprite. This can read only two data words in each raster line. This is why a normal sprite is limited to a width of 16 pixels and four colors. Since these two data words can be read in every line, the height of a sprite is limited only by that of the screen window.

*Construction of the sprite data list*

Such a data list consists of individual lines, each of which contains two data words. One of these lines is read through DMA in each raster line. They can contain either two control words to initialize the sprite, or two data words with the pixel data.

The control words determine the horizontal columns and the first and last lines of the sprite.

After the DMA controller has read these words and placed them in the corresponding registers, it waits until the electron beam reaches the starting line of the sprite. Then two words are read for each raster line and are output by Denise at the appropriate horizontal position on the screen until the last line of the sprite has been processed. The next two words in the sprite data list are again treated as control words. If they are both 0, the DMA channel ends its activity. It is also possible to specify a new sprite position, however. The DMA controller then waits for the start line and repeats the process until two control words with the value 0 are found as the end marker of the list.

Construction of a sprite data list (Start = starting address of the list in chip RAM):

| Address | Contents |
| --- | --- |
| Start+4 | 1st and 2nd data words of the 1st line of the sprite |
| Start+8 | 1st and 2nd data words of the 2nd line of the sprite |
| Start+12 | 1st and 2nd data words of the 3rd line of the sprite |
| Start+4*n | 1st and 2nd data words of the nth line of the sprite |
| Start+4*(n+1) | 0,0   End of the sprite data list |

Construction of the first control word

| Bit no.: | 15 | 14 | 13 | 12 | 11 | 10 | 9 | 8 | 7 | 6 | 5 | 4 | 3 | 2 | 1 | 0 |
| --- | --- | --- | --- | --- | --- | --- | --- | --- | --- | --- | --- | --- | --- | --- | --- | --- |
| Function: | E7 | E6 | E5 | E4 | E3 | E2 | E1 | E0 | H8 | H7 | H6 | H5 | H4 | H3 | H2 | H1 |

Construction of the second control word

| Bit no.: | 15 | 14 | 13 | 12 | 11 | 10 | 9 | 8 | 7 | 6 | 5 | 4 | 3 | 2 | 1 | 0 |
| --- | --- | --- | --- | --- | --- | --- | --- | --- | --- | --- | --- | --- | --- | --- | --- | --- |
| Function: | L7 | L6 | L5 | L4 | L3 | L2 | L1 | L0 | AT | 0 | 0 | 0 | 0 | E8 | L8 | H0 |

H0 to H8   Horizontal position of the sprite (HSTART)
E0 to E8   First line of the sprite (VSTART)
L0 to L8   Last line of the sprite + 1 (VSTOP)
AT         Attach control bit

Nine bits are provided for the horizontal and vertical position of the sprite. These bits are divided somewhat impractically between the two registers.

*Horizontal and Vertical position*

The resolution in the horizontal direction is one low resolution pixel, while in the vertical direction it is one raster line. These values cannot be changed since they are independent of the mode of the playfield(s).

The sprites are limited to the screen window (set by DIWSTRT and DIWSTOP). If the coordinates set by the control words are outside this area, the sprites are only partially visible, if at all, since all points which are not within the screen window are cut off.

The horizontal and vertical start position refer to the upper left corner of the sprite. The vertical stop position defines the first line after the sprite, that is, the last line of the sprite + 1. The number of lines in the sprite is thus VSTOP - VSTART.

The following example list displays a sprite at the coordinates 180,160, roughly in the center of the screen. It has a height of 8 lines. The last line (VSTOP) is thus 168.

If you combine the two data words together, you get numbers between 0 and 3 which represent one of the three sprite colors or the transparent pixels. This makes the sprite easier to understand:

```
0000002222000000
0000220000220000
0002200330022000
0022003113002200
0022003113002200
0002200330022000
0000220000220000
0000002222000000
```

In the data list the two values must be separated:

```
Start:
dc.w $A05A,$A800 ;HSTART = $B4, VSTART=$A0, VSTOP=$A8
dc.w %0000 0000 0000 0000,%0000 0011 1100 0000
dc.w %0000 0000 0000 0000,%0000 1100 0011 0000
dc.w %0000 0001 1000 0000,%0001 1001 1001 1000
dc.w %0000 0011 1100 0000,%0011 0010 0100 1100
dc.w %0000 0011 1100 0000,%0011 0010 0100 1100
dc.w %0000 0001 1000 0000,%0001 1001 1001 1000
dc.w %0000 0000 0000 0000,%0000 1100 0011 0000
dc.w %0000 0000 0000 0000,%0000 0011 1100 0000
dc.w 0,0 ;end of the sprite data list
```

The AT bit in the 2nd control word determines whether the two sprites are combined with each other or not. It has effect only for sprites with odd numbers (sprites 1, 3, 5, 7). For example, if it is set in sprite 1, its data bits are combined with those from sprite 0 to make four-bit pointers into the color table. The order of the bits is then as follows:

| | |
|---|---|
| Sprite 1 (odd number), second data word | Bit 3 (MSB) |
| Sprite 1, first data word | Bit 2 |
| Sprite 0 (even number), second data word | Bit 1 |
| Sprite 0, first data word | Bit 0 (LSB) |

*15 Color Sprites*

If two sprites are combined in this manner, their positions must also match. If this is not the case, the old three-color representation is automatically re-enabled. The simplest thing to do is to write the same control words in the two sprite data lists. Here is an example of a sprite data list for a fifteen color sprite.

For the sake of simplicity our sprite consists of only four lines. The digits represent the color of the corresponding pixels. In order to display all fifteen colors plus transparent, the hexadecimal digits "A" to "F" are also used.

```
0011111111111100
1123456789ABCD11
11EFEFEFEFEFEF11
0011111111111100
```

The structure of the data words needed can be seen from line 2:

| | |
|---|---|
| Colors of the sprites: | 1123456789ABCD11 |
| Sprite 1, data word 2: | 0000000011111100 |
| Sprite 1, data word 1: | 0000111100001100 |
| Sprite 0, data word 2: | 0011001100110000 |
| Sprite 0, data word 1: | 1101010101010111 |

Horizontal position (HSTART) is again 180. The first line of the sprite (VSTART) is 160, and the last line (VSTOP) 164.

The data list for the entire sprite looks as follows:

```
StartSprite0:
dc.w  $A05A,$A400 ;HSTART=$84, VSTART=$A0, VSTOP=$A4, AT=0
dc.w  %0011 1111 1111 1100,%0000 0000 0000 0000
dc.w  %1101 0101 0101 0111,%0011 0011 0011 0000
dc.w  %1101 0101 0101 0111,%0011 1111 1111 1100
dc.w  %0011 1111 1111 1100,%0000 0000 0000 0000
dc.w  0,0

StartSprite1:
dc.w  $A05A,$A480 ;HSTART=$84, VSTART=$A0, VSTOP=$A4, AT=1
dc.w  %0000 0000 0000 0000,%0000 0000 0000 0000
dc.w  %0000 1111 0000 1100,%0000 0000 1111 1100
dc.w  %0011 1111 1111 1100,%0011 1111 1111 1100
dc.w  %0000 0000 0000 0000,%0000 0000 0000 0000
dc.w  0,0
```

*Multiple sprites through one DMA channel*

After a sprite has been displayed, the DMA channel is free again. In the example above the last sprite data was read in line 163. After that the sprite DMA channel is turned off with the two zeros. But as we mentioned before, it is also possible to continue using the DMA channel. To do this, simply put two new control words in place of the two zeros in the data list. The condition is that there must be at least one line free between the first line of the next sprite and the last line of the previous one. For example, if the previous sprite extends through line 163, then the next cannot start before line 165. The reason for this is that the two control words must be read in the line in between (164). The sprite DMA then proceeds as follows:

| Line | Data through the DMA channel |
|---|---|
| 162 | second-to-last line of the 1st sprite through this channel |
| 163 | last line of the 1st sprite |
| 164 | control words of the second sprite |
| 165 | first line of the 2nd sprite |
| 166 | second line of the 2nd sprite |

The following example displays the three-color sprite from our first example in two different positions on the screen:

```
Start:
dc.w $A05A,$A800 ;HSTART = $B4, VSTART=$A0, VSTOP=$A8
dc.w %0000 0000 0000 0000,%0000 0011 1100 0000
dc.w %0000 0000 0000 0000,%0000 1100 0011 0000
dc.w %0000 0001 1000 0000,%0001 1001 1001 1000
dc.w %0000 0011 1100 0000,%0011 0010 0100 1100
dc.w %0000 0011 1100 0000,%0011 0010 0100 1100
dc.w %0000 0001 1000 0000,%0001 1001 1001 1000
dc.w %0000 0000 0000 0000,%0000 1100 0011 0000
dc.w %0000 0000 0000 0000,%0000 0011 1100 0000
;Now comes the second sprite in this DMA channel
;displayed at line 176 ($B0),horizontal position 300 ($12C)
dc.w $B096,$B800 ;HSTART=$12C, VSTART=$B0, VSTOP=$B8
dc.w %0000 0000 0000 0000,%0000 0011 1100 0000
dc.w %0000 0000 0000 0000,%0000 1100 0011 0000
dc.w %0000 0001 1000 0000,%0001 1001 1001 1000
dc.w %0000 0011 1100 0000,%0011 0010 0100 1100
dc.w %0000 0011 1100 0000,%0011 0010 0100 1100
dc.w %0000 0001 1000 0000,%0001 1001 1001 1000
dc.w %0000 0000 0000 0000,%0000 1100 0011 0000
dc.w %0000 0000 0000 0000,%0000 0011 1100 0000
dc.w 0,0 ;end of t10 the sprite data list
```

*Activating the sprites*

After a correct sprite data list has been constructed in the chip RAM and the desired colors have been written into the color table, the DMA controller must be told at what address this list is stored, before the sprite DMA can be enabled. Each sprite DMA channel has a register pair in which the starting address of the data list must be written:

*SPRxPT (SPRite x PoinTer):*

| Reg. | Name | Function |
|------|------|----------|
| $120 | SPR0PTH | Pointer to the sprite data list bits 16-18 |
| $122 | SPR0PTL | for sprite DMA channel 0 bits 0-15 |
| $124 | SPR1PTH | Pointer to the sprite data list bits 16-18 |
| $126 | SPR1PTL | for sprite DMA channel 1 bits 0-15 |
| $128 | SPR2PTH | Pointer to the sprite data list bits 16-18 |
| $12A | SPR2PTL | for sprite DMA channel 2 bits 0-15 |
| $12C | SPR3PTH | Pointer to the sprite data list bits 16-18 |
| $12E | SPR3PTL | for sprite DMA channel 3 bits 0-15 |
| $130 | SPR4PTH | Pointer to the sprite data list bits 16-18 |
| $122 | SPR4PTL | for sprite DMA channel 4 bits 0-15 |
| $134 | SPR5PTH | Pointer to the sprite data list bits 16-18 |
| $136 | SPR5PTL | for sprite DMA channel 5 bits 0-15 |
| $138 | SPR6PTH | Pointer to the sprite data list bits 16-18 |
| $13A | SPR6PTL | for sprite DMA channel 6 bits 0-15 |
| $13C | SPR7PTH | Pointer to the sprite data list bits 16-18 |
| $13E | SPR7PTL | for sprite DMA channel 7 bits 0-15 |

*DMA*
*controller*

The DMA controller uses these registers as pointers to the current address in the sprite data lists. At the start of each frame they contain the address of the first control word. With each data word read they are incremented by one word so that at the end of the picture they point to the first word after the data list. For the same sprites to be displayed in each frame, these pointers must be set back to the start of the sprite data lists before each frame. As with the bit plane pointers BPLxPT, this is easily done with the Copper in the vertical blanking gap. The corresponding section of the Copper list can look like this:

StartSpritexH = starting address of the sprite data list for sprite x, bits 16-18:

StartSpritexL = bits 0-15

```
CopperlistStart
MOVE #StartSprite0H,SPR0PTH ;initialize sprite DMA
MOVE #StartSprite0L,SPR0PTL ;channel 0
MOVE #StartSprite1H,SPR1PTH ;initialize sprite DMA
MOVE #StartSprite1L,SPR1PTL ;channel 1
MOVE #StartSprite2H,SPR2PTH ;initialize sprite DMA
MOVE #StartSprite2L,SPR2PTL ;channel 2
... ... ...                 ;same for channels 3 to 6
MOVE #StartSprite7H,SPR7PTH ;initialize sprite DMA
MOVE #StartSprite7L,SPR7PTL ;channel 7
... ... ...                 ;other copper tasks
WAIT $FFFE                  ;end of the copper list
```

There is no way to turn the sprite DMA channels on and off individually. The SPREN bit (bit no. 5) in the DMACON register turns the sprite DMA on for all eight sprite channels. If you don't want to use all of them, the unused channels must process empty data lists. To do this, their SPRxPT's are set to two memory words with the content 0. The two zeros at the end of an existing data list can be used for this.

All eight SPRxPT's must always be initialized in the vertical blanking gap. Even if the data list is nothing but the two zeros, SPRxPT points to the first word after them at the end of the frame.

Naturally, the SPRxPT registers can also be initialized by the processor in the vertical blanking interrupt.

As the last step, the sprite DMA must be enabled. As mentioned, this is done for all eight sprite DMA channels by means of the SPREN bit in the DMACON register. The following MOVE command accomplished this:

```
MOVE.W #$8220,$DFF096 ;set SPREN and DMAEN in DMACON
                      ;register
```

*Moving
sprites*

The values of the two control words in the sprite data list determine the position of a sprite. In order to move a sprite, these values must be changed step-by-step. This can be done directly with the processor by means of appropriate MOVE commands. The only thing to watch out for is that the control words must be modified at the right time. If this is not done, the following problem can occur:

The processor modifies the first control word. Before it can change the second, the DMA control reads the two words. Since they no longer belong together, what appears on the screen may not make any sense.

The easiest way to avoid this is to change the control words during the vertical blanking gap (in the vertical blanking interrupt, after the Copper has initialized the SPRxPT).

*The sprite/
playfield
priority*

The priority of a playfield or sprite determines whether it appears in front or behind the other screen elements. The sprite with the highest priority appears in front of all others. Nothing can cover it. The priority of a sprite is determined by its number. The lower the number, the higher the priority. Thus sprite 0 has priority over all other sprites.

For the playfields, a control bit determines whether number 1 or 2 appears in front.

But what is the priority of the sprites in reference to the playfields?

On the Amiga it is possible to position the playfields almost anywhere between the sprites. The sprites are always grouped into pairs when it comes to setting the priority of playfield vs. sprites. These are the same combinations as those used for the fifteen color sprites. Always one sprite with an even number and its odd successor:

Sprites 0 & 1, Sprites 2 & 3, Sprites 4 & 5, Sprites 6 & 7

The four sprite pairs can be viewed as a stack of four elements. If you look at the top of this stack, the underlying elements can only be seen through holes in the overlying stack positions. The holes correspond to the transparent points in the bit planes or sprites and the parts of the screen that a sprite cannot cover because of its size. The order of elements in the stack cannot be changed. But two other elements, namely the playfields, can be placed anywhere between the four sprite pairs. Five positions are possible for each playfield:

| Position | Order from top to bottom | | | | |
|---|---|---|---|---|---|
| 0 | PLF | SPR0&1 | SPR2&3 | SPR4&5 | SPR6&7 |
| 1 | SPR0&1 | PLF | SPR2&3 | SPR4&5 | SPR6&7 |
| 2 | SPR0&1 | SPR2&3 | PLF | SPR4&5 | SPR6&7 |
| 3 | SPR0&1 | SPR2&3 | SPR4&5 | PLF | SPR6&7 |
| 4 | SPR0&1 | SPR2&3 | SPR4&5 | SPR6&7 | PLF |

The BPLCON2 register contains the priority of the playfields with respect to the sprites:

*BPLCON2 $104 (write-only)*

```
Bit no.:  15-7   6      5     4     3     2     1     0
Function: unused PF2PRI PF2P2 PF2P1 PF2P0 PF1P2 PF1P1 PF1P0
```

PF2PRI
> If this bit is set, playfield 2 appears in front of playfield 1.

PF1P0 to PF1P2
> These three bits form a three-bit number which determines the position of playfield 1 (all odd bit planes) between the four sprite pairs. Values between 0 and 4 are allowed (see above table).

PF2P0 to PF2P2
> These three bits have the same function as the bits PF1P0 to PF1P2 except for playfield 2 (all even bit planes).

Example:

```
BPLCON2 = $0003
```

This means that playfield 1 appears before playfield 2, PF2P0-2 = 0, PF1P0-2 = 3. This yields the following order, from front to back:

```
PLF2 SPR0&1 SPR2&3 SPR4&5 PLF1 SPR6&7
```

If we look at it closely, something doesn't make sense. The PF2PRI bit is 0, so playfield 1 should appear in front of playfield 2. In spite of this, the order is as shown above. When one of the sprites 0 to 5 is between playfield 1 and 2, it appears in front of playfield 1, according to its priority. Since this is in front of playfield 2, the sprite is visible at this point, although it must actually be behind playfield 2. If only playfield 2 and the sprite are at a given position, playfield 2 covers the sprite because of its priority.

This is because the playfield/playfield priority has precedence over the sprite/playfield priority.

If the dual-playfield mode is not used, there is only one playfield which is formed from the even and odd bit planes. The PLF2PRI and the PL2P0-PL2P2 bits have no function in this case.

*Collisions between graphic elements*

It is often very useful to know whether two sprites have collided with each other or with the background. This makes writing game programs much easier.

When the pixels of two sprites overlap at a certain screen position, that is, they both have a set point (not transparent) at the same coordinates, this is treated as a collision between the two sprites. A collision of the playfield with each other or with a sprite is also possible.

Each recognized collision is noted in the collision data register, CLXDAT:

*Collision data register*

CLXDAT $00E (read-only)

| Bit no. | Collision between |
|---------|-------------------|
| 15 | unused |
| 14 | Sprite 4 (or 5) and sprite 6 (or 7) |
| 13 | Sprite 2 (or 3) and sprite 6 (or 7) |
| 12 | Sprite 2 (or 3) and sprite 4 (or 5) |
| 11 | Sprite 0 (or 1) and sprite 6 (or 7) |
| 10 | Sprite 0 (or 1) and sprite 4 (or 5) |
| 9 | Sprite 0 (or 1) and sprite 2 (or 3) |
| 8 | Playfield 2 (even bit planes) and sprite 6 (or 7) |
| 7 | Playfield 2 (even bit planes) and sprite 4 (or 5) |
| 6 | Playfield 2 (even bit planes) and sprite 2 (or 3) |
| 5 | Playfield 2 (even bit planes) and sprite 0 (or 1) |
| 4 | Playfield 1 (odd bit planes) and sprite 6 (or 7) |
| 3 | Playfield 1 (odd bit planes) and sprite 4 (or 5) |
| 2 | Playfield 1 (odd bit planes) and sprite 2 (or 3) |
| 1 | Playfield 1 (odd bit planes) and sprite 0 (or 1) |
| 0 | Playfield 1 and playfield 2 |

While on a sprite any non-transparent point can cause a collision, we can set which colors on the playfield are regarded in collision detection. Moreover, it is possible to include or exclude any odd-numbered sprite from collision detection. All of this can be set with the bits in the collision control register, CLXCON.

*Collision control register*

CLXCON $098 (write only)

| Bit no. | Name | Function |
|---------|------|----------|
| 15 | ENSP7 | Enable collision detection for sprite 7 |
| 13 | ENSP5 | Enable collision detection for sprite 5 |
| 13 | ENSP3 | Enable collision detection for sprite 3 |
| 12 | ENSP1 | Enable collision detection for sprite 1 |
| 11 | ENBP6 | Compare bit plane 6 with MVBP6 |
| 10 | ENBP5 | Compare bit plane 5 with MVBP6 |
| 9 | ENBP4 | Compare bit plane 4 with MVBP6 |
| 8 | ENBP3 | Compare bit plane 3 with MVBP6 |
| 7 | ENBP2 | Compare bit plane 2 with MVBP6 |
| 6 | ENBP1 | Compare bit plane 1 with MVBP6 |
| 5 | MVBP6 | Value for collision with bit plane 6 |
| 4 | MVBP5 | Value for collision with bit plane 5 |
| 3 | MVBP4 | Value for collision with bit plane 4 |
| 2 | MVBP3 | Value for collision with bit plane 3 |
| 1 | MVBP2 | Value for collision with bit plane 2 |
| 0 | MVBP1 | Value for collision with bit plane1 |

*ENSPx bits*      The ENSPx bits (ENable SPrite x) determine whether the corresponding odd-numbered sprite is regarded in collision detection. For example, if the ENSP1 bit is set, a collision between sprite 1 and another sprite or a playfield is registered. Such a collision sets the same bit in the collision data register as for sprite 0. Therefore it is not possible to tell, by looking at the register contents, whether sprite 0 or sprite 1 was involved in the collision. In addition, no collisions between sprites 0 and 1 are detected. These facts should be kept in mind when selecting and using sprites.

If two sprites have been combined into one fifteen-color sprite, the corresponding ENSPx bit must be set in order to have correct collision detection.

*ENBPx bits*      For the playfields, the programmer can set which bit combinations of the bit planes generate a collision and which do not. The ENBPx bits (ENable Bit Plane) determine which bit planes are considered for collision detection. If all ENBPx bits of a playfield are set, a collision is possible on all points whose bit combinations match that of the MVBP (Match Value Bit Plane x) bits.

The ENBPx bits determine whether the bits from plane x are compared with the value of MVBPx. If the bits of all planes for which the ENBPx bit is set match those of the corresponding MVBPx bits for a given pixel, then this point can generate a collision.

Complicated? An example makes it clearer:

The ENBPx bits are set, as are all of the MVBPx bits. Now only those pixels of the playfield whose bit combinations are 111111 binary can generate a collision. If only the lower three MVBPx bits are set, then a collision is possible only if the pixel in the playfield has the combination 000111.

If a collision is allowed for all pixels with bit combinations 000111, 000110, 000100 or 000101, the MVBP bits must be 000100. The lower two bits should always satisfy the collision condition, so the corresponding ENBPx bits are cleared, ENBP value: 111100.

Examples for possible bit combinations:

| ENBPx | MVBPx | Collision possible with bit pattern |
|---|---|---|
| 111111 | 111111 | 111111 |
| 111111 | 111000 | 111000 |
| 111100 | 1111xx | 111100, 111101, 111110, 111111 |
| 011111 | x00000 | 000000, 100000 |
| 000000 | xxxxxx | Collision possible with any bit pattern |

(The values of bits marked with an x are irrelevant.)

If fewer than six bit planes are active, the ENBPx bits for the unused planes must be set to 0!

The various combinations of the ENBPx and MVBPx bits allow a variety of different collision detection strategies. For example, the CLXCON register can be set so that sprites can collide only with the red and green pixels of the playfield, but not with other colors. Or so that a collision is possible only at the transparent points of playfield 1 if the underlying points of playfield 2 are black, etc.

*Other sprite*
*registers*

In addition to the SPRxPT registers, each sprite has four additional registers. They are normally supplied with values automatically by the DMA controller. It is also possible to access them by hand (through the processor), however:

| | |
|---|---|
| SPRxPOS | first control word |
| SPRxCTL | second control word |
| SPRxDATA | first data word of a line (low word) |
| SPRxDATB | second data word of a line (high word) |

(x stands for a sprite number from 0 to 7. The addresses of these registers can be found in the register overview in Section 1.5.1).

The DMA controller writes the two control words of a sprite directly into the two registers SPRxPOS and SPRxCTL. When a value is written into the SPRxCTL register, whether through DMA or by the 68000, Denise turns the sprite output off. The sprite can no longer be output to the screen.

The DMA controller now waits for the line stored in VSTART. Then it writes the first two data words into the SPRxDATA and SPRxDATB registers. This causes the sprite to be displayed, because writing to the SPRxDATA register causes Denise to enable the sprite output again. It now compares the desired horizontal position from the SPRxCTL and SPRxPOS registers with the actual screen column and displays the sprite at the correct location on the monitor.

The DMA controller writes two new data words in SPRxDATA/B in each line until the last line of the sprite is past (VSTOP). Then it fetches the next control words and places them in SPRxPOS and SPRxCTL. This turns the sprite off again until the next VSTART position is reached. If both control words were zero, the DMA controller ends the sprite DMA for the corresponding channel until the start of the next frame. At the end of the vertical blanking gap it starts again at the current address in SPRxPT.

*Displaying*
*sprites*
*without DMA*

A sprite can also be easily displayed without the DMA channel. You simply write the desired control words directly into the SPRxPOS and SPRxCTL registers. Only the HSTART position and the AT bit have to contain valid values. VSTART and VSTOP are used only by the DMA controller.

The sprite output can begin in any line by writing the two data words into the SPRxDATA and SPRxDATB registers. Since writing to SPRxDATA enables the sprite output, it is better to write SPRxDATB first.

If the data in the two registers is not changed, they are displayed again in each line. The result is a vertical column.

To turn the sprite off again, simply write some value to SPRxPOS.

---

## 1.5.7      The blitter

What is a blitter? The name *blitter* is an abbreviation of sorts for "block image transfer." This is, in fact, the main task of the blitter: moving and copying data blocks in memory, generally involving graphic data. The blitter can also perform logical operations on multiple memory areas and write the result back into memory. It accomplishes these tasks very quickly. Simple data moves are accomplished at speeds of up to 16 million pixels per second!

In addition, the blitter can fill surfaces and draw lines. The combination of these two capabilities allows filled rectangles to be drawn much faster than would be possible with the 68000.

The operating system uses the blitter for almost all graphic operations. It handles the text output, draws gadgets, moves windows, etc. In addition, it is used to decode data from the diskette, which shows that the many-sided capabilities of the blitter are not limited to graphics.

*Using the blitter to copy data*
The blitter always follows the same procedure when copying data: One to three memory areas, the data sources, are combined together using the selected logical operations and the result is written back into memory. The spectrum ranges from simple copying to complex combinations of multiple data areas. The addresses of the source data areas, named A, B and C, and the destination area D can be anywhere in the chip RAM (addresses 0 to $7FFFF).

The number of words which can be processed in a blitter operation can be up to 65536. Up to 128KB of data can be moved through the memory in one pass.

The blitter supports "rectangular memory areas." That is, the memory, like a bit map, is divided into columns and rows. It is also possible to process small areas inside a large bit map by using what are called modulo values. You can recall such modulo values that are also used in conjunction with the playfields in order to define bit planes which are larger than the screen window.

The following steps are necessary to start a blitter operation:

- Select the blitter mode: Copy data

- Select the source data areas (not all three sources have to be used) and the destination area

- Select the logical operation

- Define other operating parameters (scrolling, masking, address direction)

- Define the window in which the blitter operations take place and start the blitter

***Defining the blitter window***

You may wonder why we're starting with a discussion of the last step. Actually, the definition of the desired window is the basis of all of the other settings. But when the blitter is programmed, this value is written at the end into the corresponding register because it also starts the blitter. Therefore this point is also listed last in the list above. It is important to understand the term "blitter window" before trying to explain the other values, however.

The blitter window is a memory area in which the blitter is to perform the blitter operation. It is constructed like a bit plane, that is, divided into rows and columns, whereby a column corresponds to one word (2 bytes). The number of words in the window is equal to the product of the rows and columns: R*C.

Since the desired memory area is divided into rows and columns, the blitter is very well suited for processing bit planes.

Linear memory areas can be accessed just as well, however. The division into rows and columns is just to make the programming easier. In actuality the individual lines reside at contiguous addresses in memory. For small data fields which are not divided into rows and columns, it is also possible to set the window width or height to 1.

The blitter processes the blitter window line by line. The blitter operation begins with the first word in the first line and ends with the last word of the last line.

The BLTSIZE contains the window size:

*BLTSIZE $058 (write-only)*

```
Bit no.:  15 14 13 12 11 10  9  8   7  6  5  4  3  2  1  0
Function: H9 H8 H7 H6 H5 H4 H3 H2  H1 H0 W5 W4 W3 W2 W1 W0
```

H0-H9    These ten bits represent the height of the blitter window in lines. The window can have a height between 1 and 1024 lines ($2^{10}$ = 1024). A height of 1024 lines is set by setting the height value to 0. For all other values the height corresponds directly to the number of lines. A height of 0 lines is not possible.

W0-W5    Six bits represent the width of the window. It can vary between 1 and 64 words ($2^6$ = 64). In terms of graphic pixels this ranges up to 1024 pixels. As with the height, the maximum width of 64 words is set by making the width value = 0.

The following formula shows how to calculate the necessary BLTSIZE value from the height and width: BLTSIZE = Height*64 + Width.

To take the two extreme cases height = 1024 and Width = 64 into account, the formula is:

```
BLTSIZE = (Height AND $3FF)*64 + (Width AND $3F)
```

The BLTSIZE register should always be the last register initialized. The blitter is automatically started when a value is written to BLTSIZE.

*Source and data areas*

During a blitter operation, data are combined together from completely different areas of memory. Even though the blitter window defines the number and organization of the data to be processed, the positioning of this window within the three source and the destination data areas must be defined.

Let's assume that you want blitter to copy a small rectangular graphic stored somewhere in chip RAM into the screen memory. For this simple task there is only one source area. The selection of the blitter window is easy. The entire graphic is copied, so the width and height of the blitter correspond to those of the graphic in memory.

So that the blitter also knows where this graphic can be found, write the address of the first word in the top line into the appropriate register.

But how is the destination area defined? The graphic is copied into the screen memory, so it must be transferred to the current bit plane (for the sake of simplicity the graphic and the screen memory is assumed to consist of just one bit plane). But this bit plane is significantly wider than the small graphic. If the blitter copied it directly into the bit plane, it would look rather strange. In addition to the address of the destination area, the blitter must also know its width. This information is communicated by the modulo values. The modulo value is added to the address pointer after each processed line of the blitter window. Thus the words which are not affected are skipped and the pointer is again at the start of the next line. The source and destination areas have independent modulo registers so that they can have different widths.

*Figure 1.5.7.1*

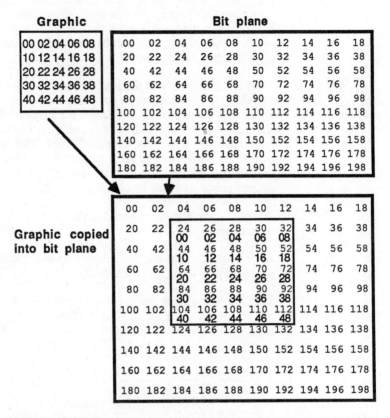

Figure 1.5.7.1 illustrates our example. The graphic consists of 5 lines, each ten words wide. The numbers stand for the address of the corresponding word in relationship to the start address of the graphic. The bit plane has a height of 20 words. How do we choose the blitter window, starting addresses and modulo values?

The blitter window must correspond to the graphic, since it is copied completely. The graphic is 5 lines high and 10 words wide, so the value which must be written to the BLTSIZE register is 330, or $014A.

The starting address of the source data is equal to the address of the first data word of the graphic. Since the width of a line of the graphic is equal to the line width of the blitter window, the modulo value for the source is 0.

The modulo value must now be calculated for the destination data area. To do this, simply take the difference of the actual line width and that of the blitter window. In our example this is 20 words minus 10 words: The modulo value for the destination data area is 10 words. The modulo value must be specified in bytes in the blitter modulo registers. Modulo value = modulo in words * 2.

Finally, the blitter needs the starting address of the destination data. This determines the position at which the graphic is copied and is equal to the starting address of the bit plane plus the address of the word at which the upper left corner of the graphic is placed. In our figure this is the address of the bit plane plus 24.

*How does the blitter operation proceed?*

After the addresses and the modulo values in our example have been defined, the blitter starts to copy the data after BLTSIZE has been initialized. It fetches the word from the starting address of the source data and stores it at the destination address. Then it adds one word to both addresses and copies the next word. This is repeated until the number of words per line set in BLTSIZE have been processed. Before the blitter continues with the next line, it adds the modulo value to the address pointers so that the next line starts at the correct address.

After all of the lines have been copied, the blitter turns off and waits for its next job.

After a blitter operation, the address registers contain the address of the last word plus 2 and plus the modulo value.

The address registers are called BLTxPT, whereby the x stands for one of the three sources A, B, C or the destination area D. As usual, the address registers consist of one register for bits 0-15 and another for bits 16-18:

| Reg. | Name | Function | |
|------|------|----------|---|
| 048 | BLTCPTH | Starting address | Bits 16-18 |
| 04A | BLTCPTL | of source data area C | Bits 0-15 |
| 04C | BLTBPTH | Starting address | Bits 16-18 |
| 04E | BLTBPTL | of source data area B | Bits 0-15 |
| 050 | BLTAPTH | Starting address | Bits 16-18 |
| 052 | BLTAPTL | of source data area A | Bits 0-15 |
| 054 | BLTDPTH | Starting address | Bits 16-18 |
| 056 | BLTDPTL | of source data area D | Bits 0-15 |

Each of the four areas has its own modulo register:

| | | |
|------|---------|------|
| 060 | BLTCMOD | Modulo value for source C |
| 062 | BLTBMOD | Modulo value for source B |
| 064 | BLTAMOD | Modulo value for source A |
| 066 | BLTDMOD | Modulo value for destination data D |

*Copying with increasing or decreasing addresses*

In our example the blitter worked with increasing addresses, that is, it started at the starting address and incremented this until the end address. The end address is thus logically higher than the starting address.

There is a case in which such addresses leads to errors. Copying a memory area to a higher address in which the source and data areas overlap in part. An example:

| Address | Source data | Destination data | Result desired | actual |
|---------|-------------|------------------|----------------|--------|
| 0 | source1 | | | |
| 2 | source2 | | | |
| 4 | source3 | | | |
| 6 | source4 | dest1 | source1 | source1 |
| 8 | source5 | dest2 | source2 | source2 |
| 10 | | dest3 | source3 | source3 |
| 12 | | dest4 | source4 | !source1! |
| 14 | | dest5 | source5 | !source2! |

The five source data words are written at the address of the destination data. If the blitter starts at source1, it overwrites source4 when it stores source1 at the desired destination address dest1 since source4 and dest1 have the same address (the two areas overlap). The same happens for source2 and dest2.

When the blitter reaches the address of source4, it finds source1 there instead. Thus source1 is copied to dest4 instead of source4 and source2 to dest5 instead of source5.

To solve this problem, the blitter has a decreasing address mode in addition to the ascending mode. In this mode it starts at the addresses in BLTxPT and decrements these values by 2 bytes after each word is copied. Also, the modulo value is subtracted instead of added. The end address is thus before the starting address.

This must naturally be taken into account when initializing the BPLxPT's. Normally these are set to the upper left corner of the blitter window in the given data area (A, B, C or D). In the descending mode the addressing is backwards. Correspondingly, BPLxPT must point to the lower right corner.

The modulo and BLTSIZE values are identical to those for the ascending mode.

In general, the following statements can be made about the two modes:

1.    No overlap between source and destination areas:

      Either ascending or descending mode; both work correctly in this case.

2.    Source and destination overlap partially, whereby the destination area is before the source:

      Only ascending mode works correctly.

3.    Source and destination overlap partially, whereby the destination area is after the source (see example):

      Only the descending mode works correctly.

*Selecting the logical operations*

As mentioned, there are three source data areas and these can be combined to form the destination data. These logical operations are always bitwise, that is, the destination bit D must be obtained from the three data bits A, B and C.

The blitter recognizes 256 different operations. These are divided into two levels:

1.　　Eight different boolean equations are applied to the three data bits. Each of these yields a 1 from a different combination of A, B and C.

2.　　The right results of the above equations are selectively combined with a logical OR. The result is the destination bit D.

The term "boolean equation" refers to a mathematical expression which represents a combination of logical operations. This type of computation is called boolean algebra after the English mathematician George Boolen (1815 to 1864). The explanations of the logical functions of the blitter can be understood without knowledge of boolean algebra, but the boolean equations are included.

There are eight possible combinations for the three bits. Each of the eight equations is true for one of them (its result is 1). By means of eight control bits LF0 to LF7 you can select whether the result of the equation has any effect on the formation of D. All result bits whose corresponding LFx bit is 1 are combined with a logical OR function. An OR operation means that the result is 1 if at least one of the input bits is 1. Put another way, a logical OR returns a 0 only if all inputs are 0.

The eight LFx bits can be used to select which combinations of the three input bits A, B and C causes the output bit D to be 1.

The term for the eight boolean input equations is "minterm."

The following table gives an overview of the input combinations for each LFx bit.

(In the minterm row a lowercase letter stands for a logical inversion of the corresponding input bit. Normally this is indicated with a bar over the letter.)

The Input bits row contains the bit combination for which the corresponding equation is true. The order of the bits is A B C.

|  | LF7 | LF6 | LF5 | LF4 | LF3 | LF2 | LF1 | LF0 |
|---|---|---|---|---|---|---|---|---|
| Minterm | ABC | ABc | AbC | Abc | aBC | aBc | abC | abc |
| Input bits: | 111 | 110 | 101 | 100 | 011 | 010 | 001 | 000 |

*Minterms*     Selecting the individual minterms is easy. For each input combination for which the output bit D should be 1, set the corresponding LFx bit.

In our first example we simply copy the source data from A directly to D. The B and C sources are not used. Which minterms must be selected for this?

D can be 1 only when A=1. Thus only the upper four terms LF4 to LF7 come into play, since A=1 only for these terms. Since B does not play a role, we choose a term in which B is 1 and a term in which B is 0, but which are otherwise identical. Now B has no effect on D because the remainder of the equation is unchanged for both values of B and its result depends only on this remainder. The same holds for C. If we look at the table of input combinations, we see that LF4 to LF7 must be activated. Then the result depends only on A since for any combination of B and C, one of these four equations is always true for A=1 and thus D is 1. If A=0, all four are false and D=0.

Those who are familiar with boolean algebra can derive the appropriate minterms formally. The required expression is A=D. Since B and C are always present in the blitter, they must be integrated into the equation as well:

    A*(b+B)*(c+C)=D

The term x+X is always true (equal to 1) and is used when the result is independent of the value of X. To get the minterms needed, just multiply it out:

1.    A*(b+B)*(c+C)=D
2.    (A*b+A*B)*(C+C)=D
3.    A*b*c+A*B*c+A*b*C+A*B*C=D

or without the AND operators:

    Abc+ABc+AbC+ABC  =  D

Now we just have to set the LFx bits of the corresponding minterms.

Here are some examples of common blitter operations and the corresponding LFx bit settings:

•     Invert a data area: a = D

LFx combination: 00001111
Boolean algebra:   a = D
                   a*(b+B)*(c+C)  =  D
                   (ab+aB)*(c+C)  =  D
                   abc+aBc+abC+aBC  =  D

• Copy a graphic in a bit plane without changing the original contents of the destination bit plane. This corresponds to logically ORing the source and destination areas: $A + B = D$

LFx combination:
```
A + B = D
A(b+B)(c+C)+B(a+A)(c+C)  = D
(Ab+AB)(c+C)+(Ba+BA)(c+C)  = D
Abc+ABc+AbC+ABC+Bac+BAc+BaC+BAC = D
Abc+ABc+AbC+ABC+aBc+aBC  = D
```

Here again is the rule for determining the LFx bits needed:

1. Determine which of the eight combinations of ABCD should be equal to 1.

2. Set the LFx bits accordingly.

3. If not all three sources are needed, all combinations in which the unused bits occur and the desired bits have the proper value must be selected.

*Shifting the input values*

For some tasks the blitter's limitation to word boundaries can cause trouble. For example, you may want to shift a certain area within a bit map by a few bits. Or perhaps you want the blitter to write a graphic at specific screen coordinates that do not match a word boundary.

In order to handle this problem, the blitter has the capability to shift the words from sources A and B to the right by up to 15 bits. This allows it to move data to the desired bit position. All bits which are pushed out to the right by the shift operation move into the free bits in the next word. Thus the entire line is shifted bit by bit. A device called a barrel shifter is used inside the blitter in order to shift the words. It requires no additional time for the shift operation, regardless of how many bits are moved.

Example for shifting data by three bits:

Before:

| Data word 1 | Data word 2 | Data word 3 |
|---|---|---|
| 00011111 10011100 | 00010101 01111111 | 11100001 11100101 |

After:

| Data word 1 | Data word 2 | Data word 3 |
|---|---|---|
| xxx00011 11110011 | 10000010 10101111 | 11111100 00111100 |

The three xxx bits depend on the previous data word from which they are shifted out.

*Masking*

It is possible to use the blitter to copy a graphic from the screen memory whose borders are not on word boundaries. The data to the left of the graphic but which are still in the first data word should not be copied along with the actual graphic data. To make this possible, the blitter can apply a mask to the first and last data words of a line. This permits undesired data to be erased from the edges of a line.

Only source A can be masked in this manner. Two registers contain the masks for the two edges. A bit is copied in the blitter operation only if it is set in the mask register. All others are cleared.

*$044 BLTAFWM Blitter source A First Word Mask*

Mask for the first data word in the line.

*$046 BLTQLWM Blitter source A Last Word Mask*

Mask for the last data word in the line.

Bits 0-15 contain the corresponding mask bits.

Example:

("1" stands for a set bit, "." for a cleared bit)

*Graphic data in the bit plane:*

| Column 1 | Column 2 | Column 3 |
|---|---|---|
| ......11111111 | 1111111111111111 | 1............11 |
| 111111.....1111 | 11..........1111 | 1111........1111 |
| ...11........11 | 1111.........111 | 11111....1111111 |
| ...11.........1 | 11111.........11 | 1111111111111111 |
| ...11.........1 | 11111.........11 | 1111111111111111 |
| ...11........11 | 1111.........111 | 11111....1111111 |
| 111111.....1111 | 11..........1111 | 1111........1111 |
| ......11111111 | 1111111111111111 | 1............11 |

| First Word Mask: | Last Word Mask: |
|---|---|
| 0000000011111111 | 1111110000000000000 |

Result:

| Column 1 | Column 2 | Column 3 |
|---|---|---|
| ......11111111 | 1111111111111111 | 1.............. |
| ...........1111 | 11..........1111 | 1111.......... |
| ............11 | 1111.........111 | 11111......... |
| .............1 | 11111.........11 | 111111........ |
| .............1 | 11111.........11 | 111111........ |
| ............11 | 1111.........111 | 11111......... |
| ...........1111 | 11..........1111 | 1111.......... |
| ......11111111 | 1111111111111111 | 1.............. |

By masking out the unwanted picture elements at the edges, you get the the desired graphic.

When the width of the blitter window is one word (BLTSIZE width=1), both masks come together. They both operate on the same input word. Only the input bits whose mask bits are set in both masks are let through.

*The blitter control register*

The blitter has two control registers, BLTCON0 and BLTCON1. The following blitter control bits are found in these two registers:

*BLTCON0 $040*

| Bit no. | Name | Function |
|---------|------|----------|
| 15 | ASH3 | ASH0-3 contain the shift distance |
| 14 | ASH2 | for the input data from source A |
| 13 | ASH1 | ASH0-3 = 0 means no shift |
| 12 | ASH0 | |
| 11 | USEA | Enables the DMA channel for source A |
| 10 | USEB | Enables the DMA channel for source B |
| 9 | USEC | Enables the DMA channel for source C |
| 8 | USED | Enables the DMA channel for destination D |
| 7 | LF7 | Selects minterm ABC (bit comb. of ABC: 111) |
| 6 | LF6 | Selects minterm ABc (bit comb. of ABC: 110) |
| 5 | LF5 | Selects minterm AbC (bit comb. of ABC: 101) |
| 4 | LF4 | Selects minterm Abc (bit comb. of ABC: 100) |
| 3 | LF3 | Selects minterm aBC (bit comb. of ABC: 011) |
| 2 | LF2 | Selects minterm aBc (bit comb. of ABC: 010) |
| 1 | LF1 | Selects minterm abC (bit comb. of ABC: 001) |
| 0 | LF0 | Selects minterm abc (bit comb. of ABC: 000) |

*BLTCON1 $042*

| Bit no. | Name | Function |
|---------|------|----------|
| 15 | BSH3 | BSH0-3 contain the shift distance |
| 14 | BSH2 | for the input data from source B |
| 13 | BSH1 | BSH0-3 = 0 means no shift |
| 12 | BSH0 | |
| 11-5 | | unused |
| 4 | EFE | Exclusive Fill Enable |
| 3 | IFE | Inclusive Fill Enable |
| 2 | FCI | Fill Carry In |
| 1 | DESC | DESC = 1 switches to descending mode |
| 0 | LINE | LINE = 1 activates the line mode |

The LINE bit switches the blitter into its line drawing mode. If you want to copy data with the blitter, LINE must be 0.

Ascending or descending addresses can be selected with the DESC bit. If DESC=0, the blitter works in ascending mode, else if DESC01, in descending mode.

The EFE and IFE bits activate the surface-filling mode of the blitter. They must both be 0 for the blitter to operate in the normal mode.

The FCI bit is used only in the fill mode.

*The blitter*
*DMA*

The data from the source areas A, B and C and the output data D are read from or written to the memory through four DMA channels. This blitter DMA can be enabled for all channels with the BLTEN bit (bit 6) in the DMACON registers. The blitter has four data registers for its DMA transfers:

| Addr. | Name | Function |
|-------|------|----------|
| 000 | BLTDDAT | Output data D |
| 070 | BLTCDAT | Data register for source C |
| 072 | BLTBDAT | Data register for source B |
| 074 | BLTADAT | Data register for source A |

The DMA controller reads the needed input values from memory and writes them into the data registers. When the blitter has processed the input data, BLTDDAT contains the result. The DMA controller then transfers the contents of BLTDDAT to the chip RAM.

The DMA transfer through these four registers can be enabled and disabled through the four USEx bits. For example, USEA=0 disables the DMA channel for data register A. The blitter continues to access the data in BLTADAT, however, each new word from the active sources is the same word always read from source A. This is why unused channels must be disabled with USEx=0 and the effect of this source must be effectively disabled by selecting the appropriate minterms. Another option is to make use of the fact that the same word is always read when the DMA channel is disabled. This can be used to fill the memory with a given pattern, for example, by writing the appropriate value directly into BLTxDAT.

In addition to BLTEN, three other bits in DMACON pertain to the blitter.

*Bit 10 BLTPRI*

This bit was already explained in the Fundamentals section. If it is 1, the blitter has absolute priority over the processor.

*Bit 14 BBUSY (read-only)*

BBUSY indicates the state of the blitter. If it is 1, it is currently performing an operation.

After the blitter window is set in BLTSIZE the blitter starts its DMA and sets BBUSY until the last word of the blitter window has been processed and written back into memory. It then ends its DMA and clears BBUSY.

At the same time BBUSY is cleared, the blitter-finished bit is also set in the interrupt request register.

*Bit 13 BZERO*

The BZERO bit indicates whether all of the result bits of a blitter operation were 0. In other words, BZERO is set when none of the operations performed on any of the data words resulted in a 1. One use of this bit is to perform collision detection. The minterms are set such that D is 1 only if the two sources are also 1. If the graphics in both sources intersect at least one point, the result is 1 and BZERO is cleared. Thus at the end of the blitter operation you can determine if a collision occurred or not. USED is set to 0 in this application so that the output data are not written to memory.

*Using the blitter to fill surfaces*

What does it mean to "fill a surface"?

The blitter understands a surface to be a two-dimensional area of memory which is filled with points. Normally this surface belongs to a graphic or bit plane.

In order to fill a surface, the blitter must recognize its boundaries. You need a definition of a boundary line which the blitter can deal with. Many fill functions exist in various drawing programs and also in AmigaBASIC with the PAINT command. These functions cause an area of the screen to be filled, starting with some initial points, until the program encounters a boundary line. This allows completely arbitrary surfaces to be filled, assuming that they are enclosed by a continuous line. The blitter is not in a position to perform such a complex fill operation. It only works line by line and fills the free space between two set bits which mark the boundaries of the desired surface. Two examples show how the blitter fill operation works:

Correct fill operation:

```
          Before:                      After:
..........1.1....................111...........
........1.......1..........111111111.........
......1...........1........1111111111111.......
.....1....1...1....1.......111111...111111......
.....1....1...1....1.......111111...111111......
......1...........1........1111111111111.......
........1.......1..........111111111..........
.....1.............1.......1111111111111.......
```

Incorrect operation due to improper border bits:

```
          Before:                      After:
..........111...................11111111111111.......
......111...111................111111111..........
.....11...111...11........11111111111111...11........
....1....1...1....1............111111...111111......
....1....1...1....1............111111...111111......
.....11...111...11........11111111111111...11........
.......1.......1..............111111111..........
.....1111111111111........11111111111111111111.......
```

In the first example the surface is bounded properly for the blitter and is thus filled correctly. Example 2 is a different matter, however. Here a closed boundary line is drawn around the figure. If you attempt to fill such a figure with the blitter, chaos results.

*The FC bit*    The reason for this is the algorithm that the blitter uses. It is extremely simple. The blitter starts at the right side of the line. It uses the Fill Carry bit (FC) to determine if it must set a bit. Normally this is 0 at the start. The blitter checks the value of the bit at the far right. If it is zero, the value of the FC bit remains unchanged. It forms the corresponding bit of the output. The blitter continues in this manner with the neighboring bits until it finds one which is set to 1. This causes the FC bit to be set. Since the output bits correspond to the current value of the FC bit, they are 1. The blitter does not clear the FC bit until it encounters another set input bit. In this manner the area between two set bits is always filled. As you can see from the second example, the fill logic gets rather confused by an odd number of set bits.

The FCI bit (Fill Carry In) in BLTCON1 determines the start value of the FC bit. If FCI is cleared, everything proceeds as described above. If FCI=1, the blitter starts to fill from the edge until it encounters the first set bit. The fill procedure is thus reversed.

Example of the effect of the FCI bit:

| Output graphic | FCI=0 | FCI=1 |
|---|---|---|
| ....1.....1....... | .....1111111...... | 1111111....111111 |
| ....1..........1... | ....11111111111... | 11111.........1111 |
| ...1....1.1.....1.. | ...111111.111111.. | 1111....111....111 |
| ...1....1.1.....1.. | ...111111.111111.. | 1111....111....111 |
| ....1..........1... | ....11111111111... | 11111.........1111 |
| ......1.....1...... | ......1111111..... | 1111111.....111111 |

In the examples up to now, the input bits (the boundaries of the surface) have been retained in the filled graphic. This is always the case when the fill mode is activated by setting the ICE (InClusive fill Enable) bit in BLTCON1.

*ECE mode*    In contrast to this is the ECE mode (ExClusive fill Enable), which is enabled by setting the bit with this name in the BLTCON1 register. In this mode the boundary bits at the left edge of a filled surface (whenever the fill carry bit changes from 1 to 0) is not retained in the output picture. This causes all surfaces to become one bit pixel smaller. Only in the ECE mode is it possible to get surfaces with a width of only one bit. This is impossible in the ICE mode because at least two boundary bits are needed to define a surface and both will then appear in the output.

Difference between the ICE and ECE modes:

```
Output graphic              ICE                     ECE
........11......11    ........11......11    .........1.......1
......1...1....1.1    ......11111....111    ......1111.....11
...1...11..1..1..1    ...111111111..1111    ....1111.111...111
1.....11...11...1    11111111111111111111   .1111111.1111.1111
..1.............1    ..1111111111111111111  ...111111111111111
....1...........1.   ....1111111111111.    .....111111111111.
......1...1...11..   ......11111...11..    .......1111....1..
```

Bitwise operation of the different fill operations:

Input pattern: 11010010

| | | | FCI = 0 | | FCI = 1 | | |
|---|---|---|---|---|---|---|---|
| Bit No. | Input bit | FC | ICE | ECE | FC | ICE | ECE |
| – | 11010010 | | FC=FCI | | FC=FCI | | |
| 0 | 0 | 0 | 0 | 0 | 1 | 1 | 1 |
| 1 | 1 | 1 | 10 | 10 | 0 | 11 | 01 |
| 2 | 0 | 1 | 110 | 110 | 0 | 011 | 00 |
| 3 | 0 | 1 | 1110 | 1110 | 0 | 0011 | 0001 |
| 4 | 1 | 0 | 11110 | 01110 | 1 | 10011 | 10001 |
| 5 | 0 | 0 | 011110 | 001110 | 1 | 110011 | 110001 |
| 6 | 1 | 1 | 1011110 | 1001110 | 0 | 1110011 | 0110001 |
| 7 | 1 | 0 | 11011110 | 01001110 | 1 | 11110011 | 10110001 |

(FC=FCI) means that the FC bit assumes the value of the FCI bit at the start of the fill operation.)

*How is a blitter fill operation started?*

The blitter can perform this fill operation in addition to a normal copy procedure. It is enabled by setting either the ICE or ECE bit in BLTCON1 according to the desired mode. Blitter forms the output data from the three sources A, B and C and the selected minterms as usual. If neither of the two fill modes is active, the blitter writes this data directly to its output data register (BLTDDAT, $000) from where it is written to memory through DMA, assuming USED=1.

In the fill mode, the output data D is used as input data for the fill circuit. The result of the fill operation is then written into the output register BLDDAT.

The following steps are necessary to perform a fill operation:

• Select the BLTxPT, BLTxMOD, and minterms such that the output data D contain the correct boundary bits for the surface to be filled.

• Select descending mode (the blitter fills from right to left and this works only when the words are accessed with ascending addresses).

• Select the desired fill mode: set ICE or ECE; set or clear FCI as desired.

- LINE = 0 (line mode off)

- Set BLTSIZE to the size of the graphic to be filled.

The blitter now starts with the fill procedure. When it is done, it sets BBUSY to 0 as usual.

The speed of the blitter is not limited by activating the fill mode. In the maximum case the blitter can fill surfaces at a speed of 16 million pixels per second. The major application of the fill mode is in drawing filled polygons. The desired polygon is drawn in an empty memory area and the blitter then fills this area.

*Using the blitter to draw lines*

The blitter is an extremely versatile tool. In addition to its excellent capabilities for copying data and filling surfaces, it has a powerful mode for drawing lines. Like the other blitter modes it is extraordinarily fast: up to a million pixels per second. Even with a 68020 this speed can be reached in software only with some effort. For the built-in 68000 it is completely impossible.

*What do "drawing lines" amount to?*

When drawing a line, two points are to connect to each other by a continuous series of points. Since the resolution of a computer graphic is limited, the optimal points cannot always be chosen. The actual points always lie either above or below the intended ideal line. Such a line usually resembles a staircase more or less. The higher the resolution, the smaller the steps, but they can never be completely eliminated.

Example of a line in a computer graphic:

```
The two points                        are connected by a line
......................                ......................
..................1...                ..............111...
......................                .............111......
......................                ..........1111.........
......................                ........111............
.....1................                .....111..............
......................                ......................
```

The blitter can draw lines up to a length of 1024 points. Unfortunately, you cannot specify the coordinates of the two end points. The lines must be defined in a blitter style.

First, the blitter needs to know the octants in which the line is located. The coordinate system is divided into eight parts, and you'll find that the octants are found in many graphic processors.

*Figure 1.5.7.2*

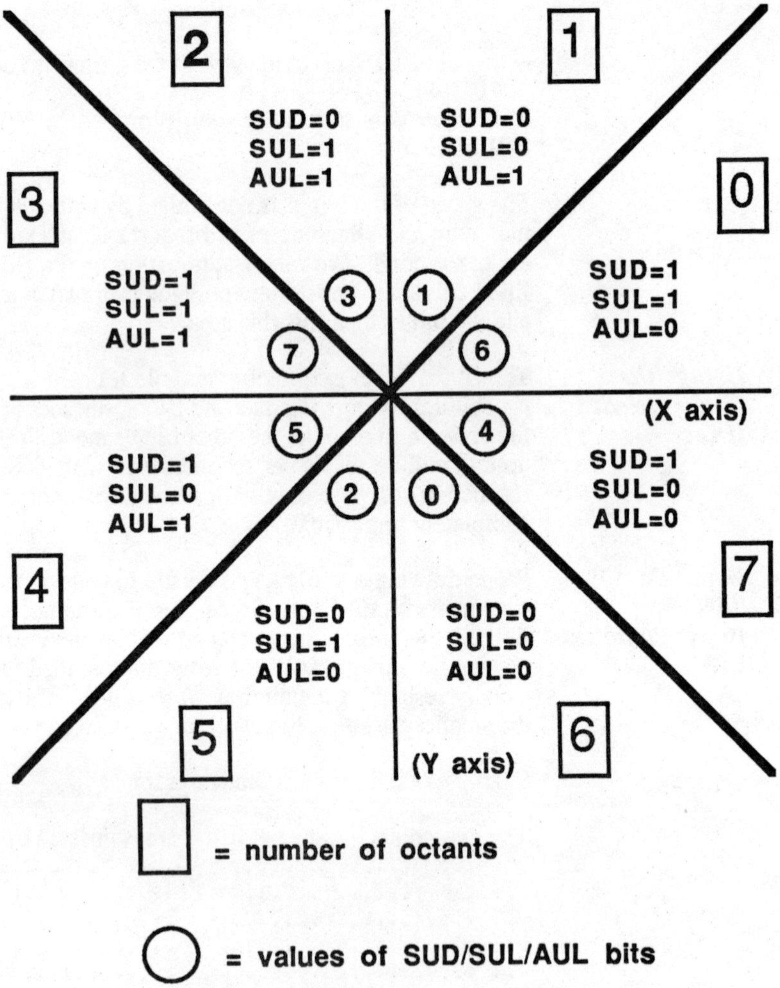

```
            2                    1

        SUD=0            SUD=0
        SUL=1            SUL=0
        AUL=1            AUL=1
  3                                    0
        SUD=1      ③  ①    SUD=1
        SUL=1            SUL=1
        AUL=1    ⑦      ⑥  AUL=0
  ─────────────────────●──────────────── (X axis)
        SUD=1    ⑤      ④  SUD=1
        SUL=0            SUL=0
        AUL=1      ②  ⓪    AUL=0
  4                                    7
        SUD=0            SUD=0
        SUL=1            SUL=0
        AUL=0            AUL=0

            5                    6
                          (Y axis)
```

☐ = number of octants

◯ = values of SUD/SUL/AUL bits

*Figure 1.5.7.3*

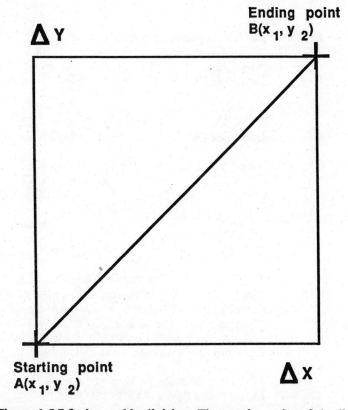

Figure 1.5.7.2 shows this division. The starting point of the line is located at the origin of the coordinate system (at the intersection of the X and Y axes). The end point is located in one of the eight octants, according to its coordinates. The number of this octant can be determined with three logical comparisons. X1 and Y1 are the coordinates of the start point and X2 and Y2 are those of the end point:

If X1 is less than X2, the end point is in octant 0, 1, 6 or 7, while if X1 is greater than X2, it is in 2, 3, 4 or 5. If X1 and X2 are equal, it is on the Y axis. Then all eight octants are possible.

Similarly: Y1 is less than Y2, possible octants of the end points are 0, 1, 2 or 3, if Y1 is greater than Y2, possible octants are 4, 5, 6 or 7. Y1=Y2: all octants.

For the last comparison we need the X and Y differences: DeltaX = |X2-X1|, DeltaY = |Y2-Y1|. If DeltaX is greater than DeltaY, the end point can be located in octant 0, 3, 4 or 7. If DeltaX is less than DeltaY, it is in octant 1, 2, 5 or 6. DeltaX = DeltaY: all octants.

The end point is located in the octant which occurred in all three comparisons. If a point is on the border between two octants, it doesn't matter which is chosen.

151

*Selecting the correct octant:*

| Point coordinates | Octant | Code | Point coordinates | Octant | Code |
|---|---|---|---|---|---|
| Y1 <= Y2<br>X1 <= X2<br>DeltaX >= DeltaY | 0 | 6 | Y1 >=Y2<br>X1 >= X2<br>DeltaX >= DeltaY | 4 | 5 |
| Y1 <= Y2<br>X1 <= X2<br>DeltaX <= DeltaY | 1 | 1 | Y1 >= Y2<br>X1 >= X2<br>DeltaX <= DeltaY | 5 | 2 |
| Y1 <= Y2<br>X1 >= X2<br>DeltaX <= DeltaY | 2 | 3 | Y1 >= Y2<br>X1 <= X2<br>DeltaX <= DeltaY | 6 | 0 |
| Y1 <= Y2<br>X1 >= X2<br>DeltaX >= DeltaY | 3 | 7 | Y1 >= Y2<br>X1 <= X2<br>DeltaX >= DeltaY | 7 | 4 |

The digits in the Code column correspond to the circled numbers in Figure 1.5.7.2. The blitter needs a special combination of three bits, depending on the octant in which the end point of the line is located. These are SUD (Sometimes Up or Down), SUL (Sometimes Up or Left), AUL (Always Up or Left). Code is the 3-bit number formed by these three bits (SUD=msb and AUL=lsb).

When programming the lines you must first determine the octant of the end point and then write the corresponding code value into the blitter.

*Lines with patterns*

When drawing a line, the blitter uses a mask to determine whether the points of the line are set, cleared or given a pattern. The mask is 16 bits wide, so the pattern repeats every 16 bits. The relationship between the pattern and the appearance of the line can best be understood with a couple of examples:

("." = 0, "1' = 1, A = start point and B = end point)

Output picture: Mask = "1111111111111111":

```
.........11111111......B.      .........11111111....11B.
.......111......111......       .......111......11111....
......11.............11....     ......11.........11.11....
....11..............11...       ....11.........111....11...
....11..............11...       ....11....111.......11...
.....11.............11....      .....11111.........11....
.......111......111......       .....11111......111......
..A......11111111........       ..A11....11111111........
```

Zero bits in the mask cause line points to be cleared:

Output picture: Mask = "0000000000000000":

```
....1111111111111111..B.    ....1111111111111111..B.
....1111111111111111....    ....11111111111111.......
....1111111111111111....    ....111111111111..111....
....1111111111111111....    ....111111111...,11111....
....1111111111111111....    ....111111...11111111....
....1111111111111111....    ....1111..11111111111....
....1111111111111111....    ....1...1111111111111....
..A.1111111111111111....    ..A..1111111111111.......
```

If we combine ones and zeros in the mask, the line takes on a pattern:

```
.A111111........................................
..........111...1...............................
................111111..........................
.......................111...11.................
.............................11111..............
.....................................111...111....
.........................................1111.B
```

*Drawing boundary lines*  In the section on filling surfaces with the blitter we explained that the boundary lines of these surfaces can only be one pixel wide. If these lines are drawn with the blitter, it can occur that several line points lie on the same horizontal line. To prevent this, the blitter can be made to draw lines with only one point per raster line:

Normal line:                    Line with one point/raster line:
```
..............1111              ................1...
............1111....            .............1......
.......1111........            ........1...........
....1111............            ....1...............
1111..............             1...................
```

*Definition of slope*  So the blitter knows where to draw the line, it needs a blitter-style definition of the slope in the line. This slope is formed from the results of three terms, all based on the DeltaX and DeltaY values as explained in the section on octants (DeltaX and DeltaY represent the width and height of the rectangle whose diagonal line forms [see Figure 1.5.7.3]).

First the two values must be compared with each other to find the larger/smaller of the two. We call the smaller delta *Sdelta* and the larger *Ldelta*. Then the three expressions required by the blitter are as follows:

1.    2*Sdelta
2.    2*Sdelta - Ldelta
3.    2*Sdelta - 2*Ldelta

In addition the blitter has a SIGN flag which must be set to 1 if 2*Sdelta < Ldelta.

*Register func-*
*tions in line*
*mode*

The blitter uses the same register when drawing lines as it does when copying data (it doesn't have any more), but the functions change:

BLTAPTL

The value of the expression 2*Sdelta-Ldelta must be written into BLTAPTL.

BLTCPT & BLTDPT

These two register pairs (BLTCPTH and BLTCPTL, BLTDPTH and BLTDPTL) must be initialized with the start address of the line. This is the address of the word in which the start point of the line is located.

BLTAMOD

The value of the expression "2*Sdelta-2*Ldelta" must be stored in BLTAMOD.

BLTBMOD

"2*Sdelta"

BLTCMOD & BLTDMOD

The width of the entire picture in which the line is drawn must be stored in these two modulo registers. As usual, this is done in the form of an even number of bytes. With a normal bit plane of 320 pixels (40 bytes) in the X direction, the value for BLTCMOD or BLTDMOD = 40.

BLTSIZE

The width (bits 0 to 5) must be set to 2. The height (bits 6 to 15) contains the length of the line in pixels. A height of 0 corresponds to a line with a length of 1024 points.

The correct line length is always the value of Ldelta.

Drawing a line is started by writing to the BLTSIZE register. Therefore it should be the last register initialized.

BLTADAT

This register must be intialized to $8000.

BLTBDAT

BLTBDAT contains the mask with which the line is drawn.

BLTAWFM

$FFFF is stored in this mask register.

*BLTCON0*

| Bit no. | Name | Function |
|---|---|---|
| 15 | START3 | The 4-bit value START0-3 contains the position of the start point |
| 14 | START2 | of line within the word |
| 13 | START1 | at the start address of the line (BLTCPT/BLTDPT) |
| 12 | START0 | Normally this is the four lower bits of the X coordinate of the start point |
| 11 | USEA = 1 | This combination of the USEx bits is necessary for the line mode |
| 10 | USEB = 0 | |
| 9 | USEC = 1 | |
| 8 | USED = 1 | |
| 7 | LF7 | The LFx bits must be initialized with $CA |
| to 0 | LF0 | (D = aC+AB) |

*BLTCON1*

| Bit no. | Name | Function |
|---|---|---|
| 15 | Texture3 | This is the value for shifting the mask |
| 14 | Texture2 | Normally it Texture0-3 is set to Start0-3 |
| 13 | Texture1 | The pattern in the mask register BLTBDAT |
| 12 | Texture0 | then starts with the first point of the line |
| 11 to 7 | = 0 | unused, always set to 0 |
| 6 | SIGN | If 2*Sdelta < Ldelta, set SIGN to 1 |
| 5 | — | unused, set to 0 |
| 4 | SUL | These three bits must be initialized |
| 3 | SUD | with the SUL/SUD/AUL code |
| 2 | AUL | of the corresponding octant (fig. 1.5.7.2) |
| 1 | SING = 1 | Draw lines with only one point per raster line |
| 0 | LINE = 1 | Put the blitter in line drawing mode |

A numerical example:

You want to draw a line in a bit plane. The bit plane is 320 by 200 pixels large and lies at address $40000. The starting point of the line has the coordinates X=20 and Y=185. The ending point lies at X=210 and Y=35 (The coordinates are in relation to the upper left corner of the bit plane). DeltaX=190, DeltaY=150.

*1st step* <u>Find the octant of the end point</u>

Three comparisons are performed to do this, result: X1<X2, Y1>Y2, and DeltaX>DeltaY. This results in octant number 7 and a value for the SUD/SUL/AUL code of 4.

*2nd step*        Address of the starting point

This is calculated as follows:

starting address of the bit plane + (number of lines - Y1 - 1) *
bytes per line + 2*(X1/16)

(The fractional portion of the division is ignored.)

After inserting the values:

$40000 + (100-185-1)*40 + 2 = $40232

This value is placed in BTLCPT and BLTDPT. The number of bytes
per line is also written into the BLTCMOD and BLTDMOD registers.

*3rd step*        Starting point of the line in START0-3

Calculation: X1 AND $F
Numerically: START0-3 = 20 AND $F = 4

*4th step*        Values for BLTAPTL, BLTAMOD, and BLTBMOD

DeltaY < DeltaX, meaning that Sdelta = DeltaY and Ldelta = DeltaX
BLTAPTL = 2*Sdelta-LDelta = 2*150-190 = 110
BLTAMOD = 2*Sdelta-2*Ldelta = 2*159-2*190 = -80
BLTBMOD = 2*Sdelta = 300

*5th step*        Length of the line for BLTSIZE

Length = Ldelta = DeltaX = 190

The value for the BLTSIZE register is calculated from the usual
formula: Length*64 + Width. Width must always be set to 2 when
drawing lines. BLTSIZE = DeltaX*64+2 = 12162 or $2F82.

*6th step*        Combining the values for the two BLTCONx registers

The START value must be stored in the correct position in BLTCON0,
in addition to $CA for the LFx bits and 1011 for USEx. In the example
this results in $ABCA.

BLTCON1 contains the octant code and the control bits. We want to
draw our line normally, so SING=0. LINE must naturally be 1. SIGN
was already calculated as is 0 in this example. Together this makes
$0011.

In assembly language the initialization of the registers can look like
this:

```
LEA $DFF000,A5                      ;base address of the custom
                                    ;chips in A5
MOVE.L #$40232, BLTCPTH(A5)         ;start address to BLTCPT
MOVE.L #$40232, BLTDPTH(A5)         ;and BLTDPT
MOVE.W #40, BLTCMOD(A5)             ;width of bit plane to BLTCMOD
MOVE.W #40, BLTDMOD(A5)             ;and BLTDMOD
MOVE.W #110, BLTAPTL(A5)
MOVE.W #-80, BLTAMOD(A5)
MOVE.W #300, BLTBMOD(A5)
MOVE.W #$ABCA, BLTCON0(A5)
MOVE.W #$11, BLTCON1(A5)
MOVE.W #12162, BLTSIZE(A5)          ;now the blitter starts
                                    ;drawing the line
```

***Other drawing modes***

Up to now we always chose $CA as the value for the LFx bits. This causes the points on the line to be set or cleared according to the mask, while the other points remain unchanged.

But other combinations of LFx are also useful. To understand this, you must know how the LFx bits are interpreted in the line mode:

The blitter can only address the memory word wise. In line mode the input data enters the blitter through source channel C. The mask is stored in the B register. The A register determines which point in the word read is the line point. It always contains exactly one set bit, which is shifted to the correct position by the blitter. The normal LFx value of $CA causes all bits for which the A bit is 0 to be taken directly from source C. If A is 1, however, the destination bit is taken from the corresponding mask bit.

If you know how the LFx bits are used, you can choose other drawing modes. $4A, for example, causes all the line points to be inverted.

***The blitter DMA cycles***

As we explained in the section on fundamentals, the blitter uses only even bus cycles. Since it thereby has priority over the 68000, it is interesting to know how many cycles are left over for the processor. This depends on the number of active blitter DMA channels (A, B, C and D). The following table shows the course of a blitter operation for all fifteen possible combinations of active and inactive DMA channels. The letters A, B, C and D stand for the corresponding DMA channels. The digit 1 is placed after the first word of the blitter operation, 3 after the last operation, and 2 after all the ones in between. A dashed line (---) indicates that this bus cycle is not used by the blitter.

*Blitter bus cycle usage:*

| A | B | C | D | Usage of even bus cycles |
|---|---|---|---|---|
| | | | | -- -- -- -- -- -- -- -- -- -- -- -- |
| | | | D | D0 -- D1 -- D2 -- -- -- -- -- -- -- |
| | | C | | C0 -- C1 -- C2 -- -- -- -- -- -- -- |
| | | C | D | C0 -- -- C1 D0 -- C2 D1 -- D2 -- -- -- |
| B | | | | B0 -- -- B1 -- -- B2 -- -- -- -- -- |
| B | | | D | B0 -- -- B1 D0 -- B2 D1 -- D2 -- -- -- |
| B | | C | | B0 C0 -- B1 C1 -- B2 C2 -- -- -- -- |
| | B | C | D | B0 C0 -- -- B1 C1 D0 -- B2 C2 D1 -- D2 |
| A | | | | A0 -- A1 -- A2 -- -- -- -- -- -- -- |
| A | | | D | A0 -- A1 D0 A2 D1 -- D2 -- -- -- -- |
| A | | C | | A0 C0 A1 C1 A2 C2 -- -- -- -- -- -- |
| A | | C | D | A0 C0 -- A1 C1 D0 A2 C2 D1 -- D2 -- -- |
| A | B | | | A0 B0 -- A1 B1 -- A2 B2 -- -- -- -- |
| A | B | | D | A0 B0 -- A1 B1 D0 A2 B2 D1 -- D2 -- -- |
| A | B | C | | A0 B0 C0 A1 B1 C1 A2 B2 C3 -- -- -- -- |
| A | B | C | D | A0 B0 C0 -- A1 B1 C1 D0 A2 B2 B3 D1 D2 |

*Comments:*

The table above is valid only when the following conditions are fulfilled:

1. The blitter is not disturbed by the Copper or bit plane DMA accesses.
2. The blitter is running in normal mode (neither drawing lines nor filling surfaces).
3. The BLTPRI bit in the DMACON register is set and the blitter has absolute priority over the 68000.

*Explanations:*

As you can see, the output datum D0 doesn't get to RAM until the A1, B1 and C1 data have been read. This results from the *pipelining* in the blitter. Pipelining means that the data are processed in multiple stages in the blitter. Each stage is connected to the output of the preceding on and the input of its successor. The first stage gets the input data (for example, A0, B0 or C0), processes it and passes it on to the second. While this stage processes the output of stage 1, the next input data is fed into the input stage (A1, B1 or C1). When the first data reaches the output stage (D0), the blitter has long since read the next data. Two data pairs are always in different processing stages of the blitter at any given time during a blitter operation.

The table also allows the processing time of a blitter operation to be calculated. Each microsecond the blitter has two bus cycles available. If it's moving a 64K block (32768 words) from A to D, it needs 2*32768 cycles. But if the same block is combined with source C, a total of 3*32768 cycles are needed because two input words must be read for each output word produced.

The table also shows that the blitter is not capable of using every bus cycle if only one blitter DMA channel is active.

*Example*
*programs*

<u>Program 1 Lines with the blitter</u>

This program can be used as a universal routine for drawing lines with the blitter. It shows how the necessary values can be calculated. The program is quite simple:

At the start of the program the memory is requested and the Copper list is constructed. The only new part is the OwnBlitter routine. Like the name says, it can be used to gain control of the blitter. Correspondingly, there is a call to DisownBlitter at the end of the program so that the blitter returns to the control of the operating system.

The program uses only one hi-res bit plane with standard dimensions of 640x200 pixels. In the main loop the program draws lines which go from one side of the screen through the center of the screen to the other side. When a screen has been filled the program shifts the mask used to draw the lines and starts again.

*Note:*

The coordinate specifications in the program start from point 0,0 in the upper left corner of the screen and are not mathematical coordinates, as were used in the previous discussions. In practice this means that when comparing the Y values the greater/less than sign is reversed.

```
;*** Lines with the Blitter

;Custom chip register


INTENA  = $9A     ;Interrupt enable register (write)
DMACON  = $96     ;DMA-Control register (write)
DMACONR = $2      ;DMA-Control register (read)
COLOR00 = $180    ;Color palette register
VHPOSR  = $6      ;Position (read)


;Copper Register

COP1LC  = $80     ;Addresse of 1st. Copper-List
COP2LC  = $84     ;Addersse of 2nd. Copper-List
COPJMP1 = $88     ;Jump to  Copper-List 1
COPJMP2 = $8a     ;Jump to Copper-List 2

;Bitplane Register

BPLCON0 = $100    ;Bit plane control register 0
BPLCON1 = $102    ;1 (Scroll value)
BPLCON2 = $104    ;2 (Sprite<>Playfield Priority)
BPL1PTH = $0E0    ;Pointer to 1st. bitplane
BPL1PTL = $0E2    ;
BPL1MOD = $108    ;Modulo value for odd Bit Planes
BPL2MOD = $10A    ;Modulo value for even Bit Planes
DIWSTRT = $08E    ;Start of screen window
DIWSTOP = $090    ;End of screen window
DDFSTRT = $092    ;Bit Plane DMA Start
```

```
DDFSTOP = $094   ;Bit Plane DMA Stop

;Blitter Register

BLTCON0 = $40    ;Blitter control register 0 (ShiftA,Usex,LFx)
BLTCON1 = $42    ;Blitter control register 1 (ShiftB,misc. Bits)
BLTCPTH = $48    ;Pointer to source C
BLTCPTL = $4a
BLTBPTH = $4c    ;Pointer to source B
BLTBPTL = $4e
BLTAPTH = $50    ;Pointer to source A
BLTAPTL = $52
BLTDPTH = $54    ;Pointer to targer data D
BLTDPTL = $56
BLTCMOD = $60    ;Modulo value for source C
BLTBMOD = $62    ;Modulo value for source B
BLTAMOD = $64    ;Modulo value for source A
BLTDMOD = $66    ;Modulo value for target D
BLTSIZE = $58    ;HBlitter window width/height
BLTCDAT = $70    ;Source C data register
BLTBDAT = $72    ;Source B data register
BLTADAT = $74    ;Source A data register
BLTAFWM = $44    ;Mask for first data word from source A
BLTALWM = $46    ;Mask for first data word from source B
;CIA-A Port register A (Mouse key)
CIAAPRA = $bfe001

;Exec Library Base Offsets

OpenLibrary = -30-522 ;LibName,Version/a1,d0
Forbid      = -30-102
Permit      = -30-108
AllocMem    = -30-168 ;ByteSize,Requirements/d0,d1
FreeMem     = -30-180 ;MemoryBlock,ByteSize/a1,d0
;Graphics Library Base Offsets

OwnBlitter    = -30-426
DisownBlitter = -30-432

;graphics base


StartList = 38

;other Labels
Execbase   = 4
Planesize  = 80*200   ;Bitplane size: 80 Bytes by 200 lines
Planewidth = 80
CLsize     = 3*4      ;The Copper-List contains 3 commands
Chip       = 2        ;allocate Chip-RAM
Clear      = Chip+$10000 ;Clear Chip-RAM first

;*** Initialization ***

Start:
```

```
;Allocate memory for bit plane
 move.l Execbase,a6
 move.l #Planesize,d0      ;Memory requirment for bit plane
 move.l #clear,d1
 jsr    AllocMem(a6)       ;Allocate memory
 move.l d0,Planeadr
 beq    Ende               ;Error! -> End
;Allocate memory for Copper-List
 moveq  #Clsize,d0
 moveq  #chip,d1
 jsr    AllocMem(a6)
 move.l d0,CLadr
 beq    FreePlane          ;Error! -> FreePlane
;Create Copper-List
 move.l d0,a0              ;Address of Copper-List from a0
 move.l Planeadr,d0        ;Address of Bitplane
 move.w #bpl1pth,(a0)+     ;First Copper coommand in RAM
 swap   d0
 move.w d0,(a0)+           ;Hi-Word of Bit plane address in RAM
 move.w #bpl1ptl,(a0)+     ;second command in RAM
 swap   d0
 move.w d0,(a0)+           ;Lo-Word of  Bitplane address in RAM
 move.l #$fffffffe,(a0)    ;End of Copper-List
;Allocate Blitter
 move.l #GRname,a1
 clr.l  d0
 jsr    OpenLibrary(a6)
 move.l a6,-(sp)           ;ExecBase from the Stack
 move.l d0,a6              ;GraphicsBase from a6
 move.l a6,-(sp)           ;and from the Stack
 jsr    OwnBlitter(a6)     ;Take over Blitter
;*** Main program ***
;DMA and Task-Switching off
 move.l 4(sp),a6           ;ExecBase to a6
 jsr    forbid(a6)         ;Task-Switching off
 lea    $dff000,a5
 move.w #$03e0,dmacon(a5)
;Copper initialization
 move.l CLadr,cop1lc(a5)
 clr.w  copjmp1(a5)
;Set color

 move.w #$0000,color00(a5)    ;Black background
 move.w #$0fa0,color00+2(a5)  ;Yellow line

;Playfield initialization

 move.w #$2081,diwstrt(a5)    ;20,129
 move.w #$20c1,diwstop(a5)    ;20,449
 move.w #$003c,ddfstrt(a5)    ;Normal  Hires Screen
 move.w #$00d4,ddfstop(a5)
 move.w #%1001001000000000,bplcon0(a5)
 clr.w  bplcon1(a5)
 clr.w  bplcon2(a5)
 clr.w  bpl1mod(a5)
 clr.w  bpl2mod(a5)
```

**161**

```
;DMA on
 move.w #$83C0,dmacon(a5)

;Draw lines

;Determine start values:

 move.l Planeadr,a0      ;Constant parameter for DrawLine
 move.w #Planewidth,a1   ;into correct register
 move.w #255,a3          ;Size of  Bitplane in Register
 move.w #639,a4
 move.w #$0303,d7        ;Start pattern

Loop:  rol.w #2,d7       ;Shift pattern
 move.w d7,a2            ;Pattern in register for DrawLine

 clr.w  d6               ;Clear loop variable
LoopX:

 clr.w  d1               ;Y1 = 0
 move.w a3,d3            ;Y2 = 255
 move.w d6,d0            ;X1 = Loop variable
 move.w a4,d2
 sub.w  d6,d2            ;X2 = 639-Loop variable

 bsr DrawLine

 addq.w #4,d6            ;Increment loop variable
 cmp.w  a4,d6            ;Test if greater than 639
 ble.s  LoopX            ;if not. continue loop

 clr.w  d6               ;Clear loop variable
LoopY:

 move.w a4,d0            ;X1 = 639
 clr.w  d2               ;X2 = 0
 move.w d6,d1            ;Y1 = loop variable
 move.w a3,d3
 sub.w  d6,d3            ;Y2 = 255-loop variable

 bsr DrawLine            ;Draw line

 addq.w #2,d6            ;Increment loop variable
 cmp.w  a3,d6            ;Is loop variable greater than 255?
 ble.s  LoopY            ;if not, continue loop

 btst   #6,ciaapra       ;Mouse key pressed?
 bne    Loop             ;No, continue

;*** End program ***

;Wait till blitter is ready

Wait: btst #14,dmaconr(a5)
 bne    Wait
```

```
;Activate old Copper-List

move.l (sp)+,a6          ;Get GraphicsBase from Stack
move.l StartList(a6),cop1lc(a5)
clr.w  copjmp1(a5)       ;Activare Startup-Copper-List
move.w #$8020,dmacon(a5)
jsr    DisownBlitter(a6) ;Release blitter
move.l (sp)+,a6          ;ExecBase from Stack
jsr    Permit(a6)        ;Task Switching on


;Release memory for Copper-List

move.l CLadr,a1          ;Set parameter for FreeMem
moveq  #CLsize,d0
jsr    FreeMem(a6)       ;Release memory

;Release Bitplane memory

FreePlane:

move.l Planeadr,a1
move.l #Planesize,d0
jsr    FreeMem(a6)


Ende:

clr.l  d0
rts                      ;Program end

;Variable

CLadr:    dc.l 0         ;Address of Copper-List
Planeadr: dc.l 0         ;Address of Bitplane


;Constants

GRname: dc.b "graphics.library",0

align                    ;even

;*** DrawLine Routine ***

;DrawLine draws a line with the Blitter.
;The following parameters are used:
;d0 = X1   X-coordinate of Start points
;d1 = Y1   Y-coordinate of Start points
;d2 = X2   X-coordinate of End points
;d3 = Y2   Y-coordinate of End points
;a0 must point to the first word of the bitplane
;a1 contains bitplane width in bytes
;a2 word written directly to mask register
;d4 to d6 are used as work registers
```

```
DrawLine:


;Compute the lines starting address

    move.l  a1,d4       ;Width in work register
    mulu    d1,d4       ;Y1 * Bytes per line
    moveq   #-$10,d5    ;No leading characters: $f0
    and.w   d0,d5       ;Bottom four bits masked from X1
    lsr.w   #3,d5       ;Remainder divided by  8
    add.w   d5,d4       ;Y1 * Bytes per line + X1/8
    add.l   a0,d4       ;plus starting address of the Bitplane
                        ;d4 now contains the starting address
                        ;of the line
                        ;Compute octants and deltas

    clr.l   d5          ;Clear work register
    sub.w   d1,d3       ;Y2-Y1  DeltaY from D3
    roxl.b  #1,d5       ;shift leading char from DeltaY in d5
    tst.w   d3          ;Restore N-Flag
    bge.s   y2gy1       ;When DeltaY positive, goto y2gy1
    neg.w   d3          ;DeltaY invert (if not positive)
y2gy1:
    sub.w   d0,d2       ;X2-X1  DeltaX to D2
    roxl.b  #1,d5       ;Move leading char in DeltaX to d5
    tst.w   d2          ;Restore N-Flag
    bge.s   x2gx1       ;When DeltaX positive, goto x2gx1
    neg.w   d2          ;DeltaX invert (if not positive)
x2gx1:

    move.w  d3,d1       ;DeltaY to d1
    sub.w   d2,d1       ;DeltaY-DeltaX
    bge.s   dygdx       ;When DeltaY > DeltaX, goto dygdx
    exg     d2,d3       ;Smaller Delta goto d2
dygdx: roxl.b #1,d5     ;d5 contains results of 3 comparisons
    move.b Octant_table(pc,d5),d5 ;get matching octants
    add.w   d2,d2       ;Smaller Delta * 2


;Test, for end of last blitter operation

WBlit:  btst #14,dmaconr(a5);BBUSY-Bit test
    bne.s   WBlit       ;Wait until equal to 0

    move.w d2,bltbmod(a5) ;2* smaller Delta to BLTBMOD
    sub.w   d3,d2        ;2* smaller Delta - larger Delta
    bge.s   signnl       ;When 2* small delta > large delta
                         ;to signnl
    or.b    #$40,d5         ;Sign flag set
signnl: move.w d2,bltaptl(a5) ;2*small delta-large delta
                              ;in BLTAPTL
    sub.w   d3,d2        ;2* smaller Delta - 2* larger Delta
    move.w d2,bltamod(a5)    ;to BLTAMOD
```

```
;Initialization other info

    move.w #$8000,bltadat(a5)
    move.w a2,bltbdat(a5)      ;Mask from a2 in BLTBDAT
    move.w #$ffff,bltafwm(a5)
    and.w  #$000f,d0           ;bottom  4 Bits from X1
    ror.w  #4,d0               ;to START0-3
    or.w   #$0bca,d0           ;USEx and LFx set
    move.w d0,bltcon0(a5)
    move.w d5,bltcon1(a5)      ;Octant in Blitter
    move.l d4,bltcpth(a5)      ;Start address of line to
    move.l d4,bltdpth(a5)      ;BLTCPT and BLTDPT
    move.w a1,bltcmod(a5)      ;Width of Bitplane in both
    move.w a1,bltdmod(a5)      ;Modulo Registers

;BLTSIZE initialization and Blitter start

    lsl.w  #6,d3              ;LENGTH * 64
    addq.w #2,d3              ;plus (Width = 2)
    move.w d3,bltsize(a5)

    rts

;Octant table with LINE =1:
;The octant table contains code values
;for each octant, shifted to the correct position


Octant_table:

    dc.b 0  *4+1 ;y1<y2, x1<x2, dx<dy = Okt6
    dc.b 4  *4+1 ;y1<y2, x1<x2, dx>dy = Okt7
    dc.b 2  *4+1 ;y1<y2, x1>x2, dx<dy = Okt5
    dc.b 5  *4+1 ;y1<y2, x1>x2, dx>dy = Okt4
    dc.b 1  *4+1 ;y1>y2, x1<x2, dx<dy = Okt1
    dc.b 6  *4+1 ;y1>y2, x1<x2, dx>dy = Okt0
    dc.b 3  *4+1 ;y1>y2, x1>x2, dx<dy = Okt2
    dc.b 7  *4+1 ;y1>y2, x1>x2, dx>dy = Okt3

    end
```

## Program 2 — Filling surfaces with the blitter

This program is very similar to the first program. It shows how filled polygons can be created by drawing boundary lines and filling them with the blitter.

Since much of it's identical to the first program, we just printed the parts which have to be changed in program 1 to get program 2.

The first part which must be changed is from the comment 'Draw lines' to the comment '*** End program ***' (page 162.) This area must be replaced by the section in the following listing labeled Part 1.

In addition, the old octant table at the end of the program must be replaced by Part 2.

The new octant table is necessary because the blitter needs only one point per boundary line when filling surfaces. The SING bit is set in addition to the LINE bit in the new octant table.

The program labeled Part 1 draws two lines and then fills the area between them with the blitter. Then it waits for the mouse button to be clicked.

```
;*** Fill area with Blitter ***

;Part 1:

;Draw filled triangle

;Set starting value

    move.l Planeadr,a0          ;Set constant parameters for
    move.w #Planewidth,a1       ;the LineDraw routine
    move.w #$ffff,a2            ;Mask from $FFFF -> no pattern

;* Draw border lines *

;Line from 320,10 to 600,200
    move.w #320,d0
    move.w #10,d1
    move.w #600,d2
    move.w #200,d3
    bsr    drawline             ;Line draw

;Line from 319,10 to 40,200
    move.w #319,d0
    move.w #10,d1
    move.w #40,d2
    move.w #200,d3
    bsr    drawline             ;draw line

;* Fill area *

;Wait till the blitter draws the last line

Wline: btst #14,dmaconr(a5) ;BBUSY test
    bne    Wline

    add.l  #Planesize-2,a0      ;Address of last word
    move.w #$09f0,bltcon0(a5)   ;USEA and D, LFx: D = A
    move.w #$000a,bltcon1(a5)   ;Inclusive Fill plus Descending
    move.w #$ffff,bltafwm(a5)   ;First- and Last word mask set
    move.w #$ffff,bltalwm(a5)
    move.l a0,bltapth(a5)       ;Address of last word of Bit-
    move.l a0,bltdpth(a5)       ;plane in the Address-Register
    move.w #0,bltamod(a5)       ;no Modulo
```

```
move.w #0,bltdmod(a5)
move.w #$ff*64+40,bltsize(a5) ;Start Blitter

;Wait for mouse button

end1:   btst #6,ciaapra   ;Mouse key pressed?
 bne.S  end1              ;no  -> continue

;End of Part 1.

;Part 2:

;Octant table with SING =1 and LINE =1:

Octant_table:

 dc.b 0 *4+3 ;y1<y2, x1<x2, dx<dy = Okt6
 dc.b 4 *4+3 ;y1<y2, x1<x2, dx>dy = Okt7
 dc.b 2 *4+3 ;y1<y2, x1>x2, dx<dy = Okt5
 dc.b 5 *4+3 ;y1<y2, x1>x2, dx>dy = Okt4
 dc.b 1 *4+3 ;y1>y2, x1<x2, dx<dy = Okt1
 dc.b 6 *4+3 ;y1>y2, x1<x2, dx>dy = Okt0
 dc.b 3 *4+3 ;y1>y2, x1>x2, dx<dy = Okt2
 dc.b 7 *4+3 ;y1>y2, x1>x2, dx>dy = Okt3
```

## 1.5.8     Sound output

*Fundamentals of electronic music*

When you hear sound, whether it's music, noise or speech, it all occurs in the form of oscillations in the air, the sound waves which reach our ears. A normal musical instrument creates these oscillations either directly, such as a flute in which the air blown through is made to oscillate, or indirectly, in which part of the instrument creates the tone (oscillation) and then the air picks it up. This is what happens for all string instruments, for example.

An electronic instrument creates electrical oscillations in its circuits, which correspond to the desired sound. You can't hear these oscillations until they're converted into sound oscillations by means of a loudspeaker. On the Amiga the speaker built into the monitor is generally used. Unfortunately, because of its size and quality it is not capable of converting the electrical oscillations into identical sound waves. In English: It sounds bad. Therefore you should connect your Amiga to a good amplifier/speaker system to get the full pleasure of its musical capabilities. But back to our theme:

167

What parameters determine the sound which comes from the computer?

*Frequency*

The first is the frequency of the sound. It determines whether the pitch sounds high or low. Seen physically, the frequency is the number of oscillations per second, measured in Hertz (Hz). One oscillation per second is 1 Hz, and a kilohertz is 1000 Hz. The human ear can respond to sounds between 16 and 16000 Hz. Those who know something about music know that the standard A is 440 Hz. The connection between frequency and pitch is as follows: With each octave the frequency doubles. The next A thus has a frequency of 880 Hz, while the A on the octave below the standard has a frequency of 220 Hz.

The frequency of sound does not have to be constant. For example, it can periodically vary around the actual pitch by a few Hz, creating an effect called vibrato.

*Volume*

The second parameter of a sound is its volume. By volume we mean the amplitude of the oscillation. The volume of a tone is measured in deci-Bels (dB). The range of human hearing is about 1 dB to 120 dB. Each increase of about 10 dB doubles the audible volume. The volume of sound is also called sound pressure.

The volume can be influenced by many parameters. The simplest is naturally the volume control on the monitor or amplifier. This does nothing other than change the amplitude of the electrical oscillation. But the distance between the listener and the speaker also has an effect on the volume. The further you are from the speaker, the softer the sound. But also the furnishings in the room, open or closed doors, etc., all this can affect the amplitude of the sound waves. Therefore the absolute volume is not that important. More interesting is the relative volume of sounds between each other, such as whether a sound is louder or softer than its predecessor.

There is a relationship between the volume of a sound and its frequency. The cause of this is the sensitivity of the human ear. High and low sounds are perceived as being softer than those in the middle range, even if they physically have the same sound pressure in decibels. This middle pitch range runs from about 1000 to 3000 Hz. In this frequency range are also the oscillations for the human voice, which is probably the reason for the higher sensitivity.

The volume of a sound can also change periodically within a given range. This effect is called tremolo. Moreover, there is the variation in volume from the start to the end of the sound. A sound can start out loud and then slowly die out. But it can also start out loud and then drop a certain amount and then stop abruptly. Or it starts softly and then slowly becomes louder. There are almost no limits to the combinations here.

*Figure 1.5.8.1*

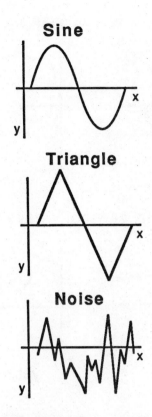

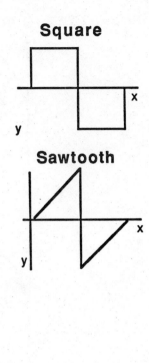

***Tone color or timbre***

The third and last parameter of a sound is somewhat more complicated. This is the timbre, and it plays an important role. There are hundreds of different instruments which can all play a sound with the same frequency and volume, but still they sound different from each other. The reason for this is the shape of the oscillation. Figure 1.5.8.1 shows four common waveforms. Why do they sound different?

Each waveform, regardless of what it looks like, can be represented as a mix of sine waves of different frequencies. For a square wave, for instance, the first wave has the fundamental frequency of the sound, the second three times the fundamental but only a third of the volume. The third harmonic has five times the frequency but a fifth of the amplitude, and so on.

*Figure 1.5.8.2* **3 combined sine waves make a square wave**

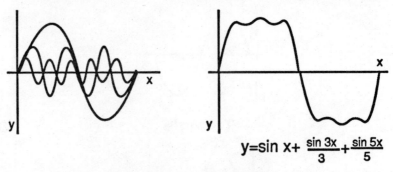

$$y=\sin x+\frac{\sin 3x}{3}+\frac{\sin 5x}{5}$$

**...or a sawtooth wave**

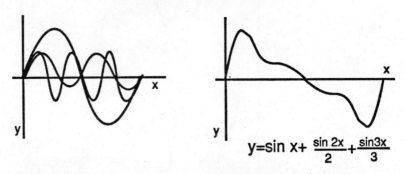

$$y=\sin x+\frac{\sin 2x}{2}+\frac{\sin 3x}{3}$$

Figure 1.5.8.2 shows this for a square wave and a sawtooth wave. For the same simplicity only the first three harmonics are shown.

As we said, all periodic waveforms can be represented as sums of sine waves. This is called the harmonic series of a sound. The pure sine wave consists only of the fundamental frequency. A square wave consists of an infinite number of harmonics. The number of harmonics and their frequency and amplitude relationship determine the timbre of the sound. The harmonic series is important because the ear reacts only to sine waves. A sound whose waveform deviates from a sound wave is divided into its harmonics by the ear. Keep these facts in mind when reading the rest of this section.

*Noises*

In addition to pitched tones there are also noises. While you can define a tone very precisely and also create it electronically, this is much more difficult for noises. They have neither a given frequency nor a defined amplitude variation and no actual waveform. They represent an arbitrary combination of sound events. The basis of many noises is called *white noise*, which is a mix of an infinite number of sounds whose frequencies and phases have no relationship to each other. The wind produces this sound, because each of the millions of air molecules put into oscillation collide with each other or with an object on the ground. These oscillations make up an undefinable mixture of sounds (noise), which is a typical sound of wind.

Figure 1.5.8.3

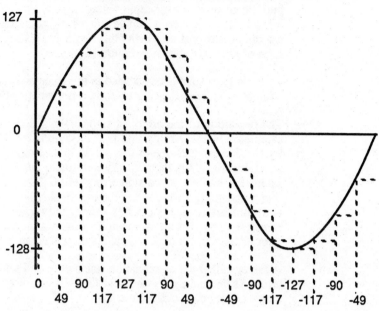

**Digitizing a waveform**

Sound
creation on
the Amiga

The main criterion for judging the acoustic capabilities of a computer is its versatility. The optimal case is where all three parameters of a sound, frequency, volume and timbre, can be set completely independent.

On the Amiga the developers tried to get as close to this goal as possible. Not to be limited to predefined waveforms, the digital equivalent of the desired waveform is stored in memory and then conversion to the corresponding electrical oscillation by a digital-to-analog converter. In other words, the oscillation is digitized and stored in the computer. During output, the digitized data are converted back to analog form and sent to the amplifier.

In Figure 1.5.8.1 you saw various waveforms. To put these into a understandable form to a computer, they must be converted into a series of numbers.

To do this you divide one cycle of the desired waveform into an even number of equal-sized sections. If possible, you want to start with a point where the wave intersects, the X axis. For each of these sections put the corresponding Y value into memory. This produces a sequence of numbers whose elements represent snapshots of the wave at given points in time. These digitized values are called *samples*.

On output, the Amiga converts the number values from memory back into the corresponding output voltages. But since the wave is divided into a limited number of samples by the digitalization, the output curve can only be reconstructed with this number. This results in the staircase form of the wave shown in Figure 1.5.8.3.

The quality of sounds reproduced in this manner in comparison to their original waveforms depends essentially on two quantities:

The resolution of the digitized signals. This is the value range of the samples. On the Amiga this is 8 bits, or from -128 to +127. Each input value can take one of 256 values in memory. Since the resolution of analog signals is theoretically unlimited, but that of the individual samples is limited, conversion errors result. These are called quanitization or rounding errors. When the input value lies somewhere between two numbers (it doesn't correspond exactly to one of the 256 digital steps), it's rounded up or down. The maximum possible quantization error is 1/256 of the digitized value (also called an error of 1 LSB).

A factor called the quantization noise is bound with the quantization error. As the name says, this reveals itself as noise matching the magnitude of the quantization error.

A value range of eight bits allows moderately good reproduction of the original wave. Higher resolution is needed for high-fidelity reproduction, however. A CD player, for example, works with 16 bits.

The second parameter for the quality of digitized sound is the sampling rate. This is the number of samples per second. Naturally, a higher number of samples result in better reproduction. The sampling rate can be set within certain bounds on the Amiga. First you must consider how many samples are used per digitized cycle of the waveform. In the example, Figure 1.5.8.3 this is 16 values. There is little audible difference between the resulting staircase waveform and a normal sine signal.

*The output of the digitized sound*

Once the desired waveform has been converted to the corresponding numbers and written into memory, you naturally want to hear it. The Amiga has four sound channels which all work according to the following principle:

A digitized wave is read from memory through DMA and output through a digital/analog conversion. This process is repeated continually so that the single cycle of the waveform creates a continuous tone.

Channels 0 and 3 are sent to the left stereo channel, while 1 and 2 are sent to the right.

Each audio channel has its own DMA channel. Since the DMA on the Amiga is performed on words, two samples are combined into one data word. This is why you need an even number of samples. The upper half of the word (bits 8-15) are always output before the lower bits (0-7). The data list for our digitized sine wave looks as follows in memory, whereby Start is the starting address of the list in chip RAM:

```
Alstart:
dc.b 0,49          ;1st data word, samples 1 and 2
dc.b 90,117        ;2nd data word, samples 3 and 4
dc.b 127,117       ;3rd data word, samples 5 and 6
dc.b 90,49         ;4th data word, samples 7 and 8
dc.b 0,-49         ;5th data word, samples 9 and 10
dc.b -90,-117      ;6th data word, samples 11 and 12
dc.b -127,-117     ;7th data word, samples 13 and 14
dc.b -90,-49       ;8th data word, samples 15 and 16
Alend:
```

The digital/analog converter requires the samples to be stored as signed two's complement 8-bit numbers. The assembler converts the negative values into two's complement for us so that you can write negative values directly in the data list.

Now you must select one of the four audio channels over which you want to output the tone. The corresponding DMA channel must then be initialized. Five registers per channel set the operating parameters. The first two form an address register pair, which you should recognize from the other DMA channels. These are called AUDxLCH and AUDxLCL, or together AUDxLC, whereby x is the number of the DMA channel:

| Reg. | Name | Function |
|------|------|----------|
| $0A0 | AUD0LCH | Pointer to the audio data, bits 16-18 |
| $0A2 | AUD0LCL | for channel 0, bits 0-15 |
| $0B0 | AUD1LCH | Pointer to the audio data, bits 16-18 |
| $0B2 | AUD1LCL | for channel 1, bits 0-15 |
| $0C0 | AUD2LCH | Pointer to the audio data, bits 16-18 |
| $0C2 | AUD2LCL | for channel 2, bits 0-15 |
| $0D0 | AUD3LCH | Pointer to the audio data, bits 16-18 |
| $0D2 | AUD3LCL | for channel 3, bits 0-15 |

The initialization of these address pointers can be accomplished with a MOVE.L command as usual:

```
LEA$DFF000, A5           ;base address of custom chips in A5
MOVE.L #Start, AUD0LCH(A5) ;write "Start" in AUD0LC
```

Next the DMA controller must be told the length of the digitized cycle, that is, the number of samples it comprises. The appropriate registers are the AUDxLEN registers:

*AUDxLEN*
*register*

| Reg. | Name | Function |
|------|------|----------|
| $0A4 | AUD0LEN | Number of audio data words for channel 0 |
| $0B4 | AUD1LEN | Number of audio data words for channel 1 |
| $0C4 | AUD2LEN | Number of audio data words for channel 2 |
| $0D4 | AUD3LEN | Number of audio data words for channel 3 |

The length is specified in words, not bytes. Thus the number of bytes must be divided by two before it is written into the AUDxLEN register.

The AUDxLEN register can be initialized with the following MOVE command. To avoid having to count all of the words, two labels are defined: Alstart is the starting address of the data list, Alend is the end address +1 (see example data list above). The base address of the custom chips ($DFF000) is stored in A5:

```
MOVE.W # (Ende-Start) /2, AUD0LEN (A5)
```

Now comes the volume of sound. On the Amiga the volume for each channel can be set separately. A total of 65 levels are available. The range runs from 0 (inaudible) or 64 (full volume). The corresponding registers are called AUDxVOL:

*AUDxVOL*
*register*

| Reg. | Name | Function |
|------|------|----------|
| $0A8 | AUD0VOL | Volume of audio channel 0 |
| $0B8 | AUD1VOL | Volume of audio channel 1 |
| $0C8 | AUD2VOL | Volume of audio channel 2 |
| $0D8 | AUD3VOL | Volume of audio channel 3 |

Let's set our audio channel to half volume:

```
MOVE.W #32, AUD0VOL (A5)
```

The last parameter is the sampling rate. This determines how often a data byte (sample) is sent to the digital/analog converter. The sampling rate determines the frequency of the sound. As explained before, the frequency equals the number of oscillations (cycles) per second. An oscillation consists of an arbitrary number of samples. In the example it is 16. If the sampling rate represents the number of samples read per second, the frequency of the sound corresponds to the sampling rate divided by the number of samples per cycle:

$$\text{Sound frequency} = \frac{\text{Sampling rate}}{\text{Samples per cycle}}$$

Unfortunately the sample rate cannot be specified directly in Hertz. The DMA controller wants to know the number of bus cycles between the output of two samples. A bus cycle takes exactly 279.365 nanoseconds (billionths of a second) or $2.79365 * 10^{-7}$ seconds.

To get from the sampling rate to the number of bus cycles, you need the inverse of the sampling rate. This yields the period of a sample. If you divide this value by the period of a bus cycle in seconds, you get the number of bus cycles between two samples, called the sample period:

$$\text{Sample period} = \frac{1}{\text{Sampling rate} * 2.79365 * 10^{-7}}$$

Let's assume that you want to play the example tone at a frequency of 440 Hz. The sampling rate is calculated as follows:

Sampling rate = frequency * samples per cycle
Sampling rate = 440 Hz * 16 = 7040 Hz

The necessary sample period can also be calculated quickly by inserting the proper values:

$$\text{Sample period} = \frac{1}{7040 * 2.79365 * 10^{-7}} = 508.4583$$

Since only integer values can be specified for the sample period, you round the result to 508. As a result the output frequency is not exactly 440 Hz, but the deviation is minimal, namely 0.4 Hz.

The sample period can theoretically be anything between 0 and 65535. The actual range has an upper limit, however. As can be gathered from Figure 1.5.3.2 in the Interrupts section, each audio channel has one DMA slot per raster line, that is, one data word, or two samples, can be read from memory in each raster line. Thus the smallest possible value for the sample period is 124. The corresponding sample frequency for this value is 28867 Hz. If the sample period is made shorter than 124, a data word can be output twice because the next one cannot be read on time.

*AUDxPER*
*register:*

| Reg. | Name | Function |
|------|------|----------|
| $0A6 | AUD0PER | Sample period for audio channel 0 |
| $0B6 | AUD1PER | Sample period for audio channel 1 |
| $0C6 | AUD2PER | Sample period for audio channel 2 |
| $0D6 | AUD3PER | Sample period for audio channel 3 |

MOVE.W #508, AUD0PER(A5) puts the sample rate you calculated into the AUD0PER register. Now all of the registers for audio channel number 0 have been supplied with the proper values for our sound. To make it audible, you have to enable the DMA for audio DMA channel 0.

Four bits in the DMACON register are responsible for the audio DMA channels:

| DMACON bit no. | Name | Audio DMA channel no. |
|---|---|---|
| 3 | AUD3EN | 3 |
| 2 | AUD2EN | 2 |
| 1 | AUD1EN | 1 |
| 0 | AUD0EN | 0 |

To enable the audio DMA for channel 0 you must set the AUD0EN bit to 1. Just to be sure, you should also set the DMAEN bit:

```
MOVE.W #$8201, DMACON(A5) ;set AUD0EN and DMAEN
```

Now the DMA controller starts to fetch the audio data from the memory and output it through the digital/analog converter. The sound can be heard through the speaker. To turn it off again, simply set AUD0EN = 0.

Whenever AUDxEN is set to 1, the DMA starts at the address in AUDxLC. There is one exception: If the DMA channel was on, AUDxEN = 1, and the bit is briefly cleared and then set back to 1 without out the DMA channel reading a new data word in the meantime, the DMA controller continues with the old address.

*Audio interrupt*

The audio DMA always starts with the data byte at the address in AUDxLC. Once the number of data words specified in AUDxLEN have been read from memory and output, the DMA starts over at the AUDxLC address. In contrast to the address registers for the blitter or the bit planes, the contents of the AUDxLC registers are not changed during the audio DMA. There is an additional address register for each audio channel. Before the DMA controller gets the first data word from memory it copies the value of the AUDxLC register into this internal address register. It also transfers the AUDxLEN value into an internal counter. As you read the section on interrupts, there is a separate interrupt bit for each of the four audio channels. The processor interrupt level 4 is reserved exclusively for these bits.

While the DMA controller now reads data words from memory, the processor can supply AUDxLC and AUDxLEN with new values, since the values of both registers are stored internally. Not until the counter which is initialized at the beginning with the value of AUDxLEN reaches 0 will the data from AUDxLC and AUDxLEN be read again. The processor then has enough time to change the values of the two registers, if necessary. This allows uninterrupted sound output.

An interrupt is generated after each complete cycle. For high frequencies this occurs very often. The interrupt enable bits (INTEN) for the audio interrupts should be set only when they are actually needed, or the processor may not be able to save itself from all of the interrupt requests.

*Modulation of*
*volume and*
*frequency*

To create specified sound effects, it's possible to modulate the frequency and/or volume. One of the DMA channels acts as a modulator which changes the corresponding parameter of another channel. This can be done very simply: The modulation fetches its data from memory as usual, but instead of sending it to the digital/analog converter, it is written to the volume or frequency register of the oscillator which it modulates (AUDxVOL or AUDxLEN). It can also influence both registers at the same time. In this case the data words read from its data list are written alternately to the AUDxVOL or AUDxLEN registers. The data words have the same format as their destination registers:

Volume:     Bits 7-15   unused
            Bits 0-6    volume value between 0 and 64
Frequency:  Bits 0-15   sample period

The following table shows the use of data words of the modulation oscillator for all three possible cases:

|        | Data word | Oscillator modulates: | |
|--------|-----------|-----------|----------------------|
| Number | Frequency | Volume    | Frequency and volume |
| 1      | Period 1  | Volume 1  | Volume 1             |
| 2      | Period 2  | Volume 2  | Period 1             |
| 3      | Period 3  | Volume 3  | Volume 2             |
| 4      | Period 4  | Volume 4  | Period 2             |

To activate an audio channel as a modulator, you must set the corresponding bits in the audio-disk control register (ADKCON). Each channel can modulate only its successor, channel 0 modulates channel 1, 1 modulates 2, 2 modulates 3. Channel 3 can also be switched as a modulator, but its data words are not used to modulate another channel and are lost. If an audio channel is used as a modulator, its audio output is disabled.

The ADKCON register contains, as its name says, control bits for the disk controller in addition to the audio circuitry, and these control bits are not explained here.

*ADKCON register $09E (write) $010 (read)*

| Bit no. | Name    | Function                                          |
|---------|---------|---------------------------------------------------|
| 15      | SET/CLR | Bits are set (SET/CLR=1) or cleared               |
| 14 to 8 |         | Used by the disk controller                       |
| 7       | USE3PN  | Audio channel 3 modulates nothing                 |
| 6       | USE2P3  | Audio channel 2 modulates period of channel 3     |
| 5       | USE1P2  | Audio channel 1 modulates period of channel 2     |
| 4       | USE0P1  | Audio channel 0 modulates period of channel 1     |
| 3       | USE3VN  | Audio channel 3 modulates nothing                 |
| 2       | USE2V3  | Audio channel 2 modulates volume of channel 3     |
| 1       | USE1V2  | Audio channel 1 modulates volume of channel 2     |
| 0       | USE0V1  | Audio channel 0 modulates volume of channel 1     |

To recap: If a channel is used for modulation, its data words are simply written into the corresponding register of the modulated channel. Otherwise the two operate completely independently of each other.

In the example we defined a cycle with 16 samples. The maximum sampling rate is 28867 Hz. This yields a maximum frequency of 28867 / 16 = 1460.4 Hz.

*Problems with digital sound generation*

If you want a higher pitch, you must decrease the number of samples per cycle. If you define a sine with half as many samples, the maximum frequency increases to 3020.8 Hz. Eight data bytes are rather few for a good sine wave, however. For even higher pitches the number of samples decreases even more. For 6041.6 Hz there are only four. Waveforms are scarcely recognizable with just four samples.

This is not all that noticeable in hearing, however. Our ear behaves exactly the same way. The higher the frequency, the more difficult it is to tell different sounds apart.

Despite this, it can improve the sound quality to use multiple cycles to define the desired waveform at high frequencies. This is illustrated in Figure 1.5.8.4.

*Figure 1.5.8.4*

# Digitizing multiple waves for improving tone quality

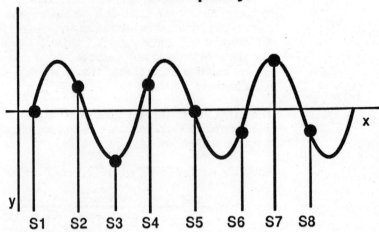

S = sample

The maximum frequency of the Amiga sound output is limited by another factor, however. When converting the digital sound data back to analog, two undesired alias frequencies arise due to oscillation facts between the sampling rate and the desired sound frequency. One of these is the sum of the sampling rate and the sound frequency and the other is the difference of these two. These phenomena are called *aliasing distortion*.

For example, with a 3 kHz sound and a 12 kHz sampling rate, the difference is 9 kHz and the sum is 15 kHz.

In order to eliminate this aliasing distortion, a device called a low-pass filter has been placed between the output of the digital/analog converter and the audio connectors. Its functions are illustrated in Figure 1.5.8.5. All frequencies up to 4 kHz pass through undisturbed. Between 4 and 7 kHz the signal decreases in amplitude until it's no longer passed above 7 kHz. Let's take the example from above: The 3 kHz tone is not affected by the low-pass filter, but both the sum and the different frequencies of 16 and 9 kHz lie above the filter's cut-off frequency of 7 kHz, and is not allowed to pass through. Thus they are not heard through the speaker either. But if you try to output the same 3 kHz tone with a sampling rate of 9 kHz, the difference between the frequency is 6 kHz and is diminished by the filter, however, it still lets through.

*Figure   1.5.8.5*                          **Low-pass  filter**

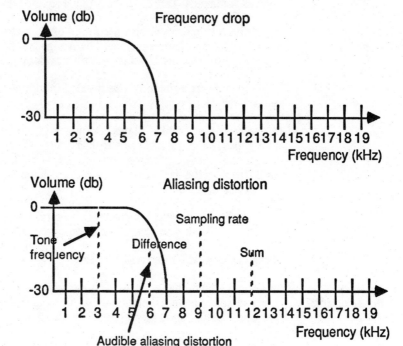

To be sure that the different frequency always lies above the cut-off frequency of the filter, the following rule must be observed:

Sampling rate > highest frequency component + 7 kHz

It's not enough to ensure that the difference between the sampling frequency and the desired output frequency is greater than 7 kHz. If a waveform with many harmonics is used, each of the harmonics produces its own different frequency with the sampling rate. This is why the highest frequency component of the waveform must be used in the expression above.

Not only does the low-pass filter hold back the aliasing distortion, it also limits the frequency range of the Amiga. To be sure, tones with a fundamental frequency between 4 and 7 kHz rarely occur in a musical piece, but the harmonics of much lower fundamentals for certain waveforms lie within this range. This is especially clear with a square wave. In Figure 1.5.8.2 you saw that a square wave consists of the combination of multiple sine waves having a set frequency relationship to each other. In the figure the square wave consists of just two harmonics and the fundamental tone. An actual square wave, however, consists of many infinite harmonics. If the higher-order harmonics are limited or removed by the filter, a deformed square wave results, as shown in Figure 1.5.8.2. In the extreme case when the fundamental frequency of the square wave approaches the cut-off frequency of the filter, only the fundamental remains. This turns the original square wave into a sine wave.

*Amplitude envelope*

In addition to the waveform the sound of an instrument is also influenced by its amplitude envelope. The Amiga can do almost anything in the area of waveforms. How are specific envelopes programmed?

The envelope of a sound can be divided into three sections: the attack, sustain and decay phases.

As soon as the sound is played the attack phase begins. It determines how quickly the volume rises from zero to the sustain value. During the sustain phase the sound remains at this volume. When the sound ends, it enters the decay phase where the volume drops from the sustain value back to zero.

The amplitude curve which this process represents is generally called an envelope. How do you program such an envelope on the Amiga?

There are basically three possibilities:

*Volume modulation*

A second sound channel is used to modulate the volume of the sound. For example, channel 0 can be used to modulate channel 1. Channel 1 can continually output the desired sound with its volume set to zero.

The desired envelope is divided into two parts: attack phase and decay phase. It is digitized (just like a waveform) and placed in memory in two data lists. When the sound is played, channel 0 is set to the address of the attack data and started. Since it modulates the volume of channel 1, the volume of the sound follows the desired attack phase exactly. When the attack phase reaches the sustain value, the data list for channel 0 has been processed. It then creates an interrupt and the data list would normally be processed again from the beginning. The processor must react to the interrupt and turn on channel 0 by means of the AUD0EN bit in the DMACON register. Channel 1 remains at the desired sustain volume.

When the tone is turned off again, set channel 0 to the start of the decay data and start it. Again wait for the interrupt signalling that the decay phase is done and then turn channel 0 off.

The channel 0 registers must be initialized as follows for this procedure:

USE0V1    This bit in the ADKCON register must be set to 1 so that channel 0 modulates the volume of channel 1.

AUD0LC    First set the data list for the attack phase and then to that for the decay phase.

AUD0VOL   Not used since the audio output of channel 0 is turned off.

AUD0PER   The contents of the AUD0PER register determines the speed at which the volume data are read from memory. This can be used to set the length of the attack/decay phase.

This method allows the desired envelope to be constructed perfectly. Unfortunately it also has a big disadvantage: Two audio channels are required for each sound. If you want four different sound channels, you have to use an alternate method:

*Controlling volume with the processor*

The desired envelope is placed in memory as described above. This time, however, the processor changes the volume. The processor fetches the current volume value from memory at regular intervals and writes it to the volume register of the corresponding sound channel. The corresponding program must be run as an interrupt routine. This can be done in the vertical blanking interrupt or one of the timer interrupts from CIA-B can be used.

The disadvantage of this method is the amount of processor time which it requires, since the control of the volume is not performed by DMA. Since the amount of time needed is reasonably limited, this is usually the best method for most applications.

*Constructing
the envelope
in the sample
data*

This method is best for short sounds or sound effects. Instead of digitizing just one cycle of the desired waveform, write the entire sound into memory. This can either be calculated by a program, or an audio digitizer can be used. This allows a sound to be digitized by means of an analog/digital converter. Several firms offer such devices for use with the Amiga. Once the data are in the Amiga, they can be played back at any pitch or speed. This allows complex effects such as laughter or screams to be produced by the Amiga with considerable accuracy.

This method also has disadvantages: It involves either difficult calculations or additional hardware in order to put the complete sound in digitized form in memory. In addition, this method requires large amounts of memory. For example, if the sound is one second long with a sampling rate of 20 kHz, the sound data takes up 20K!

## 1.5.9 Tips, tricks, and more

*Sound quality*

The value range of the digital data is from -128 to 127. This range should be used as fully as possible. The best situation is when the amplitude of the digital waveform equals 256. If it's not, the sound quality decreases audibly, since the size of the quantization error increases with a decreasing value range.

Therefore you should avoid using the amplitude of the digitialized signal to control the volume of the sound. Each channel has a AUDxVOL register for this purpose. If the volume is reduced with this register, the relationship between the desired sound and the distortion remains the same and thus the sound quality is preserved.

*Changing
waveforms
smoothly*

To avoid annoying crackling, clicks or jumps in volume when changing waveforms, the following rules must be kept in mind:

Each cycle should be digitized from zero-point to zero-point, that is, each cycle should start at a point where the waveform crosses the X axis. If this rule is kept, all waveforms in memory have the same starting and ending value, namely zero. Thus no sudden level jumps occur when switching from one waveform to another.

Second, you should make sure that the total loudness of the two waveforms is approximately the same. By this we mean the effective value of the waveform. The effective value is the same as the amplitude of a square wave signal whose surface under the curve is exactly as large as that of the waveform.

This effective value determines the volume of an oscillation. Only for a square wave does it equal the amplitude. If you change from one waveform to one with a higher effective value, this sounds louder than its predecessor.

The effective value of a cycle can be easily calculated from its digitized data:

Add the values of all the bytes and divide by the number of data bytes.

If you want to make full use of the eight bit value range for all waveforms, your effective values will not always match. The volume can then be changed accordingly with the AUDxVOL registers when changing from one waveform to another.

*Playing nodes*

Normally a musical piece is transcribed in a form of notes. If you want to play such things on the Amiga, you must convert the note values into the corresponding sample periods. To minimize the amount of calculation, it is generally best to use a table which contains the sample period values for all of the half-tones in an octave:

*Sample period values for music notes:*

| Note | Frequency (Hz) | Sample period for AUDxLEN = 16 | |
|---|---|---|---|
| C | 261.7 | 427 | (262.0) |
| C# | 277.2 | 404 | (276.9) |
| D | 293.7 | 381 | (293.6) |
| D# | 311.2 | 359 | (311.6) |
| E | 329.7 | 339 | (330.0) |
| F | 349.3 | 320 | (349.6) |
| F# | 370.0 | 302 | (370.4) |
| G | 392.0 | 285 | (392.5) |
| G# | 415.3 | 269 | (415.8) |
| A | 440.0 | 254 | (440.4) |
| A# | 466.2 | 240 | (466.0) |
| B | 493.9 | 226 | (495.0) |
| C | 523.3 | 214 | (522.7) |

(The values in parentheses represent the actual frequency for the corresponding sampling period.)

A comment about calculating the values above: The frequency of a half-tone is always greater than its predecessor by the factor "twelfth root of 2". 440 (A) * $2^{(1/12)}$ = 466.2 (A#), 466.2 * $2^{(1/12)}$ = 493.9 (B), etc.

An octave always corresponds to doubling the frequency.

If you now want to play a note from an octave which is not listed in the table, there are two options:

1. Change the sampling period. For each octave up the value must be halved. An octave lower corresponds to doubling the sampling period. This is simple, but one soon runs into certain limits. With a data field of 32 bytes (AUDxLEN = 16) as in our table, the smallest possible sampling period (124) is reached with the second A. The data list must then be reduced in size.

   In this case you get problems with lower tones, however, since the aliasing distortion then becomes audible.

A better solution is procedure 2:

2.    A separate data list is created for each octave. The sampling period value thus remains the same for each octave. It is used only to select the half-tone. If a tone from an octave above that in the table is required, you use a data list which is only half as long. Correspondingly, a list twice as long is used for the next lower octave.

The normal range of sound comprises eight octaves, meaning that you need eight data lists per waveform.

To make up for the extra work this method involves, you always get the optimal sound regardless of the pitch.

*Creating higher frequencies*

The minimal sampling period is normally 124. The reason for this is the audio DMA would not be able to read the data words fast enough to support a shorter sampling period. The old data word is then output more than once. This effect can be used to our advantage. Since the data word read contains two samples, a high frequency square wave can be created with it. With a sampling period of 1 you get a sampling frequency of 3.58 MHz and an output frequency of 1.74 MHz! To be able to use this high-frequency output signal, you must intercept it before it reaches the low-pass filter. The AUDIN input (pin 16) of the serial connector (RS-232) allows you to do this. It is connected directly to the right audio output of Paula (see the section on interfaces).

In order to create such high frequencies, AUDxVOL must be set to the maximum volume (AUDxVOL = 64).

*Playing polyphonic music*

Since the Amiga has four independent audio channels, it's easy to create four sounds at once. This allows any four-voice musical pieces to be played directly.

But there can be more. Just because there are four audio channels doesn't mean that four voices is the maximum. It has already been mentioned that each waveform is actually a combination of sine signals. Just as these harmonics together make up the waveform, you can also combine multiple waveforms into a multi-voiced sound. The output signals for audio channels 0 and 3 are also mixed together into one stereo channel inside Paula. The waveforms of the two channels are combined into a single two-voice channel.

But the same thing we do electronically with analog signals can be done by computation with digital data. Add the digital data from two completely different waveforms and output the new data to the audio channel as usual. Now you have two voices per audio channel. Theoretically, any number of voices can be played over a sound channel in this manner.

In practice the number of voices is limited by the speed of the computer, but 16 voices is certainly possible!

Calculating the summed signal from the components is very simple. At each point in time the current values of all the sounds are added and the result is divided by the number of voices.

*Audio output without DMA*    As with all DMA channels, there are also data registers for the audio DMA in which the data is stored and to which the processor can write:

*The audio data registers*

| Reg. | Name | Function |
|------|------|----------|
| $0AA | AUD0DAT | These four registers always contain the current |
| $0BA | AUD1DAT | audio data word, consisting of two samples. |
| $0CA | AUD2DAT | The sample in the upper byte (bits 8-15) |
| $0DA | AUD3DAT | is always output first. |

In order for the processor to be able to write to the audio data registers, the DMA must be turned off with AUDxEN = 0. This also changes the creation of audio interrupts. They always occur after the output of the two samples in the AUDxDAT register instead of at the start of each audio data list as before.

If a new data word is not loaded into AUDxDAT in time, the last two samples are not repeated, as for the DMA operation, but the output remains at the value of the last data byte (the lower half of the word in AUDxDAT).

The direct programming of the audio data registers costs a good deal of processing time. The audio DMA should be used except in special cases.

*A few facts:*    AUDxVOL- Value in decibels (0db=full volume)

| AUDxVOL | dB | AUDxVOL | dB | AUDxVOL | dB | AUDxVOL | dB |
|---------|------|---------|------|---------|-------|---------|-------|
| 64 | 0.0 | 48 | -2.5 | 32 | -6.0 | 16 | -12.0 |
| 63 | -0.1 | 47 | -2.7 | 31 | -6.3 | 15 | -12.6 |
| 62 | -0.3 | 46 | -2.9 | 30 | -6.6 | 14 | -13.2 |
| 61 | -0.4 | 45 | -3.1 | 29 | -6.9 | 13 | -13.8 |
| 60 | -0.6 | 44 | -3.3 | 28 | -7.2 | 12 | -14.5 |
| 59 | -0.7 | 43 | -3.5 | 27 | -7.5 | 11 | -15.3 |
| 58 | -0.9 | 42 | -3.7 | 26 | -7.8 | 10 | -16.1 |
| 57 | -1.0 | 41 | -3.9 | 25 | -8.2 | 9 | -17.0 |
| 56 | -1.2 | 40 | -4.1 | 24 | -8.5 | 8 | -18.1 |
| 55 | -1.3 | 39 | -4.3 | 23 | -8.9 | 7 | -19.2 |
| 54 | -1.5 | 38 | -4.5 | 22 | -9.3 | 6 | -20.6 |
| 53 | -1.6 | 37 | -4.8 | 21 | -9.7 | 5 | -22.1 |
| 52 | -1.8 | 36 | -5.0 | 20 | -10.1 | 4 | -24.1 |
| 51 | -2.0 | 35 | -5.2 | 19 | -10.5 | 3 | -26.6 |
| 50 | -2.1 | 34 | -5.5 | 18 | -11.0 | 2 | -30.1 |
| 49 | -2.3 | 33 | -5.8 | 17 | -11.5 | 1 | -36.1 |

(AUDxVOL = 0 corresponds to a dB value of minus infinity)

If AUDxVOL = 64, then a digital value of 127 corresponds to an output voltage of about 400 millivolts and -128 corresponds to -400 millivolts. A change of 1 LSB causes a change in the output voltage of about 3 millivolts.

*Example
programs*

<u>Creating a simple sine wave</u>

This program creates a sine wave tone with a frequency of 440 Hz. The sample table presented in the text is used. The largest portion of this program is again used to request chip RAM for the audio data list.

The sound is produced over channel 0 until the mouse button is pressed. The program then releases the occupied memory.

*Program 1*

```
;*** Create a simple sinewave ***
;Custom chip registers

intena = $9A              ;Interrupt enable register
(write)
dmacon = $96              ;DMA control register (write)

;Audio-Register

aud0lc = $A0              ;Address of audio data list
aud0len = $A4             ;Length of audio data list
aud0per = $A6             ;Sampling period
aud0vol = $A8             ;Volume
adkcon = $9E              ;Control register for modulation

;CIA-A Port register A (mouse button)

ciaapra = $bfe001

;Exec Library Base Offsets

AllocMem = -30-168        ;ByteSize,Requirements/d0,d1
FreeMem = -30-180         ;MemoryBlock,ByteSize/a1,d0

;Other labels

Execbase = 4
chip = 2                  ;Allocate chip RAM

ALsize = ALend - ALstart     ;Length of audio data list

;*** Initialization ***
start:

;Allocate memory for audio data list

    move.l  Execbase,a6
    moveq   #ALsize,d0       ;Size of audio data list
    moveq   #chip,d1
    jsr     AllocMem(a6)     ;Allocate memory
    beq     Ende             ;Error -> End program
```

```
;Copy audio data list in chip RAM

move.l    d0,a0           ;Address in chip RAM
move.l    #ALstart,a1     ;Address in program
moveq     #ALsize-1,d1    ;Loop counter

Loop:     move.b (a1)+,(a0)+ ;Data list in chip RAM
dbf       d1,Loop

;*** Main program
;Initialize audio registers

lea       $DFF000,a5
move.w    #$000f,dmacon(a5) ;Audio DMA off
move.l    d0,aud0lc(a5)      ;Set address of data list
move.w    #ALsize/2,aud0len(a5) ;Length in words
move.w    #32,aud0vol(a5)    ;Half volume
move.w    #508,aud0per(a5)   ;Frequency: 440 Hz
move.w    #$00ff,adkcon(a5)  ;Disable modulation

;Enable audio DMA

move.w    #$8201,dmacon(a5) ;Channel 0 on

;Wait for a mouse button

wait:  btst #6,ciaapra
bne       wait

;Disable audio DMA

move.w    #$0001,dmacon(a5) ;Channel 0 off

;*** End of program ***
move.l    d0,a1           ;Address of data list
moveq     #ALsize,d0      ;Length
jsr       FreeMem(a6)      ;Release assigned memory

Ende: clr.l d0
 rts

;Audio data list

ALstart:
 dc.b     0,49
 dc.b     90,117
 dc.b     127,117
 dc.b     90,49
 dc.b     0,-49
 dc.b     -90,-117
 dc.b     -127,-117
 dc.b     -90,-49
ALend:

;Program end
 end
```

*Program 2*      <u>Sine wave with vibrato</u>

This program is an extension of the previous one. The same sine wave
is output, but this time over channel 1. Channel 0 modulates the frequency of channel 1 and creates the vibrato effect. The data for the
vibrato represents a digitized sine wave whose zero point is the value of
the sampling period of 508 Hz A.

```
;*** Creating a vibrato ***

;Custom chip register

INTENA = $9A ;Interrupt enable register (write)
DMACON = $96 ;DMA control register (write)

;Audio registers

AUD0LC  = $A0 ;Address of audio data list
AUD0LEN = $A4 ;Length der audio data list
AUD0PER = $A6 ;Sampling eriod
AUD0VOL = $A8 ;Volume
AUD1LC  = $B0
AUD1LEN = $B4
AUD1PER = $B6
AUD1VOL = $B8
ADKCON  = $9E ;Control register for modulation

;CIA-A Port register A (mouse button)

CIAAPRA = $bfe001

;Exec Library Base Offsets

AllocMem = -30-168 ;ByteSize,Requirements/d0,d1
FreeMem  = -30-180 ;MemoryBlock,ByteSize/a1,d0

;Other labels

Execbase = 4
chip     = 2                  ;Allocate chip RAM
ALsize = ALend - ALstart ;Length of audio data list
Vibsize = Vibend - Vibstart ;Length of vibrato table
Size = ALsize + Vibsize      ;Total length of both lists

;*** Initialization ***
start:

;Allocate memory for data lists

    move.l  Execbase,a6
    move.l  #Size,d0          ;Length of both lists
    moveq   #chip,d1
    jsr     AllocMem(a6)      ;Allocate memory
    beq     Ende
```

```
;Copy audio data list in chip RAM
   move.l   d0,a0           ;Address in chip RAM
   move.l   #ALstart,a1     ;Address in program
   move.l   #Size-1,d1      ;Loop counter

Loop:    move.b  (a1)+,(a0)+ ;Lists in chip RAM
   dbf      d1,Loop

;*** Main program

;Initialize audio registers

   move.l   d0,d1           ;Audio data list address
   add.l    #ALsize,d1      ;Address of vibrato table
   lea      $DFF000,a5
   move.w   #$000f,dmacon(a5) ;Audio DMA off
   move.l   d1,aud0lc(a5)   ;Set to  vibrato table
   move.w   #Vibsize/2,aud0len(a5) ;Length of vibrato table
   move.w   #8961,aud0per(a5)        ;Vibrato frequency

   move.l   d0,aud1lc(a5)     ;Channel 1 from audio data list
   move.w   #ALsize/2,aud1len(a5) ;Length of audio data list
   move.w   #32,aud1vol(a5)       ;Half volume

   move.w   #$00FF,adkcon(a5) ;Disable other modulation
   move.w   #$8010,adkcon(a5) ;Channel 0 modulates period
;from channel 1

;Audio DMA on

   move.w   #$8203,dmacon(a5) ;Channels 0 and 1 on

;Wait for a mouse button

   wait:    btst #6,ciaapra
   bne      wait

;Audio DMA off

   move.w   #$0003,dmacon(a5) ;Channels 0 and 1 off

;*** End program  ***

   move.l   d0,a1           ;Address of lists
   move.l   #Size,d0        ;Length
   jsr      FreeMem(a6)      ;Release memory

Ende: clr.l d0
   rts
```

```
;Audio data list

ALstart:
  dc.b    0,49
  dc.b    90,117
  dc.b    127,117
  dc.b    90,49
  dc.b    0,-49
  dc.b    -90,-117
  dc.b    -127,-117
  dc.b    -90,-49
ALend:
;Vibrato table

Vibstart:
  dc.w    508,513,518,522,524,525,524,522,518,513
  dc.w    508,503,498,494,492,491,492,494,498,503
Vibend:

;Program end
  end
```

# 1.5.10        Mouse, joystick and paddles

Mouse, joystick and paddles—all of these can be connected to the Amiga. We'll go through them in order, together with the corresponding registers. The pin assignment of the game ports, to which all of these input devices are connected can be found in the section on interfaces. Let's start with the mouse:

*The mouse*

The mouse is the most-often used input device. It's an important device for using the user-friendly interfaces of the Amiga. But how does it work and how is the mouse pointer on the screen created and updated?

If you turn the mouse over, you'll see a rubber-coated metal ball which turns when the mouse is moved. These rotations of the ball are transferred to two shafts, situated at right angles to each other so that one turns when the mouse is moved along the X axis and the other when the mouse is moved along the Y axis. If the mouse is moved diagonally, both shafts rotate corresponding to the X and Y components of the mouse movement.

Unfortunately, rotating shafts don't help the Amiga when it wants to determine the position of the mouse. Some conversion of the mechanical movement into electrical signals is necessary.

A wheel with holes around its circumference is attached to the end of each shaft. When it rotates it repeatedly breaks a beam of light in an optical coupler. The signal which results from this is amplified and sent out over the mouse cable to the computer.

Now the Amiga can determine when and at what speed the mouse is moved. But it still doesn't know in what direction, that is, left or right, forward or backward.

A little trick solves this problem. Two optical couplers are placed on each wheel, set opposite from each other and offset by half a hole. If the disk rotates in a given direction, one light beam is always broken before the other. If the direction is reversed, the order of the two signals from the optical couplers change correspondingly. This allows the Amiga to determine the direction of the movement.

The mouse therefore returns four signals, two per shaft. They are called Vertical Pulse, Vertical Quadrature Pulse, Horizontal Pulse and Horizontal Quadrature Pulse.

*Figure 1.5.10.1*

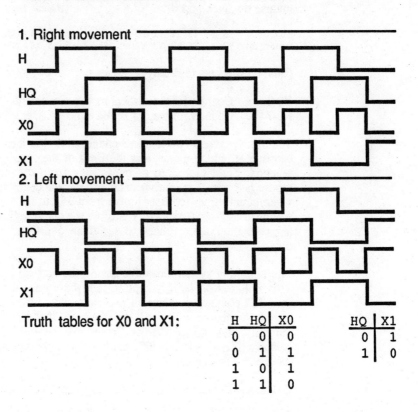

1. Right movement

H

HQ

X0

X1

2. Left movement

H

HQ

X0

X1

Truth tables for X0 and X1:

| H | HQ | X0 |
|---|----|----|
| 0 | 0  | 0  |
| 0 | 1  | 1  |
| 1 | 0  | 1  |
| 1 | 1  | 0  |

| HQ | X1 |
|----|----|
| 0  | 1  |
| 1  | 0  |

Figure 1.5.10.1 shows the phase relationship of the horizontal pulse (H) and quadrature pulse (HQ) signals, but it also holds for the vertical signals. It's easy to see how H and HQ differ from each other depending on the direction of movement. The Amiga combines these two signals to obtain two new signals, X0 and X1. X1 is an inverted HQ and X0 arises from an exclusive-OR or H and HQ. That is, X0 is 1 whenever H and HQ are at different levels (see truth table in Figure 1.5.10.1). With these two signals the Amiga controls a 6-bit counter which counts up or down on X1 depending on the direction. Together with X0 and X1 an 8-bit value is formed which represents the current mouse position.

If the mouse is moved right or down, the counter is incremented. If the mouse is moved left or up, it is decremented.

*JOYDAT0 and JOYDAT1:*  Denise contains four such counters, two per game port since a mouse can be connected to each one. They are called JOYDAT0 and JOYDAT1:

| JOY0DAT $00A | JOY1DAT $00C |
|---|---|
| (mouse on game port 0) | (mouse on game port 1) |

```
Bit no.:   15 14 13 12 11 10  9  8  7  6  5  4   3  2  1  0
Function:  Y7 Y6 Y5 Y4 Y3 Y2 Y1 Y0 X7 X6 X5 X4  X3 X2 X1 X0
```

(Both registers are read-only)

Y0-7    Counter for the vertical mouse movements (Y direction)
H0-7    Counter for the horizontal mouse movements (X direction)

The mouse creates two hundred count pulses per inch, or about 79 per centimeter, which means that the limit of the mouse counter is soon reached. Eight bits yield a count range from 0 to 255. Moving the mouse just over four centimeters overflows the counters. This can occur when counting up (counter jumps from 255 to 0) as well as counting down (jump from 0 to 255). Therefore the count registers must be read at given intervals to check to see if an overflow or underflow has occurred.

The operating system does this during the vertical-blanking interrupt. This is based on the assumption that the mouse is not moved more than 127 count steps between two successive reads. The new counter state is compared with the last value read. If the difference is greater than 127, then the counter overflowed and the mouse was moved right or down. If it's less than -127, an underflow occurred corresponding to a mouse movement left or up.

| Old state | New state | Actual difference | Mouse movement | Over/underflow |
|---|---|---|---|---|
| 100 | 200 | -100 | +100 | no |
| 200 | 100 | +100 | -100 | no |
| 50 | 200 | -150 | -105 | underflow |
| 200 | 50 | +150 | +105 | overflow |

Difference = old counter state - new counter state

If an underflow occurred, the actual mouse movement is calculated as follows:

-255 - difference, or in numbers: -255 - (50-200) = -105

For an overflow:

255 - difference, or in numbers: 255 - (200-50) = +105

A positive mouse movement corresponds to a movement right or down, a negative value to left or up.

*JOYTEST $036 (write-only)*

The mouse counters can also be set through software. A value can be written to the counter through the JOYTEST register. JOYTEST operates on both game ports simultaneously, meaning that the horizontal and vertical counters of both mouses are set to the same values (JOY0DAT = JOY1DAT).

```
Bit no.:   15 14 13 12 11 10  9  8  7  6  5  4  3  2  1  0
Function:  Y7 Y6 Y5 Y4 Y3 Y2 xx xx  7 X6 X5 X4 X3 X2 xx xx
```

As you can see, only the highest-order six bits of the counters can be affected. This makes sense when you remember that the lowest two bits are taken directly from the mouse signals and aren't located anywhere in memory, and thus cannot be changed.

*The joysticks*

When you look at the pin-out of the game ports, you see that the four direction lines for the joysticks occupy the same lines as those for the mouse. It therefore seems reasonable that they can also be read with the same registers. In fact, the joystick lines are processed exactly like the mouse signals, each pair of lines is combined into the X0 and X1/Y0 and Y1 bits. The joystick position can be determined from these four bits:

| | | |
|---|---|---|
| Joystick right | X1 = 1 | (bit 1 JOYxDAT) |
| Joystick left | Y1 = 1 | (bit 9 JOYxDAT) |
| Joystick backward | X0 EOR X1 = 1 | (bits 0 and 1 JOYxDAT) |
| Joystick forward | Y0 EOR Y1 = 1 | (bits 8 and 9 JOYxDAT) |

In order to detect whether the joystick has been moved up or down, you must take the exclusive-OR of X0 and X1 and Y0 and Y1. If the result is 1, the joystick is in the position in question. The following assembly language program reads the joystick on game port 1:

```
TestJoystick:
  MOVE.W $DFFF000C, D0   ;move JOY1DAT to D0
  BTST #1, D0      ;test bit no. 1
  BNE RIGHT        ;set? if so, joystick right
  BTST #9, D0      ;test bit no. 9
  BNE LEFT         ;set? if so, joystick left
```

```
MOVE.W D0,D1      ;copy D0 to D1
LSR.W #1,D1       ;move Y1 and X1 to position of Y0 and X0
EOR.W D0,D1       ;exclusive OR: Y1 EOR Y0 and X1 EOR Y0
BTST #0, D1       ;test result of X1 EOR X0
BNE BACK          ;equal 1? if so, joystick backward
BTST #8, D1       ;test result of Y1 EOR Y0
BNE FORWARD       ;equal 1? if so, joystick forward
BRA MIDDLE        ;joystick is in the middle position
```

The exclusive-OR operation is performed as follows in this program:

A copy of the JOY1DAT register is placed in D1 and is shifted one bit to the right. Now X1 in D1 and X0 in D0 have the same bit position as Y1 and Y0. An EOR between D0 and D1 exclusive-ORs Y0 with Y1 and X0 with X1. All you have to do is test the result in D1 with the appropriate BTST commands.

This program does not support diagonal joystick positions.

*The paddles*

The Amiga has two analog inputs per game port so potentiometers can be connected. These have a given resistance in each position which can be determined by Paula. A paddle contains such a potentiometer which can be set with a knob. Analog joysticks also work this way. One potentiometer for the X and one for the Y direction determine the joystick position exactly.

Two registers contain the four eight-bit values of the analog inputs, POT0DAT for game port 0 and POT1DAT for game port 1.

*POT0DAT $012 POT1DAT $014*

```
Bit no.:  15 14 13 12 11 10  9  8  7  6  5  4  3  2  1  0
Function: Y7 Y6 Y5 Y4 Y3 Y2 Y1 Y0 X7 X6 X5 X4 X3 X2 X1 X0
```

(Both registers are read-only)

*How is the resistance measured?*

Since a computer can process only digital signals, it needs a special circuit to convert any analog signals it wants to work with. On the Amiga the value of external resistances is determined as follows:

The potentiometers have a maximum resistance of 470 kilo Ohms (±10%). One side is connected to the five-volt output and the other to one of the four paddle inputs of the game port. These lead internally to the corresponding inputs of Paula and to one of four capacitors connected between the input and ground.

The measurement is started by means of a special start bit. Paula places all paddle outputs at ground briefly, discharging the capacitors. Also, the counters in the POTxDAT registers are cleared. After this the counters increment by one with each screen line while the capacitors charge through the resistors. When the capacitor voltage exceeds a given value, the corresponding counter is stopped. Thus the counter state corresponds exactly to the size of the resistance. Small resistances correspond to small counter values, large to high values.

*The POTGO register:*

POTGO $034 (write-only) POTGOR $016 (read-only)

| Bit no. | Name | Function |
|---------|------|----------|
| 15 | OUTRY | Switch game port 1 POTY to output |
| 14 | DATRY | Game port 1 POTY data bit |
| 13 | OUTRX | Switch game port 1 POTX to output |
| 12 | DATRX | Game port 1 POTX data bit |
| 11 | OUTLY | Switch game port 0 POTY to output |
| 10 | DATLY | Game port 0 POTY data bit |
| 9 | OUTLX | Switch game port 0 POTX to output |
| 8 | DATLX | Game port 0 POTX data bit |
| 7 to 1 | | unused |
| 0 | START | Discharge capacitors and start measurement |

(A write access to POTGO clears both POTxDAT registers.)

Normally you set the START bit to 1 in the vertical blanking gap. The capacitors then charge up while the picture is being displayed, reach the set value, and the counters stop. The valid potentiometer readings can then be read in the next vertical blanking gap.

The four analog inputs can also be programmed as normal digital input/ output lines. The corresponding control and data bits are found together with the start bit in the POTGO register. Each line can be individually set to an output with the OUTxx bits (OUTxx=1). This separates them from the control circuit of the capacitors and the value of the DATxx bit in POTGO is output on these lines.

When reading the DATxx bits in POTGO the current state of the given line is always returned.

The following must be noted if the analog ports are used as outputs:

Since the four analog ports are internally connected to the capacitors for resistance measurement (47 nF), it can take up to 300 microseconds for the line to assume the desired level due to the charging/discharging of the capacitor required.

*The input device buttons*

Each of the three input devices mentioned so far have one or more buttons. The following table shows which registers contain the status of the mouse, paddle and joystick buttons:

*Game port 0:*

| | |
|---|---|
| Left mouse button | CIA-A, parallel port A, port bit 6 |
| Right mouse button | POTGO, DATLY |
| (Third mouse button | POTGO, DATLX) |
| Joystick fire button | CIA-A, parallel port A, port bit 6 |
| Left paddle button | JOY0DAT, bit 9 (1=button pressed) |
| Right paddle button | JOY0DAT, bit 1 (1=button pressed) |

*Game port 1:*   Left mouse button        CIA-A, parallel port A, port bit 7
                 Right mouse button       POTGO, DATRY
                 (Third mouse button      POTGO, DATRX)
                 Joystick fire button     CIA-A, parallel port A, port bit 7
                 Left paddle button       JOY1DAT, bit 9 (1=button pressed)
                 Right paddle button      JOY1DAT, bit 1 (1=button pressed)

(Unless specified otherwise, all bits are zero-active, meaning that 0=button pressed.)

---

## 1.5.11          The serial interface

As we discussed in Section 1.3.4, the Amiga has a standard RS-232 interface. The various lines of this connector can be divided into two signal groups:

1.     The serial data lines
2.     The handshake lines

First about the handshake lines: The RS-232 interface has a number of handshake lines. Normally they are not all used. Moreover, the behavior of these signals is not the same from RS-232 device to device. The operation and programming of these lines was already described in Section 1.3.4.

*Serial data line*

The entire transfer of data takes place over these two data lines. The RXD line receives the data and it is sent out over TXD. RS-232 communication can thus take place in two directions at once when two devices are connected together through RXD and TXD. The RXD of one device is connected to the TXD of the other, and vice versa.

*Figure 1.5.11.1*

### Principle of serial RS-232 data transfer

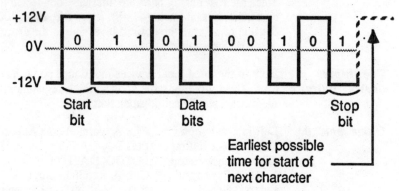

**Principle of serial RS-232 data transfer**

Since only one line is available for the data transfer in each direction, the data words must be converted into a serial data stream which can then be transmitted bit by bit. No clock lines are provided in the RS-232 standard. So that the receiver knows when it can read the next bit, the time per bit must be constant, that is, the speed with which the data is sent and received must be well defined. This is called the baud rate and it determines the number of bits transferred per second. Common baud rates are, for example, 300, 1200, 2400, 4800 and 9600. You are not limited to these baud rates, but care must be taken when using strange baud rates that the sender and receiver actually match.

One more thing required for successful transfer is that the receiver must know when a byte starts and ends. Figure 1.5.11.1 shows the transmission of a byte on one of the data lines. Each byte begins with a start bit which is no different from the normal data bits and which always has the value 0. Following this are the data bits in the order LSB to MSB. At the end are one or two stop bits which have the value 1. The receiver recognizes the transition from one byte to the next by the level change from 1 to 0 which occurs when a start bit follows a stop bit.

**The UART register**

The component which performs this serial transfer is called a Universal Asynchronous Receiver/Transmitter, or UART. In the Amiga it is contained in Paula and its registers are in the custom chip register area:

*SERPER $032 (write-only)*

| Bit no. | Name | Function |
|---------|------|----------|
| 15 | LONG | Set length of the receive data to 9 bits |
| 0 to 14 | RATE | This 15-bit number contains the baud rate |

*SERDAT $030 (write-only)*

SERDAT contains the send data

*SERDATR $018 (read-only)*

| Bit no. | Name | Function |
|---------|------|----------|
| 15 | OVRUN | Overrun of the receiver shift register |
| 14 | RBF | Receive buffer full |
| 13 | TBE | Transmit buffer empty |
| 12 | TSRE | Transmitter shift register empty |
| 11 | RXD | Corresponds to the level on the RXD line |
| 10 | — | unused |
| 9 | STP | Stop bit |
| 8 | DB8 | Depends on the data length |
| 7 | DB7 | Receiver data buffer bit 7 |
| 6 | DB6 | Receiver data buffer bit 6 |
| 5 | DB5 | Receiver data buffer bit 5 |
| 4 | DB4 | Receiver data buffer bit 4 |
| 3 | DB3 | Receiver data buffer bit 3 |
| 2 | DB2 | Receiver data buffer bit 2 |
| 1 | DB1 | Receiver data buffer bit 1 |
| 0 | DB0 | Receiver data buffer bit 0 |

One bit in the ADKCON register belongs to the UART control:

*ADKCON $09E (write)   ADKCONR $010 (read)*

Bit no. 11: UARTBRK

This bit interrupts the serial output and sets TXD to 0

---

# 1.5.12     Data transfer with the Amiga UART

*Receiving*

The reception of the serial data takes place in two stages. The bits arriving on the RXD pin are received into the shift register at the baud rate and are combined into a parallel data word. When the shift register is full its contents are written into the receiver data buffer. It is then free for the next data. The processor can only read the received data buffer, not the shift register. The corresponding data bits in the SERDATR register are DB0 to DB7 or DB8.

The Amiga can receive both eight and nine-bit data words. The UART can be set to nine-bit words with the LONG bit (=1) in the SERPER register.

The data length determines the format in the SERDATR register. With nine bits, bit 8 of SERDATR contains the ninth data bit, while the stop bit is found in bit 9. With eight data bits, bit 8 contains the stop bit. If two stop bits are present, the second lands in bit 9.

The state of the receiver shift register and the data buffer is given by two signal bits in SERDATR:

RBF stands for Receive Buffer Full. As soon as a data word is transferred from the shift register to the buffer, this bit changes to 1 and thereby signals the microprocessor that it should read the data out of SERDATR.

This bit also exists in the interrupt registers (RBF, INTREQ/INTEN bit no. 11). After the processor has read the data it must reset RBF in INTREQ. It then returns to zero in both INTREGR and in SERDATR.

```
MOVE.W #$0800,$DFF000+INTREQ
;clears RBF in INTREQ and SERDATR
```

If this is not done and the shift register has received another complete data word, the UART sets the OVRUN bit. This signals that no more data can be received because both the buffer (RBF=1) and the shift register (OVRUN=1) are full. OVRUN returns to 0 when RBF is reset. RBF then jumps back to 1 because the contents of the shift register are immediately transferred from DB0 to DB8 in order to make the shift register free for new data.

*Transmit*

The sending procedure is also performed in two stages. The transmit data buffer is found in the SERDAT register. As soon as a data word is written into this register it is transferred to the output shift register. This is signaled by the TBE bit. TBE stands for Transmit Buffer Empty and indicates that SERDAT is ready to receive more data. TBE is also present in the interrupt registers (TBE, INTREQ/INTEN, bit no. 0). Like RBF, TBE must also be reset in the INTREQ register.

Once the shift register has sent the data word, the next one is automatically loaded from the transmitter data buffer. If this is empty, the UART sets the TSRE bit (Transmit Shift Register Empty) to 1. This bit is reset when TBE is cleared.

The length of the data word and the number of stop bits are set by the format of the data in SERDAT. You simply write the desired data word in the lower eight or nine bits of SERDAT with one or two stop bits in front of it depending on the number of stop bits. An eight-bit data word with two stop bits would look like this, for example:

```
Bit no.: 15 14 13 12 11 10  9  8  7  6  5  4  3  2  1  0
Function: 0  0  0  0  0  0  1  1 D7 D6 D5 D4 D3 D2 D1 D0
```

D0 to D7 are the eight data bits.

The two ones stand for the desired stop bits.

With a nine-bit data word and one stop bit the following data must be written into SERDAT:

```
Bit no.: 15 14 13 12 11 10  9  8  7  6  5  4  3  2  1  0
Function: 0  0  0  0  0  0  1 D8 D7 D6 D5 D4 D3 D2 D1 D0
```

Eight bits plus one stop bit:

```
Bit no.: 15 14 13 12 11 10  9  8  7  6  5  4  3  2  1  0
Function: 0  0  0  0  0  0  0  1 D7 D6 D5 D4 D3 D2 D1 D0
```

The LONG bit in the SERPER register affects only the length of the data received. The format of the transmitted data is affected only by the value in the SERDAT register.

*Setting the baud rate*

The baud rate for both send and receiving data must be written in the lower 15 bits of the SERPER register. Unfortunately the baud rate can not be set directly. You must select the number of bus cycles between two bits (1 bus cycle takes $1.79365 * 10^{-7}$ seconds). If a bit is output every n bus cycles, the value n-1 must be written in the SERPER register. The following formula can be used to calculate the necessary SERPER value from the baud rate:

$$SERPER = \frac{1}{baud\ rate * 2.79365 * 10^{-7}} - 1$$

For example, for a baud rate of 4800 baud:

```
SERPER = 1/(4800*2.79365*10-7)-1 = 1/0.00134-1=744.74
```

The calculated value is rounded and written in SERPER:

```
MOVE.W #745,$DFF000+SERPER ;set SERPER, LONG = 0
or MOVE.W #$8000+745,$DFF000+SERPER ;LONG = 1
```

## 1.5.13     The disk controller

The hardware control of the disk drives is divided into two parts.

First there are the control lines which activate the desired drive, turn the motor on, move the read/write head, etc. They all lead to various port lines of the CIAs. Information about these control lines can be found in Section 1.3.5.

Excluded from these are the data lines. These carry the data from the read/write head to the Amiga and, when writing, in the opposite direction from the Amiga to the diskette. A special component in Paula, the disk controller, handles the processing of the data.

It has its own DMA channel and writes or reads data by itself to or from the disk.

*Programming the disk DMA*
Before you start the disk DMA you must be sure that the previous disk DMA is finished. If one interrupts a write operation in progress, the data on the corresponding track can be destroyed. Let's assume that the last disk DMA is done.

First we must define the memory address of the data buffer. The disk DMA uses one of the usual address register pairs as a pointer to the chip RAM. The registers are called DSKPTH and DSKPTL:

$20 DSKPTH   Pointer to data from/to disk bits 16-18
$22 DSKPTL   Pointer to data from/to disk bits 0-15

Next the DSKLEN register must be initialized. It is constructed as follows:

*DSKLEN $024 (write-only)*

| Bit no. | Name | Function |
|---------|------|----------|
| 15 | DMAEN | Enable disk DMA |
| 14 | WRITE | Write data to the disk |
| 0-13 | LENGTH | Number of data words to be transferred |

LENGTH   The lower 14 bits of the DSKLEN register contain the number of data words to be transferred.

WRITE   WRITE = 1 switches the disk controller from read to write.

DMAEN   When DMAEN is set to 1 the data transfer begins. The following points must be observed:

1.   The disk DMA enables a bit in the DMACON register (DSKEN, bit no. 4) must also be set.

2.   To make it more difficult to write to the disk accidentally, you must set the DMAEN bit twice in succession. Then the disk DMA begins. In addition, for safety's sake the WRITE bit should only be 1 during a write operation. An orderly initialization sequence for DMA disk is as follows:

   1.   Write a 0 to DSKLEN to turn DMAEN off.
   2.   If DSKEN in DMACON is not yet set, do so now.
   3.   Store the desired address in DSKPTH and DSKPTL.
   4.   Write the correct value for LENGTH and WRITE along with a set DMAEN bit to DSKLEN.
   5.   Write the same value into DSKLEN again.
   6.   Wait until the disk DMA is done (see below).
   7.   For safety's sake, set DSKLEN back to zero.

The DSKBLK interrupt (disk block finished, bit no. 1 in INTREQ/INTEN) is provided so that the processor knows when the disk controller has transferred the number of words defined in LENGTH. It is generated when the last data word is read or written.

The current status of the disk controller can be read in the DSKBYTR register:

*DSKBYTR $01A (read-only)*

| Bit no. | Name | Function |
|---------|------|----------|
| 15 | BYTEREADY | This bit signals that the data byte in the lower eight bits is valid. |
| 14 | DMAON | DMACON indicates whether the disk DMA is operating. To make DMAON=1 both DMAEN in DSKLEN and DSKEN in DMACON must be set. |
| 13 | DSKWRITE | Indicates the state of the WRITE in DSKLEN. |
| 12 | WORDEQUAL | Disk data equals DSKSYNC |
| 11 to 8 | | unused |
| 7 to 0 | DATA | Current data byte from the disk |

With the 8 DATA bits and the BYTEREADY flag you can read the data from the disk with the processor instead of through DMA. Each time a complete byte is received the disk controller sets the BYTEREADY bit. The processor then knows that the data byte in the 8 DATA bits is valid. After the DSKBYTR register is read the BYTEREADY flag is automatically reset.

Sometimes we don't want to read an entire track into memory at once. In this case the DMA transfer can be made to start at a given position. To do this, write the data word at which you want the disk controller to start into the DSKSYNC register:

*DSKSYNC $07E (write-only)*

DSKSYNC contains the data word at which the transfer is to start.

The disk controller then starts as usual after the disk DMA is enabled and reads the data from the disk, but it doesn't write it into memory. Instead, it continually compares each data word with the word in DSKSYNC. When the two match it starts the data transfer, which then continues as usual. Thus the disk controller can be programmed to wait for the synchronization mark at the start of a data block.

The WORDEQUAL bit in the DSKBYTR register is 1 as soon as the DATA read and DSKSYNC match. Since this match lasts only two (or four) microseconds, WORDEQUAL is also set only during this time span. An interrupt is also generated at the same time WORDEQUAL goes to 1:

Bit no. 12 in the INTREQ and INTEN registers is the DSKSYN interrupt bit. It is set when the data from the disk matches DSKSYNC.

*Setting the operating parameters*

The data cannot be written to the disk in the same format as they are found in memory. They must be specially coded. Normally the Amiga uses MFM coding. It is also possible to use GCR coding, however. Two steps are necessary for selecting the desired coding:

1.  An appropriate routine must encode the data before it is written to disk and decode the data read from disk.
2.  The disk controller must be set for the appropriate coding. This is done with certain bits in the ADKCON register.

*ADKCON $09E (write) ADKCONR $010 (read)*

| Bit no. | Name | Function |
| --- | --- | --- |
| 15 | SET/CLR | Set (SET/CLR=1) or clear bits |
| 14-13 | PRECOMP | These bits contain the precompensation value: |

| | Bit 14 | Bit 13 | PRECOMP time |
| --- | --- | --- | --- |
| | 0 | 0 | Zero |
| | 0 | 1 | 140 ns |
| | 1 | 0 | 280 ns |
| | 1 | 1 | 560 ns |

| Bit no. | Name | Function |
| --- | --- | --- |
| 12 | MFMPREC | 0 = GCR, 1 = MFM |
| 11 | UARTNRK | not used for the disk controller, see UART |
| 10 | WORDSYNC | WORDSYNC=1 enables the synchronization of the disk controller described above. |
| 9 | MSBSYNC | MSBSYNC=1 enables the GCR synchronization |

| 8   | FAST  | Disk controller clock rate:<br>FAST=1: 2 microseconds/bit (MFM)<br>FAST=0: 4 microseconds/bit (GCR) |
| 7-0 | AUDIO | These bits do not belong to the disk<br>controller, see Section 1.5.8. |

*The disk controller data registers*

As usual the DMA controller transfers data from the memory to and from the appropriate registers. The disk controller has one data register for data read from the disk and one for the data to be written to the disk.

*DSKDAT $026 (write-only)*

Contains the data to be written to the disk.

*DSKDATR $008 (read-only)*

Contains the data from the disk. This is a early-read register and cannot be read by the processor.

# 2
# Exec

# 2.1 Operating system fundamentals

In this chapter we'll examine the Amiga's operating system, something with which any successful programmer (or those who want to be) must be familiar with.

The operating system at the top of the address space comprises 256K ($FC0000-$FFFFFF) while the Amiga 500 and 2000 contain this in ROM. This large memory space contains a number of routines which can make the programmer's work much easier. On the Amiga these routines are grouped according to their various tasks. You can imagine the system as a number of well-matched modules which divide the various operating system tasks among themselves. The most important parts are obvious: DOS (input/output control), graphics, Intuition (a collection of large complex routines for window and screen management) and Exec.

The task of Exec is to manage the multitasking and thereby allow multiple programs to operate concurrently. Exec also represents the lowest level between the hardware and the program. From these tasks it's easy to see that Exec is the most important part of the Amiga operating system.

Each part of the system offers a number of powerful routines which can be easily used by the programmer. To make them easier to call, the routines belonging to a given part of the operating system are combined into a jump table. Section 2.3 explains how these routines are called.

The communication between Exec and the hardware is not direct, but it is handled by a device driver. Exec makes available a set of routines to access the device handlers. Naturally, it is also possible to access the Amiga hardware directly in machine language without using a device driver, but in general this means that the multitasking capabilities of the system must be forfeited.

# 2.2    Introduction to programming the Amiga

Now that we have explained the rough construction of the Amiga operating system, we want to look more closely at the actual programming.

*Note:*    All assembly language listings from the Kickstart area refer to Kickstart Version 1.2, which is built into ROM on both the Amiga 500 and 2000. For owners of an Amiga 1000, these listings apply only if this same version of Kickstart is used.

## 2.2.1    Differences between C and assembly language

Everyone knows that assembly language is faster than C. This means that assembly language solves some programming problems better than C or any other high-level language. What assembly language programmers must take into account when using operating system routines or structures is probably less well known, however.

Let's start with calling routines with parameters. In C it looks like this:

```
Entry = FindName (list,name)
  D0               A0   A1
```

FindName is a routine for finding an entry in a list. The parameters which must be passed are a pointer to the start of the linked list and the name of the entry to be found. For assembly language programmers the registers in which the parameters must be passed are listed for the routines (functions) which we describe. From the routine we get the pointer to the entry, which in this example is stored in Entry. The pointer returned by the function is passed for this and other function calls in register D0. If there is more than one return parameter, other registers are used.

The call is basically the same in assembly language. You just have to pass the parameters to the routine in the appropriate registers.

```
LEA.L        LIST,A0
LEA.L        NAME,A1
JSR          FINDNAME
MOVE.L       D0,MEMORY
               •
               •
               •
NAME:
DC.B  "NAME",0
```

First the pointer to the list must be written to A0. A1 must contain a pointer to the name for which you want to search. This string must be terminated with a zero. The routine is then called and the pointer to the entry found is returned in D0, where it can be stored somewhere else.

So much for calling routines. Next let's look at what structures look like in C and assembly language.

```
struct {
      struct Node * ln_Succ;
      struct Node *ln_Pred;
      UBYTE ln_Type;
      BYTE ln_Pri;
      char *ln_Name;
      };
```

We won't go into the meaning of the structure here. It is used only to demonstrate the differences between C and assembly language. Initializing the structure should be no problem.

Example:

```
      ln_Pri = 20;
```

With this assignment the value 20 is stored as a signed single-byte value in the structure. In assembly language such a C structure exists as a table. The values are in the same order as that given in the structure, placed in memory according to their length. You must know the base address of such a table in order to access it.

For this example it looks as follows:

```
Base + 0     $00000000     Pointer to successor ln_Succ
Base + 4     $00000000     Pointer to predecessor ln_Pred
Base + 8     $00           ln_Type
Base + 9     $00           ln_Pri
Base + 10    $00000000     Pointer to Name ln_Name
```

The zeros stand for any values and are used to show the length of the entries. To set ln_Pri to 20 as in the previous C example, you must know the base address of the structure. If this is the case, you are ready to set the ln_Pri field.

```
LEA.L        Base+9,A0
MOVE.B       #20,(A0)
```

You can see that accessing structures in assembly language doesn't represent any problems. Naturally, it isn't quite as easy as in C. Assembly language does have the advantage, however, that it is faster than C and it allows better access to the hardware. Also, assembly language allows access to some routines which cannot be used in C. These routines refer to parts of the operating system which the normal programmer has no need to access, but which are used for certain tricks, such as for managing the multitasking.

## 2.2.2    Construction of nodes

Next we want to discus. one of the most important basic structures. It is essential that you understand this material in the following sections for this to make any sense

First we present the node 'structure. It is used to create a linked list, which are very common in the Amiga. It has the following appearance:

In C:

```
struct
    struct Node * ln_Succ;
    struct Node *ln_Pred;
    UBYTE ln_Type;
    BYTE ln_Pri;
    char *ln_Name;
    };
```

in assembly language:

```
Base + 0     $00000000     Pointer to successor ln_Succ
Base + 4     $00000000     Pointer to predecessor ln_Pred
Base + 8     $00           ln_Type
Base + 9     $00           ln_Pri
Base + 10    $00000000     Pointer to Name ln_Name
```

This structure can be divided into two parts. The first is the link part (ln_Succ and ln_Pred) and the second is the data part (Type, Priority and Name).

*ln_Succ
    This is a pointer to the next node (successor).

*ln_Pred
    This is a pointer to the previous node (predecessor).

ln_Type
> The various types of the node are coded and stored in this byte.

ln_Pri
> The priority of the node. Only in certain cases, such as for a task node, does it make any sense to set this field to a value other than zero. More about this later.

*ln_Name
> In this long word a pointer to the null-terminated string is stored. It's the name of the node, which is generally chosen such that the node can be uniquely identified by its name, simplifying debugging immensely.

*Initializing a node*

Before a node is appended to a list it must first be properly initialized.

First the type must be set. Here one has a choice between various standardized types, listed below:

| Node type | Code |
|-----------|------|
| NT_TASK | 01 |
| NT_INTERRUPT | 02 |
| NT_DEVICE | 03 |
| NT_MSGPORT | 04 |
| NT_MESSAGE | 05 |
| NT_FREEMSG | 06 |
| NT_REPLYMSG | 07 |
| NT_RESOURCE | 08 |
| NT_LIBRARY | 09 |
| NT_MEMORY | 10 |
| NT_SOFTINT | 11 |
| NT_FONT | 12 |
| NT_PROCESS | 13 |
| NT_SEMAPHORE | 14 |

Thus specifying the node type is very easy. Simply find the type which goes with your node and enter its code.

Let's assume that you want to initialize a node found in a task structure. To understand how this initialization works, we'll first show how a task structure is constructed.

```
struct Task {
    struct Node tc_Node;
        .
        .
        .
};
```

The node type is initialized in C as follows:

```
struct Task mytask;  /* mytask is the name of the task
                        structure */
mytask.tc_Node.ln_Type = NT_TASK;
```

Here is the same initialization in assembly language:

```
LEA.L        mytask,A0        ;base address of the task in A0
MOVE.L       #01,8(A0)        ;set type = task (value 01)
```

After the type has been set, the priority of the node is specified in relationship to the other nodes. This can be a value between -128 and +127. The larger the value, the higher the priority, so +127 is the highest and -128 the lowest priority.

Some Exec lists are ordered according to the priorities of their entries, whereby the entry with the highest priority is placed at the front. Most Exec lists do not use the ln_Pri entry, however. It is best to set the priority of such list entries (nodes) to zero.

The priority is set as follows:

```
mytask.tc_Node.ln_Pri = 5;
```

And in assembly language:

```
LEA.L        mytask,A0        ;base address of the task in A0
MOVE.L       #05,9(A0)        ;set Pri to 5
```

Finally, we have to specify the name of the node and thereby that of the task.

In C:

```
mytask.tc_Node.ln_Name = "Example task";
```

In assembly language:

```
LEA.L        mytask,A0        ;base address of the task in A0
LEA.L        Name,A1          ;address of the name in A1
MOVE.L       A1,10(A0)        ;enter pointer to name
Name:
DC.B         "Example task",0
```

As said before, the string must be terminated with a zero byte.

This example shows that you must know the position of the corresponding entry in order to initialize the structure in assembly language. This position is called the offset from the base address. In our last example this offset was 10.

The initialization of ln_Succ and ln_Pred is discussed in the next section.

## 2.2.3    Lists

What exactly is a list and what does it contain? A list is a series of node structures which are linked together in both directions (called a doubly-linked list). In the first position of a node structure is a pointer (ln_Succ) to the next node. In the second position is a pointer (ln_Pred) to the previous node.

In order to manage a linked list better, a head node is introduced which is immediately found at the start or end of the linked list. Apart from this information, the structure also indicates what type of entries are found in the list. The list structure has the following appearance:

The numbers in front of the structure members in the following list structure are their offsets so that they can also be accessed in assembly language. The offsets do not belong to the C structure and thus are not entered along with it. They are only to aid the assembly language programmer.

```
struct List {
0      struct Node *lh_Head;
4      struct Node *lh_Tail;
8      struct Node *lh_TailPred;
12     UBYTE lh_Type;
13     UBYTE ly_pad;
};
```

*lh_Head
        is a pointer to the first entry (node) of the list

*lh_Tail
        is always zero

*lh_TailPred
        is a pointer to the last valid entry in the list

lh_Type
        specifies the type of nodes in the list. lh_Type is set as per the type of the node

lh_pad
        is contained in the structure, but is not used

The pointer ln_Succ of the last entry in the list points to lh_Tail (second entry of the list structure). lh_Tail is zero (NIL) and indicates that the node which you attempted to access is no longer valid.

The ln_Pred pointer of the first node points to lh_Tail (also in the list structure). The zero thus indicates that the previous entry read from the list was the first.

*Figure  2.2.3.1*

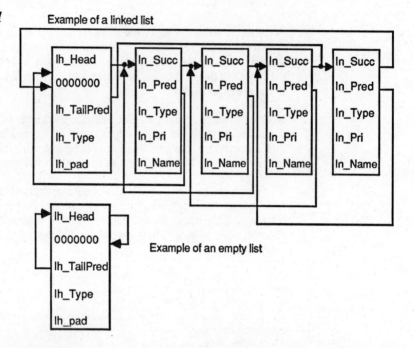

Example of a linked list

Example of an empty list

*Initializing a list*

Now that we have seen what a linked list looks like, we want to try to create one. We must first create a new list structure and designate it as empty. The initialization of a task list in C looks like this:

```
#include "exec/lists.h"
main ()
{
struct List list1;
list1.lh_Head = (struct Node *)&list1.lh_Tail;
list1.lh_Tail = 0;
list1.lh_TailPred = (struct Node *)&list1.lh_Head;
list1.lh_Type = NT_TASK;
}
```

In assembly language it looks like this:

```
LEA.L        list1,A0
MOVE.L       A0,(A0)
ADDQ.L       #04,(A0)
CLR.L        #04(A0)
MOVE.L       A0,8(A0)
MOVE.B       #01,12(A0)
```

The list we just created is, of course, empty. We'll talk about inserting nodes into the list later. Here we show how a list is recognized as empty. There are two ways of doing this. First, you can test to see if lh_Head is zero (NIL), or second, if lh_TailPRED points to the start of the list (lh_Head). If this is the case, then the list in question is empty.

This is done in C as follows:

```
if (list1.TailPred == &list1) {
    printf("list is empty");
}
```

Or:

```
if (list1.lh_Head->ln_Succ == 0) {
    printf("list is empty");
}
```

## 2.2.4        Exec routines for list management

Exec offers a variety of very useful functions for managing lists. The first function is the Insert() function. It is used to insert nodes into a list at a given position.

*Insert()*

```
Insert (list, node, predecessor)
         A0    A1    A2
```

Offset:        -234

Parameters:

list    is a pointer to the list in which the node is inserted.

node    is a pointer to the node to insert into the list.

predecessor
        is a pointer to the node after which the given node is inserted. If this pointer is set to a value other than zero, the pointer passed in the list parameter is no longer relevant. The specified list is not searched for the position of the specified node (in order to determine if the desired node actually exists). Instead, the predecessor parameter is assumed to be correct and the node is inserted. If the predecessor is zero, the node is inserted at the first position. The second way of inserting a node in the first position of a list is to set predecessor to lh_Head. Inserting at the last position is accomplished by setting the predecessor parameter to lh_TailPred. There are also separate functions for inserting in the first or last positions.

*Remove()*

```
Remove (node)
        A1
```

Offset:    -252

Description:
Like the name says, this function removes a node from a list.

Parameters:

node    Pointer to the node to be removed. If node doesn't actually point
        to a list entry, Exec tries to remove the node anyway, possibly
        leading to information loss or a system crash.

*AddHead()*

```
AddHead(list,node)
        A0   A1
```

Offset:    -240

Description:
This function is used to insert nodes at the head of a list.

Parameters:

list    is a pointer to the list in which the node is inserted.

node    is a pointer to the node to be inserted.

*RemHead()*

```
RemHead(list)
        A0
```

Offset:    -258

Description:
Removes the first node in a list.

Parameters:

list    is a pointer to the list whose first node is removed.

*AddTail()*

```
AddTail(list,node)
        A0   A1
```

Offset:    -246

Description:
Inserts a node as the last element of a list.

Parameters:

list    is a pointer to the list in which the node is inserted.

node    is a pointer to the node to be inserted.

*RemTail()*        RemTail(list)
                    A0

Offset:    -258

Description:
        Removes the last node in a list.

Parameters:

list    is a pointer to the list whose last node is removed.

*Enqueue()*      Enqueue(list, node)
                    A0  A1

Offset:    -270

Description:
        This function is used to order entries in a list according to their priority. As explained in the section on nodes, nodes with higher priorities are placed at the front of the list. If multiple nodes of the same priority are present in a list, the most recently inserted node is placed after the others.

Parameters:

list    is a pointer to the list in which the node is entered.

node  is a pointer to the node to be inserted.

*FindName()*     Entry = FindName(list, "name")
             D0             A0   A1

Offset:    -276

Description:
        FindName searches a list for a node with a given name.

Parameters:

list    is a pointer to the list to be searched.

name  is a pointer to the name for which to search. This string must be terminated with a zero.

Result:

This function returns a pointer to the node found. If an entry with the specified name is not found, a zero is returned.

The following example shows how to determine whether a name occurs twice in a node. This example cannot be run "as is" because the list must be initialized before the FindName() call or the computer crashes.

```
#include <exec/lists.h>
main()

{
struct Node *FindName(),*node;
struct List *list1;

if ((node = FindName(list1,"test node"))!=0)
    if ((node = FindName(node, "test node")) !=0)
            printf("\n the name 'test node' was found
            twice\n");
}
```

Now that we have listed the functions available for processing lists, we should clarify them with an example. Our example shows how a list is created, output, and how entries are deleted from it.

*List example:*
```
#include <exec/lists.h>

char *name[] = {"node1","node2","node3"};

struct List liste;
struct Node node[3],*np;

main ()

{
    int i;
    char n;
    liste.lh_Head = (struct Node *) &liste.lh_Tail;
    liste.lh_Tail = 0;
    liste.lh_TailPred = (struct Node *) &liste.lh_Head;
    liste.lh_Type = NT_TASK;

    for (i=0;i<=2;i++) {
        node[i].ln_Type = NT_TASK;
        node[i].ln_Name = name[i];

        AddTail (&liste,&node[i]);
    }

    output ();
    printf ("\n Output the finished list.\n");

    np = liste.lh_Head->ln_Succ;
    Remove (np);
    output();
    printf ("\n 2nd node skipped.\n");
}
```

```
output ()
{
   for (np = liste.lh_Head;
        np != &liste.lh_Tail;
        np = np->ln_Succ)
           printf ("\n %s \n",np->ln_Name);
}
```

Here is the output from the list_node.c program:

```
>list_node

node1

node2

node3

Output the finished list.

node1

node3

2nd node skipped.
```

# 2.3     Libraries

This section is intended for both C and assembly language programmers. It is essential to understand this material if you want to be able to make full use of the Amiga's capabilities.

What actually is a library? A library in this sense is a set of functions which can be used by the programmer. It is, to be precise, a large jump table from which functions can be called. Libraries are used so that programmers can use functions which are not available in C and not easily available in assembly language, but which are made available by the operating system. An example of this is the OpenScreen() function for creating a custom screen. C doesn't offer this function, so it must be called with the help of a library.

A library has the following appearance:

```
      .
      .
      .
00060A  JMP $FC2FD6
000610  JMP $FC0B28
000616  JMP $FC0AC0
      .
      .
      .
```

The libraries are divided into various function groups. Most of these are already contained in the ROM of the computer; some must be loaded in from disk as required. The following libraries are available:

- clist.lib
- console.lib
- diskfont.lib
- dos.lib
- expansion.lib
- exec.lib
- graphics.lib
- icon.lib
- intuition.lib
- layers.lib
- mathffp.lib
- mathieeedoubbas.lib
- mathtrans.lib
- potgo.lib
- ram.lib
- timer.lib
- translator.lib

The Exec library has a special status since its functions are available immediately after reset. If you want to use a function from another library, the system must be told, which then calls the corresponding library. If this library was already called, the programmer tells the program where to find the library.

Normally all that is known about a library is its base address, from which the desired function can be called with a negative offset.

A library call looks like this:

```
move.l      libBase,a6      ;base address of the library
jsr         offset(a6)
```

The offset of the corresponding function must be taken from the tables in the Appendix of this book. The parameters (if any) must be loaded into the appropriate registers before the function is called.

As we said, the Exec library functions are available immediately after a reset. To call its functions, its base address must be known. The base address of the Exec library is stored in memory location $04. You can see this base address in C by reading the standard variable SysBase.

Calling an Exec library function from C is very easy. As an example we show a call to the FindName function.

```
#include <exec/execbase.h>
struct ExecBase *SysBase;
struct Library *FindName(), *library;


main()

{
    library = FindName(&(SysBase->LibList),"dos.library");
    printf("\n %x \n",library);

}
```

This little C program searches through the list of all available libraries for the DOS library. If this is found, the address at which it is located is printed, else a zero is printed.

You can see that except for the perhaps confusing-looking assignment in the function call there is nothing unusual about Exec functions. You know from the previous section that the FindName function must be given a pointer to a list and the name of the node. The appearance of this particular function call is discussed in the section on ExecBase.

Let's take a look at how the C compiler translates this program into assembly language. If we restrict ourselves to the important parts, the translated program looks like this:

```
        global _SysBase,4
        global _library,4


        _main:

        pea *Node              ;push pointer to Node onto the stack
        move.l _SysBase,a6     ;pointer to ExecBase (from $4)
        pea 378(a6)            ;push pointer to list on the stack
        jsr _FindName          ;call FindName function
        move.l d0,_library     ;save return value in library
        move.l _library,-(a7)  ;and pass to _printf
        jsr _printf            ;on the stack
        rts


        _FindName
        movem.l 4(sp),a0/a1    ;get parameters for FindName from the
                               ;stack and load into the proper
                               ;registers
        move.l _SysBase,A6     ;get base address of the Exec library
        jmp -276(a6)           ;call function FindName
```

The complete assembly listing produced by the compiler is somewhat more comprehensive, but nothing essential to the understanding of the library function call has been omitted.

_SysBase is a pointer to the Exec library, whose functions are called with negative offsets. If you access memory with positive offsets on _SysBase, you get the values of ExecBase (the main structure of the operating system), which we'll go into later.

The compilation is a bit complicated, but it can still be readily understood.

The main program puts the pointers to the list and the node on the stack and then calls the subroutine. There the parameters just stored are loaded into the appropriate registers. Then the base address of the Exec library is fetched and written in A6. Now everything is ready to call the actual FindName function from the Exec library. The offset of this function is -276, as can be found in its description in Section 2.2.4. Thus the actual function call is "jmp -276(a6)". The parameter returned is stored in _library, pushed into the stack, and then printed with _printf.

Since the location of the Exec library is known to the system, its functions can be called without problems. If you want to call a function from another library, neither the operating system nor the compiler knows where this library can be found. Therefore the Exec library has a function with which the base addresses of the other libraries can be obtained. This function is called OpenLibrary and has the following syntax:

```
LibPtr = OpenLibrary(LibName,Version)
   D0                   A1        D0
```

*LibName*      LibName is a pointer to the zero-terminated name of the library to be opened, such as intuition.library.

*Version*      Version indicates the library version which the user wants to open. If several libraries have the same name, the version is used to distinguish them. If a new version is requested which is not available, the OpenLibrary call fails.

*LibPtr*       LibPtr contains, after the call, the base address of the desired library, assuming it was found. If it was not, a zero is returned.

The variable name in which the base address of the library is stored cannot be chosen at will. So that the C compiler knows the base address of the library from which a function is being called, it must be stored in a variable reserved for it. If this variable is declared but not initialized to the proper value, the call to the library function causes the program or computer to crash.

Listing of the predefined variables:

| Library | Variable |
| --- | --- |
| clist.lib | CListBase |
| diskfont.lib | DiskFontBase |
| dos.lib | DosBase |
| expansion.lib | ExpansionBase |
| exec.lib | SysBase |
| graphics.lib | GfxBase |
| icon.lib | IconBase |
| intuition.lib | IntuitionBase |
| layers.lib | LayersBase |
| mathffp.lib | MathBase |
| mathieeedoubbas.lib | MathIeeeDoubBasBase |
| mathtrans.lib | MathTransBase |
| potgo.lib | PotgoBase |
| translator.lib | TranslatorBase |

There are various ways to declare this reserved variable. The easiest way is to declare them as ULONG (Unsigned LONG word) to avoid pointer conversion. Naturally, when declaring them as ULONG the include file exec/types.h must also be included or the compiler won't know what ULONG means.

## 2.3.1        Opening a library

Let's take a look at an example of how to use and open a library. The
following example opens the Intuition library and then its own screen.

```
#include <exec/types.h>
#include <intuition/intuition.h>

struct NewScreen ns ={
                      0,0,
                      640,200,
                      2,
                      0,1,
                      HIRES,
                      CUSTOMSCREEN,
                      NULL,
             (UBYTE *)  "My screen",
                      NULL,
                      NULL };

ULONG IntuitionBase;

main()
{
ULONG screen;

if (!(IntuitionBase = OpenLibrary("intution.library")))
   exit(100);

screen = OpenScreen(&ns);
}
```

After exec/types.h and the Intuition structures have been included, the
screen structure is declared and IntuitionBase is declared as ULONG.
IntuitionBase must be declared globally because it must be used by the
procedures linked into the program (OpenScreen). Then the OpenLi-
brary() function of the Exec library is called. The Intuition library is
opened and the base address of the library is stored in IntuitionBase. The
OpenScreen functions are then called.

Let's take a look at what the compiler turns this program into. The
actual compiled version is somewhat longer and the unimportant parts
are omitted here.

```
_ns:                             ;initialize the screen structure
  dc.w 0
  dc.w 0
  dc.w 640
  dc.w 200
  dc.w 2
  dc.b 0
  dc.b 1
  dc.w -32768
  dc.w 15
  dc.l $0000
  dc.l .1+0
  dc.l $0000
  dc.l $0000
.1:
  dc.b "My screen",0

global _Intuitionbase,4

_main:

  movem.l version,-(sp)          ;lib version on the stack
  pea *name                      ;pointer to name on the stack
  jsr _OpenLibrary               ;call OpenLib function
  move.l d0,_IntuitionBase       ;store return value
  tst.l d0                       ;test for zero
  bne .5                         ;not zero (ok)
  pea 100                        ;number for exit
  jsr _exit                      ;exit

.5:

  pea _ns                        ;pointer to screen structure
  jsr _OpenScreen                ;call OpenScreen function
  rts                            ;return

_OpenScreen:

  move.l 4(sp),a0                ;pointer to screen structure
  move.l _IntuitionBase,a6       ;get base address from the
                                 ;IntuitionBase variable
  jmp -198(a6)                   ;call function

_OpenLibrary:

  move.l _Sysbase,a6             ;get base address from Exec
  move.l 4(sp),a1                ;get pointer to name
  move.l 8(sp),d0                ;get version from stack
  jmp -552(a6)                   ;call OpenLibrary
```

Here you can see that the program could not be compiled without the declaration of IntuitionBase, since this variable is used in OpenScreen. If it is declared, but not initialized properly (with OpenLibrary), the program crashes.

## 2.3.2        Closing a library

A library should always be closed when it is no longer needed so that
the operating system can remove this library from memory.

The Exec library offers such a function:

*CloseLibrary*        `CloseLibrary(library)`
                                  `A1`

library
        is a pointer to the open library which you want to close.

## 2.3.3        Structure of a library

The library structure is set up in a C include file as follows:

```
#define LIB_VECTSIZE            6L
#define LIB_RESERVED            4L
#define LIB_BASE                (-LIB_VECTSIZE)
#define LIB_USERDEF             (LIB_BASE-
                                (LIB_RESERVED*LIB_VECTSIZE))
#define LIBMONSTD               (LIB_USERDEF)

#define LIB_OPEN                (-6L)
#define LIB_CLOSE               (-12L)
#define LIB_EXPUNGE             (-18L)
#define LIB_EXTFUNC             (-24L)

#define LIBF_SUMMING            (1L<<0)
#define LIBF_CHANGED            (1L<<1)
#define LIBF_SUMUSED            (1L<<2)
#define LIBF_DELEXP             (1L<<3)

extern struct Library {
  0    struct                   Node lib_Node;
  14   UBYTE                    lib_Flags;
  15   UBYTE                    lib_pad;
  16   UWORD                    lib_NegSize;
  18   UWORD                    lib_PosSize;
  20   UWORD                    lib_Version;
  22   UWORD                    lib_Revision;
  24   APTR                     lib_IdString;
  28   ULONG                    lib_Sum;
  32   UWORD                    lib_OpenCnt;
  };
```

*Structure*
*entries:*

lib_Node
> is a node structure, which we have already seen. The libraries are chained into a list with the help of this structure. The type of the entry is naturally NT_LIBRARY and the name of the library is the name of the node.

lib_pad
> is an extra byte used to align the following words and long words to an even address.

lib_NegSize
> specifies the size of the area for negative offsets.

lib_PosSize
> indicates the size of the library from the base address on. This value is of interest because a library can contain more entries than are indicated in the C structure. The number of these entries and their meaning is library-dependent.

lib_Version
> specifies the library version.

lib_Revision
> indicates the library revision.

lib_IdString
> is a pointer to a string which contains more information about the library.

lib_Sum
> is a checksum for the library. If you change the library, the checksum must be recalculated.

lib_OpenCnt
> specifies how many tasks this library has open. It depends on the type of the library whether or not it is removed when no tasks have it open anymore.

The functions which a library offers to the user normally start at offset -30, although they could theoretically start at -6. If you look at the first offsets, you see that they point to functions which are used by Exec to manage the library.

These involve functions to open and close the library and are accessed by the corresponding Exec functions. Thus each library has its own open and close functions. These routines also decide whether or not the library is removed when it is no longer needed by any task.

As can be seen from the #defines in the include file, the four offsets mentioned have the following meanings:

| LIB_OPEN | -6 | Open library |
| LIB_CLOSE | -12 | Close library |
| LIB_EXPUNGE | -18 | Remove library |
| LIB_EXTFUNC | -24 | free for expansion |

The libraries which are not removed when they are no longer needed do not use the LIB_EXPUNGE jump. All unused entries should point to a routine which clears D0 and then returns.

## 2.3.4  Changing an existing library

The Exec library contains a function for changing an existing library, with which certain offset entry points can be modified. The function looks like this:

*SetFunction()*
```
SetFunction(library, offset, jump)
              A1       A0     D0
```

Offset:        -420

Description:
> This function changes the entry to the desired negative-offset function such that it points to the new routine. The library checksum is recalculated.

Parameters:

library
> is a pointer to the library to be changed.

offset  specifies the offset of the function to be changed.

entry  is a pointer to the new routine.

## 2.3.5  Creating a custom library

Now that we have discussed how libraries are used, we should show you how you can create your own libraries.

Creating a custom library is useful if several tasks are running concurrently and all use a certain group of functions. In this case it is a good idea to make a library so that each task can easily access the functions and only one copy of them need be in memory.

The Exec library offers several functions for creating libraries.

*InitStruct()*    InitStruct (initTable, memory, size)
                            A1        A2        D0
Offset:        -78

Description:
        The function initializes a structure at the specified memory location according to the table given.

Parameters:

initTable
        is a pointer to the table used for creating the structure.

memory
        is a pointer to the allocated memory.

size    indicates the size of the structure to be initialized. The memory in which the structure is created needn't be cleared, this is handled by InitStruct.

The table which is used to create the structure looks rather confusing. It consists of a command byte followed by data, the format of which depends on the command byte. After the data comes another command byte and more data. The length of the data also depends on the command byte. The end of the table is signalled by a command byte of zero.

The command byte is divided into low and high nibbles. The bit pattern in the high nibble (the upper four bits) indicates the command and the low nibble the number of command executions.

Let's look at the high nibble first. This is divided into the upper and two lower bits. The upper two bits indicate the actual command and the lower two the size of the data on which it operates. The possible data sizes are long, word or byte.

Four different commands can be coded into the top two bits:

Combination 00
        This indicates that the data starting after the command word is copied into the structure. The next two bits indicate the size of the data (long words, words or bytes).

Combination 01
        This indicates that the data byte following the command is used to fill the structure created.

**Combination 10**

This combination indicates that the byte after the command word is used as an offset into the structure. The offset is added to the starting address of the structure and the byte after this is copied into this position of the structure. After this command ends, the data which follows is copied into the position in the structure at which this command ended.

**Combination 11**

This combination indicates that the three bytes after the command byte is used as a 24-bit offset. Otherwise it is identical to the previous command.

The next two bits of the command byte (bits 4 and 5) specify the type of data involved.

| | |
|---|---|
| Combination: 00 | long word (even addresses only) |
| Combination: 01 | word (even addresses only) |
| Combination: 10 | byte |
| Combination: 11 | unused |

The low nibble of the command byte specifies how often a given function is performed; it is used as a counter. Since the counter is decremented to -1, the function is executed one more time than the count value.

The command byte must be located at an even address.

Here are two examples:

```
dc.b %00010010,$00
dc.w $FFFF,$FFFF,$1234
```

The command byte is $12 = %00010010 and indicates that the three words which follow it are copied into the structure. The zero-byte after the command byte is needed because words must start on even addresses.

```
dc.b %10000001,$10
dc.l $12341234,$ffff1111
```

The command byte indicates that two long words are copied into the structure at position 16.

*Program example:*   In this example memory space is reserved for a library structure and the structure is partially initialized.

```
;InitStruct.asm
AllocMem = -198
FreeMem = -210
MemType = $10001
InitStruct = -78
StructSize = 34
Size = $300
```

```
                move.l $4,a6
                move.l #MemType,d1
                move.l #Size,d0
                jsr AllocMem(a6)
                tst.l d0
                beq error
                lea Table,a1
                move.l d0,a2
                move.l StructSize,d0
                jsr InitStruct(a6)
error:          rts
name:           dc.b  'Test',0,0
Table:
  dc.b %01000001,$00
  dc.l 0                ;node Succ and Pred
  dc.b %00100001
  dc.b $09,0,0          ;Type and Pri
  dc.b %00011000,0
  dc.l name             ;Name
  dc.w 0,0,0,1,0        ;negS, PosS,Version,Revision
  dc.l name             ;IDString
  dc.b %00000000        ;end marker
```

*MakeLibrary()*  Library = MakeLibrary(vectors,structure,init,size,SegList)
                 D0                    A0        A1   A2   D0   D1

Offset:        -84

Description:
        With this function it is possible to create a custom library. The
        memory space, the library structure, is initialized by the func-
        tion, as well as lib_NegSize and lib_PosSize.

Parameters:

vectors
        is a pointer to a table for vectors library. The table contains
        either the pointers directly to the various functions or offsets
        which are added to the base address of the library in order to get
        the entry point. If you want to store offsets in the table, start it
        with $FFFF (-1). The end marker for the table is -1 with the
        same length as the table entries (word-length for an offset table,
        long word for pointers to the functions).

Structure
        is a pointer to an initialization table as described for the
        InitStruct function. The library structure is constructed with this
        table at the end of the MakeLibrary() function execution. The
        entries lib_NegSize and lib_PosSize are calculated and initialized
        by the function and overwrite any values stored there by the ini-
        tialization table. If the structure parameter in MakeLibrary() call
        is not defined, no table is used for creating the structure and it
        must be initialized by hand.

init
    is a pointer to a program which is executed at the end of the
    MakeLibrary() function, assuming the pointer is defined. This
    routine might initialize the library structure, for example, if this
    was not done with an initialization table. The pointer to the
    library structure is passed in D0 and the pointer to the segment
    list in A0. If the init routine changes D0, this change is returned
    when the function ends.

SegList
    is a pointer to a segment list (used by DOS) which is passed to
    the init routine in A0.

library
    is the pointer to the library structure returned by the function,
    which should not be confused with the start of the memory
    occupied by the library.

With this function it is possible to create a library of your own. This is
not inserted into the library list ExecBase structure, however. In addition, the library checksum is not calculated. The Exec Library has
another function for doing this, called AddLibrary.

*AddLibrary()*     AddLibrary(library)
                             A1

Offset:        -396

Parameters:

library
    is a pointer to the library structure previously created with the
    MakeLibrary() function.

The following example program shows how to create a custom library
and how it is used.

```
;AddLibrary.asm
MakeLib   = -84
AddLib    = -396
OpenLib   = -552
Blinker   = -30
OpenCnt   = 32
InitStruct = -78
StructSize = 34

            move.l $4,a6
            lea Vectors,a0          ;Pointer to vectors
            move.l #0,a1            ;Clear structure
            lea init,a2            ;Init routine
            move.l #StructSize,d0   ;Structure size
            clr.l d1               ;Seg list
            jsr MakeLib(a6)
            tst.l d0
```

```
                    beq Error
                    move.l d0;a1
                    jsr AddLib(a6)
                    lea name,a1                 ;Lib name
                    move.l #1,d0                ;Version
                    jsr OpenLib(a6)
                    tst.l d0
                    beq Error
                    move.l d0,LibBase
                    move.l d0,a6
                    move.l #$20000,d0           ;Value for blinker
                    jsr blinker(a6)             ;Call function
Error:              rts

init:               move.l d0,a0
                    move.b #9,8(a0)  ;Enter type
                    lea name,a1
                    move.l a1,10(a0) ;Enter name
                    move.l a1,24(a0) ;IDString = Name
                    move.w #1,20(a0) ;Version
                    rts
open:               move.l a6,d0
                    add.w #$01,OpenCnt(a6)
                    rts
close:              sub.w #$01,OpenCnt(a6)
                    clr.l d0
                    rts
expunge:            clr.l d0
                    rts
extfunc:            clr.l d0
                    rts
blink:              move.w d0,$dff180
                    sub.l #1,d0
                    bne blink
                    rts

LibBase:            dc.l 0
name:               dc.b 'test.library',0,0


Vectors:
  dc.l open, close,expunge,extfunc,blink,$ffffffff

  end
```

The program creates a library with the name test.library. One function is inserted, reachable at offset -30. The function is called Blinker and briefly changes the screen color. The parameter for the flash duration is passed in D0.

It's necessary to define entries for the library offsets -6 to -24, as described previously.

Since the structures Library, Resource and Device all contain a Library structure as their standard header, it is also possible to create a Device or Resource structure with the MakeLibrary() function.

---

## 2.3.6 The remaining library functions

*RemLibrary()*

```
Error = RemLibrary(library)
D0                   A1
```

Offset:          -402

Description:
This function removes a Library structure from the library list in the ExecBase structure. After the library is removed, it is no longer possible to open it with OpenLibrary().

Parameters:

library
is a pointer to the library structure.

error   specifies whether an error occurred in the function. If this is the case, the error message is returned in D0, else error is set to 0.

*OldOpen Library()*

```
library = OldOpenLibrary(libName)
D0                          A1
```

Offset:          -408

Description:
This function is a holdover from Kickstart Version 1.0. It is also used to open a library, but it doesn't check the version number of the library to be opened. It is kept in the Exec library only so that programs which were written for Kickstart 1.0 also work with Version 1.2.

# 2.4 Multitasking

Multitasking is one of the best features of Exec. Multitasking is the ability of the operating system to run several programs or tasks at once. Since the Amiga has only one processor, only one task can actually be processed at a time, of course. To make it seem as though several tasks are running at once, the 68000 is divided between the tasks. Each of the programs gets the processor for a certain amount of time. This is called time-multiplexing the processor among the various tasks.

Not all of the tasks which are present in the computer memory need to be executed concurrently. Many of them are activated only when needed. Otherwise they may be waiting for a certain key, a mouse movement, etc.

Thus the various tasks can be divided into the following categories (called task states):

running     This is the task to which the processor is currently assigned. Only one task is ever in the running state.

ready       All tasks which are ready to run but to whom the processor has not yet allocated time, are in the ready state.

waiting     Tasks in the waiting state are all those which are waiting for a specific event and are not ready to be processed.

In addition, a task can also find itself in the following states:

added       Such a task has just been added to the system and is not yet in one of the three states above.

removed     This task has just ended. It is no longer in one of the three states above and are removed from the system.

exception   A task exception is a special state in which the task can be interrupted by a certain event. After processing this exception it returns to one of the three states above.

A task consist basically of two elements: the actual program and the task structure. This contains all of the information about the task which Exec needs. To better understand the capabilities of a task, we should first examine the task structure.

## 2.4.1    The task structure

The task structure, as defined in the include file exec/tasks.h of a C compiler, looks as follows (The numbers in parentheses indicates the distance of an element from the base address of the structure):

```
extern struct Task {
struct Node tc_Node;
   UBYTE   tc_Flags;      /* (14) */
   UBYTE   tc_State;      /* (15) task state */
   BYTE    tc_IDNestCnt;  /* (16) counter for   Disable() */
   BYTE    tc_TDNestCnt;  /* (17) counter for Forbid()    */
   ULONG   tc_SigAlloc;   /* (18) allocated signal bits */
   ULONG   tc_SigWait;    /* (22) wait for these */
   ULONG   tc_SigRecvd;   /* (26) received signals */
   ULONG   tc_SigExcept;  /* (30) exception gen. signals */
   UWORD   tc_TrapAlloc;  /* (34) allocated trap commands */
   UWORD   tc_TrapAble;   /* (36) allowed trap commands */
   APTR    tc_ExceptData; /* (38) data for exceptions */
   APTR    tc_ExceptCode; /* (42) code for exceptions */
   APTR    tc_TrapData;   /* (46) data for trap handler */
   APTR    tc_TrapCode;   /* (50) code for trap handler */
   APTR    tc_SPReg;      /* (54) temp storage for SP */
   APTR    tc_SPLower;    /* (58) lower stack bound */
   APTR    tc_SPUpper;    /* (62) upper stack bound + 2 */
   VOID    (*tc_Switch)();/* (66) task loses CPU */
   VOID    *tc_Launc)();  /* (70) task gets CPU */
   struct List  tc_MemEntry;   /*(74) occupied memory */
   APTR    tc_UserData;   /* (88) pointer to task data */
};
```

As you can see the header of a task structure consists of the node structure we discussed in the previous section. The reason is that Exec manages the tasks in two different lists, one for the ready tasks and one for the waiting tasks. Thus the basic functions like Insert(), Remove() and FindName() can be used on the task list as well. There are also special functions for managing the task lists.

Each list also has a list header. In the case of the task lists these are in the ExecBase structure. This structure is described later. The following lines show how the task lists can be accessed:

```
#include <exec/execbase.h>

extern ExecBase *SysBase;
main()

{
struct task *waiting, *ready, *running;

waiting=(struct Task *)SysBase->TaskWait.lh_Head;
ready=(struct Task *)SysBase->TaskReady.lh_Head;
running=(struct Task *)SysBase->ThisTask;

etc.
}
```

The program places in waiting and ready, pointers to the first task structure of these lists. Running is a pointer to the running task. TaskWait and TaskReady are list headers, while ThisTask is just a pointer. Since there can be only one running task, there is naturally no list here.

*Task
switching*

Here we should say a few words about the central process which is responsible for allowing multiple tasks to use the same processor. This is called task switching, and it involves switching from one task to another. If a task is found in one of the two task lists, it is automatically brought into this process. The first question is:

How are the tasks switched?

*Switch
routine*

A task doesn't know when it gets the processor or when it has to give it up. If it looks at the ThisTask field in ExecBase, it only finds a pointer to its task there since it can only read this field when the CPU is allocated to it. In reality however it can be interrupted at any time. The whole process is triggered by an interrupt which occurs when the task has used the amount of processor time alloted to it or when a more important task must be processed immediately. The Switch routine of the operating system accomplishes the actual switching. In contrast to the task, which always runs in the user mode of the 68000, the Switch routine is run in the supervisor mode. First the processor registers D0-D7 and A0-A6 are saved on the task stack. The user stack pointer is then stored in the tc_SPReg field of the task structure, followed by the status register and the program on the user stack. They are automatically placed on the supervisor stack by the 68000 when the interrupt occurs. The task is then placed in the ready list.

The new task comes from either the ready or waiting list. It is now removed from there and entered in the ThisTask field. After this its stackpointer is fetched from its tc_SPReg field and then its registers are fetched from the stack. Exec exits the Switch routine at the end with an RTE causing a branch to the new task.

Of course, this is only a rough summary of what the Switch routine does. Actually, more data is exchanged and special cases checked. If the task is in the exception state, the Switch routine can call the routines whose addresses are in the tc_Launch and tc_Switch entries of the task structure either before or after the switch.

But as indicated, the entire switching procedure is completely automatic. You don't have to worry about it.

The second question about task switching is: When will the tasks be switched?

*Task scheduling*

Or put differently: What amount of the processor time does a given task get? The division of the processor time is called task scheduling. Exec uses the ln_Pri field of the list node structure at the start of the task structure as the basis of this. In general, the higher the priority of a task, the more processor time it gets, and thus the faster it runs. Exec starts with the task with the highest priority. It gets the processor for a given time span. After this, the processor time which it used is subtracted from its relative priority in comparison to the ready tasks. Now it is no longer the task with the highest priority and the processor moves on to the next task. This procedure ensures that even tasks with a low priority get the processor once in a while and that time-critical tasks which need the processor immediately, but for only a short time, get priority over the others.

The priority can be a value between -128 and 127. A normal task should have a priority of 0. This is also the priority of a CLI task. The remaining operating system tasks vary between -20 and 20, so it is not necessary to write extreme values in the tc_Node.ln_Pri field of a task structure.

Another field of the task structure is tc_Node.ln_Name. This contains a pointer to the name of the task (see the section on lists). This makes it easier to find a given task.

The tc_State field contains the task state. The following values are assigned to the various states:

| | |
|---|---|
| invalid | = 0 |
| added | = 1 |
| running | = 2 |
| ready | = 3 |
| waiting | = 4 |
| exception | = 5 |
| removed | = 6 |

*The task stack*    In addition to the task structure, a task also needs a stack. As mentioned before, this is a user stack. Tc_SPLower contains the lower bound of the stack and tc_SPUpper the upper bound (recall that a stack always grows from higher addresses to lower addresses).

The address in tc_SPReg is used as storage for the stack pointer. Normally tc_SPReg is set equal to tc_SPUpper, but any address between tc_SPUpper and tc_SPLower can be placed in tc_SPReg. The area between tc_SPReg and tc_SPUpper can then be used to store global variables, etc.

*A word about*       Tc_SPUpper points to the upper bound of the stack, the first address
*tc_SPUpper:*        after the stack area. The word at the last position of the stack has the address tc_SPUpper minus 2.

Since Exec saves the registers on the task stack when switching tasks, the task stack must be at least 70 bytes large. But then the task would not be able to place any variables or return addresses on the stack. Since C programs in particular make heavy use of the stack, at least 1K should be reserved for the stack.

Since a task consists of various elements, task structure, stack, program, etc., a certain amount of structure must also be reserved for it. This makes it possible to keep in the task structure a list which contains all of the memory occupied by the task. The tc_MemEntry contains the header of this list. We'll explain how such a memory list is constructed later.

*Enabling and*       Sometimes you may not want a processor to be able to leave a given
*disabling task*     task at any time. Imagine that you want to display the list of waiting
*switching*          tasks on the screen. But while your task is reading the entries, a ready task changes to the waiting state, or vice versa. The values read are then incorrect.

In general, whenever a task access data structures which are open to either the entire system or certain other tasks, the task switching must first be disabled so that the data are not changed by some other task during the access.

*Forbid() and*       The Forbid() and Permit() routines represent the first level of the task
*Permit()*           switching enabling/disabling mentioned above. Forbid() prevents task switching and Permit() allows it again. Both routines are called without parameters and do not return values (C type: void).

*Disable() and*
*Enable()*

Often it is not sufficient just to turn task switching off. Many system data structures are changed by Exec during interrupts. All interrupts can be disabled with Disable() and enabled again with Enable(). But be careful! Turning off task switching, even for a long time, doesn't hurt anything. This is not the case with interrupts, however. Their regular occurrence is necessary for the life of Exec. If the interrupts are disabled for too long, a system crash can occur when you try to re-enable multitasking. The task is completely undisturbed during Disable(), since turning off the interrupts also turns off task switching.

It is also possible to nest several Forbid() or Disable() calls. Two counters are maintained, TDNestCnt and IDNestCnt (Task Disable Nesting Counter and Interrupt Disable Nesting Counter). Everytime Forbid() is called, TDNestCnt is incremented by 1, and decremented by 1 on each call to Permit(). Task switching is possible only when TDNestCnt < 0. This means that the number of Permit() calls must be the same as the number of Forbid() calls before task switching is re-enabled. This applies to Enable(), Disable() and IDNestCnt.

The following program shows the use of the Enable() and Disable() functions. It reads the points of all the task structures of the ready and waiting tasks while the interrupts are disabled with Disable(). Afterwards they are re-enabled with Enable() and the pointers stored are used to display information about the task structures like name, stack and priority on the screen.

The program shows what tasks are present on the Amiga. Experiment with CLI commands like NEWCLI, RUN or SETTASKPRI.

The running task is also displayed, which is naturally always the task from which our program was called.

```
/** DISP-TASK.c **/

#include <exec/execbase.h>

struct ExecBase *SysBase;

main()
{
register struct Task *a_task;
APTR run, tnodes[50], wtask, ltask;
void o1(),o2();
register APTR Anode;

Disable();

Anode = tnodes;
run = (APTR)SysBase->ThisTask;

for(a_task=(struct Task *)SysBase->TaskReady.lh_Head;
 a_task->tc_Node.ln_Succ;
```

```
    *Anode=(APTR)a_task,Anode++,
    a_task=a_task->tc_Node.ln_Succ);
wtask=Anode;

for(a_task=(struct Task *)SysBase->TaskWait.lh_Head;
    a_task->tc_Node.ln_Succ;
    *Anode=(APTR)a_task,Anode++,
    a_task=a_task->tc_Node.ln_Succ);
ltask=Anode;

Enable();

printf("\nTask in the running state:\n");o1();o2(run);

printf("\nTask(s) in the ready state:\n");o1();
for(Anode=tnodes;Anode!=wtask;o2(*Anode),Anode++);

printf("\nTask(s) in the waiting state:\n");o1();
for(;Anode!=ltask;o2(*Anode),Anode++);

}

void o1()
{
printf
("Stack adrs. Stacksize Priority Signals  Name\n");
printf
("---------- ---------- -------- --------- ----------\n");
}

void o2(at)
register struct Task *at;
{
printf("%10lx%10lx%8ld%11lx  %s\n",at->tc_SPLower,
  (ULONG)at->tc_SPUpper - (ULONG)at->tc_SPLower -2L,
  (LONG)at->tc_Node.ln_Pri,
  at->tc_SigWait,at->tc_Node.ln_Name);
}
```

Since the program just saves pointers to the task structures and not the contents of these structures, errors are always possible since a task can be removed while the values are being displayed. This almost never happens, however, and since it would require much more work to store all of the task structures, we avoided it in this program. Other fields of the task structures can also be printed by changing the o1() and o2() routines.

*Creating a task*

Now that we have talked so much about tasks and task structures, we want to create a new task. What do we need?

First a task structure, then a stack, the task name (since the task structure just contains a pointer to the actual name), and finally a program, the actual task.

Some problems arise here. A different area of memory is required for each task since it must remain in memory after the program which created it has ended.

To make the program less complicated, the task structure, task name and stack are combined into the structure alltask, for which one common memory block is then allocated.

The actual task is written as a normal C function with the name "code". All it does is increment a counter until it reaches $FFFFFF. This takes several minutes. Its presence can be noticed by the fact that the Amiga reacts more slowly, since our task also gets its share of processing time. The previous example program can also be used to view the existence of our task. It has the name "Sample task".

To copy the code function to its final memory position, its name is used as a pointer to its address. The end function is just used to get the end address of the code function. Since there is no way to determine the memory requirements of a function in C, it is calculated as the difference between the starting and ending addresses.

To keep the program simple, the occupied memory is not released, but this amounts to just over a kilobyte.

```
/**** Create a task ****/

#include <exec/types.h>
#include <exec/Tasks.h>
#include <exec/memory.h>

#define STACK_SIZE 500 /* Stack size */

main()
{
void code(),end();
APTR mycode, AllocMem();
static char Taskname[] = "Sample Task";
register APTR c1,c2;

struct alltask {
struct Task tc;
char    Name[sizeof(Taskname)], Stack[STACK_SIZE];
} *mytask;

mytask = AllocMem((ULONG)sizeof(*mytask),
  MEMF_PUBLIC|MEMF_CLEAR);
if(mytask==0)
{printf("No memory for the AllTask structure!\n");
 return(0);
}

mycode = AllocMem((ULONG)end-(ULONG)code,MEMF_PUBLIC);
if(mycode==0)
{FreeMem(mytask,(ULONG)sizeof(*mytask));
```

```
printf("No memory for the task code!\n");
return(0);
}

strcpy(mytask->Name,Taskname);

mytask->tc.tc_SPLower=mytask->Stack;
mytask->tc.tc_SPUpper=mytask->Stack+STACK_SIZE;
mytask->tc.tc_SPReg=mytask->tc.tc_SPUpper;

mytask->tc.tc_Node.ln_Type=NT_TASK;
mytask->tc.tc_Node.ln_Name=mytask->Name;

for(c1=code,c2=mycode;c1<=end;*c2++=*c1++);

AddTask(mytask,mycode,0L);
}

/*** The "code" function is the task itself ***/

void code()
{
ULONG count;

for(count=0;count<0xffffff;count++);
}

void end(){}
```

As you can see, only a few of the fields in the task structure have to be initialized:

> tc_SPLower with the lower stack bound
> tc_SPUpper and tc_SPReg with the upper stack bound
> tc_Node.ln_Type with the list type NT_TASK

The name can also be omitted.

An important function was used in this program for the first time:

*AddTask()*       `AddTask(task, initialPC, finalPC)`

This function inserts a new task into the system. Normally the new task is immediately added to the ready list.

The AddTask function requires the following parameters:

task        This is a pointer to a task structure in which at least the above four fields have been initialized.

initialPC   This is the address at which the task program execution begins. In our example this is the starting address of the code function at its final address, stored in mycode.

finalPC     finalPC contains the address to which the processor jumps when the task executes an RTS command. This can be the address of a routine which releases the occupied memory, closes open files, etc. If you specify 0 as the finalPC (as in our example), Exec uses a default finalPC routine. This releases the memory to which the tc_MemEntry field of the task structure points. After this the task is removed from the system lists.

*Ending a task*     The description of finalPC brings us to the next topic. How is a task ended? The following possibilities exist:

1.     The task reaches an RTS command which does not represent the return from a JSR or BSR task. Then the procedure listed for finalPC is performed.

2.     A 68000 exception occurs which is not handled by the task, such as a bus or address error, division by zero, etc. Exec then creates its "Software error - Task Held" message or a Guru Meditation. At the end of this section we'll show how to trap such errors.

3.     A call to the RemTask function, which removes the task from the system.

## 2.4.1.1     Task functions

Exec contains certain functions for creating and removing tasks and for managing the task lists:

*AddTask()*     
```
AddTask(task, initialPC, finalPC)
        A0      A1         A2
```

Offset:     -282

Description:
     AddTask adds a new task to the system,

Parameters:

task     is a pointer to a task structure. The fields tc_SPUpper, tc_SPLower, tc_SPReg and tc_Node.ln_Type must be properly initialized.

initialPC
     is the address at which the execution of the task begins.

**finalPC**
> is the return address which is placed on the stack before the start of the task. If the task executes an extra RTS, this address is branched to. If finalPC is 0, Exec uses the address of its default finalPC routine.

*FindTask()*

```
Task = FindTask (name)
 D0               A1
```

Offset:        -294

Description:
> FindTask searches the task lists for a task with the specified name and returns a pointer to it if it found such a task. If 0 is given as the name, the function returns a pointer to the task structure of the current task.

Parameter:

name  is a pointer to the name of the task to be found.

Result:

Task  is a pointer to the task structure of the node found.

*RemTask()*

```
RemTask (task)
         A1
```

Offset:        -288

Description:
> RemTask removes a task from the system. If the tc_MemEntry field points to a MemEntry list, this memory is released. All of the other system resources occupied by the task must have been released prior to invoking this function.

Parameter:

task   Pointer to the task structure of the task to be removed. If task=0, the current task is removed.

*SetTaskPri()*

```
oldPriority = SetTaskPri (task, newPriority)
 D0                       A1      D0
```

Offset:        -300

Description:
> SetTaskPri returns the old priority of a task and sets the current priority to a new value. This performs an operation called rescheduling, meaning that the processor divides its time among the individual tasks differently as a result of the new priority. If a

task is set to a high priority, it is generally serviced immediately by the processor.

Parameters:

task   Pointer to the task structure of the task.

newPriority
new priority of the task (in the lower eight bits of D0).

Result:

oldPriority
Old priority of the task (in the lower eight bits of D0).

**Forbid()**          Forbid()

Offset:          -132

Description:
Prevents task switching and increments TDNestCnt.

**Permit()**          Permit()

Offset:          -138

Description:
Decrements TDNestCnt and permits task switching if TDNestCnt < 0.

**Disable()**          Disable()

Offset:          -120

Description:
Disables all interrupts and increments IDNestCnt.

**Enable()**          Enable()

Offset:          -126

Description:
Decrements IDNestCnt and permits interrupts again if IDNestCnt < 0.

## 2.4.2       Communication between tasks

Not every task can operate on its own. Most tasks want to exchange
data with others. This generally involves input/output processes, since
the routines which control the various I/O devices, such as the keyboard, screen and disk drives are set up as separate tasks.

It has been mentioned that some tasks just wait for signals from other
tasks before going into action. These signals are the subject of this
section.

## 2.4.2.1     The task signals

*Signal Bits*    Each task has 32 signal bits which allow it to distinguish various
events. Each task can use this signal as it desires. A given signal can
have complete meanings to two different tasks. Certain system
functions, such as Intuition, use various signals for messages. If a task
wants to use one of its signals, it must first allocate it. This is done
with the AllocSignal() function. Normally the lower 16 bits are
reserved for system functions, leaving the other 16 free.

A given signal can be allocated with AllocSignal() by passing it the
number of the desired signal as an argument, or you can let
AllocSignal() find the next free signal by passing a -1 to it.

The result returned is the number of the desired signal, provided it is not
already allocated, or a -1 as an error message. AllocSignal(-1) only
returns -1 when no more free signals could be found.

The following C program allocates the next free signal with the
AllocSignal function:

```
Signal=AllocSignal(-1L);
Signal < 0?
printf("No more free signals available"):
printf("Signal number %ld has been allocated",(long)Signal);
```

There are two ways to specify a given signal. The first is to specify its
number. This is a number between 0 and 31 which corresponds to the
bit number of the corresponding signal.

The second option is to specify the entire signal word. In this signal mask the state of a bit indicates the corresponding signal. The advantage of specifying the desired signal in the form of a signal mask is that several signals can be selected at once. AllocSignal returns the signal number. To get from this to the signal mask, the bit at the position indicated by the signal number must be set. This can be done in C as follows:

```
signal_mask=1<<signal_number
```

Or in machine language:

```
MOVE.W signal_number,D0
MOVE.L signal_mask,D1
BSET D0,D1
```

whereby signal_mask and signal_number are the addresses of the given values (not the values themselves).

The signals allocated by a task are stored as a signal mask in the tc_SigAlloc field of a task.

*Waiting for signals*

The main reason that signals are used is so that tasks can wait for them. This sounds rather strange, but it's true. Let's say that a task is waiting for a certain key. It could do this in the form of a loop, but this would waste computer time without actually doing anything. To prevent this, a task can be made to wait for an event such as a key being pressed with the help of the task signals. Any task can wait for signals and while it is waiting it is put in the waiting list and this doesn't use any processor time.

The Wait function is used to make a task wait for a signal. It needs only one parameter, a signal mask which contains the signals to be waited for. This makes it possible to wait for more than one signal at a time. As soon as one of the specified signals is set by another task, the Wait function comes back and returns a signal mask containing the signal(s) which occurred. The desired signals and the signal mask returned by Wait() can be logically ANDed to determine which signal actually occurred. The following hypothetical C fragment demonstrates this:

```
unsigned long Signals;
Signals = Wait(Key|Mouse_button|Menu);
if (Signals & Key) { /* key pressed */ }
if (Signals & Mouse_button) { /* mouse button pressed */ }
if (Signals & Menu) { /* menu option activated */ }
```

If one of the desired signals is set before the call, Wait() returns to the program immediately.

The signals for which a task is waiting are stored in its tc_SigWait field and those which it has received are stored in tc_SigRecvd.

If the task switching or interrupts are turned off before calling Wait(),
they are turned on again. The disabled state is restored when Wait()
returns to the calling program.

This is accomplished by storing the contents of the TDNestCnt and
IDNestCnt counters in the appropriate fields of the task structure:
tc_TDNestCnt and tc_IDNestCnt.

There are five important routines which have to do with task signals.
The SetSignals() function is not required for normal applications.

## 2.4.2.2   The signal functions

*AllocSignal()*
```
Signal_number = AllocSignal(Signal_number)
       D0                              D0
```

Offset:          -330

Description:
A task signal can be reserved with the AllocSignal function. If -1
is passed instead of the signal number, AllocSignal searches for
the next free signal and allocates it. If the desired signal is already
allocated, AllocSignal returns -1.

AllocSignal can only be used to allocate signals for the current
task. Also, AllocSignal should not be called within an exception.

Parameter:

Signal_number
The number of the signal to be allocated (0-31) or -1 for the next
free signal.

Result:

Signal number
The number of the allocated signal or -1 if the desired signal (or
all signals for AllocSignal(-1)) is already allocated.

*FreeSignal()*
```
FreeSignal(Signal_number)
                     D0
```

Offset:          -336

Description:
FreeSignal() is the opposite of AllocSignal. The signal with the
number specified is released. As with AllocSignal(), FreeSignal()
should not be called in an exception.

Parameter:

Signal_number
> The number of the signal to be released (0-31).

### SetSignals()

```
OldSignals = SetSignals(NewSignals,mask)
  D0                      D0        D1
```

Offset:       -306

Description:
> SetSignals() transfers the state of the signals whose correspond-
> ing bits are set in the mask from NewSignals to the task signals
> (tc_SigRecvd). If a bit in NewSignals and the mask are both 1,
> the corresponding task signal is set. If it is 0 in NewSignals and
> 1 in the mask, it is cleared. If a mask bit is 0, the corresponding
> task signal is not changed.

Parameters:

NewSignals
> contains the new state of the signals.

mask  determines which signal bits are changed.

Result:

OldSignals
> indicates the old state of the task signals.

SetSignals(0L,0L) returns the current signal state without changing any
signals.

### Signal()

```
Signal(Task, Signals)
       A1      D0
```

Offset:       -324

Description:
> This function allows the signals of another task to be set. It is
> the main function of the signal system since it allows signals to
> be sent from task to task. If the receiver task has been waiting
> for the sent signal, it returns to the ready or running state. This
> function is used mainly by the message system, discussed in the
> next section.

Parameters:

Task  Pointer to the task structure of the receiver task.

Signals
> A signal mask which contains the signal bits to be sent.

*Wait()*            Signals = Wait (Signal_mask)
                      D0                         D0

Offset:          -318

Description:
   Wait waits for the signals in the specified signal mask. This means that the task remains in the waiting state until one of the signals is set by another task or an interrupt. If one of the signals was already set before the call to the Wait function, Wait returns immediately. The result which Wait returns is a signal mask which contains all of the signals which occurred for which it was waiting.

Note:
   The function can be called only in the USER mode.

Parameter:

Signal_mask
   Wait waits for the signals in this signal mask.

Result:

Signals
   These are the signals from the signal mask which were received.

---

## 2.4.2.3          The message system

The task signals form the basis of another communication system between tasks, called the message system. This allows not only signals to be transferred, but also messages which can contain any data. This system also forms queues automatically if the receiver isn't fast enough to react to a message. Something called a message port is used as the basis for this type of communication. This is another data structure. In C it has the following format (exec/ports.h):

```
struct MsgPort {
  struct Node mp_Node;
  UBYTE mp_Flags;              /* (14) flags for action mode */
  UBYTE mp_SigBit;             /* (15) signal bit of the task */
  struct Task *mp_SigTask;  /* (16) pointer to receiver task*/
  struct List mp_MsgList;/* (20) list header or message list */
};
```

A message port serves as a collecting point for messages to a task (or software interrupt). Any task can send data to a message port, but only one task is informed when messages arrive.

The individual fields of a message port structure have the following meanings:

*mp_Node*

The mp_Node is a node structure as presented in section 1. A pointer to the name of the message port is stored in its ln_Name field. This makes it easier to find a given message port.

The node type in ln_Typ is always NT_MSGPORT for a message port.

The other fields of the node structure are used only when you want to put a message port in a list. This can be either a private list or a list of the public ports. This is the list of all message ports which are known to Exec.

*mp_Flags*

The lower two bits in this field determine what happens when the message port receives a message. The following options are available (the corresponding bit combinations are contained in the include file "exec /ports.h"):

PA_IGNORE (2)
　　This combination of flag bits determines that nothing happens when a message is received.

PA_SIGNAL (0)
　　Each time the message port receives a message, the signal from the mp_SigBit field is sent to the destination task.

PA_SOFTINT (1)
　　A software interrupt is generated each time a message is received. More about software interrupts can be found in the next section.

*mp_SigBit*

In this field is stored the number of the signal bit which is set to the task when mp_Flags = PA_SIGNAL. This is a signal number between 0 and 31, so that only one signal bit of a message port can be affected.

*mp_SigTask*

This field must contain a pointer to the task structure of a task to which the signal in mp_SigBit is sent.

If the PA_SOFTINT mode is set, mp_SigTask contains a pointer to the interrupt structure of the corresponding software interrupt instead.

*mp_MsgList*

This is the list header for the list of all messages received. Each message received is appended to the end of this list and this either causes nothing to happen (PA_IGNORE), a software interrupt to be generated (PA_SOFTINT), or a signal to send to the receiver task (PA_SIGNAL). This list header must be initialized properly. This can be done with NewList(), for example.

*Construction of a message*

Each message consists of a message structure and a message, which can be a maximum of 64K long. The message is appended directly to the message structure. This structure is also contained in the include file exec/ports.h:

```
struct Message {
  struct Node mn_Node;
  struct MsgPort *mn_ReplyPort; /* (14) reply port */
  UWORD mn_Length; /* (18) length of the message in bytes */
};
```

mn_Node

> mn_Node is a normal node structure. It is used to chain the message in the list of received messages. The ln_Typ field is set to the node type NT_MESSAGE. A message can be given a name, but this is not necessary.

mn_Length

> mn_Length contains the length of the message in bytes. As mentioned, the message is appended immediately after the mn_Length field.

*Sending a message*

A message is sent to a port by means of the PutMsg function.

PutMsg(Message_port, Message) sends Message to Message_port. Both are pointers to the appropriate structures. The following example sends a string as a message to a hypothetical message port:

```
{
extern APTR Port;   /* pointer to the message port */
static char text[] = "This is a sample message";
static struct {
struct Message msg;
char contents[sizeof(text)];
} mes;
mes.msg.mn_Node.ln_Type = NT_MESSAGE;
strcpy(mes.contents,text);
PutMsg(Port,&mes);
}
```

When a message is sent it is simply appended to the list of received messages, the mp_Msglist. This is done as usual with the ln_Succ and ln_Pred fields in the node structure of the message, mn_Node. The message is not copied! This means that the entire message is still part of the task which sent it. Sending a message thus allows the receiver task to use part of the memory area of the sender task.

*Receiving a message*

Receiving a message normally consists of two parts. First a task waits for a signal from the message port, and when this signals that a message has been received, it is then read.

Assuming that the message port has been properly initialized, there are two ways for a task to wait for the arrival of a message at the message port:

It can use either the Wait() function or WaitPort().

```
Message = WaitPort(Port);
```

This function waits for a message to be received at the message port "Port". If one or more messages are already present there, WaitPort() returns to the program immediately. Otherwise, like the Wait function, it puts the task in the waiting state until a message arrives. WaitPort() returns a pointer to the message structure of the first message, but the message is not removed from the message port.

When should Wait() or WaitPort() be used?

*Wait()*

Wait() has the advantage that it can be used to wait for more than one signal at a time. This is the best function to use in cases where you want to wait for multiple events. But if the task is really only waiting for a message on a given message port, WaitPort() is better. This function waits only when the message port is empty. Wait(), on the other hand, works with signals. For example, if the message port has already received two signals before Wait(), the following problem occurs:

The first Wait() call returns immediately because the two messages have already set the corresponding signal. If Wait() is now used to wait for the next message, it can wait forever, since the desired message has long since arrived. The cause of this problem is that a signal is set only once, even if several messages arrive. Thus you must test to see if the next message has arrived before the second Wait(). This is why it is better to use WaitPort() if the task is just waiting for a message.

The GetMsg function is used to get a message from a port:

```
Message = GetMsg(Port);
```

This function gets the first message from the specified port and returns a pointer to its message structure. The message is then removed from the message port list. GetMsg() gets the message from the first position of this list. Since new messages are appended at the end, the list represents a FIFO buffer or queue. FIFO stands for First In, First Out and means that the element which was first placed in the list is the first taken from it.

Thus you can use GetMsg() to get all of the message received by a port in order. If no more messages are present, GetMsg() returns with a 0.

The following example uses WaitPort() and GetMsg() to get a message from a hypothetical port:

```
extern struct MsgPort *Port;
struct Message *GetMsg();
int signal;

if ((signal=AllocSignal(-1L))<0)
{ printf("No more free signals"); return(0); }

Port->mp_FLags = PA_SIGNAL;
Port->mp_SigBit = signal;
```

```
Port->mp_SigTask = FindTask(0); /* this task */

WaitPort(Port);
message = GetMsg(Port);
```

*Replying to a message*

Once a task has sent a message, it probably wants to know if it was received. The reason for this is that the entire message, including the message structure, belongs to it. By sending it, the task gave the receiver permission to read the memory in which the message was located. In addition the receiver can also store various replies or results in the message. Since the sender probably wants to use the memory for other purposes, like a new message, it has to know when the receiver has received and processed it. It can't just simply erase it without knowing whether it has been read or not. Therefore a reply port is set up. A reply port can be any port belonging to the sender task. There is a field in the message structure which is used to tell the receiver the address of this port:

mn_ReplyPort

> mn_ReplayPort contains the address of the reply port of the sender task. In order to reply to a message, the receiver simply sends a message to this port after it has read and processed the first one. The sender thus knows that the message has been received. It can now re-use the memory which the message occupied or simply return it to the system.

ReplyMsg(Message) is used to reply to a message.

*Creating a new message port*

To create a new message port, all that has to be done is to place a correctly initialized message port structure in memory. The easiest way to do this is with a C structure with the memory class static. The necessary memory can also be obtained from the system with AllocMem() and initialized.

Once a message port structure has been completed, you must decide whether it is inserted into the list of public message ports. This can be done with the AddPort function. This function also initializes the mp_MsgList field of the structure and makes it unnecessary to call NewList(). AddPort requires as its parameter the address of the message structure. The advantage of placing a message port in the list of public ports is that another task can easily find this port by its name. If a port is not added to this list, every task which communicates with it must be told the address of the message port.

The FindPort function is used to find a port based on its name:

```
Port = FindPort(Name);
```

searches for a message port with the specified name and, if it finds it, returns its address. If you add a port to the system with AddPort(), you should first check to make sure that a port with this name is not already present.

If a port is no longer needed, it can simply be deleted after all outstanding messages have been received and acknowledged with ReplyMsg().

If the message port is in the public list, it must be removed from the system with RemPort(Port) before it can be deleted (or its memory released).

A CreatePort function makes it easier to create a new message port. This function is not part of the operating system, but is found in the run-time library of an Amiga C compiler (amiga.lib). Its C source code goes like this:

```
#include <exec/exec.h>

extern APTR AllocMem();
extern UBYTE AllocSignal();
extern struct Task *FindTask();

struct MsgPort *CreatePort(Name, Pri)
char *name;
BYTE Pri;
{
BYTE Signal;
struct MsgPort *Port;

if ((Signal = AllocSignal(-1)) == -1)
      return((struct MsgPort *)0);

Port = AllocMem((ULONG)sizeof(*Port),MEMF_CLEAR
|MEMF_PUBLIC);

if (port == 0) {
      FreeSignal(Signal);
      return((struct MsgPort *)0);
}

Port->mp_Node.ln_Name = Name;
Port->mp_Node.ln_Pri = Pri;
Port->mp_Node.ln_Type = Type;

Port->mp_Flags = PA_SIGNAL;
Port->mp_SigBit = Signal;
Port->mp_SigTask = FindTask(0);

if (name != 0)
      AddPort(Port);
else
      NewList(&(Port->mp_MsgList));

return(Port);
}
```

This function creates a message port with the specified name and priority. It returns the address of the new port or 0 if no memory or signals are free. If the pointer to the name is not zero, the port is added to the list of public ports. This function can be used to quickly build a reply port, for example.

There is also a function in amiga.lib for deleting a port:

```
DeletePort(Port)
        struct MsgPort *Port;
{
if ((Port->mp_node.ln_Name) != 0)
        RemPort(Port);

Port->mp_Node.ln_Type = 0xFF;
Port->mp_MsgList.lh_Head=(struct Node *)-1;

FreeSignal(Port->mp_SigBit);

FreeMem(Port,(ULONG) sizeof(*Port));
}
```

DeletePort() deletes the specified port. If it has a name it is also removed from the public list.

*Task*
*exception*

There are some cases where we want a task to keep on running while it is waiting for a signal. Let's say that a task is drawing a mathematical function. Since this takes a long time, we want to have the option of stopping the process by pressing a key. This is indicated through a message port. We would have to continually test inside the drawing loop to see if the port has a received message. This slows the drawing loop down, however. But we don't have to live with this unsatisfactory solution on the Amiga. We can make use of something called a task exception.

Similar to an interrupt, the task is interrupted by the occurrence of a signal. This can happen at any time. The exception handler is then called. This is part of the original task and thus has access to its data (provided they are not local). In our example it could set the loop variable to the end value and thus stop the drawing. In machine language you have more options and the task can be manipulated directly.

The following steps are needed to make task exceptions possible:

1.    The start address of the exception handler must be placed in the corresponding field of the task structure, tc_ExceptCode. A pointer to common data can also be written in tc_ExceptData.

2.    The signals which are allowed to cause an exception must be determined. The tc_SigExcept field in the task structure determines this. Each set signal there generates an exception when it is received by a task. There a special function makes it easier to set and clear the bits in the field: SetExcept. Its exact descrip-tion is found in the function overview at the end of this section.

If an exception occurs, Exec first places the current contents of the processor registers (PC, SR, D0-D7 and A0-A6) on the task stack in order to allow the task to be continued at the end of the exception.

Then a signal mask containing the exception signals which occurred is placed in D0. The address in the tc_ExceptData field is copied into A1. The exception code is then executed starting at the address in tc_ExceptCode.

An RTS must be at the end of an exception. Exec then restores the old register contents from the stack and continues with the task.

During an exception Exec prohibits other exceptions from occurring. To allow other exceptions to occur at the end of the current one, you must place the same value back in D0 as was passed in it at the beginning.

If a signal occurs during an exception which generates a new exception, this new exception is processed at the end of the current one.

If a signal was already set before it was permitted with SetExcept, the exception occurs immediately.

*Processor traps*

Another type of exception are the traps. These are the 68000 processor exceptions, as they are called by Motorola, and should not be confused with the task exceptions described above. The following 68000 exceptions are viewed as traps by Exec:

Traps:

| | |
|---|---|
| 2 | Bus error |
| 3 | Address error |
| 4 | Illegal instruction |
| 5 | Division by zero |
| 6 | CHK instruction |
| 7 | TRAPV instruction |
| 8 | Privilege violation |
| 9 | Trace |
| 10 | Line 1010 emulator |
| 11 | Line 1111 emulator |
| 32-37 | Trap instructions |

A trap is always the direct result of an instruction in the program. It can be either desired (CHK, TRAP, TRAPV, 1010, 1111 or Trace) or it can occur as a result of a program error (bus or address error, division by zero or privilege violation).

When a processor trap occurs, Exec jumps to its trap handler. The address of this handler is fetched from the tc_TrapCode field. Normally a pointer to the standard Exec trap handler is found there. This (unfortunately) creates the "Software error - Task held" requester or even a Guru Meditation.

The address in tc_TrapCode can be redirected to a custom handler, however. This handler can either react to all traps, or just certain ones, passing on the rest to the standard handler.

A trap handler is jumped to almost directly. Exec simply places the trap number (see list above) on the stack. This has the following results:

First, the computer goes into the supervisor mode with the supervisor stack. Task switching is thus disabled during the trap handler. Second, the contents of the stack can vary. Normally it has the following format:

| | |
|---|---|
| Stack pointer (SSP) | Trap number (long word) |
| Stack pointer +4 | Status register (word) |
| Stack pointer +2 | Return address (long word) |

More information is placed on the stack if an address or bus error occurred, however. Also, this changes completely with new members of the 680x0 family, such as the 68010 and 68020. A good 68000 book is recommended as a reference if you try to make your trap handler handle all cases.

Otherwise, you could jump to the Exec trap handler when an address or bus error occurs, since there usually isn't anything that can be done about these errors.

To exit the trap handler, the trap number is removed from the stack (it's a long word) and an RTE (ReTurn from Exception) instruction is executed. Since Exec doesn't save any other registers on the stack, the contents of the processor register cannot be changed by the trap handler.

The following example uses a trap handler to catch a division by zero error. Since trap handlers cannot be written well in C, it is written in machine language and integrated into the source code with #asm and #endasm. Since not all C compilers recognize these preprocessor instructions (the program was written for Aztec C), the C and machine language portions may have to be compiled/assembled separately and then linked together.

```
/****  Trapping a  68000 exception  ****/

#include <exec/execbase.h>

extern struct ExecBase *SysBase;

main()
{
/*** Inserting the trap handler ***/

extern APTR Trap;
APTR oldtrap;
USHORT digit1,digit2;
struct Task *ThisTask;
```

```
oldtrap=SysBase->ThisTask->tc_TrapCode;
SysBase->ThisTask->tc_TrapCode=&Trap;
SysBase->ThisTask->tc_TrapData=(APTR)0;

/*** Configure a "Division by zero" trap ***/

digit1 = 10; digit2 = 0;
digit1 = digit1/digit2;

if((ULONG)SysBase->ThisTask->tc_TrapData==0)
 printf("Haven't reached this point!");
else
 printf
 ("Exception recognized, since tc_TrapData =
  TrapNumber:%ld\n",
 SysBase->ThisTask->tc_TrapData);

/*** Remove trap handler ***/

SysBase->ThisTask->tc_TrapCode=oldtrap;

}

/*** Trap-Handler ***/
/** RUNS WITH AZTEC C ONLY **/
/** TAB before opcode necessary! **/

#asm

_Trap move.l a0,-(sp)
      move.l 4,a0             ;SysBase
      move.l 276(a0),a0       ;SysBase->ThisTask
      move.l 4(sp),46(a0)     ;Trap-Number after
                              ;SysBase->ThisTask->tc_TrapData
      move.l (sp),a0
      add.l  #8,sp
      rte

#endasm
```

Without the trap handler this program would crash with a "Software error - Task held" because digit1 (10) is divided by 0. The If command proves that this has really generated a trap. Only the track can set tc_TrapData to a non-zero value after it was previously cleared by the task. But immediately after the illegal division Exec jumps to the trap handler. This takes the trap number off the supervisor stack and writes it in the tc_TrapData field. This is why the printf() call prints the number 5, the number of the division-by-zero trap, on the screen.

**The trap commands**

A trap generated by one of the 16 trap commands (trap numbers 32 to 47) also causes a jump to the trap handler. It is possible to allocate specific traps in advance, similar to the way signals are allocated and released. Allocating and releasing traps is just for preserving order so that it is always clear which traps are being used and which are not. If a trap command occurs, the trap handler is always called, regardless of whether a trap command is allocated with AllocTrap or not.

## 2.4.2.4  Message system, trap and exception functions

**AddPort()**

```
AddPort(Port)
        A1
```

Offset:        -354

Description:

AddPort() inserts the specified message port into the list of public ports. This list is ordered according to priority. The list header of this list can be accessed through SysBase->PortList. AddPort() also initializes the mp_MsgList structure in the message port.

Parameters:

Port    Pointer to a message port structure.

**AllocTrap()**

```
Trap_number = AllocTrap(Trap_number)
   D0                              D0
```

Offset:        -342

Description:

AllocTrap allocates one of the 68000 trap commands. A number between 0 and 15 can be specified as the trap number in order to allocate the corresponding trap command. If -1 is passed as the trap number, AllocTrap searches for the next free trap commands.

Parameter:

Trap_number
        A number between 0 and 15 for a given trap number or -1 for the first free one.

Result:

Trap_number
        contains the actual allocated trap command or -1 if the desired trap command was not free or no more trap commands were free.

*FindPort()*
```
Port = FindPort (Name)
D0                 A1
```

Offset:          -390

Description:
FindPort() searches the list of public message ports for the next one with the specified name. If such a port exists, it returns a pointer to this port.

Parameter:

Name
The name of the port to be found.

Result:

Port   A pointer to a message port with the specified name, or zero if no such port exists.

*FreeTrap()*
```
FreeTrap (Trap_number)
              D0
```

Offset:          -348

Description:
FreeTrap releases the trap command with the specified number.

Parameter:

Trap_number
The number of the trap command (0 to 15).

*PutMsg()*
```
PutMsg (port, message)
         A0      A1
```

Offset:          -366

Description:
PutMsg sends a message to the message port specified. There it is appended to the list of received messages and the appropriate action is initiated based on the contents of the mp_Flags field.

Parameters:

port   The address of the message port structure.

message
Pointer to the message structure of the message.

**RemPort()**
```
RemPort (port)
        A1
```

Offset:        -360

Description:

This function removes a message port from the list of public ports. It is then no longer possible to access it with FindPort.

Parameter:

port    Pointer to the message port.

**ReplyMsg()**
```
ReplyMsg (message)
         A1
```

Offset:        -378

Description:

ReplyMsg() sends a message back to its reply port. If the mn_ReplyPort field of the message structure is zero, nothing is done.

Parameter:

message
        Pointer to the message structure.

**SetExcept()**
```
OldSignals = SetExcept (NewSignals, mask)
  D0                              D0          D1
```

Offset:        -312

Description:

SetExcept determines which signals can generate an exception. The exact behavior of this function corresponds to that of SetSignals().

Parameters:

NewSignals
        are the new states of the exception signals.

mask    The mask determines which exception signals are changed.

Result:

OldSignals
        are the states of the exception signals before the change.

*WaitPort()*        Message = WaitPort (port)
                                        A0

                    Offset:          -384

                    Description:
                          WaitPort waits for a message to be received on the given port.
                          When a message arrives or if a message had already arrived before
                          WaitPort() was called, WaitPort returns with the address of this
                          message. The message is not removed from the list of received
                          messages, however. GetMsg() must be used for this.

                    Parameter:

                    port    Address of the port

                    Result:

                    Message
                          Pointer to the first message in the list

# 2.5    Amiga memory management

The Amiga uses dynamic memory management, which means that screen memory, disk storage, etc. as well as the programs loaded are not placed at any predefined location in memory but can be assigned a different location each time they are loaded. This dynamic memory management makes it possible to run several programs in memory at once, since no program is assigned a specified area of memory as is the case on other computers, such as the C64.

The system need only be told that memory is needed, whereupon it is assigned to the user, assuming that it is still free. The system doesn't make note of which program (task) was allocated the memory, only that it is no longer available for use by other tasks. More precisely: the system doesn't keep track of what memory is allocated, only what is still free.

When a task no longer needs a given area of memory, it should tell the system this so that the memory can be assigned to another task. If the unneeded memory isn't returned to the system, it remains allocated until a reset is performed. The result is naturally a drastic decrease in available memory.

Memory can be allocated only in eight-byte steps. If the amount of memory requested is not a multiple of eight, the system rounds it up to the next eight-byte increment. Thus the minimal amount of memory which can be allocated is eight bytes.

The Exec library contains several functions for allocating and releasing memory. These two are used most often: AllocMem() and FreeMem().

When allocating memory you must tell the system what type of memory you want and whether it should have certain properties.

These requirements, which can be chosen, are:

MEMF_CHIP
    specifies that the memory must be in chip memory. Chip memory is the lower 512K range which can be addressed by chips like the blitter. Graphics, sound, etc. must be in this area. Even if you only have 512K and therefore this condition is always fulfilled you should still specify it when necessary in order to maintain compatibility with devices with more memory. The code for this requirement is $02 and, like the other requirements, is defined in C by the memory include file.

MEMF_FAST
specifies that the memory to be allocated lies outside the lower 512K. This works only when using a RAM expansion, however. The code for the requirement is $04.

MEMF_PUBLIC
specifies that the memory cannot be moved after it has been allocated. Memory blocks aren't moved anyway in the current version of the operating system, but it should be used for tasks, interrupts, message ports, etc. for sake of future compatibility. The code for this requirement is $01.

MEMF_CLEAR
specifies that the allocated memory should be cleared with zeros. The code is $10000.

MEMF_LARGEST
specifies that the allocated memory should be the largest available memory block. The code for this is $20000.

If you want to have multiple requirements, like chip and clear, the codes must be ORed together. If neither chip memory nor fast memory is specified, the operating system attempts to allocate fast RAM first. If this fails, it tries the chip RAM.

*Note:*
You should not try to allocate or release memory inside an interrupt routine because the routines which perform these operations on the Amiga do not disable interrupts. If a task is in a routine for managing memory and is interrupted by an interrupt which also accesses the memory routines, the system can get in big trouble. The same applies for any routines called from an interrupt which must not be interrupted but which do not disable interrupts.

---

## 2.5.1    The AllocMem() and FreeMem() functions

*AllocMem()*
```
Memory = AllocMem(MemSize, requirements)
  D0                 D0           D1
```

Description
The function searches for a free memory area which corresponds to the specified requirements and marks it as allocated. The starting address of the memory is returned in D0. If it's not possible to allocate the desired memory, a zero is returned in D0 as an error message.

Parameters:

MemSize
indicates the amount of memory to be allocated.

requirements
> are the requirements described before which are passed to the
> AllocMem() function and which governs the search for a suitable
> area of memory.

AllocMem() cannot be used to allocate a specific area of memory, just
one of specific size. The operating system determines where in memory
it is located.

*FreeMem()*          FreeMem (MemBlock, Size)
                             A1       D0

Offset:        -210

Description:
> This function releases the previously allocated block of memory
> back to the system and allows it to be used by other tasks. The
> parameters passed to the function are rounded.

Parameters:

MemBlock
> is a pointer to the start of the memory area to be returned to the
> system. The pointer is rounded to the next multiple of eight.

Size    specifies how much memory is released. The size is also rounded
        to the next multiple of eight.

*Note:*         If an attempt is made to release memory which is already marked as
        free, a crash with Guru number 81000009 occurs.

The following C program shows how memory can be allocated and
released again.

```
#include <exec/memory.h>
#include <exec/types.h>

#define SIZE 1000

main()
{
    ULONG mem;

    mem = AllocMem(SIZE,MEMF_CHIP | MEMF_PUBLIC);
    if (mem = 0) {
    printf("\n Memory could not be allocated\n");
    exit(0);
    }
    printf("\n Memory allocated\n");
    FreeMem(SIZE, mem);
}
```

The starting address of the allocated memory is stored in mem.

## 2.5.2    The memory list structure

Often it is necessary to allocate several different areas of memory. To do
this you could call the AllocMem() function for each individual area.
You can clearly see that this can be a lot of work. Therefore the Exec
library has two functions which make this task easier for us. These
functions are called AllocEntry() and FreeEntry().

Before these functions can be called (how could it be otherwise on the
Amiga) a structure must be initialized from which the functions get
their parameters.

*The MemList*
*structure:*

The structure is called MemList and looks like this:

```
struct MemList {
0       struct Node ml_Node;
14      UWORD ml_NumEntries;
16      struct MemEntry ml_ME[1];
};
```

ml_Node
> is a node structure for chaining multiple MemList structures
> together.

ml_NumEntries
> specifies how many memory areas are allocated.

ml_ME[1]
> is another structure in which you enter the requirements for the
> memory to be reserved and the size of the memory block. This
> structure looks like this:

```
struct    MemEntry {
          union {
                              ULONG meu_Reqs;
                              APTR meu_Addr;
          } me_Un;
          ULONG me_Length;
};

#define me_un me_Un
#define me_Reqs me_Un.meu_Reqs
#define me_Addr me_Un.meu_Addr
```

me_Un

The contents of me_Un can vary due to the union. me_Un can contain the requirements for the memory allocation or a pointer to the reserved memory. When creating the MemEntry structure for calling the AllocEntry() function this contains the requirements (such as MEMF_CHIP) for the memory allocation, and after the call it contains the starting address of the allocated memory.

me_Length

specifies the length of memory to be allocated.

*AllocEntry()*
```
List = AllocEntry(MemList)
D0                    A0
```

Offset:        -222

Description:

The function is passed a pointer to the MemList structure in A0. The function then tries to allocate all of the memory blocks entered in the structure. If an area is allocated, a pointer replaces the requirements in the structure.

Result:

List   is a pointer to the newly-created MemList structure. If an error occurred during the allocation, the requirements of the unavailable memory is returned in D0, whereby the top bit (bit 31) is set. In this case no memory is allocated, even if other entries could have been allocated successfully.

*FreeEntry()*
```
FreeEntry(List)
          A0
```

Offset:        -228

Description:

This function returns all of the memory blocks in the MemList structure back to the system.

Parameter:

List   is a pointer to the MemList structure returned from the AllocEntry() function.

It is not possible to manage multiple chained MemList structures with either the AllocEntry() or FreeEntry() functions.

You may ask how it is possible to initialize multiple entries with a MemList structure, since there is clearly only one MemEntry structure (ml_ME[1]) in the MemList structure. A trick is used to initialize multiple entries. A custom structure must be created, one such as this:

```
struct {
    struct MemList me_Head;
    struct MemEntry me_More[3];
} myList;
```

Now you pass the pointer to this structure to AllocEntry() instead of the pointer to a MemList structure. This structure allows multiple entries to be initialized. In the example above four memory blocks are allocated by the AllocEntry function.

Let's look at an example of how the AllocEntry() function is used.

```
#include <exec/memory.h>
#include <exec/types.h>

struct mList {
struct MemList me_Head;
struct MemEntry me_More[2]; };

main()
{
struct MemList *MemoryList, *AllocEntry();

struct mList MyList;

myList.me_Head.ml_NumEntries = 3;
myList.me_Head.ml_me[0].me_Reqs = MEMF_CLEAR;
myList.me_Head.ml_me[0].me_Length = 100;
myList.me_Head.ml_me[1].me_Reqs = MEMF_CLEAR | MEMF_FAST;
myList.me_Head.ml_me[1].me_Length = 1900;
myList.me_Head.ml_me[2].me_Reqs = MEMF_PUBLIC | MEMF_CHIP;
myList.me_Head.ml_me[2].me_Length = 300;

MemoryList = AllocEntry(&MyList);

if ( ((ULONG)MemoryList) >> 30) {
    printf("\n Not all entries could be allocated\n");
    exit(0);        }

}
```

## 2.5.3    Memory management and tasks

When memory is allocated by a task, it's a good idea to allocate the memory with the AllocEntry() function. A list structure (tc_MemEntry) is included in the task structure which the allocated memory can be chained in the form of a MemList structure. The memory in this list can then be easily released by the routine which invoked the task.

Another advantage to entering the memory used in a list is that the task can also find out what memory blocks it has allocated.

Naturally it's also possible to allocate a block of memory with AllocMem() and then enter it in such a list.

---

## 2.5.4            Internal memory management

Now that you know how to reserve memory for your purposes, we want to look at how the memory is managed internally.

As you might guess, the memory is managed with a structure. This structure looks as follows:

*The*
*Memheader*
*structure:*

```
struct Memheader {
0       struct Node mh_Node;
14      UWORD mh_Attributes;
16      struct MemChunk *mh_First;
20      APTR mh_Lower;
24      APTR mh_Upper;
28      ULONG mh_Free;
}

#define MEMF_PUBLIC         (1L<<0)
#define MEMF_CHIP           (1L<<1)
#define MEMF_FAST           (1L<<2)
#define MEMF_CLEAR          (1L<<16)
#define MEMF_LARGEST        (1L<<17)
#define MEM_BLOCKSIZE 8L
#define MEM_BLOCKMASK 7L
```

mh_Node
>     is a node structure used to put the MemHeader structure in a list.

mh_Attributes
>     specifies the requirements for memory, such as MEMF_FAST.

*mh_First
>     is a pointer to the first MemChunk structure. The construction and purpose of this structure is explained later.

mh_Lower
>     is a pointer to the start of memory managed by the header.

mh_Upper
>     is a pointer to the end of memory managed by the header.

mh_Free
>     specifies how much memory is available through this header.

*MemChunk*        As we've already mentioned, the system doesn't keep track of what
                  memory is allocated, but what memory is still free. The unallocated
                  memory blocks are combined with the help of a MemChunk structure.
                  The size and position of the free memory blocks can easily be deter-
                  mined with these structures. The structure has the following appearance:

```
struct MemChunk {
0       struct MemChunk *mc_Next;
4       ULONG mc_Bytes;
}
```

                  *mc_Next
                       is a pointer to the next MemChunk structure.

                  mc_Bytes
                       specifies how many bytes are free in this memory block.

                  The mh_First entry in the MemHeader structure points to the first
                  MemChunk structure, which is at the start of the first free memory
                  block. The first four bytes of this free block are the pointer to the next
                  free memory area (and the next MemChunk structure). The next four
                  bytes specify how large the memory area is. In the last MemChunk
                  structure the mc_Next pointer is set to zero and mc_Bytes indicates how
                  many bytes are between the current memory position and the value in
                  mh_Upper.

                  One MemHeader structure manages the entire chip memory and the fast
                  memory, if this is present. These structures are chained into a list con-
                  tained in the ExecBase structure. This list is called MemList and is at
                  offset 322.

                  The MemHeader priority for the fast memory area is zero and the prior-
                  ity for the chip memory area is -10. This is why Exec always tries to
                  allocate memory in fast RAM first and then chip RAM.

                  When a task now wants to allocate memory, Exec looks in the
                  MemList of the ExecBase structure to see if the requirements in the
                  AllocMem() function match the requirements in the MemHeader struc-
                  ture. Second, it checks to see if the free memory indicated in mh_Free
                  is sufficient to reserve the quantity of memory requested. If one of the
                  conditions is not fulfilled, Exec checks to see if another MemHeader
                  structure is present. If no more are reachable, a negative value is
                  returned to the AllocMem() function. Otherwise the pointer mh_First is
                  fetched and the first MemChunk structure is checked to see if it contains
                  enough memory to satisfy the request. If not, the next MemChunk
                  structure is checked. If no sufficiently large contiguous block of mem-
                  ory is found, a negative value is returned. If a suitable block is found,
                  the amount of free memory left is calculated and a MemChunk structure
                  is inserted at the position where the free memory begins and this is
                  inserted in the list. The newly allocated block is removed from the list
                  and the number of allocated bytes are subtracted from the total.

## 2.5.5          The Allocate and Deallocate functions

It is possible to create a MemHeader structure and manage a separate
memory area with the Allocate() and Deallocate() functions. These functions only allow memory to be allocated and released, however.
Requirements may not specified.

*Allocate()*        Memory = Allocate (MemHeader, ByteSize)
                      D0                      A0        D0

Offset:          -186

Description:
             The function allocates the specified memory managed by the
             specified MemHeader structure.

Parameters:

MemHeader
             is a pointer to a MemHeader structure.

ByteSize
             specifies how much memory is allocated.

Result:

Memory
             is a pointer to the allocated memory. If no memory was found, a
             zero is returned.

*Deallocate()*      Deallocate(MemHeader, Memory, ByteSize);
                               A0         A1        A0

Offset: -192

Description:
             This function releases the allocated memory back to the
             MemHeader structure.

Parameters:

MemHeader
             is a pointer to the MemHeader structure.

Memory
             is a pointer to the start of memory to be released.

ByteSize
             indicates how much memory is released.

The following program illustrates how these functions are used.

```c
#include <exec/execbase.h> /* Aztec C use option +L */
#include <exec/memory.h>
#include <exec/types.h>

#define Byte_Size 10000

struct ExecBase *SysBase;

main()
{
    struct MemHeader *header;
    struct MemChunk *chunk;
    APTR Amtmemory, AllocMem(), Allocate();

    header = (struct MemHeader *)
             AllocMem(sizeof(struct MemHeader)
                          ,MEMF_PUBLIC | MEMF_CLEAR);
    if (Amtmemory == 0) {
        printf ("\n AlloMem 1 unsuccessful\n");
        exit (0);
    }

    Amtmemory = AllocMem(Byte_Size
                          ,MEMF_PUBLIC | MEMF_CLEAR);
    if (Amtmemory == 0) {
        printf ("\n AlloMem 2 unsuccessful\n");
        FreeMem(header,sizeof(struct MemHeader));
        exit (0);
    }

    chunk = (struct MemChunk *) Amtmemory;
    chunk ->mc_Next = 0;
    chunk ->mc_Bytes = Byte_Size;

    header ->mh_Node.ln_Type = NT_MEMORY;
    header ->mh_Node.ln_Pri  = -100;
    header ->mh_Node.ln_Name = "MemHeader";
    header ->mh_Attributes = MEMF_PUBLIC | MEMF_CHIP;
    header ->mh_First = chunk;
    header ->mh_Lower = Amtmemory;
    header ->mh_Upper = Amtmemory + Byte_Size;
    header ->mh_Free  = Byte_Size;

    AddTail (&SysBase ->MemList,header);

    Amtmemory = Allocate (header,500);
    if (Amtmemory == 0) {
        printf ("\n Allocate unsuccessful\n");
        exit (0);
    }
    Deallocate (header,Amtmemory,500);
    printf ("\n Allocate and deallocate successful!\n");

}
```

## 2.5.6    Remaining functions

*AvailMem()*     AvailMem(Requirements)
                                D1

Offset:        -216

Description:
This function returns the size of memory relative to the requirements.

*AllocAbs()*     Memory = AllocAbs(ByteSize, Position)
                   D0                  D0         A1

Offset:        -204

Description:
This function allows a specific memory area to be allocated.

Parameters:

ByteSize
specifies the amount of memory to be allocated.

Position
is a pointer to the memory to be allocated.

Result:

Memory
Is a pointer to the allocated memory, which also corresponds to
Position. If it was not possible to allocate the specified memory,
a zero is returned as an error message.

# 2.6    I/O handling on the Amiga

In this section we'll show how Exec performs the I/O management. Less emphasis is placed on various devices themselves. The DOS part of this book shows how the Amiga input/output control is used in programs. Knowledge of the DOS chapter is recommended for understanding this material.

## 2.6.1    The IORequest structure

To conduct input and output processes you need an IORequest structure to transfer your commands to the device.

There are two kinds of IORequest structures, called IORequest and IOStdReq (IO Standard Request). The IOStdReq structure is an extension of the IORequest structure. The structures look like this:

```
struct IORequest {
0        struct Message io_Message;
20       struct Device *io_Device;
24       struct Unit *io_Unit;
28       UWORD io_Command;
30       UBYTE io_Flags;
31       BYTE io_Error;
}
```

io_Message
> is a message structure as described in Section 2.4. It's needed so that the device can tell us that it's done processing the I/O command. The message structure must be initialized correctly before the I/O can function.

*io_Device
> is a pointer to the device structure to be used, described shortly.

*io_Unit
> is a pointer to a unit structure, described below.

io_Command
> is a word in which the command to be executed is passed.

io_Flags

is needed in order to pass device-specific status messages or commands. The byte is divided into high and low nibbles. The lower four bits are used by Exec for internal purposes. The upper four bits can be used by the programmer to communicate with the device.

io_Error

is used to pass error messages to the programmer.

Often this structure is not sufficient to use a device. In this case there is another structure which offers the user more possibilities. It looks like this:

```
struct IOStdReq {
0       struct Message io_Message;
20      struct Device *io_Device;
24      struct Unit *io_Unit;
28      UWORD io_Command;
30      UBYTE io_Flags;
31      BYTE io_Error;
32      ULONG io_Actual;
36      ULONG io_Length;
40      APTR io_Data;
44      ULONG io_Offset;
}
```

io_Actual

indicates the number of bytes transferred. The value cannot be read until the end of the transfer.

io_Length

specifies the number of bytes to be transferred. This value must be initialized before the transfer. Often the value is set to -1 to transfer a variable number of bytes.

io_Data

is a pointer to the data buffer in which the data are placed.

io_Offset

specifies the offset, which is device specific. With a TrackDevice the block to be used is passed in the offset.

## 2.6.2    Construction of a device

The device structure looks like a library:

```
struct Device {
      struct Library dd_Library;
}

#define DEV_BEGINIO (-30L)
#define DEV_ABORTIO (-36L)
#define IOB_QUICK (0L)
#define IOF_QUICK (1L<<0)
#define CMD_INVALID (0L
#define CMD_RESET 1L
#define CMD_READ 2L
#define CMD_WRITE 3L
#define CMD_UPDATE 4L
#define CMD_CLEAR 5L
#define CMD_STOP 6L
#define CMD_START 7L
#define CMD_FLUSH 8L
#define CMD_NONSTD 9L
```

To use a device, it must first be opened. The command for opening a device is:

```
Error = OpenDevice (Name, Unit, IORequest, flags)
D0                   A0    D0    A1         D1
```

The IORequest structure must be initialized before the OpenDevice function is used.

Like the libraries, each device has a jump table in which the entries are reached with negative offsets. The functions reached through the jump table are used to open and close a device as well as to perform I/O. Such a routine is necessary so that a function like OpenDevice() can open any device, even when the tasks to be accomplished vary from device to device. The OpenDevice() function thus jumps to the routine for the corresponding device for the device-specific processes.

The most important functions which each device offers are:

| Offset | Function |
|--------|----------|
| -36 | AbortIO |
| -30 | BeginIO |
| -12 | Close |
| -6 | Open |

Let's take a closer look at the assembly language routine to see what happens when a device is opened.

The routine shown here is the most important part of the OpenDevice() function, but it is not called by the Exec library directly but by a routine in the RAM library.

*Routine entry parameters:*

D0 = Unit
D1 = flags
A0 = pointer to the device name
A1 = pointer to IORequest
A6 = pointer to ExecBase

```
fc0666 move.l    A2,-(A7)         save A2
fc0668 move.l    A1,A2            pointer to IORequest in A2
fc066a clr.b     31(A1)          clear error flag
fc066e movem.l   D1-D0,-(a7)     save D0 and D1
fc0672 move.l    A0,A1           pointer to name in A1
fc0674 lea       350(A6),A0      pointer to DeviceList in A0
fc0678 addq.b    #1,295(A6)      forbid
fc067c bsr.l     $fc165a         find name in DeviceList
                                 (FindName())

fc0680 move.l    D0,A0           pointer to device in A0
fc0682 movem.l   (a7)+,D1-D0     restore D0 and D1
fc0686 move.l    A0,20(A2)       enter pointer to device in
                                 IORequest
fc068a beq.s     $fc06ac         error, device not present
fc068c clr.l     24(A2)          clear pointer to Unit
fc0690 move.l    A2,A1           pointer to IORequest in A1
fc0692 move.l    A6,-(A7)        save A6
fc0694 move.l    A0,A6           pointer to Device in A6
fc0696 jsr       -6(A6)          jump to OpenDevice
fc069a move.l    (A7)+,A6        restore A6
fc069c move.b    31(A2),D0       error flag in D0
fc06a0 ext.w     D0              sign-extend error
fc06a2 ext.l     D0              sign-extend error
fc06a4 jsr       -138(A6)        Permit()
fc06a8 move.l    (A7)+,A2        restore A2
fc06aa rts                       return
```

*Entry for device not found (error):*

```
fc06ac moveq     #$ff,D0         error value in D0
fc06ae move.b    D0,31(A2)       write in error flag
fc06b2 bra.s     $fc06a4         unconditional branch
```

The following routine is the most important portion of the CloseDevice() function.

The routine is entered with:

A1 = pointer to IORequest
A6 = pointer to ExecBase

```
fc06b4 addq.b    #1,295(A6)      Forbid
fc06b8 move.l    A6,-(A7)        save A6
fc06ba move.l    20(A1),A6       pointer to device in A6
fc06be jsr       -12(A6)         jump to CloseDevice
fc06c2 move.l    (A7)+,A6        restore A6
fc06c4 jsr       -138(A6)        Permit
fc06c8 rts                       return
```

We use the OpenDevice routine of the TrackDisk device as an example of a OpenDevice routine which is called through offset -6 from the device and which performs device-specific tasks when opening the device.

For the TrackDevice the unit number specifies the number of the drive to be accessed. A pointer in the device structure is reserved for each of the four possible drives which points to the corresponding message port for the drive, assuming that the drive is present. This port, like the device itself, has additional entries in addition to the standard entries defined in the C structure, such as a counter for the number of accesses to the message port structure.

The routine is called with:

D0 = Unit number
D1 = flags
A1 = pointer to IORequest
A6 = pointer to device

```
fe9f42 movem.l   A4/A2/D2,-(A7)  save D2, A2, A4
fe9f46 move.l    A1,A4           pointer to IORequest to A4
fe9f48 move.l    D0,D2           drive number to D2
fe9f4a cmpi.l    #$00000004,D0   number too large?
fe9f50 bcs.s     $fe9f56         branch if number ok
fe9f52 moveq     #$20,D0         else error number in D0
fe9f54 bra.s     $fe9f82         return error, done
fe9f56 lsl.w     #2,D0           number*4 for offset
fe9f58 lea       36(A6),A2       pointer to drive port
fe9f5c adda.l    D0,A2           add offset
fe9f5e move.l    (A2),A0         drive port to A0
fe9f60 move.l    A0,D0           is drive present?
fe9f62 bne.s     $fe9f70         branch if everything ok
fe9f64 bsr.l     $fe9d3e         else determine drive port
fe9f68 tst.l     D0              port found?
fe9f6a bne.l     $fe9f82         branch if not found
fe9f6e move.l    A0,(A2)         enter port in device
fe9f70 move.l    A0,24(A4)       enter port in IORequest
fe9f74 addq.w    #1,32(A6)       increment number of
                                 accesses to device
fe9f78 addq.w    #1,36(A0)       increment number of access
                                 to drive port
fe9f7c movem.l   (A7)+,A4/A2/D2  restore D2, A2, A4
fe9f80 rts                       return
```

*Entry for error in drive port assignment:*
```
fe9f82 move.b    D0,31(A4)       error number in error flag
fe9f86 move.w    #$ff,D0         error number in D0
fe9f88 move.l    D0,24(A4)       clear pointer to unit
fe9f8c move.l    D0,20(A4)       clear pointer to device
fe9f90 bra.s     $fe9f7c         unconditional branch
```

*TrackDisk*    The CloseDevice() function jumps to a device-specific routine at offset -12. The routine for the TrackDisk device looks like this:

```
fe9f92 movem.l    A3-A2,-(A7)    save A2 and A3
fe9f96 move.l     A1,A2          pointer to IORequest to A2
fe9f98 move.l     24(A2),A3      pointer to drive port to A3
fe9f9c subq.w     #1,36(A3)      decrement number of accesses
fe9fa0 bne.s      $fe9fa8        branch is drive still needed
fe9fa2 bset       #3,64(A3)      set flag
fe9fa8 subq.w     #1,32(A6)      decrement number of accesses
                                 to the device
fe9fac moveq      #$ff,D0        load clear value
fe9fae move.l     D0,24(A2)      clear pointer to port
fe9fb2 move.l     D0,20(A2)      clear pointer to device
fe9fb6 movem.l    (A7)+,A3-A2    restore A2 and A3
fe9fba moveq      #$00,D0        return message zero in D0
fe9fbc rts                       return
```

## 2.6.3      I/O control with functions

For each device there is always a task where commands can be passed.
The following routines are used to send commands to a device:

*DoIO()*

```
Error = DoIO(IORequest)
D0              A1
```

Offset:        -456

Description:
    This function is usually used for I/O control. It waits until the
    command passed has been completed and then returns to the call-
    ing program. In the intervening time the task is set to wait.

*SendIO()*

```
SendIO(IORequest)
       A1
```

Offset:        -462

Description:
    This function is used to send a I/O request to the corresponding
    device, but it doesn't wait for it to finish.

*CheckIO()*

```
done = CheckIO(IORequest)
D0               A1
```

Offset:        -468

Description:
    The function checks if a given I/O process has been processed. If
    this is the case, a pointer to the corresponding IORequest struc-
    ture is returned in D0. If the process is not finished, a zero is
    returned.

*WaitIO()*         WaitIO(IORequest)
                        A1

                   Offset:        -474

                   Description:
                        This function waits until the I/O process has been completed.
                        During this time the current task is set to wait so that other
                        tasks can be processed. The SendIO and WaitIO functions
                        together are equivalent to DoIO.

*AbortIO()*        AbortIO(IORequest)
                        A1

                   Offset:        -480

                   Description:
                        This function terminates an I/O process.

                   After this brief description of the functions, let's look at how they
                   appear in the operating system.

*DoIo  routine*    The DoIO assembly language routine looks like this:

                   A pointer to the initialized IORequest structure is in A1.

```
fc06dc move.l    A1,-(A7)          save A1
fc06de move.b    #$01,30(A1)       set quick bit
fc06e4 move.l    A6,-(A7)          save A6
fc06e6 move.l    20(A1),A6         get pointer to device
fc06ea jsr       -30(A6)           jump to IO execution
fc06ee move.l    (A7)+,A6          get A6
fc06f0 move.l    (A7)+,A1          get A1
```

                   Here begins the WaitIO function which is used by the DoIO function.

```
fc06f2 btst      #0,30(A1)           test quick bit
fc06f8 bne.s     $fc0744             done if set
fc06fa move.l    A2,-(A7)            save A2
fc06fc move.l    A1,A2               pointer to IORequest to A2
fc06fe move.l    14(A2),A0           pointer to Reply port
fc0702 move.b    15(A0),D1           get signal bit for port
fc0706 moveq     #$00,D0             clear D0
fc0708 bset      D1,D0               set bit for signal
fc070a move.w    #$4000,$dff09a      disable
fc0712 addq.b    #1,294(A6)          macro
fc0716 cmpi.b    #$07,8(A2)          type of msg = reply msg?
fc071c beq.s     $fc0724             branch if type ok
fc071e jsr       -318(A6)            else wait for msg (wait())
fc0722 bra.s     $fc0716             unconditional jump
fc0724 move.l    A2,A1               IORequest to A1
fc0726 move.l    (A1),A0
fc0728 move.l    4(A1),A1            remove node
fc072c move.l    A0(A1)              from reply msg list
```

```
fc072e move.l    A1,4(A0)
fc0732 subq.b    #1,294(A6)       enable
fc0736 bge.s     $fc0740
fc0738 move.w    #$c000,$dff09a macro
fc0740 move.l    A2,A1            pointer to IORequest to A1
fc0742 move.l    (A7)+,A2         restore A2
fc0744 move.b    31(A1),D0        error flag to D0
fc0748 ext.w     D0               sign extend
fc074a ext.l     D0               sign extend
fc074c           rts              return
```

In the routine above, the quick bit is set immediately. Then the pointer
to the device is placed in A6 and the BeginIO function is called, which
is described later for the TrackDisk device. This routine checks the
command to be performed for validity and then passes it on to the
TrackDisk task. When the program returns from this routine, the
message type in the IORequest structure is always set to "message."
The task is passed the IORequest structure as a message.

The command passing is all done now. You just have to wait for it to
finish. If the quick bit has not been cleared, the routine ends. Otherwise
it checks to see if the I/O process is done. To do this it simply checks
to see if the type of the message structure is "reply message." If this is
not the case, the task waits until the appropriate message is received.

It may be necessary to explain more clearly why it suffices to test the
substructure Message in the IORequest structure for the type reply
message.

The BeginIO routine (the routine which the device makes available at
offset -30) sends a message to the corresponding task which executes
the command. The message which is sent is our IORequest structure,
sent with the PutMsg() function. The type of the message to be sent is
automatically set to "message" (byte value 05). Our IORequest structure
has the same location in memory, but it's now appended to the message
list of the task by its Node structure. The task processes your command
and sends a reply message to indicate that it's finished. The message
returned is the IORequest structure again. The type of message sent is
automatically set to ReplyMsg (byte value 07) by the ReplyMsg()
function and appends to the message list of the reply port. The WaitIO()
function checks the type of the message structure in your IORequest
structure, determines that it is a reply message, and removes it from the
ReplyMsg list.

*The SendIO*
*function:*

The pointer to the IORequest structure is in A1:

```
fc06ca clr.b     30(A1)           clear all flags
fc06ce move.l    A6,-(A7)         save A6
fc06d0 move.l    20(A1),A6        get pointer to device
fc06d4 jsr  -30(A6)               jump to BeginIO
fc06d8 move.l    (A7)+,A6         get A6
fc06da rts                        return
```

You can see that the SendIO function is no different from the start of the DoIO function.

**The CheckIO function:**

A pointer to the IORequest structure is in A1.

```
fc074e btst    #0,30(A1)     test if quick bit is set
fc0754 beq.s   $fc075a       branch if not set
fc0756 move.l  A1,D0         else return OK message
fc0758 rts                   return
fc075a cmpi.b  #$07,8(A1)    type of message structure =
                             ReplyMsg?
fc0760 beq.s   $fc0766       yes, then positive return
fc0762 moveq   #$00,D0       else negative return message
fc0764         rts           return
fc0766 move.l  A1,D0         return OK message
fc0768 rts                   return
```

The CheckIO function tests to see if a reply message has arrived. If this is the case, a pointer to the IORequest structure is returned in D0, else a zero is sent in D0.

This routine checks to see if a reply message has arrived, but it does not remove it from the list of reply messages. When using CheckIO the reply message must be removed by hand, such as with the GetMsg() function, as long as the quick bit is not set.

**The AbortIO function:**

A pointer to the IORequest structure is in A1.

```
fc076a move.l  A6,-(A7)      save A6
fc076c move.l  20(A1),A6     pointer to device in A6
fc0770 jsr     -36(A6)       jump to AbortIO
fc0774 move.l  (A7)+,A6      restore A6
fc0776 rts                   return
```

As we have mentioned, each device has a jump table for managing the device-dependent routines. Let's use the TrackDisk device as an example to see what's behind the routine which actually performs the I/O. It is called with offset -30 and is used by the DoIO and SendIO functions.

A pointer to the IORequest structure is in A1 and a pointer to the device in A6.

```
fe9fbe clr.b   31(A1)            clear error flag
fe9fc2 move.w  #$00,D0           clear D0
fe9fc4 move.b  29(A1),D0         io_Command to D0
fe9fc8 cmpi.b  #$16,D0           legal command?
fe9fcc bcc.s   $fea016           branch if not
fe9fce move.l  24(A1),A0         pointer to device port
fe9fd2 move.l  #$000c61c2,D1     command code bits
fe9fd8 btst    D0,D1             execute command
                                 directly?
fe9fda bne.s   $fe9ff0           yes
fe9fdc andi.b  #$7e,30(A1)       clear flags except
                                 quick bit
fe9fe2 move.l  A6,-(A7)          save A6
```

```
fe9fe4 move.l 52(A6),A6              get ExecBase
fe9fe8 jsr     -366(A6)             PutMsg (pass IORequest
                                    to TrackDisk task)
fe9fec move.l (A7)+,A6              get A6
fe9fee bra.s  $fea014              unconditional branch
fe9ff0 bset   #7,30(A1)            set flag for execution
fe9ff6 move.b #$05,8(A1)           set type in IORequest
                                    structure to message so
                                    that WaitIO has to wait
fe9ffc movem.l A3-A2,-(A7)         save A2 and A3
fea000 move.l A0,A3                pointer to drive port
                                    in A3
fea002 move.l A1,A1                pointer to IORequest in
                                    A2
fea004 lea    762(PC)($=fea300),A0 pointer to command
                                    table
fea008 lsl.w  #2,D0                command*4 to get offset
fea00a move.l 0(A0,D0.W),A0        get entry
fea00e jsr    (A0)                 jump
fea010 movem.l (A7)+,A3-A2         restore A2 and A3
fea014 rts                         return
```

# 2.7 Interrupt handling on the Amiga

In this section we want to look at how the Amiga uses the seven interrupt levels available to the processor and how you can use them as well.

To better understand this material you should have read the parts of Chapter 1 pertaining to interrupts.

In this section we'll look at the interrupt after the processor has received the appropriate signal from the 4703 chip's interrupt logic.

After the processor has received an interrupt signal and it was not disabled, it loads the address corresponding to the priority into its program counter and executes the routine it finds there. The vector for the interrupt service routines are at address $0064 to $007F, whereby the first four bytes of the vector are for level 1 and bytes $007C to $007F contain the vector for interrupt level 7.

Since the Amiga uses more interrupts than the processor has available, all interrupts go through a register which manages the 15 different interrupts. The interrupts which arrive are checked to see if they are allowed with the help of an interrupt enable register. If a given interrupt is permitted, an interrupt is sent to the processor. Since there are only seven priorities for 15 interrupt sources, more than one interrupt is assigned to the same processor priority. Since their priorities are the same, various interrupts have the same vector and the corresponding interrupt service routine must determine the source of the interrupt. The following table shows the priorities of the various interrupts. By pseudo-priority we mean the priority by which the software checks the sources. The number corresponds to the bit number of the interrupt stored in the interrupt request register.

*An example:* The interrupt which is generated when the raster beam reaches screen line 0 has the same priority as the interrupt for the end of the blitter activity. The two interrupts are indicated by bits 5 and 6 of the interrupt request register. In software the interrupt with the higher bit number (the higher pseudo-priority) is checked before the lower. In this case the blitter interrupt is checked before the raster beam interrupt.

The next table lists the fifteen interrupts on the Amiga and their processor and pseudo-priorities.

| Pseudo-priority | Name | Processor priority | Function |
|---|---|---|---|
| 14 | INTEN | (6) | Enable interrupts |
| 13 | EXTER | 6 | Interrupt from CIA-B or expansion port |
| 12 | DSKSYN | 5 | Disk sync value recognized |
| 11 | RBF | 5 | Input buffer of the serial port full |
| 10 | AUD3 | 4 | Audio data on channel 3 output |
| 9 | AUD2 | 4 | Audio data on channel 2 output |
| 8 | AUD1 | 4 | Audio data on channel 1 output |
| 7 | AUD0 | 4 | Audio data on channel 0 output |
| 6 | BLIT | 3 | Blitter done |
| 5 | VERTB | 3 | Start of the vertical blanking gap |
| 4 | COPER | 3 | Reserved for Copper interrupts |
| 3 | PORTS | 2 | Interrupt from CIA-A or expansion port |
| 2 | SOFT | 1 | Reserved for software interrupts |
| 1 | DSKBLK | 1 | Disk DMA transfer ended |
| 0 | TBE | 1 | Output buffer of the serial port empty |

## 2.7.1 The interrupt structure

It shouldn't surprise you that there is a structure specifically for managing interrupts on the Amiga.

The structure looks like this:

```
struct Interrupt {
0       struct Node is_Node;
14      APTR is_Data;
18      VOID (*is_Code)();
}
```

is_Node
    is a standard node structure.

is_Data
> is a pointer to a data buffer which can be used by the interrupt. The size of the buffer can be set to any value when the structure is created.

is_(*Code)()
> is a pointer to the actual interrupt program to be executed.

There are two ways to use an interrupt. A program, called an interrupt handler or interrupt service routine, can be executed during the interrupt, or an interrupt can be used to call several programs, which is done with an interrupt server.

Every permitted interrupt is noted in the ExecBase structure. In this structure there is a small substructure for each of the fifteen possible interrupts, the initialization of which is very important for the interrupt. The substructure is called IntVector and looks like this:

```
struct IntVector {
0      APTR iv_Data;
4      VOID (*iv_Code)();
8      struct Node *iv_Node;
}
```

The initialization of the IntVector structure is different depending on whether the corresponding interrupt is managed by an interrupt handler or server. For the interrupt handler the initialization goes like this:

iv_Data
> is a pointer to the same data buffer mentioned in the Interrupt structure.

(*iv_Code)()
> is a pointer to the interrupt program to be executed.

*iv_Node
> is a pointer to the interrupt structure described.

For the interrupt server it looks like this:

iv_Date
> is a pointer to a ServerList structure, explained shortly.

(*iv_Code)()
> is a pointer to a routine which handles the management of multiple interrupt programs.

*iv_Node
> is not used here and has the value zero.

These interrupt vector structures don't have to be initialized by hand if you want to use an interrupt handler. The initialization is done by calling the Exec function SetIntVector. To use an interrupt with an interrupt handler the interrupt structure must be initialized and the SetIntVector function called.

Let's look at how an interrupt is processed after it has been started by the processor. As an example, the following listing is an interrupt handler which manages a level 3 (priority 3) interrupt.

$FC0CD8 is the entry where the processor jumps after recognizing a level-3 interrupt. This address applies only to Kickstart 1.2 in ROM in the Amiga 500 or 2000. On the Amiga 1000 the routine is the same, but shifted slightly depending on the version of Kickstart.

```
movem.l A6-A5/A1-A0/D1-D0,-(A7)  save registers on the
                                 stack
lea      $dff000,A0              start of register to A0
move.l   $0004,A6                SysBase to A6
move.w   28(A0),D1               read interrupt enable
                                 register
btst     #14,D1                  test master bit
beq.l    L1                      no interrupts allowed
and.w    30(A0),D1               filter out the allowed
                                 interrupts with the interrupt
                                 request register
btst     #6,D1                   test bit for blitter done
beq.s    L2                      no, test other bit
movem.l  156(A6),A5/A1           get pointers to data and
                                 program from IntVector
                                 structure
pea      -36(A6)                 set return to ExitInter
jmp      (A5)                    jump to interrupt

L2:

btst     #5,D1                   test bit for RasterInter
beq.s    L3                      no, keep testing
movem.l  144(A6),A5/A1           get pointers to data and
                                 program from IntVector
                                 structure
pea      -36(A6)                 set return to ExitInter
jmp      (A5)                    jump to interrupt

L3:

btst     #4,D1                   test bit for copper interrupt
beq.s    L1                      no, then done
movem.l  132(A6),A5/A1           get pointers to data and
                                 program from IntVector
                                 structure
pea      -36(A6)                 set return to ExitInter
jmp      (A5)                    jump to interrupt
```

```
L1:

movem.l   (A7)+,A6-A5/A1-A0/D1-D0   restore registers
rte                                 return
```

From the assembly listing you can see which registers you can use in your interrupt program and which contain specific values you can use.

The registers D0, D1, A0, A1, A5 and A6 are saved on the stack before the actual interrupt program is executed. The return address is also saved on the stack so that the interrupt program must be terminated with RTS.

*Description of*   D0   contains no useful information
*the registers:*   D1   contains the AND of IntEnaReg and IntReqReg and thus shows
                        which interrupts are currently enabled
                   A1   is a pointer to the start of the hardware registers
                   A5   is a pointer to the code to be executed
                   A6   is a pointer to SysBase

None of these registers need be restored to their old values before the interrupt program returns.

When an interrupt handler is used, the actual interrupt program is executed with "jmp (a5)". The interrupt program must be terminated with RTS.

When interrupts are managed by an interrupt server the individual interrupt programs which are executed when an interrupt occurs must be linked into a list by their interrupt structures. The processing order corresponds to the priorities stored in their is_Node structures.

The list structure in which the interrupts are stored looks like this:

```
struct ServerList {
0       struct List sl_List;
14      UWORD sl_IntClr1;
16      UWORD sl_IntSet;
18      UWORD sl_IntClr2;
20      UWORD sl_pad;
}
```

sl_List
        is a list structure.

sl_IntClr1 and sl_IntClr22
        are words in which the bit responsible for the interrupt in the interrupt request register is set. The Clr/Set bit (#15), explained in Chapter 1, is cleared here. If this value is written into the interrupt request register, the interrupt bit is cleared.

sl_IntSet
>   is a word with the same contents as sl_IntClr but with the Clr/
>   Set bit set.

sl_pad
>   is a word which is always zero.

This structure is not included into any include file and must be declared
by hand if it is needed.

Since we now want to use an interrupt server, the initialization of the
interrupt vector structure is such that (*iv_Code)() is a pointer to a routine which manages an interrupt list.

This routine is called with "jmp (A5)", lies at address $FC12FC, and
looks like this:

A1 contains the pointer to the ServerList structure.

```
fc12fc move.w  18(A1),-(A7)    read and store sl_IntClr
fc1300 move.l  A2,-(A7)        save A2
fc1302 move.l  (A1),A2         pointer to first interrupt
fc1304 move.l  (A2),D0         see if interrupt present
fc1306 beq.s   $fc1316         branch if not present
fc1308 movem.l 14(A2),A5/A1    a1 = is_Data and a5 =
                               (*is_Code)()
fc130e jsr     (A5)            jump to interrupt program
fc1310 bne.s   $fc1316         branch if return message is
                               not zero
fc1312 move.l  (A2),A2         set pointer to next
                               interrupt
fc1314 bra.s   $fc1304
fc1316 move.l  (A7)+,A2        restore A2
fc1318 move.w  (A7)+,$dff09c   clear interrupt bit in
                               interrupt request register
fc131e rts                     return
```

When one interrupt is processed, the next one is called immediately,
assuming another one is present and the previous one returned a zero
value. The return value is generally passed in D0.

The same registers are free here as for the interrupt handler. The only
difference is in the values which they pass.

*Description of*   **D0**   is a pointer to the next interrupt
*the registers:*   **D1**   unknown value
               **A1**   is a pointer to the interrupt buffer
               **A5**   is a pointer to the actual interrupt program
               **A6**   unknown value

To make it easier to understand the management of an interrupt through an interrupt server, we'll explain the process using the port interrupt generated by CIA-A as an example.

The interrupt vector structure for this interrupt is at offset 120 from the ExecBase structure and is initialized as follows:

iv_Data
>points to the ServerList structure.

(*iv_Code)()
>is a pointer to a subroutine which manages the server list. This routine is at $FC12FC on the Amiga 500 and 2000 (1.2.)

*iv_Node
>is not initialized because the interrupt structures are linked in the ServerList structure.

The initialized ServerList structure looks like this:

sl_List
>is initialized like any list structure. The interrupt structures are linked together in this list.

sl_IntClr and sl_IntSet
>have the value $0008 since bit 3 of the interrupt request register is responsible for this interrupt.

sl_IntSet
>has the value $8008.

---

## 2.7.2      Soft interrupts

Like the name says, these are interrupts which are generated by software. These interrupts have a higher priority than tasks, but lower than hardware interrupts and can be used to execute various synchronous processes.

*The Cause()*   The Cause() function is used to call such a function. When this is called
*function*   the running task is interrupted and the interrupt is executed. If the Cause() function is called by a hardware interrupt service routine, it is ended before the soft interrupt is generated.

To create a software interrupt, the interrupt structure must first be initialized, as for all interrupts. The Cause() function can then be called,
whereby the pointer to the structure is passed in A1.

A soft interrupt can be assigned only five different priorities: -32, -16,
0, +16, +32. This is because there is a SoftIntList structure in the
ExecBase structure for each priority and there is only room for five
structures.

Each of the structures looks like this:

```
struct SoftIntList {
0       struct List sh_List;
14      UWORD sh_Pad;
}
```

sh_List
        is a standard list structure.

sh_Pad
        is a word which is used only to align the structure to a long word
        boundary. It is always zero.

Five of these structures are found in the ExecBase structure. They are
stored consecutively and start at offset 434.

The following assembly language programs show how Exec manages
these interrupts.

First is the documentation for the Cause() routine:

```
fc1320 move.w  #$4000,$dff09a disable all interrupts
fc1328 addq.b  #1,294(A6)        increment IdNestCount
fc132c cmpi.b  #$0b,8(A1)        test type for SoftInt
fc1332 beq.s   $fc1370           branch if type SoftInt
fc1334 move.b  #$0b,8(A1)        else enter new
fc133a moveq   #$00,D0
fc133c move.b  9(A1),D0          priority in D0
fc1340 andi.w  #$00f0,D0         clear unpermitted bits
fc1334 ext.w   D0                and sign extend
fc1346 lea     466(A6),A0        pointer to int. with pri. 0
fc134a adda.w  D0,A0             determine position of the
                                 SoftIntList by the priority
fc134c lea     4(A0),A0          pointer to lh_Tail
fc1350 move.l  4(A0),D0          pointer to last member in D0
fc1354 move.l  A1,4(A0)          enter new interrupt as last
fc1358 move.l  A0,(A1)           set int. successor to zero
fc135a move.l  D0,4(A1)          set pointer to predecessor
fc135e move.l  D0,A0             pointer to previous int.
fc1360 move.l  A1,(A0)           successor to current
fc1362 bset    #5,292(A6)        permit SoftInt in SysFlag
fc1368 move.w  #$8004,$dff09c generate interrupt
fc1370 subq.w  #1,294(A6)        decrement IdNestCount
```

```
fc1374 bge.s    $fc137e         branch if int. cannot be
                                allowed yet
fc1376 move.w   #$c000,$dff9a   enable interrupts
fc173e rts                      return
```

The listing shows how a soft interrupt is created. Before the interrupt can be executed it must first be entered in one of the five SoftIntList structures. The priority determines which of these structures it is placed in. From the way the structure is determined you can see why only priorities -32, -16, 0, +16 and +32 are allowed. Each SoftIntList structure is 16 bytes long. A pointer to the middle structure is created. The priority is added to this pointer, yielding the position of the desired structure.

After the appropriate SoftIntList structure has been determined, the structure of the interrupt to be created is appended to the list as the last member and SysFlags in the ExecBase is updated to indicate that a soft interrupt is present. The bit for executing a soft interrupt is set in the interrupt request register and it is indicated as allowed in the ExecBase structure. After all this is done, the interrupts, which were disabled at the start of the routine, are enabled again.

The soft interrupt is now executed and the pointer to the program to be executed, which manages the SoftIntList structures, is fetched from the interrupt vector structure. This program lies at $FC1380.

```
fc1380 move.w   #$0004,$dff09c  clear interrupt request bit
fc1388 bclr     #5,292(A6)      clear SysFlag bit, test
fc138e bne.s    $fc1392         branch if interrupt allowed
fc1390 rts                      return
fc1392 move.w   #$0004,$dff09a  clear interrupt enable bit
fc139a bra.s    $fc13c2
fc139c move     #$2700,SR       enable all processor
                                interrupts
fc13a0 move.l   (A0),A1         pointer to first interrupt
fc13a2 move.l   (A1),D0         is node valid?
fc13a4 beq.s    $fc13ae         branch if no more int.
fc13a6 move.l   D0,(A0)         remove first interrupt from
                                list
fc13a8 exg      D0,A1           exchange A1 and D0
fc13aa move.l   A0,4(A1)        set ln_Pred to list
fc13ae move.l   D0,A1           pointer to first interrupt
fc13b0 move.b   #$02,8(A1)      set ln_Type to int.
fc13b6 move     #$2000,SR       disable all interrupts
fc13ba movem.l  14(A1),A5/A1    A1 = is_Data, A5 =
                                (*is_Code)()
fc13c0 jsr      (A5)            jump
fc13c2 moveq    #$04,D0         number of int. lists -1
fc13c4 lea      498(A6),A0      pointer to int. list with
                                highest priority
fc13c8 move.w   #$0004,$dff09c  clear int request bit
fc13d0 cmpa.l   8(A0),A0        list empty?
fc13d4 bne.s    $fc139c         branch if not empty
```

```
fc13d6 lea      -16(A0),A0     else set pointer to int
                                list with lowest priority
fc13da dbf      D0,$fc13d0     branch if not all lists
                                searched
fc13de move     #$2100,SR      disable all interrupts
                                except pri. 1
fc13e2 move.w   #$8004,$dff09a allow soft interrupt again
fc13ea rts                     return
```

First the routine above checks to see if the bit which indicates the soft interrupts are allowed is set, as it is by the Cause() function. If this is the case, the routine is executed. Next the interrupt request bit is cleared and the soft interrupt lists are searched for their interrupt structures. Once a list is processed or if it is empty the next list is searched. The lists are processed in descending order of priority.

## 2.7.3          The CIA interrupts

Now that we've discussed interrupt handling on the Amiga in general, we should make special mention of the interrupts generated by the CIAs. The processor priorities of the two components are 6 for CIA-B and 2 for CIA-A and both are managed by an interrupt server. Therefore the iv_Code element of the interrupt vector structure points to a ServerList structure and (*iv_Code)() points to the routine for managing the server list. The interrupt vector structures for CIA-A are at offset 120 and for CIA-B at offset 240 in the ExecBase structure.

## 2.7.3.1        The CIA resource structure

Normally there is only one interrupt structure in the interrupt server list. But in this case the interrupt structure is part of the CIA resource structure. The is_Data pointer points to the resource structure and (*is_Code)() points to a routine which manages the resource structure.

The routine, with help from the structure, manages all of the CIA interrupts:

- Timer A interrupt
- Timer B interrupt
- Real-time clock alarm interrupt
- Serial port or keyboard interrupt
- Flag line interrupt

*CIA resource*  The CIA resource structure is basically a library structure which has
*structure*     been extended with some additional entries. The CIA resource structure
                looks like this (breakdown of the substructures indented):

| Offset | Meaning | |
|--------|---------|---|
| 0 | struct Nodelib_Node | |
| | 0 | Pointer to next resource |
| | 4 | Pointer to the previous resource |
| | 8 | Node type |
| | 9 | Node pri |
| | 10 | Pointer to resource name |
| 14 | UBYTE lib_Flags | \* $00 *\ |
| 15 | UBYTE lib_pad | \* $00 *\ |
| 16 | UWORD lib_NegSize | \* $0018 *\ |
| 18 | UWORD lib_PosSize | \* $007C *\ |
| 20 | UWORD lib_Version | \* $0000 *\ |
| 22 | UWORD lib_Revision | \* $0000 *\ |
| 24 | APTR lib_IdString | \* $00000000 *\ |
| 28 | ULONG lib_Sum | \* $00000000 *\ |
| 32 | UWORD lib_OpenCnt | \* $0000 *\ |
| 34 | APTR CiaStartPtr | |
| 38 | WORD IntRequestBit | |
| 40 | BYTE IntEnableCia | |
| 41 | BYTE IntRequestCia | |
| 42 | struct Interrupt cia_Interrupt | |
| | 42 | Pointer to the next interrupt |
| | 46 | Pointer to the previous interrupt |
| | 50 | Node type |
| | 51 | Node pri |
| | 52 | Pointer to the interrupt name |
| | 56 | Pointer to data buffer (here resource) |
| 60 | Pointer to code to be executed | |
| 64 | struct IntVector Timer A | |
| | CIA-A and CIA-B | |
| | 64 | not initialized (00000000) |
| | 68 | not initialized (00000000) |
| | 72 | not initialized (00000000) |
| 76 | struct IntVector Timer B | |
| | CIA-A: | |
| | 76 | Pointer to data buffer |
| | 80 | Entry at $FE9726 |
| | 84 | Pointer to interrupt structure |
| | | |
| | CIA-B: | |
| | 76 | not initialized (00000000) |
| | 80 | not initialized (00000000) |
| | 84 | not initialized (00000000) |

| Offset | Meaning |
|--------|---------|
| 88 | struct IntVector TOD Alarm |

CIA-A:
88    not initialized (00000000)
92    not initialized (00000000)
96    not initialized (00000000)

CIA-B:
88    Pointer to graphic.library
92    Entry at $FC6D68
96    Pointer to interrupt structure

| 100 | struct IntVector serial data |

CIA-A:
100   Pointer to keyboard.device
104   Entry for keyboard read ($FE571C)
108   Pointer to interrupt structure

CIA-B:
100   not initialized (00000000)
104   not initialized (00000000)
108   not initialized (00000000)

| 112 | struct IntVector Flag line |

CIA-A:
112   not initialized (00000000)
116   not initialized (00000000)
120   not initialized (00000000)

CIA-B:
112   Pointer to disk.resource
116   Entry at $FC4AB0
120   Pointer to interrupt structure

We should make a few comments about some of the structure components.

**CiaStartPtr**
is a pointer to the start of the CIA register. For CIA-A this is $BFE001 and for CIA-B $BFD000.

**IntRequestBit**
is the bit which is set in the interrupt request register when the interrupt is generated. For CIA-A this is $0008 and for CIA-B $2000.

**IntEnableCia**
is a byte which stores information on which interrupts are allowed and which are not.

**IntRequestCia**
is a byte which indicates which CIA interrupt occurred.

The vectors for the individual CIA interrupts are stored in the IntVector structure. Uninitialized structures are not used by the operating system and can be used by the programmer.

## 2.7.3.2 Managing the resource structure

Now that you know what the structure looks like, we'll look at the routines which manage it. The start of the resource structure is stored in A1.

Entry for CIA-B:

```
fc4610 movem.l   A2/S2,-(A7)   save D2 and A2
fc4614 move.b    $bfdd00,D2    Int. Cont. Reg. to D2 (CIA-B)
fc461a bra.s     $fc4626       unconditional jump
```

Entry for CIA-A:

```
fc461c movem.l   A2/D2,-(A7)   save D2 and A2
fc4620 move.b    $bfed01       Int. Cont. Reg to D2 (CIA-A)
fc4626 blcr      #7,D2         clear top bit
fc462a or.b      41(A1),D2     OR old bits with new
fc462e move.b    D2,41(A1)     and enter in Int. Req. byte
fc4632 and.b     40(A1),D2     AND req. with enable bte
fc4636 beq.s     $fc4658       branch if int. not allowed
fc4638 move.l    A1,A2         pointer to resource in A2
fc463a eor.b     D2,41(A2)     clear bits of the interrupt
to be pro-                     cessed in the request reg.
fc463e lsr.b     #1,D2         bit for timer A into carry
fc4640 bcs.s     $fc465e       branch if timer A int.
fc4642 lsr.b     #1,D2         bit for timer B into carry
fc4644 bcs.s     $fc4668       branch if timer B int.
fc4646 beq.s     $fc4658       branch if no interrupts left
fc4648 lsr.b     #1,D2         bit for TOD alarm into carry
fc464a bcs.s     $fc4672       branch if TOD alarm
fc464c beq.s     $fc4658       branch if no interrupts left
fc464e lsr.b     #1,D2         bit for serial data into
                               carry
fc4650 bcs.s     $fc467c       jump is serial data int.
fc4652 beq.s     $fc4658       branch is no interrupts left
fc4654 lsr.b     #1,D2         bit for flag int. into carry
fc4656 bcs.s     $fc4686       branch if flag interrupt
fc4658 movem.l   (A7)+,A2/D2   restore A2 and D2
fc465c rts                     return
```

This routine immediately enters each arriving interrupt into the interrupt request byte of the resource structure, checks to see if the interrupt is allowed, and clears the corresponding request bits if it is allowed. Then the bits of the occurring interrupts are systematically shifted into the carry flag and checked to see if they are allowed. If so, the corresponding interrupt is executed. The routines for executing an interrupt are described below.

The pointer to the resource structure is in A2.

*Timer A interrupt:*

```
fc465e movem.l  64(A2),A5/A1   get entry and data pointer
fc4664 jsr      (A5)           jump to routine
fc4666 bra.s    $fc4642        back to the int. evaluation
```

*Timer B interrupt:*

```
fc4668 movem.l  76A2),A5/A1    get entry and data pointer
fc466e jsr      (A5)           jump to routine
fc4670 bra.s    $fc4648        back to the int. evaluation
```

*TOD alarm interrupt:*

```
fc4672 movem.l  88(A2),A5/A1   get entry and data pointer
fc4678 jsr      (A5)           jump to routine
fc467a bra.s    $fc464e        back to the int. evaluation
```

*Serial data interrupt:*

```
fc467c movem.l  100(A2),A5/A1  get entry and data pointer
fc4682 jsr      (A5)           jump to routine
fc4684 bra.s    $fc4654        back to the int. evaluation
```

*Flag interrupt:*

```
fc4686 movem.l  112(A2),A5/A1  get entry and data pointer
fc468c jsr      (A5)           jump to routine
fc468e bra.s    $fc4658        back to the int. evaluation
```

Like a library, the resource structure also has routines available to make managing it easier. These functions are accessed with negative offsets from the base address. The CIA resource structure has four functions. They are:

| Offset | Function |
|--------|----------|
| -6     | SetInterrupt |
| -12    | ClrInterrupt |
| -18    | Clr/Set EnableBits |
| -24    | ExecuteInterrupt |

SetInterrupt

Set IntVector structure according to specifications and allow interrupt (enable bit). The pointer to the interrupt structure must be in A1 and the number of the interrupt in D0. The number 0 stands for the timer A interrupt and 4 for the Flag interrupt. With this function it's not possible to change already initialized IntVector structures. To do this the structure must first be erased with ClrInterrupt. The specified interrupt is also enabled.

ClrInterrupt

Erase IntVector structure and disable interrupt. D0 contains the number of the IntVector structure to be erased. The specified interrupt is also disabled.

Clr/Set EnableBits

Set the interrupt enable bits in the hardware register and the resource structure. The bits to be changed must be set in D0. Bit 7 indicates whether these bits are cleared or set. If bit 7 is cleared, the specified bits are also cleared in the interrupt enable register. With D0 = $03 both timer interrupts are disabled. The return value in D0 is the old state of the hardware interrupt register.

ExecuteInterrupt

With this function it is possible to generate in software a CIA interrupt with a specified source. In D0 the bit which stands for a given interrupt source in the CIA interrupt request register must be set. In addition, bit 7 of D0 must be set. The function must be called with D0 = $81 to create a Timer A interrupt. The return value in D0 is the old state of the hardware interrupt request register.

The functions can be called successfully only if the pointer to the resource structure is in A5.

```
move.b #$02,d0
move.l ResourceBase,a6
jsr -18(A6)
```

disables the Timer B interrupt.

Here are the assembly language listings of the individual functions.

*SetInterrupt:*

```
fc4690 moveq     #$00,D1           clear D1
fc4692 move.b    D0,D1             int. number to D1
fc4694 mulu      #$000c,D1         calculate proper offset
fc4698 move.l    $0004,A0          ExecBase in A0
fc469c move.w    #$4000,$dff90a    disable
fc46a4 addq.b    #1,294(A0)        macro
fc46a8 lea       64(A6,D1.W),A0    determine start of
                                   structure
fc46ac move.l    8(A0),D1          was structure already
                                   initialized?
fc46b0 bne.s     $fc46e2           branch if so
fc46b2 move.l    A1,8(A0)          set *iv_node
fc46b6 move.l    18(A1),4(A0)      set (*iv_Code)()
fc46bc move.l    14(A1),0(A0)      set iv_Data
fc46c2 move.w    #$0080,D1         set Clr/Set bit to set
fc46c6 bset      D0,D1             enter bit to be set
fc46c8 move.w    D1,D0             transfer value to D0
fc46ca bsr.s     $fc470a           to function Clr/Set
                                   EnableBit
fc46cc moveq     #$00,D0           clear D0
fc46ce move.l    $0004,A0          ExecBase to A0
fc46d2 subq.b    #1,294(A0)
fc46d6 bge.s     $fc46e0           enable
fc46d8 move.w    #$c000,$dff09a    macro
fc46e0 rts                         return
fc46e2 move.l    D1,D0             section of program
fc46e4 bra.s     $fc46ce           not used
```

| | | | |
|---|---|---|---|
| ***ClrInterrupt:*** | fc46e6 moveq | #$00,D1 | clear D1 |
| | fc46e8 move.b | D0,D1 | structure number to D1 |
| | fc46ea mulu | #$000c,D1 | calculate proper offset |
| | fc46ee move.l | $0004,A0 | ExecBase in A0 |
| | fc46f2 move.w | #$4000,$dff90a | disable |
| | fc46fa addq.b | #1,294(A0) | macro |
| | fc46fe lea | 64(A6,D1.W),A0 | determine start of structure |
| | fc4702 clr.l | 8(A0) | clear pointer to interrupt structure to indicate that structure is empty |
| | fc4706 moveq | #$00,D1 | clear D1 |
| | fc4708 bra.s | $fc46c6 | clear EnableBits |
| ***Clr/Set*** | fc470a move.l | $0004,A0 | ExecBase in A0 |
| ***EnableBits:*** | fc470e move.w | #$4000,$dff90a | disable |
| | fc4716 addq.b | #1,294(A0) | macro |
| | fc471a move.l | 34(A6),A0 | CiaStartPtr to A0 |
| | fc471e move.b | 40(A6),A1 | pointer to IntEnableCia |
| | fc4722 lea | 40(A6),A1 | pointer to IntEnableCia |
| | fc4726 bra.s | $fc474c | Set bits |
| ***Execute*** | fc4728 move.l | $0004,A0 | ExecBase in A0 |
| ***Interrupt:*** | fc472c move.w | #$4000,$dff90a | disable |
| | fc4734 addq.b | #1,294(A0) | macro |
| | fc4738 move.l | 34(A6),A0 | CiaStartPtr to A0 |
| | fc473c move.b | 3328(A0),D1 | Read Cia Int Con Reg |
| | fc4740 bclr | #7,D1 | clear top bit |
| | fc4744 or.b | D1,41(A6) | OR with IntRequestCia |
| | fc4748 lea | 41(A6),A1 | set pointer to IntRequestCia |
| ***Entry from*** | fc474c moveq | #$00,D1 | clear D1 |
| ***CLR/Set*** | fc474e move.b | (A1),D1 | IntRequestCia to D1 |
| ***EnableBits*** | fc4750 tst.b | D0 | is D0 set? |
| ***from $FC4726*** | fc4752 beq.s | $fc4762 | branch if not set |
| | fc4754 blcr | #7,D0 | clear top bit |
| | fc4758 bne.s | $fc4760 | if set then branch to set bits |
| | fc475a not.b | D0 | negate bits to clear |
| | fc475c and.b | D0,(A1) | clear corresponding bits |
| | fc475e bra.s | $fc4762 | |
| | fc4760 or.b | D0,(A1) | set corresponding bits |
| | fc4762 move.b | 40(A6),D0 | check if an |
| | fc4766 and.b | 41(A6),D0 | interrupt is allowed |
| | fc476a beq.s | $fc477a | end if not allowed |
| | fc476c move.w | 38(A6),D0 | get IntRequestBit from structure |
| | fc4770 ori.w | #$8000,D0 | set Clr/Set bit |
| | fc4774 move.w | D0,$dff09c | Generate interrupt |
| | fc477a move.l | $0004,A0 | get ExecBase |
| | fc477e subq.b | #1,294(A0) | |
| | fc4782 bge.s | $fc478c | enable |
| | fc4784 move.w | #$c000,$dff09a | macro |
| | fc478c move.l | D1,D0 | return previous request bits |
| | fc478e rts | | return |

## 2.7.4        Description of interrupt functions

*SetIntVector()*    Interrupt = SetIntVector(intNum, int)
                    D0                      D0    A1

Offset:        -162

Description:
> This function initializes the IntVector structure to be used with an interrupt handler. The return parameter is a pointer to the previous interrupt structure used for this interrupt.

Parameters:

intNum
> specifies the number of the interrupt to be used. Number 1, for example, is the interrupt handler for "Disk block processed".

int    is a pointer to the initialized interrupt structure.

Result:

Interrupt
> A pointer to the previously used interrupt structure is returned in D0.

*AddIntServer()*    AddIntServer(intNum, int)
                                 D0     A1

Offset:        -168

Description:
> This function inserts the specified interrupt structure to the interrupt server list. The priority in the node structure determines where the interrupt is inserted into the list. An interrupt with a higher priority is executed before an interrupt with lower priority.

Parameters:

intNum
> specifies the number of the interrupt to be used.

int    is a pointer to the initialized interrupt structure.

*RemInt*
*Server()*

```
RemIntServer(intNum, int)
            D0       A1
```

Offset:        -174

Description:
>    The specified interrupt structure is removed from the interrupt server list.

Parameters:

intNum
>    specifies the number of the interrupt to be used.

int    is a pointer to the initialized interrupt vector.

*Cause()*

```
Cause(interrupt)
         A1
```

Offset:        -180

Description:
>    An interrupt can be generated in software by a task or another interrupt. The priority of this interrupt is lower than that of a hardware interrupt, but higher than that of a task and thereby is used to start synchronous control processes.

Parameters:

interrupt
>    is a pointer to the initialized interrupt pointer.

---

## 2.7.5        Example of an interrupt server

Now that we've discussed the theory of interrupt programming, we have an example of a practical application of what we have learned.

The following program, which in this form is only of interest to owners of a RAM expansion, makes is possible to allocate all of the fast memory with F10 and release it again with F9. F1 is used to turn off the interrupt. The program can be modified so that other processes can also be executed with certain keys.

```
mem          = $20004
Availmem     = -216
memtype      = $10004
numData      = 300
Allocmem     = -198
Freemem      = -210
```

```
addIntServer = -168
RemIntServer = -174
akey         = $bfec01
pri          = 100
Type         = 2
intNum       = 3
is_Data      = 14
is_Code      = 18
ln_Type      = 8
ln_Pri       = 9
ln_Name      = 10


        move.l  $4,a6
        move.l  #numData,d0
        move.l  #memtype,d1      ;fast,CLR
        jsr     Allocmem(a6)
        tst.l   d0
        beq     error
        move.l  d0,a2
        add.l   #32,d0           ;start of data storage
        move.l  d0,is_Data(a2)
        move.b  #pri,ln_Pri(a2)
        move.b  #Type,ln_Type(a2)
        move.l  #Ende-Start+8,d0 ;Code size set for program
        jsr     Allocmem(a6)
        tst.l   d0               ;error?
        bne     ok1              ;NO
        move.l  a2,a1            ;*Interrupt
        move.l  #numData,d0
        jsr     Freemem(a6)      ;Free up memory
        jmp     error

ok1:    move.l  d0,a3
        move.l  a3,is_Code(a2)
        move.l  a2,a1            ;*Interrupt structure

        lea     Start,a2
        move.l  #Ende-Start,d0
11:     move.b  (a2)+,(a3)+
        dbf     d0,11

        move.l  #intNum,d0       ;For key Int
        jsr     addIntServer(a6)
        rts

error: rts

;A1 is pointer to data storage
;Used only with d0,d1,a1,a5,a6

Start: move.l  d0,a5            ;*Next interrupt
        move.b  akey,d0
        not     d0
        ror.b   #1,d0
        cmp.b   #$59,d0          ;F10
        beq     Memoryout
```

```
        cmp.b   #$58,d0         ;F9
        beq     Memoryin
        cmp.b   #$50,d0         ;F1
        beq     Readout
error1:clr.l   d0
 rts

Memoryout:


        move.l  a1,a5
        tst.l   (a5)
        bne     error1
        move.l  #$ffffffff,(a5)+
        move.l  $4,a6
16:     move.l  #mem,d1
        jsr     Availmem(a6)
        tst.l   d0
        beq     end1
        move.l  d0,(a5)+
        jsr     Allocmem(a6)
        tst.l   d0
        beq     end1
        move.l  d0,(a5)+
        bra     16
end1:   clr.l   (a5)
        bra     blink

Memoryin:
        move.l  a1,a5
        move.l  $4,a6
        tst.l   (a5)
        beq     error1
        clr.l   (a5)+
17:     tst.l   (a5)
        beq     end2
        move.l  (a5)+,d0
        move.l  (a5)+,a1
        jsr     Freemem(a6)
        bra     17
end2:   bra     blink

Readout:
        move.l  4(a5),a1        ;Interrupt after a1
        move.l  #intNum,d0
        move.l  $4,a6
        jsr     RemIntServer(a6)
        bra     blink

blink:  move.l  #$2000,d0
15:     move.w  d0,$dff180
        sub.l   #$01,d0
        bne     15
        rts
Ende:
 end
```

With this program an interrupt structure is opened and inserted into the keyboard interrupt. Since the priority of our interrupt structure is higher than the one which reads the keyboard, our interrupt routine is executed first. Here we test for certain keys. If F10 was pressed, all of the fast memory is allocated and the pointer to the allocated areas with their lengths are stored in the interrupt data buffer. If F9 is pressed, the pointers saved in the interrupt data buffer are used to release the memory again. When F1 is pressed, the interrupt structure is removed from the interrupt server list and F9 and F10 are no longer read.

As a signal that a key has been pressed and the command was executed, the screen flashes briefly.

# 2.8     The ExecBase structure

*The Exec*
*Library*

The ExecBase structure is the main structure of Exec in which all of the important parameters are stored, such as which task is currently running. The base address of the structure is also the base address of the Exec library and can be addressed from C with SysBase. SysBase is a standard variable which stores the position of the Exec library.

In order to access the structure in assembly language, you must first determine its base address, which is always at memory location $000004.

Move.l $4,a6 moves the base address of the Exec library or ExecBase structure into register A6.

Since this structure is initialized by the reset routine at power up, its base address is always the same. It is moved only when the size of the location of RAM changes. After this change its position is always constant again.

On an Amiga with 512K of RAM, the position of the ExecBase structure is $676, as long as Kickstart Version 1.2 is used. When expanded to 1MB, the ExecBase structure moves to $C00276, but this applies only if the additional RAM lies at $C00000.

*The ExecBase*
*structure:*

| Offset | | Address for | | | | |
|---|---|---|---|---|---|---|
| Dec | Hex | 512KB | 1MB | | | |
| | | | | struct ExecBase { | | |
| 0 | $000 | $676 | $c000276 | struct | Library LibNode; | |
| 34 | $022 | $698 | $C00298 | UWORD | SoftVer; | |
| 36 | $024 | $69A | $C0029A | WORD | LowMemChkSum; | |
| 38 | $026 | $69C | $C0029C | ULONG | ChkBase; | |
| 42 | $02A | $6A0 | $C002A0 | APTR | ColdCapture; | |
| 46 | $02E | $6A4 | $C002A4 | APTR | CoolCapture; | |
| 50 | $032 | $6A8 | $C002A8 | APTR | WarmCapture; | |
| 54 | $036 | $6AC | $C002AC | APTR | SysStkUpper; | |
| 58 | $03A | $6B0 | $C002B0 | APTR | SysStkLower; | |
| 62 | $03E | $6B4 | $C002B4 | ULONG | MaxLocMem; | |
| 66 | $042 | $6B8 | $C002B8 | APTR | DebugEntry; | |
| 70 | $046 | $6BC | $C002BC | APTR | DebugData; | |
| 74 | $04A | $6C0 | $C002C0 | APTR | AlertData; | |
| 78 | $04E | $6C4 | $C002C4 | APTR | MaxExtMem; | |
| 82 | $052 | $6C8 | $C002C8 | UWORD | ChkSum; | |
| | | | | struct IntVector IntVects[16]; | | |
| 84 | $054 | $6CA | $C002CA | | Serial output | Pri1 |
| 96 | $060 | $6D6 | $C002D6 | | Disk block | Pri1 |
| 108 | $06C | $6E2 | $C002E2 | | SoftInterrupt | Pri1 |
| 120 | $078 | $6EE | $C002EE | | CIA-A | Pri2 |
| 132 | $084 | $6FA | $C002FA | | Copper | Pri3 |

*The ExecBase*
*structure:*

| Offset |  | Address for |  |  |  |  |
|---|---|---|---|---|---|---|
| Dec | Hex | 512KB | 1MB |  |  |  |
| 144 | $090 | $706 | $C00306 |  | Raster beam | Pri3 |
| 156 | $09C | $712 | $C00312 |  | Blitter done | Pri3 |
| 168 | $0A8 | $71E | $C0031E |  | Audio channel 0 | Pri4 |
| 180 | $0B4 | $72A | $C0032A |  | Audio channel 1 | Pri4 |
| 192 | $0C0 | $736 | $C00336 |  | Audio channel 2 | Pri4 |
| 204 | $0CC | $742 | $C00342 |  | Audio channel 3 | Pri4 |
| 216 | $0D8 | $74E | $C0034E |  | Serial input | Pri5 |
| 228 | $0E4 | $75A | $C0035A |  | Disk sync. | Pri5 |
| 240 | $0F0 | $766 | $C00366 |  | CIA-B | Pri6 |
| 252 | $0FC | $772 | $C00372 |  | Internal interrupt | Pri6 |
| 264 | $108 | $77E | $C0037E |  | NMI | Pri7 |
| 276 | $114 | $78A | $C0038A | struct | Task *ThisTask; |  |
| 280 | $118 | $78E | $C0038E | ULONG | IdleCount; |  |
| 284 | $11C | $792 | $C00392 | ULONG | DispCount; |  |
| 288 | $120 | $796 | $C00396 | UWORD | Quantum; |  |
| 290 | $122 | $798 | $C00398 | UWORD | Elapsed; |  |
| 292 | $124 | $79A | $C0039A | UWORD | SysFlags; |  |
| 294 | $126 | $79C | $C0039C | BYTE | IDNextCnt; |  |
| 295 | $127 | $79D | $C0039D | BYTE | TDNestCnt; |  |
| 296 | $128 | $79E | $C0039E | UWORD | AttnFlags; |  |
| 298 | $12A | $7A0 | $C003A0 | UWORD | AttnResched; |  |
| 300 | $12C | $7A2 | $C003A2 | APTR | ResModules; |  |
| 304 | $130 | $7A6 | $C003A6 | APTR | TaskTrapCode; |  |
| 308 | $134 | $7AA | $C003AA | APTR | TaskExceptCode; |  |
| 312 | $138 | $7AE | $C003AE | APTR | TaskExitCode; |  |
| 316 | $13C | $7B2 | $C003B2 | ULONG | TaskSigAlloc; |  |
| 320 | $140 | $7B6 | $C003B6 | UWORD | TaskTrapAlloc; |  |
| 322 | $142 | $7B8 | $C003B8 | struct | List MemList; |  |
| 336 | $150 | $7C6 | $C003C6 | struct | List ResourceList; |  |
| 350 | $15E | $7D4 | $C003D4 | struct | List DeviceList; |  |
| 364 | $16C | $7E2 | $C003E2 | struct | List IntrList; |  |
| 378 | $17A | $7F0 | $C003F0 | struct | List LibList; |  |
| 392 | $188 | $7FE | $C003FE | struct | List PortList; |  |
| 406 | $196 | $80C | $C0040C | struct | List TaskReady; |  |
| 420 | $1A4 | $81A | $C0041A | struct | List TaskWait; |  |
| 434 | $1B2 | $828 | $C00428 | struct | SoftIntList<br>SoftInts[5]; |  |
| 514 | $202 | $878 | $C00478 |  | LastAlert[4]; |  |
| 530 | $212 | $888 | $C00488 | UBYTE | VBlankFrequency; |  |
| 531 | $213 | $889 | $C00489 | UBYTE | PowerSupplyFrequency; |  |
| 532 | $214 | $88A | $C0048A | struct | List SemaphoreList; |  |
| 546 | $222 | $898 | $C00498 | APTR | KickMemPtr; |  |
| 550 | $226 | $89C | $C0049C | APTR | KickTagPtr; |  |
| 554 | $22A | $8A0 | $C004A0 | APTR | KickCheckSum; |  |
| 558 | $22E | $8A4 | $C004A4 | UBYTE | ExecBaseReserved[10]; |  |
| 568 | $22F | $8AE | $C004AE | UBYTE | ExecBaseNewReserved[20]; |  |
|  |  |  |  | } |  |  |

```
#define SYSBASESIZE ((long)sizeof(struct ExecBase))
#define AFB_68010 0L
#define AFB_68020 1L
#define AFB_68881 4L
#define AFF_68010 (1L<<0)
#define AFF_68020 (1L<<1)
#define AFF_68881 (1L<<4)
#define AFB_RESERVED8 8L
#define AFB_RESERVED9 9L
```

### LibNode - Offset 0

is the library structure of the Exec library, with a positive size of $24C and a negative size of $276 bytes. From positive size you can see that the ExecBase structure really is quite a large library structure.

### SoftVer - Offset 34
### LowMemChkSum - Offset 36

can be used by the programmer to equalize the checksum calculated over the range 34 to 78 if custom vectors are inserted. How the actual checksum is calculated and discussed under ChkSum (offset 82).

### Chkbase - Offset 38

is used to check the position of ExecBase on reset. The position of ExecBase is added to ChkBase, whereby the result must be $FFFFFFFF. If this isn't the case, a significant error must have occurred, in which case it's best to recreate the ExecBase structure. Otherwise time is saved and the structure is not completely initialized.

### ColdCapture - Offset 42

is a vector which can be used by the programmer to branch to a custom routine during a reset. If this vector is not used, it points to zero. The reset routine detects when the vector has been set and branches to the specified routine. The return address is placed in A5. Before the jump the vector is automatically reset to zero. Up to this time nothing noteworthy has happened beyond disabling interrupts and DMA. In this custom routine no operations which affect the stack should be performed because it has not been initialized correctly yet. This is also true when the return address is passed in A5 and the routine is not called through JSR.

### CoolCapture - Offset 46

can also be used to branch to a user routine during a reset. The difference between ColdCapture and CoolCapture is that the CoolCapture routine is called considerably later. CoolCapture is not reset by the reset routine. Since the stack, the memory, the exception table and the Exec library have already been initialized by this time, this vector is better suited for most applications than the ColdCapture vector. Control is returned to the reset routine with RTS.

### WarmCapture - Offset 50

is another reset vector, but to the best of our knowledge it is never called.

### SysStkUpper - Offset 54

indicates the upper limit of the supervisor stack.

SysStkLower - Offset 58
:   specifies the lower limit of the supervisor stack.

MaxLocMem - Offset 62
:   specifies the maximum addressable chip memory, which in 1.2 is 512KB or $80000 bytes.

DebugEntry - Offset 66
:   is a pointer to the entry to the Amiga debugger.

DebugData - Offset 70
:   is a pointer to the debugger data buffer (zero).

AlertData - Offset 74
MaxExtMem - Offset 78
:   indicates the upper limit of the available memory. With a memory expansion to 1MB this is $C80000.

ChkSum - Offset 82
:   is a checksum over the range from offset 34 to 78 and is checked before the jump to ColdCapture. If custom vectors are placed in this range, the checksum must be recalculated or equalized in LowChkSum. The checksum is calculated as follows:

```
fc0440 lea     34(A6),A0     set pointer to start
fc0444 move.w  #$0016,D0     number of words-1 in
                             counter
fc0448 add.w   (A0)+,D1      add words
fc044a dbf     D0,$fc0448    decrement counter
fc044e not.w   D1            negate and
fc0450 move.w  D1,82(A6)     store in checksum
```

IntVects[0] - Offset 84
:   Interrupt on serial output. Not initialized after reset.

IntVects[1] - Offset 96
:   Interrupt after a disk block has been transferred. After reset this is an interrupt handler.

IntVects[2] - Offset 108
:   Soft interrupt. For exact description see Section 2.6.

IntVects[3] - Offset 120
:   CIA-A interrupt. After reset this interrupt serves mainly for reading the keyboard (interrupt server).

IntVects[4] - Offset 132
:   Copper interrupt

IntVects[5] - Offset 144

>Interrupt which is generated when the raster beam passes raster line zero. This interrupt is also the clock signal for task switching (interrupt server).

IntVects[6] - Offset 156

>The interrupt is generated when the blitter finishes its work (interrupt handler).

IntVects[7] - Offset 168

>Audio channel 0 (interrupt handler).

IntVects[8] - Offset 180

>Audio channel 1 (interrupt handler).

IntVects[9] - Offset 192

>Audio channel 2 (interrupt handler).

IntVects[10] - Offset 204

>Audio channel 3 (interrupt handler).

IntVects[11] - Offset 216

>The interrupt is generated when a serial input arrives (not initialized after reset).

IntVects[12] - Offset 228

>This interrupt signals disk synchronization (interrupt handler).

IntVects[13] - Offset 240

>The interrupt is generated when an interrupt is created by CIA-B (interrupt server).

IntVects[14] - Offset 252

>This interrupt can only be generated through software (not initialized after reset).

IntVects[15] - Offset 264

>Non-maskable interrupt. The interrupt is not used but it's initialized as an interrupt server.

*ThisTask - Offset 276

>is a pointer to the task structure which is currently being processed. You cannot read the pointer to this task structure from a program that runs in a task and gets useful results because you always get the pointer to the same task structure. The only way to get useful values is to read the value from an interrupt. Interrupt 5 (raster beam) is used for this.

idleCount - Offset 280
DispCount - Offset 284
Quantum - Offset 288
Elapsed - Offset 290
SysFlags - Offset 292
> Various system flags are stored in this location.

> Bit 5: 0 = soft interrupt disabled, 1 = enabled

IDNestCnt - Offset 294
> specifies whether interrupts are allowed or not. If IDNestCnt is $FF (-1), interrupts are allowed, otherwise they are disabled with the Disable function. Each time the Disable function is called IDNestCnt is incremented by one. The Enable function decrements IDNestCnt by one. The interrupts are enabled again when IDNestCnt reaches -1 (the master bit is set again).

TDNestCnt- Offset 295
> indicates whether the Forbid function has been called. If it was, TDNestCnt is incremented by one. Task switching is enabled when TDNestCnt is at -1. The Permit function decrements TDNestCnt again and enables task switching when TDNestCnt reaches -1.

AttnFlags - Offset 296
> specifies which processors are connected:

```
#define AFF_68010 (1L<<0)
#define AFF_68020 (1L<<1)
#define AFF_68881 (1L<<4)
```

AttnResched - Offset 298
ResModules - Offset 300
> is a pointer to resident modules. These are structures whose routines are called from a routine $FC0AF0. The modules are called at reset. There is also a function for searching for these modules by name. It is called FindResident.

TaskTrapCode - Offset 304
TaskExceptCode - Offset 308
TaskExitCode - Offset 312
TaskSigAlloc - Offset 316
TaskTrapAlloc - Offset 320
MemList - Offset 322
> is a pointer to the memory list which indicates which memory areas are free and which are allocated.

ResourceList - Offset 336
> is a list structure in which the resource structures are linked.

DeviceList - Offset 350
> is a list structure in which the device structures are linked.

IntList - Offset 364
>   Not used

LibList - Offset 378
>   is a list structure in which the library structures are linked.

PortList - Offset 392
>   is a list structure in which the port structures are linked.

TaskReady - Offset 406
>   is a list structure in which the Task structures which are currently ready are linked.

TaskWait - Offset 420
>   is a list structure in which the task structures which are currently waiting are linked.

SoftInts[0] - Offset 434
>   is a list structure of the soft interrupts which are waiting for processing and which have priority -32 are linked.

SoftItnts[1] - Offset 450
>   is a list structure in which the soft interrupts which are waiting for processing and which have priority -16 are linked.

SoftInts[2] - Offset 466
>   is a list structure in which the soft interrupts which are waiting for processing and which have priority 0 are linked.

SoftInts[3] - Offset 482
>   is a list structure in which the soft interrupts which are waiting for processing and which have priority +16 are linked.

SoftInts[4] - Offset 498
>   is a list structure in which the soft interrupts which are waiting for processing and which have priority +32 are linked.

LastAlert[4] - Offset 514
>   here the data for the alert are stored after they have been fetched by the reset routine.

VBlankFrequency - Offset 530
>   specifies the frequency at which the raster beam constructs a picture.

PowerSupplyFrequency - Offset 531
>   specifies the frequency of the line voltage.

SemaphoreList - Offset 532
>   is a list structure in which all of the semaphore structures used are linked.

KickMemPtr - Offset 546
>   is a pointer to a MemList structure whose memory is allocated
>   on a reset.

KickTagPtr - Offset 550
>   is a pointer to a resident table which is linked in when creating
>   the main resident table.

KickCheckSum - Offset 554
>   is the checksum calculated by the SumKickData() function.

ExecBaseReserved[10] - Offset 558
>   are 10 bytes which are reserved for the ExecBase structure so that
>   Exec can store values there. (Not used)

ExecBaseReserved[20] - Offset 568
>   are twenty bytes which are reserved for the ExecBase structure so
>   that Exec can store values there. (Not used)

# 2.9 Reset routine and reset-proof programs

In this section we'll discuss exactly what the reset routine does, how the memory size is determined, and whether it is possible to write reset-proof programs.

## 2.9.1 Documentation of the reset routine

```
fc00d2 lea      $040000,A7              set stack pointer
fc00d8 move.l   #$00020000,D0           value for delay loop
fc00de subq.l   #1,D0                   decrement value
fc00e0 bgt.s    $fc00de                 branch if not
                                        decremented
fc00e2 lea      -228(PC)(=$fc0000),A0   set pointer to
                                        Kickstart ROM
fc00e6 lea      $f00000,A1              load comparison value
fc00ec cmpa.l   A1,A0                   is Reset at $F00000
fc00ee beq.s    $fc00fe                 branch if so
fc00f0 lea      12(PC)(=$fc00fe),A5     set pointer to
                                        program continuation
fc00f4 cmpi.w   #$1111,(A1)             is module at $F00000?
fc00f8 bne.s    $fc00fe                 branch if not
fc00fa jmp      2(A1)                   else enter
fc00fe move.b   #$03,$bfe201            switch port to output
fc0106 move.b   #$02,$bfe001            turn LED off
fc010e lea      $dff000,A4              pointer to chip
                                        addresses
fc0114 move.w   #$7fff,D0               load value
fc0118 move.w   D0,154(A4)              disable all
                                        interrupts
fc011c move.w   D0,156(A4)              clear interrupts
fc0120 move.w   D0,150(A4)              disable DMA
fc0124 move.w   #$0200,256(A4)
fc012a move.w   #$0000,272(A4)
fc0130 move.w   #$0444,384(A4)          set color
fc0136 move.w   #$0008,A0               set pointer to
                                        exceptions
fc013a move.w   #$002d,D1               counter for number of
                                        vectors
fc013e lea      1140(PC)(=$fc05b4),A1   set pointer to hard
                                        error routine
fc0142 move.l   A1,(A0)+                enter exceptions
fc0144 dbf      D1,$fc0142              branch if not done
fc0148 bra.l    $fc30c4                 check guru
```

This routine checks if a reset resulted from a guru meditation. If so, put guru number in D7 and memory pointer in D6. Otherwise $FFFFFFFF is loaded into D6. The reset is then continued.

```
fc014c move.l  $0004,D0           get ExecBase
fc0150 btst    #0,D0              ExecBase at even address?
fc0154 bne.s   $fc01ce            error if odd
fc0156 move.l  D0,A6              Execbase to D0
fc0158 add.l   38(A6),D0          add ChkBase
fc015c not.l   D0                 invert result
fc015e bne.s   $fc01ce            branch if error
```

The error occurs when the pointer to the Execbase structure is incorrect.

```
fc0160 moveq   #$00,D1            clear D1 for checksum
fc0162 lea     34(A6),A0          set pointer to ChkBase
fc0166 moveq   #$18,D0            value for loop counter
fc0168 add.w   (A0)+,D1           generate checksum
fc016a dbf     D0,$fc0168         branch until checksum
                                  generated
fc016e not.w   D1                 invert result
fc0170 bne.s   $fc01ce            error if not zero
fc0172 move.l  42(A6),D0          ColdCapture to D0
fc0176 beq.s   $fc0184            branch if not set
fc0178 move.l  D0,A0              pointer to A0
fc017a lea     8(PC)(=$fc0184),A5    return pointer
fc017e clr.l   42(A6)             clear ColdCapture
fc0182 jmp     (A0)               jump
fc0184 bchg    #1,$bfe001         turn LED on
fc018c move.l  -382(PC)(=$fc0010),D0 compare Kickstart
                                  version
fc0190 cmp.l   20(A6),D0          with that of Execlib
fc0194 bne.s   $fc01ce            error if versions differ
fc0196 move.l  62(A6),A3          upper limit of chip RAM
fc019a cmpa.l  #$00080000,A3 512KB   chip RAM?
fc01a0 bhi.s   $fc01ce            error if larger
fc01a2 cmpa.l  #$00040000,A3 256KB   chip RAM?
fc01a8 bcs.s   $fc01ce            error if smaller
fc01aa move.l  78(A6),A4          MaxExtMem to A4
fc01ae move.l  A4,D0              check for external memory
fc01b0 beq.l   $fc0240            branch if not
fc01b4 cmpa.l  #$00dc0000,A4      upper limit at $DC0000?
fc01ba bhi.s   $fc01ce            error if higher
fc01bc cmpa.l  #$00c40000,A4      upperlimit at $C40000?
fc01c2 bcs.s   $fc01ce            error if smaller
fc01c4 move.l  A4,D0              ???, A4 = D0
fc01c6 andi.l  #$0003ffff,D0      is boundary on even addr?
fc01cc beq.s   $fc0240            yes, else error
```

Here begins the part of the routine which is called only when
something is wrong with the initialization of the ExecBase structure. It
must be reinitialized.

```
fc01ce lea     $0400,A6          lowest possible RAM area
fc01d2 suba.w  #$fd8a,A6         find address of ExecBase,
                                 if no fast memory
fc01d6 lea     $c00000,A0        lowest fast memory area
fc01dc lea     $dc0000,A1        highest possible RAM
                                 limit
fc01e2 lea     6(PC)(=$fc01ea),A5  return pointer
fc01e6 bra.l   $fc061a           get upper memory limit
```

The routine called here determines where the upper limit of the fast
RAM is. It returns a pointer to the end of RAM in A4. If no fast RAM
is available, a zero is returned in A4. This recognition of the fast RAM
works only if the RAM is at $C00000. Owners of an Amiga 1000 can
modify the Kickstart disk to make an auto-configuring memory
expansion which does not lie at $C00000.

```
fc01ea move.l  A4,D0            fast RAM present?
fc01ec beq.s   $fc0208          branch if not present
fc01ee move.l  #$00c00000,A6    lower limit in A6
fc01f4 suba.w  #$fd8a,A6        find position on
                                ExecBase
fc01f8 move.l  A4,D0            upper limit in D0
fc01fa lea     $c00000,A0       lower limit in A0
fc0200 lea     6(PC)(=$fc0208),A5  return pointer
fc0204 bra.l   $fc0602          clear memory
```

The fast RAM area is cleared with zeros in this routine.

```
fc0208 lea     $0000,A0         lowest RAM bound
fc020c lea     $200000,A1       upper limit of contiguous
                                memory
fc0212 lea     6(PC)(=$fc021a),A5  return pointer
fc0216 bra.l   $fc0592          get lower memory size
```

The lower memory area may lie from $0000 to $200000. The routine
checks to see how large the lower contiguous memory is. The memory
size is returned in A3.

```
fc021a cmpa.l  #$00040000,A3    area smaller than 256KB?
fc0220 bcs.s   $fc0238          yes, then error, hard
                                reset
fc0222 move.l  #$00000000,$0000  clear $0000
fc022a move.l  A3,D0            upper memory bound in D0
fc022c lea     $00c0,A0         determine lower bound
fc0230 lea     14(PC)(=$fc0240),A5  return pointer
fc0234 bra.l   $fc0602          clear lower memory
```

This routine was just used to clear the fast RAM. It clears the area from
$00C0 to the upper memory bound of the lower contiguous memory.

```
fc0238 move.w   #$00c0,D0    screen color for reset
fc023c bra.l    $fc05b8      hard reset (flash LED 11 times)
```

In this reset entry the LED is flashed 11 times, whereupon the boot ROM is called and the reset is restarted. This routine is also called if an exception error occurs during the first part of the reset.

```
fc0240 lea      $dff000,A0       pointer to chip addresses
fc0246 move.w   #$7fff,150(A0)   disable DMA
fc024c move.w   #$0200,256(A0)
fc0252 move.w   #$0000,272(A0)
fc0258 move.w   #$0888,384(A0)   set screen color
fc025e lea      84(A6),A0        pointer to first IntVector
fc0262 movem.l  546(A6),D4-D2    store KickMemPrt,
                                 KickTagPrt,KickCheckSum
fc0268 moveq    #$00,D0          clear D0
fc026a move.w                    #$007d,D1  set counter
fc026e move.l   D0,(A0)+         clear from A0 to ExecBase
fc0270 dbf      D1,$fc026e       branch if not done
fc0274 movem    l D4-D2,546(A6)  set KickMemPrt, KickTagPrt
                                 and KickCheckSum
fc027a move.l   A6,$0004         set ExecBase pointer
fc027e move.l   A6,D0            pointer to D0
fc0280 not.l    D0               calculate ChkBase
fc0282 move.l   D0,38(A6)        enter ChkBase
fc0286 move.l   A4,D0            upper RAM limit to D0
fc0288 bne.s    $fc028c          branch if fast RAM
                                 available
fc028a move.l   A3,D0            else set upper chip RAM
fc028c move.l   D0,A7            limit as system stack
fc028e move.l   D0,54(A6)        and enter
fc0292 subi.l   #$00001800,D0    subtract length of stack
fc0298 move.l   D0,58(A6)        and set as lower limit
fc029c move.l   A3,62(A6)        set limit of chip RAM
fc02a0 move.l   A4,78(A6)        set limit of fast RAM
fc02a4 bsr.l    $fc30e4          enter Last Alert
```

The values fetched from $FC0148 and stored in D6 and D7 are written into the spaces reserved for them (Last Alert (offset 514)).

```
fc02a8 bsr.l    $fc0546          processor test
```

This routine tests which processors are attached. Recognized: 68000, 68010, 68020 and 68881. Bits in D0 are set as appropriate.

```
fc02ac or.w     D0,296(A6)          set bits in AttnFlags
fc02b0 lea      32(PC)(=$fc02d2),A1 pointer to table

fc02b4 move.w   (A1)+,D0            offset in D0
fc02b6 beq.l    $fc033e             end if no more offsets
fc02ba lea      0(A6,D0.W),A0       set pointer to position
fc02be move.l   A0,(A0)             enter list header
fc02c0 addq.l   #4,(A0)             point to lh_Tail
fc02c2 clr.l    4(A0)               clear lh_Tail
fc02c6 move.l   A0,8(A0)            set lh_TainPred
```

```
fc02ca move.w  (A1)+,D0           get lh_Type
fc02cc move.b  D0,12(A0)          and set
fc02d0 bra.s   $fc02b4            unconditional jump
```

The routine just described places the following list structures in Exec-Base:

**MemList**
**ResourceList**
**DeviceList**
**LibList**
**PortList**
**TaskReady**
**TaskWait**
**InterList**
**SoftIntList (all 5)**
**SemaphoreList**

```
            fc02d2
              •
              •
              •
```

Tables for creating the lists

```
              •
              •
            fc030c
              •
              •
```

Values for creating the Exec library structure.

```
              •
              •
            fc0326
              •
```

ASCII strings: chip RAM

```
              •
              •
            fc0332
              •
              •
```

ASCII strings: fast RAM

```
              •
              •
            fc033e
```

```
fc033e lea     11380(PC)(=$fc2fb4),A0 set pointer to
                                      TaskTrapCode
fc0342 move.l  A0,304(A6)             enter in TaskTrapCode
fc0346 move.l  A0,308(A6)             .enter in
                                      TaskExceptCode
fc034a move.l  #$00fc1cec,312(A6)     enter TaskExitCode
fc0352 move.l  #$0000ffff,316(A6)     enter TaskSigAlloc
fc035a move.w  #$8000,320(A6)         enter TaskTarpAlloc
fc0360 lea     8(A6),A1               pointer to
                                      LibNode.ln_Type
```

**319**

```
fc0364 lea      -90(PC)(=$fc030c),A0   pointer to table
fc0368 moveq    #$0c,D0                set counter
fc036a move.w   (A0)+,(A1)+            create Exec library
                                       structure
fc036c dbf      D0,$fc036a            branch if not done
fc0370 move.l   A6,A0                 pointer to ExecBase
                                       in A0
fc0372 lea      5836(PC)(=$fc1a40),A1 pointer to table
fc0376 move.l   A1,A2
fc0378 bsr.l    $fc1576               function:
                                      MakeFunction()
```

Execlibrary is created in the routine called here. The table is at
$FC1A40. The length of the library is returned in D0.

```
fc037c move.w   D0,16(A6)             enter library length
fc0380 move.l   A4,D0                 is fast RAM present?
fc0382 beq.s    $fc03a8               branch if no fast RAM
fc0384 lea      88(A6),A0             pointer to end of
                                      ExecBase
fc0388 lea      -88(PC)(=$fc0332),A1  String Fast Mem.
fc038c moveq    #$00,D2               priority of the
                                      MemHeader
fc038e move.w   #$0005,D1             memory attributes
                                      (Public,Fast)
fc0392 move.l   A4,D0                 pointer to end of
                                      fast RAM
fc0394 sub.l    A0,D0                 subtract ExecBase
                                      structure
fc0396 subi.l   #$00001800,D0         subtract SysStack
fc039c bsr.l    $fc19ea               create MemHeader
                                      structure
```

The routine at $FC19EA creates a MemHeader structure with the
specified data. The size of the available memory area is in D0.

```
fc03a0 lea      $0400,A0              start of chip RAM
fc03a4 moveq    #$00,D0               clear D0
fc03a6 bra.s    $fc03b2               unconditional jump
fc03a8 lea      588(A6),A0            pointer to ExecBase
                                      end
fc03ac move.l   #$ffffe800,D0
fc03b2 move.w   #$0003,D1             memory attributes
                                      (Public,Chip)
fc03b6 move.l   A0,A2                 pointer to start of
                                      RAM
fc03b8 lea      -148(PC)(=$fc0326),A1 String Chip Mem.
fc03bc moveq    #$f6,D2               priority of the
                                      MemHeaders
fc03be add.l    A3,D0                 calculating the
fc03c0 sub.l    A0,D0                 effective memory
                                      area
fc03c2 bsr.l    $fc19ea               create MemHeader
                                      structure
fc03c6 move.l   A6,A1                 ExecBase to A1
```

```
fc03c8 bsr.l    $fc140c                    calculate library
                                           checksum
```

**The Exec library is linked into the LibList and its checksum calculated.**

```
fc03cc lea      938(PC)(=$fc0778),A0  pointer to exceptions
fc03d0 move.l   A0,A1                 pointer to exceptions
                                      in A1
fc03d2 move.w   #$0008,A2             pointer to destination
                                      in A2
fc03d6 bra.s    $fc03de               unconditional branch
fc03d8 lea      0(A0,D0.W),A3         calculate address
fc03dc move.l   A3,(A2)+              and enter
fc03de move.w   (A1)+,D0              get offset
fc03e0 bne.s    $fc03d8               branch if not done
fc03e2 move.w   296(A6),D0            get AttnFlags
fc03e6 btst     #0,D0                 68010 used?
fc03ea beq.s    $fc041e               branch if not present
fc03ec lea      1166(PC)(=$fc087c),A0 pointer to new traps
fc03f0 move.w   #$0008,A1             pointer to destination
fc03f4 move.l   A0,(A1)+              enter exceptions
fc03f6 move.l   A0,(A1)+              enter exceptions
fc03f8 move.l   #$00fc08ba,-28(A6)    enter expansion
fc0400 move.l   #$42c04e75,-528(A6)   enter expansion
fc0408 btst     #4,D0                 68881 used?
fc040c beq.s    $fc041e               branch if not present
fc040e move.l   #$00fc108a,-52(A6)    enter expansion
fc0416 move.l   #$00fc10e8,-58(A6)    enter expansion
fc041e bsr.l    $fc125c               enter interrupt
                                      structure
fc0422 lea      $dff000,A0            pointer to chip
                                      addresses
fc0428 move.w   #$8200,150(A0)        allow blitter DMA
fc042e move.w   #$c000,154(A0)        allow interrupts
fc0434 move.w   #$ffff,294(A6)        clear IDNestCnt
fc043a bsr.l    $fc22fa               install debugger
fc043e moveq    #$00,D1               clear D1
fc0440 lea      34(A6),A0             pointer to SoftVer
fc0444 move.w   #$0016,D0             counter to D0
fc0448 add.w    (A0)+,D1              calculate checksum
fc044a dbf      D0,$fc0448            branch if not done
fc044e not.w    D1                    invert value
fc0450 move.w   D1,82(A6)             and store in ChkSum
fc0454 lea      118(PC)(=$fc04cc),A0  pointer to MemList
                                      structure
fc0458 bsr.l    $fc191e               AllocEntry()
```

**In this routine a MemList structure is created and $1024 bytes are reserved for the task and its stack.**

```
fc045c move.l   D0,A2                 pointer to MemList
                                      structure
fc045e lea      4112(A2),A0           pointer to start for
fc0462 lea      8(A0),A1              calculate MemEntry
fc0466 addi.l   #$00000010,D0         add MemList
```

```
fc046c move.l   D0,58(A1)              set SpLower
fc0470 move.l   A0,62(A1)              set SpUpper
fc0474 move.l   A0,54(A1)              set SpReg
fc0478 move     A0,USP                 also set as stack
fc047a clr.b    9(A1)                  clear pri
fc047e move.b   $0001,8(A1)            in tc_Type value for
fc0484 move.l   #$00fc00a8,10(A1)      pointer to name
```

The name of the task is exec.library. It will be removed later.

```
fc048c lea      74(A1),A0              pointer to tc_MemEntry
fc0490 move.l   A0,(A0                 lists
fc0492 addq.l   #4,(A0)                for MemEntries
fc0494 clr.l    4(A0)                  create
fc0498 move.l   A0,8(A0)
fc049c exg      A2,A1                  exchange MemList and task
                                       pointers
fc049e bsr.l    $fc15d8                AddHead()
fc04a2 exg      A2,A1                  swap back
fc04a4 move.l   A1,276(A6)             enter task as ThisTask
fc04a8 suba.l   A2,A2                  initPc
fc04aa move.l   A2,A3                  and clear finalPC
fc04ac bsr.l    $fc1c48                AddTask()
fc04b0 move.l   276(A6),A1             pointer to task in A1
fc04b4 move.b   #$02,15(A1)            zet tc_State to RUN
fc04ba bsr.l    $fc1600                Remove() task from list
```

The task is set to running and removed from the TaskReady list, which means that the current running program is processed as a task.

```
fc04be andi.w   #$0000,SR              disable all interrupts
fc04c2 addq.b   #1,295(A6)             set SysFkag
fc04c6 jsr      -138(A6)               Permit() (task)
fc04ca bra.s    $fc0500
               fc04cc
                 •
                 •
```

*Data for*
*MemList*
*structure*

```
                 •
                 •
               fc04fe

fc0500 lea      -30(PC)(=$fc04e4),A0
fc0504 bsr.l    $fc0900                find resident structure
```

The routine finds all of the resident structures in ROM and places the pointers to these structures in a table. It also checks to see if the KickMemPtr, KickTagPtr and KickCheckSum values are all set in the ExecBase structure. If this is the case, the specified memory areas are allocated and the specified resident structures are placed in the table, terminated with zero. The order of the entries in the table corresponds to the priorities of the resident structures. The pointer to the table is stored in ResModules.

```
fc0508 move.l  D0,300(A6)
fc050c bclr    #1,$bfe001     turn LED on (is already on)
fc0514 move.l  46(A6),D0      get CoolCapture
fc0518 beq.s   $fc051e        branch if not set
fc051a move.l  D0,A0          CoolCapture to A0
fc051c jsr     (A0)           jump
fc051e moveq   #$01,D0        set startClass
fc0520 moveq   #$00,D1        set Version
fc0522 bsr.l   $fc0af0        process InitCode(), resident
                              structures
```

The following program fragment is no longer accessed

```
fc0526 move.l  50(A6),D0      get WarmCapture
fc052a beq.s   $fc0530        branch if not set
fc052c move.l  D0,A0          WarmCapture to A0
fc052e jsr     (A0)           jump
fc0530 moveq   #$0d,D0        set value for counter
fc0532 clr.l   -(A7)          clear stack
fc0534 dbf     D0,$fc0532              branch if not done
fc0538 movem.l (A7)+,A5-A0/D7-D0
fc053c jsr     -114(A6)       jump to debugger
fc0540 move.l  $0004,A6       ExecBase to A6
fc0544 bra.s   $fc053c
```

---

## 2.9.2    Resident structures

To better understand how it is possible to "build in" reset-proof
modules, we first have to explain what resident structures are and how
they are managed.

*Resident
structures*

Resident structures are structures in the operating system which are
located on a reset. They are found using their identification code, which
is stored at the start of the structure. The positions of all found resident
structures are stored in a table and a pointer to this table is stored in
ResModules (in the ExecBase structure).

As the reset progresses, the pointer to the previously created table is
fetched and the InitCode() function is executed. The resident structures
are located again with the help of the pointers in the table.

It is in this function that the purpose of the resident structures first
become clear. Such a structure contains, among other things, a pointer
which points either to a table for the registers for a call to MakeLib() or
a program to be executed, depending on the flags stored in the resident
structure. Simply stated, a resident structure allows a program or the
MakeLib function to be called.

*Calling the*
*MakeLib()*
*function*

If you want to call the MakeLib() function, other variations are possible. You can decide whether the structure created by MakeLib() is inserted in the library list with AddLibrary(), the device list with AddDevice() or the resource list with AddResource(). These options are possible because the library, device and resource structures are all similar and can all be created by MakeLib().

A resident structure has the following appearance:

```
struct Resident {
0     UWORD rt_MatchWord;
2     struct Resident *rt_MatchTag;
6     APTR rt_EndSkip;
10    UBYTE rt_Flags;
11    UBYTE rt_Version;
12    UBYTE rt_Type;
13    BYTE rt_Pri;
14    char *rt_Name;
18    char *rt_IdString;
22    APTR rt_Init;
}

#define RTC_MATCHWORD 0x4AFCL
#define RTF_AUTOINIT (1L<<7)
#define RTF_COLDSTART (1L<<0)
#define RTM_WHEN 3L
#define RTW_NEVER 0L
#define RTW_COLDSTART 1L
#endif
```

rt_MatchWord
    is a word by which the structure is recognized. After reset the computer searches for this identification word to find the resident structures. The word must have the value $4AFC so that the structure is found.

rt_MatchTag
    is a pointer to the structure itself and is used to recognize the structure in memory. After the match word is found, the computer checks to see if the word after it points to the structure. If it does, then the resident structure is recognized.

rt_EndSkip
    is a pointer to the end of the structure. With this pointer it is possible to make the structure long and store important data in it.

rt_Flags
    indicates whether or not the resident structure should be processed at all, and if so, whether only the specified command is executed or whether the specified program is executed. If the uppermost bit (bit 7) is cleared, the program stored in the structure is called.

If it is set, then rt_Init points to a table needed for the MakeLib()
function.

rt_Version
:   indicates the version of the structure.

rt_Type
:   indicates which command is performed.

rt_Name
:   is a pointer to the name of the structure.

rt_idString
:   is a pointer to the string which explains the structure.

rt_Init
:   is a pointer to the program to be executed or a pointer to the
table of the register contents to be loaded when MakeLib() is
called. If the MakeLib() function is called, the following registers
must be placed in the table in the specified order:

$$D0 = DataSize$$
$$D1 = CodeSize$$
$$A0 = FuncInit$$
$$A1 = StructInit$$
$$A2 = LibInit$$

The following table shows what a table of pointers to resident structures to which ResModules points (in the ExecBase structure) looks
like. The end marker of the table is the last long word which has the
value zero.

The table is normally created by the reset routine.

If the uppermost bit (bit 31) of a long word in the table is set, it means
that the rest of the word is a pointer to the continuation of the table.

| | | | | | | | |
|---|---|---|---|---|---|---|---|
| 00fc | 00b6 | 00fc | 4afc | 00fe | 4880 | 00fe | 4fe4 |
| 00fc | 450c | 00fc | 4794 | 00fe | 4774 | 00fe | 49cc |
| 00fc | 5378 | 00fe | 502e | 00fe | 507a | 00fe | 90ec |
| 00fc | 34cc | 00fe | 50c6 | 00fe | 0d90 | 00fe | 510e |
| 00fe | 98e4 | 00fd | 3f5c | 00fc | 323a | 00fe | 424c |
| 00fe | b400 | 00ff | 425a | 00fe | 8884 | 0000 | 0000 |

Let's look at the second resident structure in the table. It looks like this:

```
fc4afc 4afc 00fc 4afc 00fc 516c 8121 096e 00fc.................
fc4b0c 4b48 00fc 4b16 00fc 4b38 6578 7061 6e73 ..........expans
fc4b1c 696f 6e20 3333 2e31 3231 2028 3420 4d61 ion 33.121 (4 Ma
fc4b2c 7920 3139 3836 290d 0a00 0000 0000 01c8 y 1986).........
fc4b3c 00fc 4b86 00fc 4b5a 00fc 4bee 6578 7061 ............expa
fc4b4c 6e73 696f 6e2e 6c69 6272 6172 7900 e000 nsion.library...
```

To better complete the initialization of the structure, the appropriate values are listed again in the following structure:

```
struct Resident {
0       UWORD rt_MatchWord;              $4AFC
2       struct Resident *rt_MatchTag;    $FC4AFC
6       APTR rt_EndSkip;                 $FC516C
10      UBYTE rt_Flags;                  %10000001
11      UBYTE rt_Version;                33
12      UBYTE rt_Type;                   Library
13      BYTE rt_Pri;                     110
14      char *rt_Name;                   expansion.library
18      char *rt_IdString;               $FC4B16
22      APTR rt_Init;                    $FC4B38
}
```

The rt_Flag byte is set to %10000001. The top bit is set, so rt_Init points to data for the registers needed for the call to the AddLibrary() function. Here AddLibrary() is called because the type of the resident structure is "library" (NT_LIBRARY = 09).

The following options are available:

| Type         | Function call |
|--------------|---------------|
| 03 = Device   | AddDevice()   |
| 08 = Resource | AddResource() |
| 09 = Library  | AddLibrary()  |

The InitCode() function is responsible for searching for the resident structures. When called the two parameters StartClass and Version are passed. Only resident structures whose version component matches the version password is executed. The value passed in StartClass is ANDed with rt_Flags. If the result is not zero, the structure is executed, with the initResident structure. StartClass and rt_Flags thus determine which resident structures are executed when the InitCode function is called.

On a reset the InitCode function is called with the parameters StartClass = 01 and version = 00. Only resident structures whose bit 0 is set in rt_Flags is executed.

To show you how the routines just described work in detail, here are the assembly language listings.

*InitCode()*

InitCode(StartClass, Version)
               D0           A2

| | | |
|---|---|---|
| FC0AF0 | MOVEM.L D2-D3/A2,-(A7) | Reserve register |
| FC0AF4 | MOVEA.L 300(A6),A2 | Pointer to Resmodule |
| FC0AF8 | MOVE.B D0,D2 | Startclass to D2 |
| FC0AFA | MOVE.B D1,D3 | version to D3 |
| FC0AFC | MOVE.L (A2)+,D0 | Get Pointer from table |
| FC0AFE | BEQ.S $FC0B22 | Branch at end mark |
| FC0B00 | BGT.S $FC0B0A | Branch if Top Bit |
| FC0B02 | BCLR #31,D0 | (Bit 31) is unset |
| FC0B06 | MOVEA.L D0,A2 | Else Clear Bit 31 |
| FC0B08 | BRA.S $FC0AFC | Save pointer |
| FC0B0A | MOVEA.L D0,A1 | Frontable as a new pointer |
| FC0B0C | CMP.B 11(A1),D3 | uncondition jump |
| FC0B10 | BGT.S $FC0AFC | Pointer to resident (A1) |
| FC0B12 | MOVE.B 10(A1),D0 | Resident version too old |
| FC0B16 | AND.B D2,D0 | Get rt_flags |
| FC0B18 | BEQ.S $FC0AFC | compare w/start class |
| FC0B1A | MOVEQ #0,D1 | branch if not starting |
| FC0B1C | JSR -102(A6) | set seglist to null |
| FC0B20 | BRA.S $FC0AFC | unconditional jump |
| FC0B22 | MOVEM.L (A7)+,D2-D3/A2 | get registers back |
| FC0B26 | RTS | Return |

*InitResident*

InitResident(resident, segList)
                  A1        D1

| | | |
|---|---|---|
| FC0B28 | BTST #7,10(A1) | Test Bit 7 from rt_flags |
| FC0B2E | BNE.S $FC0B3C | If not set, |
| FC0B30 | MOVEA.L 22(A1),A1 | Execute command |
| FC0B34 | MOVEQ #0,D0 | Else GOTO beginning |
| FC0B36 | MOVEA.L D1,A0 | Clear D0 |
| FC0B38 | JSR (A1) | Seglist to A0 |
| FC0B3A | BRA.S $FC0B7E | Beginning |
| FC0B3C | MOVEM.L A1-A2,-(A7) | Unconditional jump |
| FC0B40 | MOVEA.L 22(A1),A1 | Reserve register |
| FC0B44 | MOVEM.L (A1),D0/A0-A2 | Get pointer from register |
| FC0B48 | JSR -84(A6) | Get register for function |
| FC0B4C | MOVEM.L (A7)+,A0/A2 | Return register |
| FC0B50 | MOVE.L D0,-(A7) | Get return message |
| FC0B52 | BEQ.S $FC0B7C | If its an error, END |
| FC0B54 | MOVEA.L D0,A1 | pointer from library to A1 |
| FC0B56 | MOVE.B 12(A0),D0 | rt_type to D0 |
| FC0B5A | CMPI.B #3,D0 | rt_type = device |
| FC0B5E | BNE.S $FC0B66 | Branch if not device |
| FC0B60 | JSR -432(A6) | else ADDDEVICE() |
| FC0B64 | BRA.S $FC0B7C | Unconditional jump |

```
FC0B66    CMPI.B #9,D0          rt_type = LIBRARY?
FC0B6A    BNE.S $FC0B72         Branch if not library
FC0B6C    JSR -396(A6)          Else ADDLIBRARY()
FC0B70    BRA.S $FC0B7C         unconditional jump
FC0B72    CMPI.B #8,D0          re_type = resource
FC0B76    BNE.S $FC0B7C         Branch if it isn't
                                resource
FC0B78    JSR -486(A6)          Else Addresource
FC0B7C    MOVE.L (A7)+,D0       RETURN D0
FC0B7E    RTS                   RETURN
```

## 2.9.3    Reset-proof programs and structures

Now that we have taken care of all the prerequisites, we can now discuss how to write reset-proof programs and structures.

There are two ways. First, you can branch to user programs through the ColdCapture and CoolCapture vectors, and second, memory areas can be reallocated with the help of the KickMemPrt and KickTagPrt vectors and insert the resident structure in the resident vector table. All of these vectors are located in the ExecBase structure.

To simply avoid resets, the ColdCapture entry is the best. All you have to do is set this vector to a routine which resets the ColdCapture vector and then runs in an infinite loop.

When initializing the ColdCapture vector you must also recalculate the checksum which is formed from the first ExecBase vectors. A routine to disable the reset might look like this:

```
run:
allocMem      = -198
require       = 1
ColdCapture   = 42


          move.l    $4,a6
          move.l    #ende-start,d0
          move.l    #require,d1
          jsr       allocMem(a6)
          tst.l     d0
          beq       error
          move.l    d0,a1
          move.l    a1,ColdCapture(a6)
          move.w    #ende-start,d0
          lea.l     start,a0
11:       move.b    (a0)+,(a1)+
          dbf       d0,11

; recalculate checksum
```

```
        clr.l    d1
        lea.l    34(a6),a0
        move.w   #$16,d0
12:     add.w    (a0)+,d1
        dbf      d0,12
        not.w    d1
        move.w   d1,82(a6)
error:  rts

; routine which is executed on reset
start:  lea.l    start(pc),a0
        move.l   $4,a6
        move.l   a0,ColdCapture(a6)
13:     jmp      13(pc)
ende:
 end
```

The program first allocates the memory required, copies the program which is executed on reset to this area, enters the starting address of the program in ColdCapture and recalculates the checksum.

Resetting the ColdCapture vector is necessary because it is cleared by the reset routine.

When the program is started and a reset performed, only turning the computer off will save you.

ColdCapture causes a routine to be executed very early in the reset routine. You can see the jump to the documented reset routine at $FC0172. Up to this time not much has happened. The screen color has been set to black, all interrupts and DMA disabled, and the checksum of the ExecBase structure calculated.

If the ColdCapture is set, it is cleared again by the reset routine, the address where the reset routine is continued is passed in A5, and the routine specified by ColdCapture is called. This routine cannot use the stack and cannot call subroutines, since the stack has not been initialized yet.

The reset routine is continued with JMP (A5).

The other vector which can be used to branch to a user program out of the reset routine is called CoolCapture. When the user program is called, the memory has been organized again, the ExecBase structure and the Exec library created, the interrupts are set up, and the exceptions are set back to their proper values.

CoolCapture is called with JSR (A0) and thus can be terminated with a normal RTS. This vector can be used to activate a memory expansion that is not automatically activated. The jump from the reset routine is at $FC051C.

The procedure is the same as for the ColdCapture vector. The vector is entered and the checksum of the ExecBase structure is recalculated. The example program for the ColdCapture vector shows how the checksum can be calculated.

*KickSumData function:*

The best way to get reset-proof programs and structures is to create them with the help of the ExecBase entries KickMemPtr, KickTagPtr and KickCheckSum.

By using these entries you can allocate memory areas with their old values and insert new resident structures in the table of resident structure pointers. To do this, KickMemPtr must point to a MemList structure, whose entries are reallocated during an interrupt. KickTagPtr is a pointer to a resident table which looks like the one ResModules points to in the ExecBase. The resident structures saved in the table are linked independent of their priorities in the table of all resident structures, to be created later.

These two pointers are used only when KickCheckSum (the check sum of the resident table and the MemList structures) is correct. The Exec library function KickSumData() is used to calculate the checksum.

*KickSum Data()*

```
Sum = KickSumData()
D0
```

Offset:        -612

Description:
>The function calculates the checksum of the MemList structure specified in KickMemPtr as well as the resident table specified by KickTagPtr. The result of the calculation is returned in D0.

If you would like to reallocate certain areas of memory after a reset without losing data, these areas must be stored in a MemList structure and allocated with AllocEntry(). The MemList structure itself must also be allocated. It is also possible to chain multiple MemList structures together.

If you also want to execute custom programs during a reset, then you must create resident structures with which the desired programs are called. The pointers to the resident structures must be combined into a table which is terminated with zero. The memory which the resident structures occupy as well as the resident table must also be allocated with a MemList structure and inserted into the list of the memory to be allocated on a reset. The pointer to the resident table is entered in KickTagPtr.

After these steps have been taken, the KickSumData() function is called and the calculated checksum is stored in KickCheckSum.

Now the specified memory areas are reset-proof and the programs stored in the resident structures are executed on a reset.

To give you an idea of what priorities the custom resident structures must have in order to be executed at a given time, the following table shows which resident structures with which priorities are executed on a reset.

| Pri. | Resident pos. | Description |
|------|---------------|-------------|
| 120  | $FC00B6       | Create Exec lib (not allowed) |
| 110  | $FC4AFC       | Create Exception lib |
| 100  | $FE4880       | Create Potgo lib |
| 80   | $FC450C       | Create CIA resources |
| 70   | $FC4794       | Create disk resource |
| 70   | $FE4774       | Create misc resource |
| 70   | $FE49CC       | Create RAM lib (not allowed) |
| 65   | $FC5378       | Create graphics lib |
| 60   | $FE502E       | Create keyboard device |
| 60   | $FE507A       | Create gameport device |
| 50   | $FE90EC       | Create timer device |
| 40   | $FC34CC       | Create audio device |
| 40   | $FE50C6       | Create create input device |
| 31   | $FE0D90       | Create Layers lib |
| 20   | $FE510E       | Create console device |
| 20   | $FE98E4       | Create trackdisk device |
| 10   | $FD3F5C       | Create intuition lib |
| 5    | $FC323A       | Output gurus if present |
| 0    | $FE424C       | Create Math lib |
| 0    | $FEB400       | Workbench task (not allowed) |
| 0    | $FF425A       | Create DOS lib (not allowed) |
| -60  | $FE8884       | Jump to boot procedure |

Since the last resident structure doesn't return to the InitCode() function, no more resident structures can be executed after it. Therefore it doesn't make any sense to have a priority lower than -60.

# 3
# AmigaDOS

# 3.1    The DOS library

For the user, the most important part of the Amiga operating system is DOS, the Disk Operating System. Its task is to take care of all input/output functions, such as disk operations or keyboard inputs. The various functions which are required for this are made available to the user in the form of a library, which is constructed similar to the Exec library.

Like the Exec library, the DOS library doesn't exist as a file on the disk, like the Intuition library. If must still be opened before it can be used. As a result of this process the opening program can access the DOS functions through a pointer table.

## 3.1.1    Loading the DOS library

If a program or function wants to use the DOS library, it must first be opened. An Exec function by the name of OldOpenLibrary is used to do this. This function is passed a pointer to the name of the library. The name must be in lowercase and terminated with a zero. The OpenLibrary function can also be used, which must be passed an additional parameter: the desired version of the library. If the version number of the library is greater than or equal to this number, it is opened. Therefore a zero is usually passed for the version so that any version is opened.

In C this is quite simple. Through the line

```
DOSBase = OpenLibrary("dos.library",0);
```

a pointer to the DOS library is transferred by Exec to DOSBase. The pointer doesn't have to be saved or used explicitly later—the C compiler takes care of this. The value returned can only be used to check if the DOS library was opened properly: it is zero if an error occurred. This can be done as follows:

```
if (DOSBase == 0) exit (DOS_OPEN_ERROR);
```

In machine language this is not so simple, but it is still easy to understand. Opening the DOS library is programmed as follows:

```
EXEC_Base = 4
OldOpenLibrary = -408

        move.l    EXEC_BASE,a6        ;pointer to Exec base in a6
        lea       DOS_Name,a1         ;pointer to library name
        jsr       OldOpenLibrary(a6)  ;open library
        move.l    d0,DOS_Base         ;save pointer to DOS base
        beq       error               ;error occurred
        ...
error:                                ;error handling
        ...
Dos_Base: dc.l      0                 ;space for DOS base
DOS_Name: dc.b"dos.library",0
```

The pointer contained in D0 is needed for each subsequent call to a DOS function. If the library was not opened successfully, a zero is returned in D0 and in this program the error handling routine "error" is called.

In the program above the DOS library is made available through the pointer. The library is constructed similarly to the Exec library and is thus used in the same manner. The entry addresses of the individual functions lie below the DOS_Base base address and are called with negative offsets.

---

## 3.1.2     Calling functions and passing parameters

To call a DOS function, you need to know its address and you usually need to pass some parameters to it. These parameters are passed in the processor data registers D1 to D4.

An example: The DOS Open() function is used to open a simple window. The following parameters are needed:

- A pointer to the name of the file, terminated with a zero byte, in register D1. For our example the name of the window definition CON: is used.
- The file access mode must be specified in D2. This mode indicates whether the file already exists or is created. For the window to be opened in the example, pass the mode "old" so that you can also read from the window.

The assembly language program for this example looks something like this:

```
Open         = -30
Mode_old     = 1005

        ...
        move.l    #FileName,d1    ;pointer to file definition
        move      #Mode_old,d2    ;mode: old
```

```
        move.l    DOS_Base,a6        ;DOS base address in A6
        jsr       Open(a6)           ;open file (window)
        move.l    d0,ConHandle       ;save file handle pointer
        beq       error              ;error occurred!
        ...

ConHandle:    dc.l 0                 ;space for file handle
FileName:     dc.b "CON:10/10/620/170/** Test window **",0
```

A later section explains the exact use of the standard channel CON:.

---

# 3.1.3        The DOS functions

## 1)      *General I/O functions*

This section contains all of the DOS functions. The offsets are specified, as well as the registers in which the various parameters must be passed.

**Open()**

```
Handle = Open(name,mode)
D0       -30    D1    D2
```

Open file

Opens the file defined by the zero-terminated string to which D1 points.

The mode in D2 can be Mode_readwrite (1004 for DOS 1.2) for reading and writing, Mode_old (1005) for reading, or Mode_new (1006) for writing to the file.

A pointer to the file handle structure is returned in D0, or a zero if the function could not be executed. The file handle structure has the following appearance:

| Offset | Name | Meaning |
|--------|------|---------|
| 0 | Link | Unused |
| 4 | Interact | If <>0, the file is interactive |
| 8 | ID | File identification number |
| 12 | Buffer | Pointer to internal memory required |
| 16 | CharPos | Internal pointer |
| 20 | BufEnd | Internal pointer |
| 24 | ReadFunc | Pointer to routine called when buffer is empty |
| 28 | WriteFunc | Pointer to routine called when buffer is full |
| 32 | CloseFunc | Pointer to routine called when file is closed |
| 36 | Argument1 | |
| 40 | Argument2 | File-type-dependent arguments |

Most entries are reserved for internal use by AmigaDOS. These values should not be manipulated.

*Close()*
```
Close(handle)
-36    D1
```

Close file

Closes the file opened with Open. The pointer passed in D1 is the pointer to the file handle structure returned by the Open function.

*Read()*
```
Number = Read(handle, buffer, length)
D0       -42   D1      D2      D3
```

Read data

Reads up to length bytes into memory at address buffer from the file specified by handle.

The value returned in D0 is the number of bytes actually read. If this number is 0, the end of the file was reached. If an error occurs, -1 is returned.

*Write()*
```
Number = Write(handle, buffer, length)
D0       -48    D1      D2      D3
```

Write data

Writes length bytes from memory at address buffer to the file specified by handle.

The number of bytes actually written is returned in D0. If this value is -1, an error occurred.

*Seek()*
```
Position = Seek(handle, distance, mode)
D0         -66    D1      D2        D3
```

Set file pointer

This function sets the internal pointer in the file specified by handle. The mode determines whether the value in distance is treated as relative to the start of the file, to the current file position, or to the end of the file. Distance can be a signed value, allowing the file pointer to be moved backwards.

The possible modes are:     OFFSET_BEGINNING     -1
                            OFFSET_CURRENT        0
                            OFFSET_END            1

The return value indicates the current position of the pointer after the function was executed. This function can be used to determine the current pointer position by using the "relative to current position" mode (OFFSET_CURRENT) and moving 0 bytes: the return value is then the same as the old pointer position.

*Input()*

```
Handle = Input ()
DO        -54
```

Determine standard input channel

This function returns the handle of the channel from which the standard inputs are read. If the program has been called from the CLI, then this is the handle of the CLI window. If input redirection was used in the CLI command which called the program, the handle of the selected channel is returned. An example:

```
>program_name <DF0:filename
```

allows inputs through Read within the program called to come from the file filename.

*Output()*

```
Handle = Output ()
```

Determine standard output channel

This function returns the handle of the channel to which the standard outputs are written. If the program has been called from the CLI, then this is the handle of the CLI window. If output redirection was used in the CLI command which called the program, the handle of the selected channel is returned. An example:

```
>program_name >PRT:
```

sends the standard outputs from the called program to the printer.

*WaitForChar()*

```
Status = WaitForChar (handle, timeout)
DO          -204            D1    D2
```

Wait for a character

This function waits the number of microseconds specified by timeout for a character to be received from the channel specified by handle (such as RAW: window, wait for a keypress). If no character is received in this time, a 0 is returned, else the value -1. The character can be read with the Read function.

This function is accessible only when the channel is interactive (virtual term.), such as a RAW: window, in which input and output can occur simultaneously and the data doesn't necessarily arrive on command.

*IsInteractive()*

```
Status = IsInteractive (handle)
DO          -216            D1
```

Determine channel type

A true value (-1) is returned if the channel specified by handle is a virtual terminal, with which input and output can occur. Otherwise a false value (0) is returned.

*IoErr()*

```
Error = IoErr ()
D0      -132
```

Determine I/O error

If an error is signalled after calling a function, generally by returning zero in D0, the exact error message can be determined by calling IoErr(). D0 contains the number of the previous error (cf. CLI WHY command).

The next section contains a list of the error values.

## 2)    Disk operations

*CreateDir()*

```
Lock = CreateDir (name)
D0      -120     D1
```

Create subdirectory

The subdirectory name is created in the current directory.

The return value is a pointer to a file structure (lock), which has the following construction:

| Offset | Name | Description |
|---|---|---|
| 0 | NextBlock | Pointer to the next lock chained to this one, or zero |
| 4 | DiskBlock | Block number of the directory or the file header |
| 8 | AccessType | -1 = exclusive access, -2 = general access |
| 12 | ProcessID | Identification number |
| 16 | VolNode | Pointer to disk info |

This structure is the "key" to the file or directory, since it can be used to access it (cf. CLI MAKEDIR command).

*Lock()*

```
lock = Lock (name, mode)
D0     -84   D1   D2
```

Determine file key

The disk is searched for a file or directory of name and a structure is created for it. The mode determines the type of access to the file. If it is read (-2), then multiple tasks can read from this file, if it is written (-1) then only this program can write to it.

*CurrentDir()*

```
oldLock = CurrentDir (lock)
D0         -126        D1
```

Make current working directory

The directory specified by lock is made the current working directory (see CLI CD command).

The value returned is a pointer to the previous directory (its lock).

ParentDir()     newLock = ParentDir(lock)
                D0           -210        D1

Determine the parent directory

The parent directory of the one specified by lock is determined and its lock is returned in D0. If lock belongs to the root directory, a zero is returned in D0.

DeleteFile()    Status = DeleteFile(name)
                D0           -72         D1

Delete file

The specified tile is deleted. The name must be a zero-terminated string. An error message is returned in D0 if the function could not be executed (file not found, file write-protected, directory not empty, etc.).

If a directory is specified to be deleted, it must be empty.

Rename()        Status = Rename (oldName, newName)
                D0           -78         D1          D2

Rename file

The file or directory with the name oldName is renamed to newName. If a file with the new name already exists, the function is terminated and an error returned.

The two name parameters can also contain paths. In this case the file is moved from one directory to the other. This works only on the same disk.

DupLock()       newLock = DupLock(lock)
                D0           -96         D1

Copy lock

The old lock is copied into a new one. D0 points to the new structure. This can be used if multiple processes want to access the same file. No locks which are write access can only be copied, since only exclusive access is allowed to such a file.

UnLock()        UnLock(lock)
                -90          D1

The lock structure created with Lock(), DupLock() or CreateDir() is removed and the memory it occupied is released.

*Examine()*

```
Status = Examine (lock, InfoBlock)
D0        -102     D1      D2
```

Get file information

The structure to which D2 points is filled with information about the file specified by lock. This structure is called FileInfoBlock and is constructed as follows:

| Offset | Name | Description |
|--------|------|-------------|
| 0 | DiskKey.L | Disk number |
| 4 | DirEntryType.L | Entry type (+=directory, -=file) |
| 8 | FileName | 108 bytes with the filename |
| 116 | Protection.L | File protected? |
| 120 | EntryType.L | Entry type |
| 124 | Size.L | File length in bytes |
| 128 | NumBlocks.L | Number of allocated blocks |
| 132 | Days.L | Creation date |
| 136 | Minute.L | Creation time |
| 140 | Tick.L | Creation time |
| 144 | Comment | 116 bytes comment |

D0 contains zero if the function could not be executed.

*ExNext()*

```
Status = ExNext (lock, InfoBlock)
D0        -108     D1      D2
```

Determine next directory entry

This function is passed the InfoBlock filled by Examine() as well as the lock of the selected directory. The information about the first matching entry in this directory is placed in the InfoBlock. The next time ExNext() is called, the next matching entry in this directory is found and its information returned. If no more entries can be found or another error occurred, a zero is returned in D0.

The directory of a disk can be read with the Lock(), Examine() and ExNext() commands as follows:

1.  The key to the desired directory is created with Lock().
2.  The directory name or disk name can be read with Examine(). At the same time, the FileInfoBlock is created which is needed for the next function.
3.  The individual directory entries are read with multiple calls to the ExNext() function and the information transferred to the FileInfoBlock. This is repeated until the ExNext() function returns zero: no more entries.

Here is a short assembly language program which performs these steps. The print routine called is not listed here—it could print the names and lengths of the files on the screen, for example.

The DOS library must be opened and the DOSbase address placed in DOSbase before this routine is called.

```
Lock            = -84
Examine         = -102
ExNext          = -108
IoErr           = -132
...
directory:                          ;* directory of DF0:
    move.l      dosbase,a6          ;DOS base address in A6
    move.l      #name,d1            ;pointer to path/filename
    move.l      #-2,d2              ;'read' mode
    jsr         Lock(a6)            ;find file
    tst.l       d0                  ;found?
    beq         Error               ;no!
    move.l      d0,locksav          ;else save key

    move.l      dosbase,a6          ;DOS base address
    move.l      locksav,d1          ;key in D1
    move.l      #fileinfo,d2        ;pointer to FileInfoBlock
    jsr         Examine(a6)         ;get disk name
    tst.l       d0                  ;OK?
    beq         error               ;no (rarely occurs)
    bra         outpuff             ;else output name

loop:                               ;* read filename
    move.l      dosbase,a6          ;DOS base address
    move.l      locksav,d1          ;key in D1
    move.l      #fileinfo,d2        ;pointer to FileInfoBlock
    jsr         ExNext(a6)          ;find next file
    tst.l       d0                  ;found?
    beq         error               ;no: done

outpuff:                            ;* output name
    bsr         Print               ;output/evaluate name
    bra         loop                ;and continue...

error:                              ;* determine I/O status
    move.l      dosbase,a6          ;DOS base address in A6
    jsr         IoErr(a6)           ;get status
    rts                             ;end...

name:           dc.b 'DF0:',0
align           ;even
locksav:        blk.l 0
fileinfo:       blk.l 260
```

After this routine ends the error code from the IoErr() function is returned in D0. The code should be 232 (no_more_entries), otherwise something has gone wrong.

*Info()*            Status = Info(lock, InfoData)
                    D0        -104  D1        D2

Get disk information

The parameter block to which D2 points is filled with information about the disk used. This block must start on a long-word-aligned address (divisible by 4).

Lock must be for the disk, file or directory on the disk.

*InfoData*          The parameter block InfoData has the following structure:
*structure*

| Offset | Name | Description |
|--------|------|-------------|
| 0 | NumSoftErrors | Number of disk errors |
| 4 | UnitNumber | Installed disk device |
| 8 | DiskState | Disk status |
| 12 | NumBlocks | Number of blocks on the disk |
| 16 | NumBlocksUsed | Number of blocks used |
| 20 | BytesPerBlock | Number of bytes per block |
| 24 | DiskType | Disk type (see below) |
| 28 | VolumeNode | Pointer to the disk name |
| 32 | InUse | <>0 if disk is active |

DiskState indicates the status of the disk. The following values are possible:

| | |
|---|---|
| 80 | Disk is write-protected |
| 81 | Disk is being repaired (validated) |
| 82 | Disk OK and writable |

DiskType contains the type of disk, if one is inserted as a string. The possible values are:

| | |
|---|---|
| -1 | No disk inserted |
| BAD | Disk unreadable (improper format) |
| DOS | DOS diskette |
| NDOS | Format OK, but not a DOS disk |
| KICK | Kickstart disk |

*SetComment()*      Status = SetComment(name, comment)
                    D0        -180      D1        D2

Set file comment

The file or directory name has a comment associated with it. The comment can be up to 80 characters long and must be terminated with a zero byte.

*SetProtec*  `Status = SetProtection(name,mask)`
*tion()*     `D0        -186            D1    D2`

Set file status

The read/write status of the specified file or directory is set. The lower four bits of the mask have the following meanings:

| Bit | Meaning. if set |
|-----|-----------------|
| 0   | File not deletable |
| 1   | Not executable |
| 2   | Not overwritable |
| 3   | Not readable |

*CreateProc()*  `Process = CreatePorc(name,pri,segment,stack)`
                `D0        -138         D1   D2      D3      D4`

Create a new process

A new process structure is created under the name to which D1 points. This process runs with the priority set by pri and has a stack of size stack.

A pointer to a segment list in which the program code to start is defined is passed in segment. The program should thus start in the first segment of the list.

The result of the function is the new process ID, or a 0 if an error occurred.

*DateStamp()*  `DateStamp(vector)`
               `-192      D1`

Determine date and time

A pointer to a table of three long words is returned in D1. If the time in the Amiga is not set, all of these long words contain 0. Otherwise the first long word contains the days elapsed since January 1, 1978, the second the number of minutes since midnight, and the third the number of sixteenths of a second elapsed in this minute. This value is always a multiple of 60, however, so this value is just the number of seconds times 60.

*Delay()*  `Delay(time)`
           `-198    D1`

The running process is paused

The running process is stopped for the number of sixteenths of a second specified by time.

*DeviceProc()*    Process = DeviceProc (name)
                  D0            -174        D1

Determine the process using I/O

The identification of the process which is currently using the I/O channel specified by name is returned, or a 0 if no process was found.

If the name refers to a disk channel, a pointer to the lock structure of the corresponding directory can be returned with the IoErr() function.

*Exit()*          Exit (parameter)
                  -144    D1

End program

The current program is stopped. If the program was called from the CLI, control is returned to the CLI and the integer value passed in parameter is interpreted as a return value from the program. If the program was started as a process, this process is removed by Exit() and the stack, segment and process memory it occupied is released.

*Execute()*       Status = Execute (command, input, output)
                  D0            -222        D1        D2        D3

Call CLI command

The CLI command string to which D1 points is executed. The input and output of the CLI command can be directed to any channels by passing their handles as input and/or output. If 0 is specified for input or output, the standard channel is used.

These commands make it easy to create your own CLI, which, for instance, opens its own window and then calls Execute() with the window handle for input and an empty command string. The command is then entered in the window and the output is also sent to this window. This CLI can also be ended with the ENDCLI command, whereby the RUN program must be in the C: directory.

*LoadSeg()*       Segment = LoadSeg (name)
                  D0              -150      D1

Load program file

The program filename is loaded into memory. The program can be divided up among several memory modules if not enough contiguous memory is available. The resulting segments are linked together in that the first entry of segment is a pointer to the next segment in the list. If this pointer is 0, then this is the last segment.

If an error occurs during this process, all loaded segments are released and a 0 is returned in D0. Otherwise D0 contains a pointer to the first segment.

The loaded program can be started with CreateProc() or removed again with UnLoadSeg().

**UnLoadSeg()**

```
UnLoadSeg (segment)
-156        D1
```

Remove loaded program file

The program file loaded with LoadSeg is removed and the memory it occupied is released. The pointer in D1 points to the first segment in the list (see LoadSeg).

**GetPacket()**

```
Status = GetPacket (WaitFlag)
D0          -162        D1
```

Get packet

Packet sent from another process is fetched. If the WaitFlag is true (-1), the function waits for the reception of the packet, otherwise it will not wait and returns a zero if no packet is present.

**QueuePacket()**

```
Status = QueuePacket (packet)
```

Send packet

The packet to whose structure D1 points is sent. If this is done successfully, then a non-zero value is returned in D0.

---

## 3.1.4    DOS error messages

The following is a list of the error codes returned by IoErr() or the CLI WHY command and their names and descriptions.

*103*    insufficient free store

Not enough memory is free.

*104*    task table full

There are already 20 processes active—this is the maximum.

*120*    argument line invalid or too long

The argument list for this command is incorrect or contains too many arguments.

*121*    file is not an object module

The called file cannot be executed.

*122*  invalid resident library during load

The resident library called is invalid.

*202*  object in use

The specified file or directory is currently being used by another program and cannot be used for other applications.

*203*  object already exists

The specified filename already exists.

*204*  directory not found

The directory selected does not exist.

*205*  object not found

The channel with the name specified does not exist.

*206*  invalid window

The parameters specified for the window to be opened are not correct.

*209*  packet requested type unknown

The desired function is not possible on the specified device.

*210*  invalid stream component name

The filename is not valid (too long or contains illegal characters).

*211*  invalid object lock

The specified lock structure is invalid.

*212*  object not of required type

Filename and directory name were interchanged.

*213*  disk not validated

Either the disk was not recognized by the system or it is defective.

*214*  disk write-protected

The disk is write-protected.

*215*  rename across devices attempted

The rename function is possible only on the same drive.

*216*  directory not empty

A non-empty directory cannot be deleted.

*218*  device not mounted

The disk selected is not inserted.

*219*  seek error

The Seek() function had illegal parameters.

*220*  comment too big

The file comment is too long.

*221*  disk full

The disk is full or does not have enough room for this operation.

*222*  file is protected from deletion

The file cannot be deleted or is delete-protected.

*223*  file is protected from writing

The file cannot be overwritten.

*224*  file is protected from reading

The file cannot be read. With the last three error messages you can use the LIST command to check the status of the files in question.

*225*  not a DOS disk

This disk is not in AmigaDOS format.

*226*  no disk in drive

There is no disk in the specified drive.

*232*  no more entries in directory

The last ExNext() function could not find a matching file in the directory.

# 3.2   Disks

The Amiga is very heavily disk-oriented, that is, it often has to load
something from disk. Therefore it is important that the information on
a disk is stored securely and can be retrieved quickly again. In this section we'll look at the structure of the disk and the interpretation of the
data on it.

The basic structure of the disk is as follows:

- Side of head number (0 or 1)
- Track or cylinder (0 or 79)
- Sector (0-10)

Every Amiga disk is double-sided. Each side of the disk is in turn divided into 80 tracks which are arranged as concentric rings about the center.
The outer track is numbered 0 and the inner 79. These tracks are also
sometimes called cylinders.

*Figure  3.2.1*

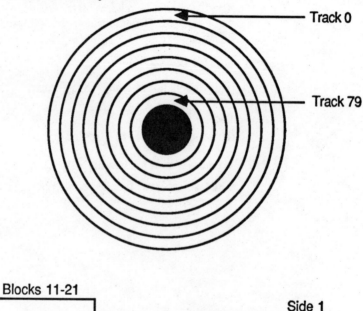

Each of these tracks is in turn divided into 11 sectors, which are numbered from 0 to 10. The sectors are also sometimes referred to as blocks, but while the sectors are numbered from 0 to 10, the blocks are numbered from 0 to 1759, since these designate the logical sector numbers of the disk.

Each of these sectors contains 512 bytes of available information, whereby each disk can contain 512*11*80*2 = 901120 bytes. Not all of this is available for storing user data, since managing the data also requires some space.

The first logical sector, the first block on the disk, lies on side 0, track 0, sector 0. The following block is the next sector of this track, and so on. Block 11 is not the first sector of the second track, but the first sector of the first track on the other side of the disk (side 1). The disk is always read or written on alternating sides in this manner.

---

## 3.2.1    The boot procedure

The first contact with the disk takes place when the Amiga is turned on. After some hardware initializations in the computer have been completed, drive 0 starts to run. What is going on?

Regardless of whether Kickstart is built into the Amiga or not, it always tries to load something from the disk in this drive. If Kickstart is not built in, the computer loads it from disk, otherwise it looks for a Workbench diskette. This loading process when the computer is turned on is called *booting*.

The first thing loaded from the inserted diskette are the boot blocks, which occupy the first two sectors (0 and 1) of the disk. These contain information about the type of diskette. The possible types are:

- Kickstart
- DOS, a loadable DOS diskette (Workbench)
- Unformatted or non-Amiga-format disk

The first four bytes of the first block of the disk indicate its type. Here there are either the letters DOS with a terminating zero byte for a DOS diskette or KICK for a Kickstart disk. If something else is found here, then the disk is not recognized (BAD).

The four bytes which follow represent the checksum of the boot block as a long word. If this sum is correct, the Amiga assumes that the disk is a Workbench disk.

The next long word contains the number of the disk block called the root block, which is normally $370 (880). The meaning of this block is explained shortly.

A program starts at the seventh word. This program, if the checksum is correct, is executed. A pointer to the Exec base is passed in A6 so that Exec functions can be called.

*Boot block (sector 0)*

| L-word | Name | Contents | Description |
| --- | --- | --- | --- |
| 0 | Disk type | DOS, KICK | Four letter disk type |
| 1 | Checksum | ??? | Block checksum |
| 2 | Root block | $370 | Number of the root block |
| 3-127 | Data | | Boot program |

The program which is usually located here uses the FindLibrary() function of Exec to determine if the DOS library is present. If this is not the case, the value -1 is returned in D0. If so, a zero is returned in D0 and a pointer to the DOS initialization routine in A0.

With a custom program the entire boot procedure and thereby the initialization of the Amiga can be customized here. This allows you to create your own Workbench disk, since several disk monitor programs can create the checksum. This checksum is absolutely necessary if the Amiga is to recognize this block as a boot block.

## 3.2.2     File structures and data distribution

In order to store data on a disk with a capacity of about 880K in a manner such that it can be retrieved again later, there are some rules about the distribution of data. These rules are naturally known to AmigaDOS, so you don't necessarily have to know them. But if an error ever occurs on the disk, you have to know how to be able to save the remaining data.

This is the purpose of the DISKDOCTOR program. To understand the operation of this rescuer, you have to look at various aspects of the disk format.

An important point is the distribution of files on the disk and the structure of the directory.

## 3.2.2.1    Disk layout

In contrast to many disk formats, the directory of the Amiga disk is not found in a group of contiguous sectors. This is why the output of the directory takes so long.

This method has advantages and disadvantages. The disadvantage is the long access time to the directory. This disadvantage is offset by a significant advantage, however: the possibility of "repairing" a damaged diskette.

If an error occurs in the directory track of another system, such as the Atari ST, big problems result. The position of the data and the corresponding sectors is no longer known and the data can be saved only with an enormous effort (if at all).

This is not the case with the Amiga. As the existence of the DISK-DOCTOR makes clear, the individual files are relatively easy to find without a central directory. This is achieved through substantial redundancy, which takes up room on the disk, but which also increases the security of the data.

How does this work? To understand how the data are distributed on the disk, we must first look at the structure of the various disk sectors.

*Root block*      Aside from the boot sectors, the root block is found at a defined location on the disk. This is normally side 0, track 40, sector 0, and thus block number 880 ($370). The third long word of the boot sector also contains this number.

This block contains the root of the entire disk. Here lies the top directory as well as the disk name and its creation date. The structure of this block is as follows (all values are long words, 4 bytes):

| Word | Name | Contents | Description |
|---|---|---|---|
| 0 | Type | 2 | Type 2 (T.SHORT) means that this block is the starting block of a structure. |
| 1 | Header Key | 0 | has no meaning here |
| 2 | HighSeq | 0 | has no meaning here |
| 3 | HT size | $48 | This is the size of the table in which the starting blocks of the files and subdirectories are listed (hash table), linked together. |
| 4 | reserved | 0 | has no meaning here |
| 5 | Checksum | ??? | Contains a value which brings the sum of all words in this block to zero |

| Word | Name | Contents | Description |
|------|------|----------|-------------|
| 6 | Hash table | | Here begins the table in which the starting blocks of the files and directories are stored. |
| 78 | BM flag | -1 | This flag contains -1 (true) if the disk bit map is valid |
| 79 | BM pages | | The following table contains pointers to the blocks which contain the bit map. Usually this is only one block so that the remaining pointers in the table are zero. |
| 105 | Days | | Contains the date when the disk was last modified |
| 106 | Mins | | Time of modification |
| 107 | Ticks | | Seconds of modification |
| 108 | Disk name | | Name of the disk as a BCPL string, that is, the first byte contains the number of characters in the name (max. 30) |
| 121 | Create days | | Creation date of the disk |
| 122 | Create mins | | Creation time |
| 123 | Create ticks | | Creation seconds |
| 124 | Next hash | 0 | always zero |
| 125 | Parent dir | 0 | Pointer to the parent directory, always zero |
| 126 | Extension | 0 | always zero |
| 127 | Sec. type | 1 | This word represents the secondary type of the block. For the root block this is 1. |

The values in the hash table specify the blocks in which the file or directory chains start within the root directory. Since this table doesn't contain enough values, chains are formed from the files and directories whose names have a certain relationship.

A value is calculated from the file/directory name which lies between 6 and 77. The long word in the hash table which indicates that the chain begins is accessed with this value.

The function used to calculate this value is:

```
Hash=length of the name
per letter of the name
   Hash=Hash *13
   Hash=Hash +ASCII value of character (always uppercase)
   Hash=Hash & $7FF (logical AND)
Hash=Hash modulo 72
Hash=Hash +6
```

The section about the TrackDisk device contains an assembly language program for evaluating the hash table to illustrate how this algorithm can be programmed.

The start of the chain thus lies where the calculated pointer in the hash table points. The 124th long word of this block contains the number of the next entry in the chain, and so on, until a zero in the pointer indicates the end of the chain.

These blocks, which form the start of a file or directory structure, are specially constructed. Let's start with the first block of a file, the file header block.

*File header block*

This block contains information about the corresponding file. This includes its name, time of creation, and a comment about the file as well as the size and location of the file on the disk.

The structure of this block is as follows:

| Word | Name | Contents | Description |
|------|------|----------|-------------|
| 0 | Type | 2 | Type 2 (T.SHORT) means that this block is the starting block of a structure. |
| 1 | Header key | | The block number |
| 2 | High seq | | Contains the total number of blocks in this file |
| 3 | Data size | 0 | |
| 4 | First data | 0 | Here is the number of the first data block in the file. This value is also in word no. 77. |
| 5 | Checksum | ??? | Contains a value which makes the sum of all words in the block zero |
| 6 | Data blocks | | Here begins the table in which the data blocks of the file are listed. The table starts at word no. 77 and works backwards. |
| 78 | reserved | 0 | |
| 79 | reserved | 0 | |
| 80 | Protect | | This word contains the status of the file in the lower four bits: Bit Protected against, if set 0 Delete 1 Modification 2 Write 3 Read |
| 81 | Byte size | | Length of the file in bytes |
| 82 | Comment | | Here begins the file comment as a BCPL string (max. 22 characters) |
| 105 | Days | | Contains the date when the file was created |
| 106 | Mins | | Time of creation |
| 107 | Ticks | | Seconds of creation |
| 108 | Filename | | Name of the file as a BCPL string, that is, the first byte contains the number of characters in the name (max. 30) |
| 124 | Hash chain | | Block number of the next file in this chain or zero |

| Word | Name | Contents | Description |
|------|------|----------|-------------|
| 125 | Parent | | Pointer to the directory in which this file appears |
| 126 | Extension | 0 | Pointer to the extension block or zero |
| 127 | Sec. type | -3 | This word represents the secondary type of the block. For the file header block this is -3 ($FFFD). |

Entry no. 126 is always non-zero when the data block table is not long enough to store all of the blocks for this file. If this is the case, it points to a block in which this list is continued.

*File list block*  This block, which continues the block list, is called the file list block and is constructed is follows:

| Word | Name | Contents | Description |
|------|------|----------|-------------|
| 0 | Type | $10 | Type $10 (T.LIST) means that this block is an extension of a file structure. |
| 1 | Header key | | The block number |
| 2 | High seq | | Contains the total number of entries in the data block table |
| 3 | Data size | 0 | |
| 4 | First data | 0 | Here is the number of the first data block in the file. This value is also in word no. 77. |
| 5 | Checksum | ??? | Contains a value which makes the sum of all words in the block zero |
| 6 | Data blocks | | Here begins the table in which the data blocks of the file are listed. The table starts at word no. 77 and works backwards. |
| 78 | info | 0 | reserved |
| 124 | Hash chain | | Block number of the next file in this chain (always zero) |
| 125 | Parent | | Pointer to the file header block |
| 126 | Extension | 0 | Pointer to the extension block or zero |
| 127 | Sec. type | -3 | This word represents the secondary type of the block. |

*User directory block*  Each directory starts with such a block, constructed similarly to the root block:

| Word | Name | Contents | Description |
|------|------|----------|-------------|
| 0 | Type | 2 | Type 2 (T.SHORT) means that this block is the starting block of a structure. |
| 1 | Header Key | 0 | The block number |
| 2 | HighSeq | 0 | has no meaning here |
| 3 | HT size | 0 | has no meaning here |

| Word | Name | Contents | Description |
|---|---|---|---|
| 4 | reserved | 0 | has no meaning here |
| 5 | Checksum | ??? | Contains a value which brings the sum of all words in this block to zero |
| 6 | Hash table | | Here begins the table in which the starting blocks of the files and directories are stored. |
| 78 | reserved | 0 | has no meaning here |
| 80 | Protect | | This word contains the status of the file in the lower four bits: |

|  | Bit | Protected against, if set |
|---|---|---|
|  | 0 | Delete |
|  | 1 | Modification |
|  | 2 | Write |
|  | 3 | Read |

| Word | Name | Contents | Description |
|---|---|---|---|
| 82 | Comment | | Here begins the directory comment as a BCPL string (max. 22 characters) |
| 105 | Days | | Contains the date when the directory was created |
| 106 | Mins | | Time of creation |
| 107 | Ticks | | Seconds of creation |
| 108 | Dir. name | | Name of the directory as a BCPL string (max. 30) |
| 124 | Next hash | | Next entry of the same chain |
| 125 | Parent dir | | Pointer to the parent directory |
| 126 | Extension | 0 | Always zero |
| 127 | Sec. type | 2 | This word represents the secondary type of the block. For the user directory block this is 2. |

Of course, in addition to these structure blocks there are also data blocks on the disk. These have the simplest structure:

**Data block**

| Word | Name | Contents | Description |
|---|---|---|---|
| 0 | Type | 8 | Type 8 (T.DATA) means that this is a data block |
| 1 | Header key | | Here is the block number of the file header |
| 2 | Seq num | | Running number of the data blocks in this file |
| 3 | Data size | $1E8 | Valid data words in this block ($1E8 or fewer). |
| 4 | Next data | | Number of the next data block of this file |
| 5 | Checksum | ??? | Contains a value which brings the sum of all words in this block to zero |
| 6 | Data | | Here the data itself starts |

Now all we're missing is the block containing the bit map mentioned in conjunction with the root block. This block contains one bit for each block on the disk, indicating whether the block is free or allocated. The structure of the bit map block is very simple:

*Bit map block*

| Word | Name | Contents | Description |
|------|------|----------|-------------|
| 0 | Checksum | ??? | Block checksum |
| 1-55 | Bit map | | Allocation bits for all blocks. Bit 0 of the first long word stands for block 2, etc. A set bit indicates a free block. |

After this look at the layout of the files on the disk, we'll now see how such a file is constructed.

# 3.2.2.2    Program structure

Actually a program is nothing more than a set of binary data words forming a machine language program. On the "good old eight-bitters" storing such a program wasn't a problem: just write the program from memory onto disk and you're done.

A machine like the Amiga, however, presents a number of problems which make this method unusable. The first problem is the allocation of memory. If the memory in which the program was run the first time is already occupied the next time it's called, it would no longer be possible to just do a "straight load" of the program. The program must be loaded at a different location in memory, which for a normal machine language program which uses absolute addresses means that it won't run.

This program was solved on the Amiga by storing a program on the disk such that all absolute addresses in the program are set up for a start address of $0000. If the program is then started at $20000, for instance, then all of these incorrect addresses must be corrected before the program can be started, that is, they must be incremented by $20000. So that the DOS, which accomplishes this, can find the addresses in the program which needs to be changed, a table must be stored along with the actual program. This table contains all of the offsets which point to a long word to be changed.

So now there are two sections which have to be saved in a program file: the program itself and the table, called the relocation table. But there is a whole set of such pieces which the Amiga uses. A program fragment composed of such parts is called a *hunk*. One or more hunks make up a program unit, of which one or more form an object file. A load file consists of one or more object files, and this load file is the executable program.

The difference between these two file types is that an object file contains a not-yet executable program that was created by a compiler or assembler, for example. If you wish to make an executable program out of one or more of these files, a linker must be used. This is a program which links object files together into a single program, which is then stored as a load file. The result can be started simply by entering its name in the CLI.

The advantage of this method is that various parts of a program which call each other can be created and compiled separately. The main program, which might be written in C and which contains the main routine, can then simply call the functions in the other files. Removing the functions from the main program makes the program more readable, since it can be much shorter than the entire program.

The reason that the individual programs cannot run separately becomes clear. Parts of the program are called which are not actually contained in this program! Not until the sections are processed by the linker are all functions combined into a single program file.

Let's start with the smallest sections which make up hunks. Some of these program file parts occur only in object files, some only in load files. They start with a given long word, which is listed in hexadecimal in parentheses in the following list.

*Overview of possible hunk parts:*

hunk_unit ($3E7)
> A program unit in an object file starts with this part. After the code $3E7 comes the length of the name of this unit and then the name itself, which must end on a long word boundary.

hunk_name ($3E8)
> Here lies the hunk name: After the $3E8 comes the length of the name and then the name itself, which must end on a long word boundary.

hunk_code ($3E9)
> This part contains a program fragment which can run after the absolute addresses have been corrected. After the code $3E9 comes the number of long words in the program and then the long words themselves.

hunk_data ($3EA)
> This is also the start of a program segment, but it contains initialized data for the program. Some of these data can also require address correction. Following the code is the number of data and the data themselves.

hunk_bss ($3EB)
> The data in this section belongs to the program itself, but they have no defined contents. Thus after the code is only the number of long words needed, but not the data itself.

hunk_reloc32 ($3EC)
>This block contains the offsets which point to the address long words in the program to be corrected. These offsets are valid for the entire program. The division of this block is as follows:

After the code $3EC comes the number of offsets contained in the first table. The next long word indicates the number of the hunk to which these offsets refer, followed by the offsets themselves. The next long word is again a number, followed by the hunk number for this table, etc., until a zero occurs as the number and this hunk section ends.

- $3EC (hunk_reloc32)
- Number of offsets
- Hunk number
- Offsets...
- Number of offsets (or 0: end)
- Hunk number
- Offsets...
  - .
  - .
  - .
- 0: end of hunk_reloc32

In this manner the table can cover all hunks which make up the program.

hunk_reloc16 ($3EC)
>This table is constructed just like hunk_reloc32 except that these offsets refer to 16-bit addresses. Such addresses occur only for PC-relative addressing.

hunk_reloc8 ($3EE)
>This table also has the same format as hunk_reloc32. The offsets contained here are used for 8-bit addresses, which occur in PC-relative addressing.

hunk_ext ($3EF)
>This block contains the names of the external references. Such references occur only in object files. These involve addresses of functions or subroutines which are unknown to the program fragment and which must be resolved by the linker.

Following the code are several "symbol data units," which are terminated by a zero word. These symbol definitions have the following structure:

1 byte: symbol type. Possible values:

| Name | Value | Symbol type |
|------|-------|-------------|
| ext_symb | 0 | Symbol table for debugging |
| ext_def | 1 | Definition to be corrected |
| ext_abs | 2 | Absolute definition |
| ext_res | 3 | Reference to resident library |
| ext_ref32 | 129 | 32-bit correction |
| ext_common | 130 | General 32-bit correction |
| ext_ref16 | 131 | 16-bit correction |
| ext_ref8 | 132 | 8-bit correction |

3-byte value for the length of the name (in long words)

*Symbol value and other data*

hunk_symbol ($3F0)

This block contains symbols with their names and values. These symbols are of interest to the debugger, not the linker. A debugger is a program for debugging other programs and this table allows the debugger to refer to addresses in the program by name rather than number. The code $3F0 is followed by symbol data units, terminated by a zero.

hunk_debug ($3F1)

The construction of this block is not completely defined. It can contain information about the program which can be accessed by the debugger. The block must simply start with $3F1 followed by the number of long words it contains.

hunk_end ($3F2)

This is the necessary block in the hunk. It consist only of the code, which is also the last long word of a program on the disk.

hunk_header ($3F3)

A load file starts with this block. Here is specified the number of hunks in the program to be loaded and how large they are. In addition this block contains the names of the resident libraries which must be loaded along with this program. The structure is as follows:

- Hunk header ($3F3)
- Length of the name of the first hunk (in long words)
- Hunk name
- Length of the name of the second hunk (or 0: end)
- Hunk name

    .
    .
    .

- 0: end of the name list
- Highest hunk number + 1: table length
- Number of hunk to be loaded first
- Number of hunk to be loaded last
- Here start the program hunks

hunk_overlay ($3F5)
This block is needed when working with overlays. This is when a memory area occupied by the program is overwritten by another program or data segment. The table after the $3F5 code contains specifications about the table size, the highest level of overlays (the number of overlay processes) and the data to be loaded itself.

hunk_break ($3F6)
This code marks the end of the overlay program section.

To take some of the confusion out of this program structure and to demonstrate it, here is a short example. In Section 3.3 we presented a short machine language program which represented the CLI command FONT. You can use the TYPE command of the CLI to see how the program was placed on the disk (by the assembler) by listing the contents of the program file Font. Your output may differ depending on what assembler you used. This can be done on the screen with

>type Font opt h

or on the printer with

>type Font to PRT: opt h

You then get the following output:

```
0000:    000003F3    00000000    00000002    00000000
0010:    00000001    00000024    00000001 /  000003E9
0020:    00000024 /  53406700    00180C18    00206600
0030:    000A51C8    FFF66000    000813E0    0000007F
0040:    2C790000    000443F9    00000072    70004EAE
0050:    FE6823C0    00000088    67000028    2C790000
0060:    00884EAE    FFC42200    243C0000    007E263C
0070:    00000009    2C790000    00884EAE    FFD06000
0080:    0008203C    FFFFFFFF    22002C79    00000088
0090:    4EAEFF70    4E75646F    732E6C69    62726172
00A0:    79009B30    3B33313B    34306D00    00000000
00B0:    3B4F7065 /  000003EC    00000007    00000000
00C0:    00000018    00000024    00000030    0000003A
00D0:    00000046    00000052    00000068    00000000 /
00E0:    000003F2 /  000003EB    00000001 /  000003F2
```

The slashes are not in the output—we just added them to separate the individual hunk sections. Let's take a look at these sections:

At the start is the code $3F3, hunk_header. The $0 which follows it indicates that there is no hunk name. The $2 indicates that this program file consists of only two hunks. The first hunk to be loaded is number $0, the last is number $1. The sizes of these two hunks are $24 and $1.

The section containing the program code starts with the code $3E9 (hunk_code). The length is specified by $24. Following this are $24 (36) long words of program code.

After this is the table of offsets for correcting the addresses, starting with the code $3EC (hunk_reloc32). The number is specified by $7 and these offsets refer to hunk number $0. Now come the seven offsets themselves. The first of these offsets, $18, refers to the value $0000007F, which is the $18th word of the code. When the program is loaded the starting address is added to this long word so that the effective memory address of the addressed byte results. The same is done with the other offsets in the reloc32 list.

The list is followed by a $0, which marks the end of the hunk_reloc32 list.

The $3F2 code (hunk_end) which follows indicates the end of the first hunk. The second follows, with a length of $1.

After this is the code $3EB (hunk_bss), followed by the number $1. This means that one long word is reserved, in which the program stores the DOS base address.

The conclusion is the code $3F2 (hunk_end) which signals the end of the second hunk and also the program.

---

# 3.2.2.3    The IFF format

IFF stands for Interchange File Format, so IFF format is a little redundant. This is a format in which diverse data files are constructed so that they can be read and evaluated by other programs.

Actually this does not belong in an Amiga programmer's book, since IFF is not directly related to the Amiga. It was developed by the Electronic Arts company and has become such a standard that has appeared in many places since. This is why we want to present an overview of the IFF structure here.

Why do you need a standardized format? Imagine that you have drawn a picture on the Amiga with some program. This picture consists of data which causes the various colors to appear on the screen.

If you want to save these data on the disk so that they can be retrieved again later, some problems arise: How large should the picture containing these data be? What color mixes should be used?

As you can see, the screen data alone are not enough. You must store additional information in the file in such a manner that other programs can retrieve it.

This problem was solved by the introduction of the IFF. Here data are stored in a predefined manner. Each of the various data blocks has a header which consists of four words and a data word containing the block length.

The word FORM marks the start of an IFF file, meaning that this is the start of a given user form (text, graphic, etc.). The long word which follows specifies the length of the form. This form is a combination of data blocks, called chunks. An IFF file can theoretically consist of multiple forms, such as text and graphic files combined. Generally a file consists of just one form, however, since it is usually just a text, graphics or sound file.

After the word FORM comes a long word with the length of this form in bytes, which is usually the file length -8. Then comes another four-letter word which specifies the type of the file (ILBM, WORD, etc.).

Immediately after the type is the code for the first chunk, followed by its length. After this are the data, padded to an even address if necessary, then the next chunk, and so on until the end of the form is reached.

An overview:

| | |
|---|---|
| "FORM" | ;start of an IFF form |
| Form length | ;length of the form in bytes |
| Type | ;code, such as ILBM, WORD, SMUS, 8SVX |
| Chunk name | ;name of the chunk, such as NAME, AUTH, BODY |
| Chunk length | ;length of the chunk in bytes |
| etc. | |

There are a large number of chunk types. Here is an overview of the most important types, along with their codes and descriptions:

*Text file*
*(WORD)*

| | |
|---|---|
| BODY | Main data section for graphics |
| COLR | Color of the text |
| DOC | Document style |
| FOOT | Footer |
| FONT | Text font |
| FSCC | Text color information |
| HEAD | Header line |
| PARA | Layout information (margins, etc.) |
| PCTS | Information about the graphics to integrate into the text |
| PINF | Information about the graphics themselves |
| TABS | Tab information |
| TEXT | Actual text section |

| *Graphics file* | BMHD | Graphics control data |
|---|---|---|
| *(ILBM)* | CMAP | Color table |
| | BODY | Graphics data |

| *Music file* | SHDR | Sound control data (tempo, volume, sound channel) |
|---|---|---|
| *(SMUS)* | NAME | Name of the music piece |
| | (c) | Copyright notice |
| | AUTH | Name of the author |
| | ANNO | Comment about the piece |
| | TRAK | Channel specification |

| *8-bit digitized* | VHDR | Control data (type, tempo, octave, volume) |
|---|---|---|
| *sound file* | NAME | Name of the sound |
| *(8SVX)* | (c) | Copyright notice |
| | AUTH | Name of the author |
| | ANNO | Comment about the sound |
| | BODY | Sound data |
| | ATAK | Attack information |
| | RLSE | Release information |

If you have an IFF file on a disk, you can look at its structure. The following assembly language program displays all of the codes and chunk lengths in a window. The name of the file is inserted directly into the program.

```
;***** IFF Demo program 6/87 S.D. *****
;*Start from CLI only

OpenLib      =-408
closelib     =-414
ExecBase     =4

Open         =-30
Close        =-36
Seek         =-66
Read         =-42
Write        =-48
mode_old     =1005

key = $bfec01                      ;special key status

run:
     move.l   execbase,a6           ;Pointer to Exec library
     lea      dosname(pc),a1
     moveq    #0,d0
     jsr      openlib(a6)           ;open DOS library
     move.l   d0,dosbase
     beq      error

     move.l   #consolname,d1        ;console definition
     move.l   #mode_old,d2
     move.l   dosbase,a6
     jsr      open(a6)              ;CON: open window
     beq      error
```

```
          move.l      d0,conhandle

          move.l      #filename,d1
          move.l      #mode_old,d2
          move.l      dosbase,a6
          jsr         open(a6)           ;open file
          beq         error
          move.l      d0,filehandle

loop:
          cmp.b       #$37,key           ;Alternate pressed?
          beq         qu                 ;yes, quit

          move.l      #-1,d0
del:
          dbra        d0,del             ;short pause for reading...


          bsr         read4              ;read decelerator
          beq         qu                 ;EOF
          bmi         error              ;Error

          move.l      conhandle,d1
          move.l      #buffer,d2         ;buffer address
          move.l      #6,d3              ;4 characters
          jsr         write(a6)          ;outpuff declarator
          beq         error

          move.l      buffer,d5          ;save declarator
          cmp.l       #'FORM',d5         ;FORM?
          bne         noform             ;no
          st          flag               ;else set flag
          bra         form               ;and continue

noform:
          tst         flag               ;code?
          beq         form               ;no
          clr         flag               ;else clear flag
          move.l      #'----',outbuff    ;identification
          bsr         print
          bra         loop               ;and continue

form:
          bsr         read4              ;read length
          beq         qu                 ;EOF
          bmi         error              ;Error
          move.l      buffer,d0          ;value in D0
          bsr         phex               ;and display

          cmp.l       #'FORM',d5         ;FORM?
          beq         loop               ;yes: next

          move.l      filehandle,d1
          move.l      buffer,d2
          addq.l      #1,d2
          bclr        #0,d2              ;on even address
```

```
        move.l    #0,d3              ;mode: OFFSET_CURRENT
        jsr       Seek(a6)           ;find next part
        bra       loop               ;continue...

qu:
        move.l    conhandle,d1
        move.l    #endtext,d2        ;end of text
        move.l    #25,d3
        jsr       Write(a6)          ;output

        move.l    conhandle,d1
        move.l    #buffer,d2         ;buffer address
        move.l    #1,d3              ;1 character
        jsr       Read(a6)           ;read
        bra       ende

error:
ende:
        move.l    conhandle,d1       ;close window
        move.l    dosbase,a6
        jsr       Close(a6)

        move.l    filehandle,d1      ;close file
        jsr       Close(a6)

        move.l    dosbase,a1         ;close DOS.lib
        move.l    execbase,a6
        jsr       CloseLib(a6)

        rts                          ;done!

read4:                              ;read 4 characters
        move.l    filehandle,d1
        move.l    #buffer,d2         ;buffer address
        move.l    #4,d3              ;read 4 characters
        jmp       Read(a6)

phex:                               ;output D0 in hexadecimal
        lea       outbuff,a0
        move      d0,d2
        move      #3,d3              ;4 digits
niblop:
        rol       #4,d2              ;shift left nibble down
        move      d2,d1
        and       #$f,d1             ;mask
        add       #$30,d1            ;convert to ASCII
        cmp       #'9',d1            ;digit?
        bls       nibok              ;yes
        add       #7,d1              ;else correct
nibok:
        move.b    d1,(a0)+           ;character in output buffer
        dbra      d3,niblop          ;continue loop
        move.b    #$a,(a0)           ;return to end

print:
        move.l    dosbase,a6
```

```
        move.l    conhandle,d1
        move.l    #outbuff,d2      ;output buffer
        move.l    #5,d3            ;5 characters
        jmp       Write(a6)        ;output

 align                             ;even
dosbase:      dc.l 0
conhandle:    dc.l 0
filehandle:   dc.l 0
flag:         dc.w 0
outbuff:      dc.b '    '
buffer:       dc.b '    '
consolname:   dc.b 'RAW:0/10/400/240/** IFF format ',0
dosname:      dc.b 'dos.library',0
filename:     dc.b 'IFF file ',0
endtext:      dc.b '***** Press any key *****'
 align                             ;even
```

The program opens a window and outputs the codes and lengths of the
chunks in the file. The name of the file must be entered as filename: in
the program. A short delay loop is included in the output to make the
output easier to read. If it is taking too long for you or the file is not an
IFF file, you can end the program by pressing the Alternate key. It then
waits for a keypress and the window is closed.

# 3.3 Programs

A program created by a linker or directly by an assembler can be started simply by entering its name in the CLI. If you want to start it from the Workbench, an .info file must also be created which contains the icon of the program that is displayed in the **Workbench** window. This icon can then be clicked to start the program.

## 3.3.1 Program start and parameters

As you already know from the CLI command, it is possible to specify parameters in the line calling the program which can then be read and evaluated by the program. Such a line cannot be entered when starting from the Workbench, of course. There is a distinct difference between passing parameters to a program between the CLI and Workbench.

The program which is being called must therefore distinguish which user interface it is being called from and then get its parameters accordingly. Let's first look at the simpler case, starting the program from the CLI.

## 3.3.1.1 Calling from the CLI

A program started from the CLI gets information about its parameters in two registers. The address register contains the address in memory of the text following the program name entered in the CLI. In addition, the number of characters behind the actual program name is passed in D0.

With these two pieces of information the program can easily read and evaluate the parameters. In order to demonstrate this, a short assembly language program follows which can be called with or without parameters.

This program is a CLI command which you can also copy to the C directory. It has the job of changing the appearance of the text that follows the call. For example, you can use it in your startup sequence if you want to display a message underlined or in italics.

If you have saved the program in the C folder under the name Font, it can be called with the command:

>Font n

The parameter n can also be omitted and the program switches back to normal text.

If you specify a parameter, it must be a digit between 0 and 7. The effects of these digits are:

0    Normal
1    Bold
3    Italic
4    Underline
7    Inverse video

You can also set bold and underline by calling Font 1 and Font 4 in succession.

Here is the program:

```
;*****  FONT command *****

; EXEC offsets

OpenLib  = -30-378
ExecBase = 4

; AmigaDOS offsets

Write   = -30-18
Output  = -30-30
Exit    = -30-114

run:
      subq     #1,d0             ;byte number-1
      beq      normal            ;no parameters?
search:
      cmp.b    #$20,(a0)+        ;find argument
      bne      found             ;found
      dbra     d0,search
      bra      normal            ;set normal font

found:
      move.b   -(a0),ftext+1      ;set style

normal:
      move.l   execbase,a6       ;pointer to Exec library
      lea      dosname,a1
      moveq    #0,d0
      jsr      OpenLib(a6)       ;open DOS library
      move.l   d0,dosbase
      beq      error             ;didn't work
```

```
        move.l    dosbase,a6
        jsr       Output(a6)              ;get standard output handle

        move.l    d0,d1                   ;output handle in D1
        move.l    #ftext,d2               ;text address in D2
        move.l    #tende-ftext,d3         ;length in D3
        move.l    dosbase,a6
        jsr       Write(a6)               ;output text
        bra       ende                    ;OK: done

error:
        move.l    #1,d0                   ;error status
ende:
        move.l    d0,d1                   ;return parameter
        move.l    dosbase,a6
        jsr       exit(a6)                ;end of the program

        rts                               ;never returns

dosbase:  dc.l 0

dosname:  dc.b 'dos.library',0
ftext:      dc.b $9b,'0;31;40m'
tende:
```

It's easy to write a C program which uses parameters. You just have to use the startup.o file as the first element in the linker instruction, which is generally done anyway. The parameter line is found in the variable argv and the number of characters in argc.

The startup program actually does even more. It also opens the DOS library and sets up the standard I/O channels with the DOS functions Input() and Output(). The handles of these channels are then in stdin and stdout. The routine then starts the main routine of your C program.

Another piece of information that can be passed to the program from the CLI is the size of the stack area to be reserved. This lies below the return address of the CLI on the stack and can be read with the command:

MOVE.L 4(SP),D0

This way the program can check to see if it has enough room on the stack for its special requests.

In addition to these parameters, several others are passed by the CLI. These parameters offer many possibilities for simplifying a CLI program. More information is found in the section on transient CLI commands.

This is the process for initializing a program started from the CLI. Let's look at the other case: starting a program from the Workbench.

## 3.3.1.2    Starting from the Workbench

When you start a program by double-clicking on its icon in the **Workbench** window, the program is started under the displayed name. This program has then passed parameters, but this time in the form of a message rather than a text line.

*Startup program*

If you have written a program in C and provided it with the startup program through the linker, then you don't have to worry about this message, called the start-up message. The startup program does the following tasks when it determines that it's been started from the Workbench:

1.    First it opens the DOS library.

2.    It waits for the startup message (WaitPort).

3.    The message is fetched (GetMsg).

4.    The number of arguments in the message is tested. If it is 0, the next step is skipped.

5.    The arguments which were passed are interpreted as a lock structure and a corresponding directory is made in the current directory.

6.    The sm_ToolWindow argument is tested. If it is 0, the specified window is opened and its handle, if it was opened successfully, is made the standard input.

What does a program have to look like which does not have this startup program available, such as an assembly language program?

Even if you don't need the message which the Workbench sends to your program, you still have to fetch it. Otherwise the guru inside your computer starts to meditate. At the next I/O function, such as opening a window, a message arrives at the message port which is not suitable for this function.

You have to perform the same functions in your program that the startup program does. First you call the Exec FindTask() function to get a pointer to the structure of the process, your program. As an argument, pass a zero in A1:

```
execbase = 4
FindTask = -294
WaitPort = -384
GetMsg   = -372
```

```
move.l   execbase,a6        ;Exec base address in A6

suba.l   a1,a1              ;clear argument A1
jsr      FindTask(a6)       ;get pointer
```

In D0 you get a pointer to your process structure. This structure contains information about whether the process was started from the CLI or the Workbench:

```
move.l   d0,a4              ;pointer to process in A4
tst.l    $ac(a4)            ;pr_CLI: CLI or Workbench?
bne      fromCLI            ;it was CLI!
```

If the tested argument is zero, the program was started from the Workbench.

If this is the case, you have to wait for the receipt of the startup message. This is done with the WaitPort() function:

```
lea      $5c(a4),a0         ;pr_MsgPort: MessagePort in A0
jsr      WaitPort(a6)       ;wait for message
```

This function waits for a message to arrive at the message port. In our case this is the startup message from the Workbench. This message must now be fetched so that it is removed from the message queue. The GetMsg() function is used:

```
lea      $5c(a4),a0         ;RastPort address in A0
jsr      GetMsg(a6)         ;get message
```

You can now evaluate this message if necessary. In D0 you get a pointer to the message structure with the name WBStartup.

This message contains the following elements:

| Offset | Name | Description |
|--------|------|-------------|
| $14 | sm_Process | Process descriptor |
| $18 | sm_Segment | Program segment descriptor |
| $1C | sm_NumArgs | Number of arguments passed |
| $20 | sm_ToolWindow | Description of the window to open |
| $24 | sm_ArgList | Pointer to the arguments themselves |

sm_ArgList points to the elements of the arguments passed. These arguments contain the information about the activated icons at the time the program was started. Some programs use this so that a data file can be selected along with the program by shift-clicking and then loaded and processed by the program. The arguments of the list to which sm_ArgList points consist of pointers:

| | |
|--|--|
| wa_Lock | file lock (directory description) |
| wa_Name | pointer to filename |

To demonstrate the use and programming of this message evaluation, we'll write a program which determines and outputs the tool types. These tool types are the entries which can be written to the given file with the Workbench INFO program. To do this, select a file (click once) and then select the Info option in the Workbench menu. A dialog window opens in which you can make entries in the input mask. You can select tool types by clicking on Add. These entries are used by some programs (such as Notepad).

These data are stored in the .info file which belong to the program. This file also contains the data for the icon, its position in the window and much more. To access this data from within a program there is another library on the Workbench disk in the LIBS directory: the Icon library.

*Icon library*     This library contains functions for processing the .info file. One of them is the GetDiskObject() function, which loads the .info file and returns a pointer to its structure. Our program also uses this function. Before we go into the details of the icon library and the DiskObject structure, here is the program:

```
;** Workbench and .info evaluation demo  S.D. **

execbase = 4                    ;EXEC base address
FindTask = -294                 ;find task
WaitPort = -384                 ;wait for message
GetMsg   = -372                 ;fetch message

OpenLib  = -408                 ;open library
CloseLib = -414                 ;close library
Open     = -30                  ;open channel
Close    = -36                  ;close channel
Read     = -42                  ;read data
Write    = -48                  ;output data
CurrentDir = -126               ;set current directory
mode_old = 1005                 ;mode for open

GetDiskObject = -78             ;load DiskObject

run:
        move.l  execbase,a6     ;Exec base address

        suba.l  a1,a1
        jsr     FindTask(a6)    ;find task

        move.l  d0,a4           ;pointer in A4
        tst.l   $ac(a4)         ;pr_CLI: CLI or Workbench?
        bne     fromCLI         ;CLI! done...

        lea     $5c(a4),a0      ;WBench message
        jsr     WaitPort(a6)    ;wait

        jsr     GetMsg(a6)      ;get message
        move.l  d0,message      ;save pointer
; **** Open libraries and window ****
```

```
; **** Open libraries and window ****

        lea     iconname,a1     ;"icon.library"
        clr.l   d0
        jsr     OpenLib(a6)     ;open ICON.library
        move.l  d0,iconbase     ;save base
        beq  ^  end3            ;error occurred!

        lea     dosname,a1      ;"dos.library"
        clr.l   d0
        jsr     OpenLib(a6)     ;open DOS
        move.l  d0,dosbase
        beq     end2            ;error occurred!

        move.l  d0,a6
        move.l  #conname,d1
        move.l  #mode_old,d2
        jsr     Open(a6)        ;open CON window
        move.l  d0,conbase
        beq     end1            ;error occurred!

;**** Set the current directory, if necessary ****

        move.l message,a0       ;pointer to WBMessage
        move.l $24(a0),a0       ;sm_ArgList:
                                ;pointer to arguments
        beq     ende            ;no arguments!

        move.l (a0),d1          ;D1 => Lock
        move.l dosbase,a6
        jsr    CurrentDir(a6)   ;set current directory

; **** Load DiskObject (.info file) ****

        move.l message,a0
        move.l $24(a0),a0       ;sm_ArgList pointer
        move.l 4(a0),a0         ;wa_Name: pointer to name

        move.l iconbase,a6
        jsr    GetDiskObject(a6) ;load DiskObject

; **** Output tool type entries in window ****

        move.l d0,a1        ;pointer to DiskObject structure
        move.l $36(a1),a1       ;do_ToolTypes:
                                ;pointer to ToolType array
        move.l a1,typetext      ;save text pointer

typesloop:
        move.l typetext,a1      ;load text pointer
        move.l (a1)+,a0         ;pointer to test in A0
        cmp.l  #0,a0            ;test present?
        beq    nomore           ;no: end of output
        move.l a1,typetext      ;else save pointer

        move.l a0,d2            ;= text address for output
```

```
lenlop:
        tst.b  (a0)+            ;find end
        bne    lenlop
        sub.l  a0,d3            ;calculate length of text
        not.l  d3               ;and correct

        move.l dosbase,a6
        move.l conbase,d1
        jsr    Write(a6)        ;output text in window

        move.l conbase,d1
        move.l #1f,d2            ;Linefeed:
        move.l #1,d3
        jsr    Write(a6)        ;next line

        bra    typesloop        ;to next entry!

; **** That's all, now wait for a key ****

nomore:
        move.l conbase,d1
        move.l #1,d3             ;a character
        move.l #buffer,d2        ;in buffer
        jsr    Read(a6)          ;read (wait for Return)

; **** Program end: close everything and return ****

ende:   move.l conbase,d1
        move.l dosbase,a6
        jsr    Close(a6)        ;close window
end1:
        move.l execbase,a6
        move.l dosbase,a1
        jsr    Closelib(a6)     ;close DOS
end2:
        move.l iconbase,a1
        jsr    Closelib(a6)     ;close ICON.library

fromCLI:
end3:
        rts                     ;End of program

; **** Data fields ****

dosbase:  blk.l 1         ;DOS base address
conbase:  blk.l 1         ;Window base
iconbase: blk.l 1         ;icon.library base
message:  blk.l 1         ;pointer to WBMessage
typetext: blk.l 1         ;text pointer

dosname:  dc.b 'dos.library',0
iconname: dc.b 'icon.library',0
conname:  dc.b 'CON:10/20/300/100/** Message output ',0
1f:       dc.b $a
buffer:   blk.b 2
 end
```

This program works only when it's started from the Workbench. Otherwise it is simply terminated (from CLI). In order to be able to start it you have to make an icon for the program. This can be easily done with the icon editor. Then it must be saved under the same name as the program above—the suffix .info is appended automatically.

Once this is done you can click on the icon and select the Info item in the Workbench menu. In the menu which appears you can then make one or more entries in tool types and save them with SAVE.

When you then activate your icon with a double click, the corresponding program is loaded and started. The program then executes the required steps to get and evaluate the Workbench startup message (WBStartup) and the DiskObject structure.

*The DiskObject structure*

| Offset | Name | Contents |
|---|---|---|
| 0 | do_Magic | A "magic number" which indicates that this file is valid ($E310) |
| 2 | do_Version | Version number (1) |
| 4 | do_Gadget | Here begins a gadget structure which determines the appearance and position of the icon |
| $30 | do_Type | Object type (tool, project, etc.) |
| $32 | do_DefaultTool | Standard program for disk |
| $36 | do_ToolTypes | Pointer to text field for types |
| $3A | do_CurrentX | |
| $3E | do_CurrentY | Icon position in window |
| $42 | do_DrawerData | Pointer to subdirectory window structure |
| $46 | do_ToolWindow | Standard window for tools |
| $4A | do_StackSize | Stack size for tools |

The pointer do_ToolTypes points to a pointer list whose entries point to the strings of the tool types entered in the `Info` window and end with zero. These pointers can be used in the program to output the strings.

From the example program you can easily see how you can access the tool types of your program. The tool types can contain basic entries which control the function of the program. This is also used in the Workbench Notepad program, where the tool types parameter is used to set the size of the input window, the file type and the font used.

The tool type entries are generally of the form:

```
NAME=<parameter>[|<parameter>]
```

This is also required by the Notepad. The advantage of this entry method is that there are two functions in the icon library which can check these lines.

The first function, FindToolType(), with offset -96, searches the entries of the tool types for a specific name. In the Notepad example, it searches for a line with the name WINDOW. A pointer is then returned to the parameters following the equals sign, or a zero if no line with this name was found.

This pointer is then passed to another function, MatchToolType() with offset -102, together with another pointer to a comparison parameter. The resulting value indicates whether the comparison parameter appeared in the line or not.

This is used, for example, when a program can read files, but it is only supposed to read certain types of files. If these types are entered in the tool types, then you can check the type of the file to be loaded with the types of those allowed.

## 3.3.2      Structure of the transient CLI commands

As you already know, the commands of the normal CLI are all transient, that is, they are stored as programs on the diskette in the C directory. When you enter something in the CLI, a check is made to see if it's a filename in the current directory or if it's a command, whose name is found in the C directory. If this is the case, the corresponding program is called.

Almost all commands need access to the DOS library in order to perform the desired function. So that these programs open the DOS library again, the programs do not have to pass parameters in the processor registers.

The registers D0 and A0 contain the length and address of the parameter string which is entered after the command. This was explained earlier in conjunction with the FONTS example.

The other registers contain values of more intrest:

| Register | Contents |
|----------|----------|
| D0 | Number of parameter characters |
| A0 | Address of the parameter string |
| A1 | Pointer to start of stack |
| A2 | Pointer to internal DOS library |
| A3 | Pointer to stack size |
| A4 | Pointer to start of program |
| A5 | Pointer to routine for function call |
| A6 | Pointer to return routine |

Let's look at registers A2, A5 and A6. With these registers you can write a CLI command which doesn't have to open the DOS library itself.

The convention for calling these routines is somewhat different from
normal DOS calls. At the address to which A2 points lie a set of jump
addresses which point to individual DOS routines. They are not called
directly, however, but with the address in A4 through JSR (A5). The
return parameter is passed in D1, not D0. Also, the offsets in the table
are different from those in a normal call.

These offsets are not permanently set, since they are not documented by
Commodore. The offsets listed below are correct for the current Amiga
version.

Before listing the offsets for direct calls to DOS functions, we should
first explain how to use them. Below is a short program which does
nothing more than open a small window, wait for the Return key to be
pressed, and close the window again. These are three DOS functions
which are called without opening the DOS library.

A macro is used here for the function call. This macro is inserted wherever the macro name (doscall) appears in the program. The parameter
specified can also be inserted where \1 appears. This parameter is our
offset.

```
;*****from the CLI: Basic DOS functions  6/87  S.D.*****

Open    =$ff                    ;DOS command: Open
Close   =$5d                    ;             Close
Read    =$fd                    ;             Read


mode_old=1005
s
;*** Defined using AssemPro Amiga other assemblers macro
;                                     call may differ ****
; **** Definition of the macro 'doscall' ****

doscall: MACRO $\1                      ; ** direct DOS call **
        move.b  #\1,d0
        ext.w   d0                      ;offset in long words
        ext.l   d0                      ;convert
        lsl     #2,d0
        move.l  0(a2,d0),a4             ;function address
        moveq   #$c,d0
        jsr     (a5)                    ;function call
        ENDM

; **** Start of program ****

run:
        move.l  #consolname,d1          ;console definition
        move.l  #mode_old,d2            ;mode
        doscall Open                    ;open CON: window
        move.l  d1,conhandle

        move.l  conhandle,d1
        move.l  #inbuff,d2              ;buffer address
```

```
        move.l  #1,d3                ;1 character
        doscall Read                 ;read character (Return)

        move.l  conhandle,d1         ;close window
        doscall Close                ;with Close

        clr.l   d0                   ;Status: OK
        jsr     (a6)                 ;end of the program

; **** Data fields ****

conhandle: dc.l 0
inbuff:    blk.b 8
consolname: dc.b 'RAW:100/50/300/100/** Test window ',0
        end
```

You see how easy it is to write a CLI command. Three DOS functions were performed in a total of 12 lines of program text. The FONTS program presented earlier can also be made shorter using this method.

The function offsets of the DOS functions are, as you can see, different from those for the normal DOS calls. Here is a list of DOS commands and the offsets which are valid for the direct-call method:

*DOS*
*commands*

| Offset | Function name | Offset | Function name |
|--------|---------------|--------|---------------|
| $FF | Open | $EF | IoErr |
| $5D | Close | $EE | CreateProc |
| $FD | Read | $02 | Exit |
| $FA | Write | $ED | LoadSeg |
| $41 | Input | $52 | UnLoadSeg |
| $42 | Output | $EC | GetPacket |
| $F8 | Seek | $EB | QueuePacket |
| $F7 | Delete | $EA | DeviceProc |
| $F6 | Rename | $E9 | SetComment |
| $F5 | Lock | $E8 | SetProtect |
| $6D | UnLock | $E7 | DateStamp |
| $71 | DupLock | $2F | Delay |
| $F4 | Examine | $57 | WaitForChar |
| $F3 | ExNext | $23 | ParentDir |
| $F2 | Info | $E6 | IsInteractive |
| $F1 | CreateDir | $E5 | Execute |
| $F0 | CurrentDir | | |

Actually, these are not really offsets but the number of the vectors to be used in the table to which A2 points. The values over $7F are negative values, meaning that an address below the address in A2 is used.

# 3.4    Input/Output

A very important part of a program is the exchange of data with the outside world, through the screen, keyboard, diskettes or other interfaces and devices. This input/output (I/O) is what allows a program to make full use of the computer on which it runs. There are three basic ways to accomplish this.

The first is I/O through the appropriate DOS functions like Open(), Close(), Read() and Write(). This method is clearly the easiest because it requires the least effort when programming. The disadvantage is that the function must be completed before your program can continue.

The second method doesn't have this disadvantage. The magic word here is "device". With these devices you can make the I/O run independently while your program continues to run. The I/O thus runs in the background, parallel to your program, and costs relatively little useful processor time. The disadvantage of this technique is that it requires significantly more programming effort.

The third method for I/O is to program the hardware of the Amiga directly. This assumes very precise knowledge of the system, however, and has further disadvantage that it can lead to major complications in the multitasking mode. More information about this method can be found in the hardware section of this book.

Let's start by looking at I/O programming by the standard method: using the DOS functions.

## 3.4.1    Standard I/O

As already mentioned, there are four DOS functions Open(), Close(), Read() and Write() which are responsible for input and output of data. Most of the functions which a program requires can be performed with these.

*I/O channels*   There is a whole set of I/O channels available which DOS knows by name. These names can then be used in an Open command. The standard channels are:

DFn:        Designates the disk drive with the number n, which can be 0, 1, 2 or 3.

SYS:        Designates the drive from which the system was loaded.

RAM:    Stands for the RAM disk, which is always available and whose size conforms to the data it contains. It can be used like a disk drive except that the information is stored in the RAM of the computer instead of on a diskette.

NIL:    This channel is a blackhole for data: data written to it is thrown away and doesn't affect anything. This is sometimes quite useful, such as when a program wants to output things which you don't need.

SER:    Stands for the serial interface (RS-232) and allows I/O through this port.

PAR:    Designates the parallel printer port, which contains eight input/output lines. You can read or write parallel data directly with this port.

PRT:    Also stands for the parallel printer port, except that this channel is used to address a printer. If the printer is defined for the serial interface, then it is accessed through this channel. The printer definitions can be made with the Preferences program.

CON:    Supplies a window for input/output. This window is automatically opened when the channel is opened. The window parameters are specified as follows:

CON:x/y/w/h/Name

x and y represent the coordinates of the upper left-hand corner of the window on the screen, w and h are the width and height of the window in pixels, and Name is the title of the window. Thus:

CON:20/10/200/100/Test window

defined a window with the name Test window which starts and positions x=20 and y=10 and which is 200 pixels wide and 100 high.

RAW:    Represents a window and echoes input and output in this window. In contrast to CON:, no functions are provided (such as editing a line) so that this window can only be used in certain ways.

*       Stands for the current window.

Let's start with probably the most important application: keyboard input and screen output.

## 3.4.1.1     Keyboard and screen

As you can see in the previous table, AmigaDOS offers three options for screen I/O: CON:, RAW: and *.

*CON: window*   The DOS Open() function is used to open a CON: window. The function expects a pointer to the name of the channel to be opened and the mode in which it is opened. The mode can be one of:

Mode_new
>   for a channel for writing only

Mode_old
>   for a channel also used for reading, and

Mode_readwrite
>   in DOS Version 1.2, for a channel which can be both read and written.

The Mode_old mode is used for opening a CON: or RAW: window since the channel is already known and you can also read from it.

To demonstrate this, here is a short assembly language program which when started from the CLI, opens the CON: window, outputs a string in it, waits for an input and then closes the window:

```
;*****  Simple CON: I/O  *****

OpenLib   = -408
closelib  = -414
ExecBase  = 4

; Amiga DOS offsets

Open      = -30
Close     = -36
Read      = -42
Write     =-48
Exit      =-144

Mode_old = 1005

run:
        move.l    execbase,a6       ;pointer to Exec library
        lea       dosname,a1
        moveq     #0,d0
        jsr       openlib(a6)       ;open DOS library
        move.l    d0,dosbase
        beq       error             ;didn't work
```

```
            move.l   dosbase,a6          ;DOS base address in A6

            move.l   #name,d1            ;pointer to name
            move.l   #mode_old,d2        ;mode
            jsr      Open(a6)            ;open window
            move.l   d0,conhandle        ;save handle
            beq      error

            move.l   conhandle,d1        ;window handle in D1
            move.l   #ttext,d2            ;text address in D2
            move.l   #tende-ttext,d3     ;length in D3
            jsr      Write(a6)           ;output text

            move.l   conhandle,d1        ;window handle
            move.l   #buffer,d2          ;buffer address
            move.l   #80,d3              ;max. length
            jsr      Read(a6)            ;wait for input

            move.l   conhandle,d1
            jsr      Close(a6)           ;close window

            bra ende                     ;done

error:
            move.l   #-1,d0              ;error status
ende:
            move.l   d0,d1
            move.l   dosbase,a6
            jsr      Exit(a6)            ;end of the program

            rts                          ;never occurs

dosname:    dc.b 'dos.library',0
name:       dc.b 'CON:20/10/200/100/** Test window ',0
ttext:       dc.b 'Enter some text!      ',0
tende:
buffer:     blk.b 80
     align
dosbase:    dc.l 0
conhandle:  dc.l 0
     end
```

*RAW: window*   The program above can also be run with RAW: instead of CON:. If you try this you will see the difference immediately. While the CON: version waits for you to press Return, the RAW: version returns immediately after any key is pressed. This also holds for the cursor and function keys, which are not recognized by the CON: window.

A CON: window offers greater ease of use when entering strings, but a RAW: window makes the whole keyboard available.

Both windows support more than the normal character representation. Other styles, like underline and bold can be used. In addition, other functions can be used to manipulate the window. The window contents can be cleared, moved up or down, etc. All of these functions are called through control sequences, sometimes with parameters, output in the window.

Here is a list of the control characters which perform functions. These characters are listed in hexadecimal.

| Sequence | Function |
| --- | --- |
| 08 | Backspace |
| 0A | Linefeed, cursor down |
| 0B | Cursor one line up |
| 0C | Clear window |
| 0D | Carriage Return, cursor in first column |
| 0E | Switch to normal display (reverse 0F) |
| 0F | Switch to special characters |
| 1B | Escape |

The following sequences start with the characters $9B, the CSI (Control Sequence Introducer). The characters following this generate a function. The values in square brackets can be omitted. The specification n is given as one or more number in ASCII characters. The value assumed for n if it's omitted is given in parentheses.

| Sequence | Function |
| --- | --- |
| 9B [n] 40 | Insert n spaces |
| 9B [n] 41 | Cursor n (1) lines up |
| 9B [n] 42 | Cursor n (1) lines down |
| 9B [n] 43 | Cursor n (1) characters right |
| 9B [n] 44 | Cursor n (1) characters left |
| 9B [n] 45 | Cursor n (1) lines down n column 1 |
| 9B [n] 46 | Cursor n (1) lines up in column 1 |
| 9B [n] [3B n] 48 | Set cursor in line; column |
| 9B 4A | Clear window at cursor |
| 9B 4B | Clear line at cursor |
| 9B 4C | Insert line |
| 9B 4D | Delete line |
| 9B [n] 50 | Delete n characters at cursor |
| 9B [n] 53 | Move n lines up |
| 9B [n] 54 | Move n lines down |
| 9B 32 30 68 | From now on: Linefeed => Linefeed+Return |
| 9B 32 30 6C | From now on: Linefeed => nur Linefeed |
| 9B 6E | Send the cursor position. A string of the following form is returned: 9B (line) 3B (column) 52 |

9B (style);(foreground color);(background color) 6D

The three parameters are decimal numbers in ASCII format. They mean:

Style: 0=normal
       1=bold
       3=italic
       4=underline
       7=inverse video

Foreground color:
  30-37: Colors 0-7 for text

Background color:
  40-47: Colors 0-7 for background

| | | |
|---|---|---|
| 9B (length) 74 | Sets maximum number of displayed lines |
| 9B (width) 75 | Sets maximum line length |
| 9B (margin) 78 | Defines the left margin in number of pixels |
| 9B (margin) 79 | Defines the top margin in pixels |

The last four functions can be used to return to the normal settings by omitting the parameters.

| | |
|---|---|
| 9B 30 20 70 | Make cursor invisible |
| 9B 20 70 | Make cursor visible |
| 9B 71 | Send window dimensions. A string of the following form is returned: |

9B 31 3B 31 3B (lines) 3B (columns) 73

To demonstrate the use of these control characters, output the following text in your window from the previous program:

```
text:   dc.b  $9b,"4;31;40m"
        dc.b  "underlined"
        dc.b  $9b,"3;33;40m",$9b,"5;20H"
        dc.b  "** Hello, world! **",0
```

The parameters for the control sequences are simply specified as ASCII strings.

These sequences are received just as they are sent, when a function key or cursor key is pressed on the keyboard. The characters which are received are as follows (<CSI> stands for $9B):

| Key | Without shift | With shift |
|---|---|---|
| F1 | <CSI>0~ | <CSI>10~ |
| F2 | <CSI>1~ | <CSI>11~ |
| ... | | |
| F9 | <CSI>8~ | <CSI>18~ |
| F10 | <CSI>9~ | <CSI>19~ |
| | | |
| HELP | <CSI>?~ | <CSI>?~ |
| | | |
| up | <CSI>A | <CSI>T~ |
| down | <CSI>B | <CSI>S~ |
| left | <CSI>C | <CSI> A~ |
| right | <CSI>D | <CSI> @~ |

In this manner the program can determine almost everything the user does with the keyboard. If this is still not sufficient, there is another source of information: the RAW input events. These are events which can be reported by a sequence, if desired. The DOS can translate the message from these events into a sequence which looks like this:

```
<CSI>n{
```

The n stands for a number between 1 and 16 which corresponds to the event. These events are as follows:

1   Key pressed
2   Mouse button pressed
3   Window was activated
4   Mouse moved
5   unused
6   Timer
7   Gadget selected
8   Gadget released
9   Requester enabled
10  Menu selected
11  Window closed (see console device)
12  Window size changed
13  Window refreshed
14  Settings changed
15  Disk removed from drive
16  Disk inserted

Some of these events (10, 11) are not available in this case since a window opened with DOS cannot access menus or the close symbol. These things become interesting if you construct your own console window, however. This is possible only through the combination of Intuition and devices and is discussed later in the section on the console device.

When an event occurs (such as the insertion of a disk), a sequence of the following format is sent:

```
<CSI><class>;<subclass>;<key>;<status>;<X>;<Y>;<seconds>;
<microseconds>|
```

where:

CSI        The control sequence introducer $9B
Class      The event number
Subclass   Not used, always zero
Key        Key code of the last key or mouse button
Status     Keyboard status

| Bit | Mask | Description |
|-----|------|-------------|
| 0 | 0001 | left Shift key |
| 1 | 0002 | right Shift key |
| 2 | 0004 | Caps Lock key |
| 3 | 0008 | Control |
| 4 | 0010 | left Alternate key |

| Bit | Mask | Description |
|---|---|---|
| 5 | 0020 | right alternate key |
| 6 | 0040 | left Amiga key |
| 7 | 0080 | right Amiga key |
| 8 | 0100 | keypad |
| 9 | 0200 | key repeat |
| 10 | 0400 | interrupt (unused) |
| 11 | 0800 | active window |
| 12 | 1000 | left mouse button |
| 13 | 2000 | right mouse button |
| 14 | 4000 | middle mouse button (unused) |
| 15 | 8000 | relative mouse coordinates |
| X and Y | | Coordinates of the mouse pointer at the mouse event |

Seconds
Microseconds   System time of event

The values which are obtained by this method are decimal numbers in ASCII. If you want to evaluate these values in a program, they must first be converted.

**\* window**

Most CLI commands use \*, since this is the simplest method. Since this specifies the current window, which is naturally open, no channel has to be opened and closed.

The Read() and Write() functions need the handle of a channel from which to read or write the data to, so you have to find out what it is.

**Input() and Output()**

The DOS functions Input() and Output() are provided for this purpose. These functions require no parameters and return the handle of the corresponding standard channel. This is the CLI window if the program was simply called from the CLI. If the input or output was redirected with < or > in the CLI, the handle derived from these functions is returned by Input() or Output().

---

## 3.4.1.2   Disk files

Disk files can be opened and processed in the same manner as the CON: or RAW: windows. The mode used when opening a file plays a big role: if Mode_old is chosen, DOS looks for an existing file on the disk, which can be read only. For Mode_new a file is created or an existing file with the same name is erased. The file opened in this manner can only be written. With Mode_new an existing file can be both read and written.

The DOS functions Read(), Write() and Close() operate the same way as for screen I/O. However, some additional functions are available which are very useful for working with disk files.

Since data can be read again and again from a file, the system must have some way of noting the last location accessed in the file. This is accomplished with a pointer, which can also be set directly. The Seek() function allows the file pointer to be moved forward and backward. The new position can be specified as an absolute position, relative to the current position, relative to the start of the file, or relative to the end of the file.

Another DOS function allows a file to be removed from the disk: the Delete() function. This can also be used to delete directories, provided they are empty.

The names of files can be changed with the Rename() function. Here the old and new filenames are simply passed to the function. An interesting feature of this function is that you can change not only the name of a file, but also its location in the logical structure of the disk. If a different path is specified in the new name, the file is moved (not copied) to this new directory. This cannot be used to move a file from one disk to another.

A disk file can also be protected against various operations. This is determined by a mask passed to the SetProtection() function. The first four bits of this mask (bits 0-3) indicate whether the file is protected against the following actions:

| Bit | Meaning, if set |
| --- | --- |
| 0 | File cannot be deleted |
| 1 | File cannot be executed |
| 2 | File cannot be overwritten |
| 3 | File cannot be read |

## 3.4.1.3    Serial interface

The serial interface can be treated just like the screen I/O. A channel with the name SER: is opened and read and write can be performed with this channel. However, three problems can occur in this process:

1)    When the Read() function is called the Amiga waits for one or more characters to be received from the serial interface. If none arrive, the Amiga waits in vain. Therefore, a program which wants to read data from this interface but is not absolutely sure that any arrive should use the WaitForChar() function before calling Read(). This function can be used to wait for a specified length of time (given in microseconds) for a character to arrive. If nothing arrives in this time, a zero is returned and the program can output an error message and quit. If something arrived, a -1 is returned and it can then be read.

2)    Data were received, but it does't know how many. The problem described under 1) can occur. This is also why you never see anything if you try to use COPY SER: TO * from the CLI. The CLI doesn't know when the data start and stop. Unfortunately, such a command can be stopped only with reset.

3)    A program wants to send or receive data over the interface, but the settings do not match. The Preferences program can be used to change the settings and the process can be restarted, but this is rather inconvenient. The program can make these changes itself. This cannot be done with a simple DOS function, however, and requires the serial device I/O functions as described in the corresponding section.

## 3.4.1.4    Parallel interface

Programming the parallel interface is normally unnecessary because the printer is usually connected to it. This device is quite interesting because it can be used to both send and receive data.

The simplest way to program this interface is directly through the hardware registers. This has the disadvantage that problems can occur with multitasking if another program wants to access this interface. Thus it is better to access it through DOS. The data format is then predefined but you lose the ability to program individual bits as inputs and outputs, however.

# 4
# Devices

# 4.    Devices

The devices represent one of the major strengths of the Amiga. These involve program packages which perform certain tasks. These tasks are assigned to the devices by a running program which can then either wait for the result or continue. This allows a program to make easy use of multitasking.

*How devices are programmed*

The basic structure of such a device has already been explained in the Exec chapter. In this chapter we concern ourselves with the practical application. First a look at the general manner in which devices are programmed:

1.    Since the device uses a message to report when it has finished a task, the receiver of this message, the program which initiated the task must be determined. This is done with the FindTask() function of Exec by passing it a zero as a parameter. The value received is used in the next step.

2.    A port is set up with the AddPort function for the message from the device. This is a reply port. The pointer to the task structure just obtained is entered in the SigTask entry (port address + $10) of the message port structure.

3.    The device is opened by means of the OpenDevice() function. A pointer to the device name and one to the I/O structure must be passed.

4.    The parameters for the desired function are then entered in the I/O structure. The number and types of these parameters differ widely from function to function.

5.    The device operation is started with DoIo() or SendIo(). With DoIO() the calling program waits for the OK signal from the reply port, while SendIO() simply starts the process and the program can continue.

Here two structures appeared which control the communication between the user program and the devices. These are the port and I/O structures, which have already been described in other places. Here again is the standard structure for I/O operations:

| *STRUCT* | Offset | Name | Description |
|---|---|---|---|
| *MsgNode* | 0 | Succ | Pointer to the next entry |
| | 4 | Pred | Pointer to the previous entry |
| | 8 | Type | Entry type |
| | 9 | Pri | Priority |
| | 10 | Name | Pointer to name |
| | 14 | Reply port | Pointer to reply port |
| | 18 | MNLength | Node length |

| *STRUCT* | Offset | Name | Description |
|---|---|---|---|
| *IOExt* | 20 | IO_DEVICE | Pointer to device node |
| | 24 | IO_UNIT | Internal unit number |
| | 28 | IO_COMMAND | Command |
| | 30 | IO_FLAGS | Flags |
| | 31 | IO_ERROR | Error status |

| *STRUCT* | Offset | Name | Description |
|---|---|---|---|
| *IOStdExt* | 32 | IO_ACTUAL | Number of bytes transferred |
| | 36 | IO_LENGTH | Number of bytes to be transferred |
| | 40 | IO_DATA | Pointer to data buffer |
| | 44 | IO_OFFSET | Offset (for TrackDisk device, for example) |
| | 48 | | Begins the extended structure |

The normal I/O functions are performed by standard commands which belong to the I/O definitions.

| | | |
|---|---|---|
| CMD_INVALID | (0) | Invalid command |
| CMD_RESET | (1) | Reset the device to original state |
| CMD_READ | (2) | Read from the device |
| CMD_WRITE | (3) | Write to the device |
| CMD_UPDATE | (4) | Process the buffer |
| CMD_CLEAR | (5) | Clear all buffers |
| CMD_STOP | (6) | Insert pause |
| CMD_START | (7) | Continue after pause |
| CMD_FLUSH | (8) | Stop current task |

In addition to these commands, there are additional ones for each device which are explained in the examples which follow.

On a normal Workbench diskette some devices are found in the DEVS directory. Other devices are not in the directory, but can still be accessed because they are resident in the Amiga.

We'll look at examples of programming the more important devices.

# 4.1 TrackDisk device: Accessing disks

The TrackDisk device is the connection to the disks provided by the operating system. This is also used by DOS. It offers the ability to access the disks directly without having to access hardware registers.

The extended I/O structure contains the following two entries (long words) which are only necessary for the extended commands:

IOTD_COUNT          Number of disk changes allowed

IOTD_SECLABEL       Pointer to the sector header field, which must contain 16 bytes per sector to be read.

The device has a number of additional commands. A distinction is made between the normal and extended TrackDisk command. Here is a list of all valid TrackDisk commands:

| | | | |
|---|---|---|---|
| *Standard commands:* | CMD_READ | (2) | Read one or more sectors from the disk |
| | CMD_WRITE | (3) | Write one or more sectors to the disk |
| | CMD_UPDATE | (4) | Write track buffer back to the disk |
| | CMD_CLEAR | (5) | Declare track buffer invalid |
| *TrackDisk commands:* | TD_MOTOR | (8) | Turn drive motor on/off |
| | TD_SEEK | (10) | Position read/write head to a given track |
| | TD_FORMAT | (11) | Initialize one or more tracks |
| | TD_REMOVE | (12) | Install interrupt routine which is called when the disk is changed |
| | TD_CHANGENUM | (13) | Determine number of disk changes |
| | TD_CHANGESTATE | (14) | Determine if disk is inserted |
| | TD_PROTSTATUS | (15) | Determine if disk is write protected |
| | TD_RAWREAD | (16) | Read the unprocessed diskette contents |
| | TD_RAWWRITE | (17) | Write unprocessed disk contents |
| | TD_GETDRIVETYPE | (18) | Determine drive type (1=3 1/2, 2=5 1/4 inch) |
| | TD_GETNUMTRACKS | (19) | Determine total number of tracks |
| | TD_ADDCHANGEINT | (20) | Install interrupt routine which is called when the disk is changed |
| | TD_REMCHANGEINT | (21) | Disable above routine |
| | TD_LASTCOMM | (22) | Determine last command |

Extended commands (all numbers +32768 [$8000]):

Same functions as above, except the disk must not have been changed:

ETD_READ          (2)
ETD_WRITE         (3)
ETD_UPDATE        (4)
ETD_CLEAR         (5)
ETD_MOTOR         (9)
ETD_SEEK          (10)
ETD_FORMAT        (11)
ETD_RAWREAD       (16)
ETD_RAWWRITE      (17)

Now let's look at a short assembly language program which uses the TrackDisk device. For a simple example we'll just read a few sectors from the disk into memory. If you have an assembler/debugger package such as AssemPro Amiga, you can view the result directly. Otherwise you can also write the data to a file on the disk with the Open() and Write() AmigaDOS functions and then output it to the screen or printer with TYPE and the H option.

```
;*** Trackdisk device demo: Read sectors 6/87  S.D. ***
ExecBase  = 4                ;Exec base address
FindTask  = -294             ;Find task structure
AddPort   = -354             ;Create port
RemPort   = -360             ;Remove port
OpenLib   = -408             ;Open library
CloseLib  = -414             ;Close library
OpenDev   = -444             ;Open device
CloseDev  = -450             ;Close device
DoIo      = -456             ;Start I/O and wait

run:
      move.l  execbase,a6        ;Pointer to Exec library
      sub.l   a1,a1             ;this task
      jsr     FindTask(a6)       ;find it
      move.l  d0,readreply+$10  ;SigTask: this task

      lea     readreply,a1

      jsr     AddPort(a6)        ;Add reply port

      lea     diskio,a1          ;I/O structure

      move.l  #0,d0             ;drive DF0:
      clr.l   d1                ;no flags
      lea     trddevice,a0       ;device name
      jsr     OpenDev(a6)        ;open trackdisk.device
      tst.l   d0                ;OK?
      bne     error             ;no: error occurred!

      lea     diskio,a1
      move.l  #readreply,14(a1) ;set reply port
      move    #2,28(a1)         ;command: READ
      move.l  #diskbuff,40(a1)  ;buffer
```

```
        move.l  #2*512,36(a1)        ;length: 2 sectors
        move.l  #880*512,44(a1)      ;offset: 880 sectors
                                     ;(root)
        move.l  execbase,a6          ;Exec base address
        jsr     DoIo(a6)             ;read sectors
        move.l  diskio+32,d6         ;IO_ACTUAL in D6
        lea     diskio,a1
        move    #9,28(a1)            ;command: TD_MOTOR
        move.l  #0,36(a1)            ;Turn motor off
        jsr     DoIo(a6)


        lea     readreply,a1
        jsr     RemPort(a6)          ;Remove port


        lea     diskio,a1
        jsr     closedev(a6)         ;Close TrackDisk device

error:
        rts                          ;End
trddevice:  dc.b 'trackdisk.device',0
        align
diskio:     blk.l 20,0
readreply:  blk.l 8,0
diskbuff:   blk.b 512*2,0
        end
```

In this example sectors 880 and 881 are loaded from drive 0 into memory at diskbuff. Sector 880 is the root block containing the diskette name and other information.

Then DoIO() is called to turn the drive motor off again (to turn it on we had to write a 1 in 36(A1)).

*About the*
*program:*

A pointer to the current task structure is returned by calling the Find-Task() function with a zero as the argument in A1. This pointer is then stored in the port structure so that the system knows what task to wake up after the I/O.

Next, this port is installed in the system.

The TrackDisk device is opened. In D0 you can select which drive this function uses. If you want to use several drives at the same time, you must prepare multiple I/O structures and make multiple calls to OpenDevice().

If an error occurs while opening the device, the program branches to the error label, where the program is ended. Otherwise the I/O structure is provided with the necessary data:

- The pointer to the reply port structure for receiving the OK message

- The command to be executed at the next I/O operation (here: 2=CMD_READ)

- A pointer to the buffer memory to be filled

- The length of this memory

- The offset of the sectors to be read from the start of the diskette, which corresponds to the sector or block number * 512

This I/O structure is then passed to the system with DoIO() and the selected function is performed. The program waits until the I/O operation is done. A return parameter, such as that returned by the TD_PROTSTATUS command, is then returned in IO_ACTUAL and loaded into data register D6 with the subsequent MOVE.L instruction. In the example above this is the value $400, which corresponds to the number of bytes read. The data register is not used after this, but can be examined with a debugger.

Following this is another call to the DoIO() function, this time with the TD_MOTOR command (9). The parameter in IO_LENGTH (diskio +36) specifies whether the motor should be turned on (1) or off (0).

When this is done, the port is removed and the device is closed. That's it.

If a function fails, a status value is returned in the IO_ERROR byte. The possible values here are:

| 20 | NotSpecified    | Unknown error              |
|----|-----------------|----------------------------|
| 21 | NoSecHdr        | No sector header present    |
| 22 | BadSecPreamble  | Invalid sector header       |
| 23 | BadSecID        | Invalid sector ID           |
| 24 | BadHdrSum       | Incorrect header checksum   |
| 25 | BadSecSum       | Incorrect sector checksum   |
| 26 | TooFewSecs      | Not enough sectors available |
| 27 | BadSecHdr       | Illegal sector header       |
| 28 | WriteProt       | Diskette write-protected    |
| 29 | DiskChanged     | Diskette was changed        |
| 30 | SeekError       | Track not found             |
| 31 | NoMem           | Not enough memory           |
| 32 | BadUnitNum      | Illegal sector number       |
| 33 | BadDriveType    | Illegal drive type          |
| 34 | DriveInUse      | Drive already active        |
| 35 | PostReset       | Reset phase                 |

This was one direction. The other, writing data to the diskette, works just the same except that the command must be changed to 3 (CMD_WRITE). Be sure to try this only on diskettes where loss of data doesn't matter, however.

Another command is quite interesting, TD_FORMAT. With this command one or more tracks of the diskette can be formatted. The data, which must be prepared in memory and to which the IO_DATA pointer points, are written to each of the specified tracks. No test is made for a diskette change. This command can be used not only to format diskettes but also to copy them by reading the sectors from one diskette and then writing them back to the second with TD_FORMAT. The advantage of this method over CMD_WRITE is simply that the destination diskette doesn't have to be formatted.

*Formatting*  If you want to format an entire diskette and don't want to use the FORMAT command of the CLI, remember that the data for the tracks must be prepared in a certain format (see the diskette section), which means quite a bit of work. To use the TD_FORMAT command requires so much effort that it really isn't worth it.

Now we'll turn to an application of the TrackDisk device which can be used to learn various information about the distribution of data on the diskette. The assembly language program presented next can be used as a diagnosis program, either out of curiosity or to determine if files have been lost as a result of a diskette error.

The program is called from the CLI, whereby a filename must be supplied as a parameter. The program calculates the hash number from this name and outputs it. Then it loads the root sector of the diskette and outputs the diskette name. With the help of the hash number, the hash chain is then searched for the desired name. If it is not found or the entry in the hash table is unoccupied, -unknown- is printed and the program stops.

If the file or directory header is found, its block number and the number of data blocks occupied by the file is printed.

All of these data blocks are then loaded in order and their numbers are printed. It would also be possible to get these block numbers from the file header block and its extension block, if present, but there would be no guarantee that they would be in order. If the requester with the message "Disk structure corrupt" appears, you can use this program to check your important files.

To preserve the readability of the program, it is not possible to test files in subdirectories. This can be done by modifying the program so that it uses the hash table of a directory header block instead of the root block.

Here is the program. It contains several interesting functions which you may want to use in your own programs. The program was written with the AssemPro Amiga assembler, but adapting it to other assemblers should be easy.

```
;*****  File tracer;  6/87 S.D.  *****
;Assemble to Chip RAM
ExecBase  = 4         ;Exec base address
FindTask  = -294      ;find task structure
AddPort   = -354      ;create port
RemPort   = -360      ;remove port
OpenLib   = -408      ;open library
CloseLib  = -414      ;close library
OpenDev   = -444      ;open device
CloseDev  = -450      ;close device
DoIo      = -456      ;start I/O and wait
output    = -60       ;determine standard output
write     = -48       ;output data

run:
      move.l  a0,commpnt
      move.l  d0,commlen
      move.l  execbase,a6
      lea     dosname,a1          ;name: dos.library
      clr.l   d0
      jsr     openlib(a6)         ;open DOS
      move.l  d0,dosbase
      beq     nodos
      move.l  dosbase,a6
      jsr     output(a6)          ;standard output channel
      move.l  d0,outbase

      sub.l   #1,commlen          ;correct length of name
      move.l  commpnt,a0          ;* calculate hash value *
      move.l  commlen,d0          ;Hash=length
      clr.l   d2
      move.l  d0,d1
      subq    #1,d1               ;counter=length-1

hashloop:
      mulu    #13,d0              ;hash=hash*13
      move.b  (a0)+,d2
      bsr     upper               ;convert to upper case
      add     d2,d0               ;hash=hash+character
      and     #$7ff,d0            ;AND $7FF
      dbra    d1,hashloop         ;loop

      divu    #72,d0
      swap    d0                  ;hash modulo 72
      addq    #6,d0               ;+6
      move    d0,hash             ;hash calculated!

      move.l  #hashtxt,d2
      bsr     prtxt               ;output "Hash:"
      move    hash,d0
      bsr     phex                ;output hash number

      move.l  execbase,a6         ;pointer to Exec library
      sub.l   a1,a1               ;this task
      jsr     FindTask(a6)        ;find task
      move.l  d0,readreply+$10    ;set SigTask
```

```
        lea     readreply,a1
        jsr     AddPort(a6)         ;add reply port

     lea diskio,a1
        clr.l   d0
        clr.l   d1
        lea     trddevice,a0
        jsr     OpenDev(a6)         ;open trackdisk.device
        tst.l   d0
        bne     error

        move.l  #880,d0            ;sector 880 (root sector)
        bsr     loadsec            ;load in disk buffer

        move.l  #voltxt,d2
        bsr     prtxt              ;output "Volume:"
        move.l  dosbase,a6
        move.l  outbase,d1
        move.l  #diskbuff+433,d2 ;name address
        clr.l   d3
        move.b  diskbuff+432,d3    ;name length
        jsr     write(a6)          ;output disk name

        lea     diskbuff,a0
        clr.l   d0
        move    hash,d0
        lsl     #2,d0              ;hash*4=sector pointer
        move.l  0(a0,d0),d0        ;get sector number
        tst.l   d0 ;Zeiger da?
        beq     none               ;no: hash entry empty!
loadloop:
        move.l  d0,sector
        bsr     loadsec            ;load next sector

        move.l  commpnt,a0
        lea     diskbuff+432,a1    ;name length from header
        move.l  commlen,d0
        cmp.b   (a1)+,d0           ;does length match?
        bne     nextsec            ;no
        subq    #1,d0

namelop:
        move.b  (a1)+,d2
        bsr     upper              ;character to upper case
        move    d2,d1
        move.b  (a0)+,d2
        bsr     upper              ;character to upper case
        cmp.b   d1,d2              ;compare characters
        bne     nextsec            ;wrong
        dbra    d0,namelop
        bra     sectorok           ;name matches

nextsec:
        move.l  diskbuff+496,d0    ;pointer to next sector
        tst.l   d0                 ;is one there?
```

```
            bne       loadloop          ;yes: continue

none:                                   ;else
            move.l    #unknown,d2
            bsr       prtxt             ;print "-unknown-"
            bra       ende              ;and quit

sectorok:
            move.l    #header,d2
            bsr       prtxt             ;output "Header:"
            move.l    sector,d0         ;sector header number
            bsr       phex              ;output
            cmp.l     #2,diskbuff+508   ;dir header?
            bne       nodir             ;no
            move.l    #dirtxt,d2
            bsr       prtxt             ;print "Directory"
            bra       ende              ;and quit

nodir:
            move.l    diskbuff+504,d0   ;extension
            tst.l     d0                ;existent?
            beq       noextens          ;no
            move.l    d0,-(sp)          ;save D0
            move.l    #extxt,d2
            bsr       prtxt             ;output "Extension"
            move.l    (sp)+,d0          ;get sector #
            bsr       phex              ;and print

noextens:
            move.l    #crtxt,d2
            bsr       prtxt             ;output CR
            move.l    diskbuff+8,d0
            bsr       phex              ;output sector number
            move.l    #sectxt,d2
            bsr       prtxt             ;output "sectors"
            clr       counter           ;column counter=0
            bra       seclop1           ;output sectors

secloop:
            move.l    sector,d0
            bsr       phex              ;output sector number
            add       #1,counter        ;counter+1
            cmp       #8,counter        ;8 numbers printed?
            bne       seclop1           ;no
            clr       counter           ;else clear counter
            move.l    #crtxt,d2
            bsr       prtxt             ;and output CR

seclop1:
            move.l    diskbuff+16,d0    ;next sector
            tst.l     d0                ;present?
            beq       ende              ;no: done
            move.l    d0,sector
            bsr       loadsec           ;load next sector
            bra       secloop           ;etc...
```

```
ende:
      move.l    #crtxt,d2
      bsr       prtxt                 ;output CR
      move.l    execbase,a6
      lea       readreply,a1
      jsr       RemPort(a6)           ;remove port
      lea       diskio,a1
      jsr       closedev(a6)          ;close TrackDisk device
error:
      move.l    dosbase,a1
      jsr       closelib(a6)          ;close DOS
nodos:
      rts                             ;done

loadsec:                             ;load sector D0
      lea       diskio,a1
      move.l    #readreply,14(a1)    ;set reply port
      move      #2,28(a1)             ;command: READ
      move.l    #diskbuff,40(a1)     ;buffer
      move.l    #512,36(a1)           ;length: 1 sector
      mulu      #512,d0
      move.l    d0,44(a1)             ;offset: sector number+512
      move.l    execbase,a6
      jsr       DoIo(a6)              ;read sector
      lea       diskio,a1
      move      #9,28(a1)             ;TD_MOTOR
      move.l    #0,36(a1)             ;motor off
      jsr       DoIo(a6)
      rts

phex:                                ;output D0 in hex
      lea       outpuff,a0
      move      d0,d2
      move      #3,d3                 ;4 digits
niblop:
      rol       #4,d2                 ;left nibble down
      move      d2qd1
      and       #$f,d1                ;mask
      add       #$30,d1               ;convert to ASCII
      cmp       #'9',d1               ;digit?
      bls       nibok                 ;yes
      add       #7,d1                 ;else correct

nibok:
      move.b    d1,(a0)+              ;character in output buffer
      dbra      d3,niblop             ;continue loop
      move.b    #$20,(a0)             ;space at end
      move.l    dosbase,a6
      move.l    outbase,d1
      move.l    #outpuff,d2           ;output buffer
      move.l    #5,d3                 ;5 characters
      jmp       Write(a6)             ;print

prtxt:                               ;output text at (D2)
      move.l    dosbase,a6
      move.l    outbase,d1
```

```
            move.l   #12,d3              ;12 char length
            jmp      Write(a6)           ;print string

      upper:                            ;convert D2 to uppercase
            cmp.b    #'a',d2             ;char <'a'?
            blo      upperx              ;yes: leave it along
            cmp.b    #'z',d2             ;char >'z'?
            bhi      upperx              ;yes: leave it alone
            sub      #$20,d2             ;else correct
      upperx:
            rts                          ;done

      trddevice:  dc.b  'trackdisk.device',0
      dosname:    dc.b  'dos.library',0

      hashtxt:    dc.b  $a,'Hashnum:    '
      voltxt:     dc.b  $a,'Volume:     '
      unknown:    dc.b  $a,'-unknown-   '
      header:     dc.b  $a,'Header:     '
      extxt:      dc.b  $a,'Extension:  '
      dirtxt:     dc.b  $a,'Directory ',$a
      sectxt:     dc.b  'Sectors:    ',$a
      crtxt:      dc.b  '            ',$a

      data

         align
      outpuff:    blk.b 6        ;buffer for hex output
      sector:     blk.l 1        ;sector scratch storage
      counter:    blk.w 1        ;counter for output formatting
      dosbase:    blk.l 1        ;DOS base address
      outbase:    blk.l 1        ;standard output handle
      hash:       blk.w 1        ;hash number
      commpnt:    blk.l 1        ;pointer to input line
      commlen:    blk.l 1        ;length of input line

      diskio:                    ;disk I/O structure
      message:    blk.b 20,0
      io:         blk.b 12,0
      ioreq:      blk.b 16,0

      readreply:  blk.l 8,0
      diskbuff:   blk.b 512,0
```

This technique can be used to write a program which loads a file from diskette without using DOS. It only has to copy the actual data out of the data blocks into memory.

# 4.2    Console device:
# Editor window

This device, where keyboard I/O can be prepared and processed, is little out of the scope of standard devices. It cannot simply be opened and used but must be used in connection with a window. This window is then used for I/O with the console device.

Before the device itself can be opened you must first open a window. To do this you have to open the Intuition library, a screen and then a window. The pointer to the window structure obtained by this is then passed when the console device is opened.

The result is a window on its own screen in which the cursor is visible in the upper left corner. This cursor has no function yet; you have to program the output of characters in the window first.

You need two I/O structures, one for inputs and one for outputs. Naturally these also have message ports associated with them so that the device can determine where the data is to go/come from.

Before we continue with such dry theory, you should first take a look at the following program, which performs the steps described above. It opens a screen and a window in which I/O then occurs through the console device. The characters entered through the keyboard are output again in the window, Return and Backspace are handled separately. If the close box of the window is clicked with the mouse, the program is ended. Additional actions of the mouse can also be evaluated.

Here is the program:

```
** Demo program for the console device  6/87  S.D. **

openlib      = -408      ;open library
closelib     = -414      ;close library
AddPort      = -354      ;create port
RemPort      = -360      ;remove port
OpenDev      = -444      ;open device
CloseDev     = -450      ;close device
execbase     = 4         ;Exec base address
GetMsg       = -372      ;get message
FindTask     = -294      ;determine task
DoIo         = -456      ;perform I/O
SendIo       = -462      ;start I/O

;     ** Intuition functions **
openscreen   = -198            ;open screen
```

```
            closescreen  = -66              ;close screen
            openwindow   = -204             ;open window
            closewindow  = -72              ;close window


    run:
            bsr     openint                 ;open Intuition
            bsr     scropen                 ;open Screen
            bsr     windopen                ;open screen

            move.l  execbase,a6             ;pointer Exec library

            sub.l   a1,a1                   ;this task
            jsr     FindTask(a6)            ;find task
            move.l  d0,readreply+$10        ;set SigTask

            lea     readreply,a1
            jsr     AddPort(a6)             ;add read reply port

            lea     writerep,a1
            jsr     AddPort(a6)             ;add write reply port

            lea     readio,a1
            move.l  windowhd,readio+$28     ;our window
            move.l  #48,readio+$24          ;length of the structure
            clr.l   d0
            clr.l   d1
            lea     devicename,a0
            jsr     OpenDev(a6)             ;open console device
            tst.l   d0
            bne     error

            move.l  readio+$14,writeio+$14  ;copy DEVICE and
            move.l  readio+$18,writeio+$18  ;UNIT

    go:
            bsr     queueread               ;start input

    loop:                                   ;* evaluate events *
            move.l  execbase,a6
            move.l  windowhd,a0
            move.l  86(a0),a0               ;window user port
            jsr     GetMsg(a6)
            tst.l   d0
            bne     wevent                  ;window event

            lea     readreply,a0
            jsr     GetMsg(a6)              ;console event (key)?
            tst.l   d0
            beq     loop                    ;no event

    cevent:                                 ;* process key *
            bsr     conout                  ;output character
            cmp.b   #$d,buffer              ;Return?
            bne     no1                     ;no
            move.b  #$a,buffer              ;else output LF
```

```
        bsr     conout

no1:
        cmp.b   #$8,buffer          ;Backspace?
        bne     no2
        move.b  #' ',buffer         ;else erase character
        bsr     conout
        move.b  #8,buffer
        bsr     conout              ;and back again

no2:
        bra     go                  ;and so on

wevent:                             ;* evaluate window event *
        move.l  d0,a0
        move.l  $16(a0),d6          ;message in D6
        cmp.l   #$2000000,d6        ;window close?
        beq     ende                ;yes: end

        ;* additional evaluations can take place here: *

        move.l  windowhd,a0
        move.l  12(a0),d5           ;mouse position in D5

        ;* e.g. set cursor to mouse position... *


ende:               ;* End of program: close everything *
        lea     readreply,a1
        jsr     RemPort(a6)         ;remove port
        lea     readio,a1
        jsr     closedev(a6)        ;close device
        lea     writerep,a1
        jsr     RemPort(a6)         ;remove port
error:
        bsr     windclose           ;close window
        bsr     scrclose            ;clsoe screen
        bsr     closeint            ;close Intuition

        rts                         ;* end *


;** Subroutines **

queueread:                  ;* start console input *
        move.l  execbase,a6
        lea     readio,a1
        move    #2,28(a1)           ;command: READ
        move.l  #buffer,40(a1)      ;buffer
        move.l  #1,36(a1)           ;length:
        move.l  #readreply,14(a1)   ;set reply port
        jsr     sendIo(a6)          ;perform function
        rts

conout:                             ;* output 1 character *
        move.l  execbase,a6
```

```
          lea       writeio,a1
          move      #3,28(a1)           ;command: WRITE
          move.l    #buffer,40(a1)      ;buffer
          move.l    #1,36(a1)           ;length:
          move.l    #writerep,14(a1)    ;set reply port
          jsr       DoIo(a6)            ;execute function
          rts

openint:                               ;* open Intuition *
          move.l    execbase,a6
          lea       intname,a1          ;library name
          jsr       openlib(a6)
          move.l    d0,intbase
          rts

closeint:                              ;* close Intuition *
          move.l    execbase,a6
          move.l    intbase,a1
          jsr       closelib(a6)
          rts

scropen:                               ;* open screen *
          move.l    intbase,a6
          lea       screen_defs,a0
          jsr       openscreen(a6)
          move.l    d0,screenhd
          rts

scrclose:                              ;* close screen *
          move.l    intbase,a6
          move.l    screenhd,a0
          jsr       closescreen(a6)
          rts

windopen:                              ;* open window *
          move.l    intbase,a6
          lea       windowdef,a0
          jsr       openwindow(a6)
          move.l    d0,windowhd
          rts

windclose:                             ;* close window *
          move.l    intbase,a6
          move.l    windowhd,a0
          jsr       closewindow(a6)
          rts

screen_defs:          ;* screen structure *
          dc.w 0,0            ;position
          dc.w 640,200        ;size
          dc.w 4              ;bit maps
          dc.b 0,1            ;colors
          dc.w $800           ;mode
          dc.w 15             ;type
          dc.l 0              ;standard font
          dc.l titel          ;screen title
```

```
        dc.l 0              ;standard title
        dc.l 0              ;no gadgets

windowdef:                  ;* window structure *
    dc.w 10,20              ;position
    dc.w 300,150            ;size
    dc.b 0,1               ;colors
    dc.l $208              ;IDCMP flags
    dc.l $100f             ;window flags
    dc.l 0                ;no gadgets
    dc.l 0                ;no menu checks
    dc.l windname          ;window name

screenhd: dc.l 0           ;screen structure pointer
    dc.l 0                ;no bit map
    dc.w 100,50            ;min. size
    dc.w 300,200           ;max. size
    dc.w $f               ;screen type

titel:      dc.b "Editor screen",0
windname:   dc.b "Console window ",0
intname:    dc.b "intuition.library",0
devicename: dc.b 'console.device',0
 align                                  ;even
windowhd:   blk.l 1
intbase:    blk.l 1
conbase:    blk.l 1

readio:
message:    blk.b 20,0
io:         blk.b 12,0
ioreq:      blk.b 16,0

writeio:
            blk.b 20,0
            blk.b 12,0
            blk.b 16,0

readreply:  blk.l 8,0
writerep:   blk.l 8,0
buffer:     blk.b 80,0

 end
```

The sequences used to perform various functions in DOS **RAW:** and
**CON:** windows can also be used here.

# 4.3  Narrator device: speech output

The narrator is a device which allows the Amiga to express itself verbally, to speak out loud. The narrator is a program package which is constructed as a device. It can be used to output text while the computer is performing other tasks. The extended I/O structure of the narrator device is constructed as follows:

| Word | Name | Description |
|------|------|-------------|
| 0 | RATE | Speech speed in words/minutes |
| 1 | PITCH | Basic speech frequency in Hertz |
| 2 | MODE | Speech mode (0=with, 1=without expression) |
| 3 | SEX | Sex of voice (0=male, 1=female) |
| 4 | CHMASKS | Pointer to channel mask field |
| 6 | NUMMASKS | Number of channel masks |
| 7 | VOLUME | Volume |
| 8 | SAMPFREQ | Sampling rate |
| 9 | MOUTHS | Mouth creation flag (byte) |
|  | CHANMASK | Current channel (internal meaning only) |

***Programming the narrator device***

Programming the narrator device is similar to the other devices. An additional component is using the translator, which converts normal text into the notation of the narrator. This translator is not a device but a library, which contains only one function.

Here is an assembly language program which outputs an example text. You can experiment with this program by changing the parameters and trying out the result. It's helpful to use an assembler with a built-in debugger like AssemPro, which this program was written with.

```
;***** Narrator-Demo  6/87  S.D. CHIP RAM  *****

ExecBase  = 4       ;EXEC-Base address
FindTask  =-294     ;Find Task
AddPort   =-354     ;Add Port
RemPort   =-360     ;Remove Port
OpenLib   =-408     ;Open Library
closelib  =-414     ;Close Library
OpenDev   =-444     ;Open Device
CloseDev  =-450     ;Close Device
DoIo      =-456     ;Do I/O
SendIo    = -462    ;Send I/O
Translate =-30      ;Translate Text

run:                ;** Initialize and open system **
     move.l  execbase,a6
```

```
        lea     transname,a1
        moveq   #0,d0
        jsr     openlib(a6)         ;Open Translator Library
        move.l  d0,tranbase
        beq     error

        sub.l   a1,a1           ;Task Number = 0: Your own task
        move.l  execbase,a6
        jsr     FindTask(a6)        ;Find Task

        move.l  d0,writerep+$10     ;set SigTask

        lea     writerep,a1
        jsr     addport(a6)         ;Add Reply-Port

        lea     talkio,a1
        move.l  #writerep,14(a1)    ;Enter Reply
        clr.l   d0
        clr.l   d1
        lea     nardevice,a0
        jsr     opendev(a6)         ;Open Narrator.device
        tst.l   d0
        bne     error

        lea     talkio,a1
        move.l  #writerep,14(a1)    ;set Reply-Port (*)
        move    #150,48(a1)         ;Rate (40-400)
        move    #110,50(a1)         ;Pitch (65-320)
        move    #0,52(a1)           ;Mode: inflected (0/1)
        move    #0,54(a1)           ;Gender:male (0/1)
        move.l  #amaps,56(a1)       ;Masks (*)
        move    #4,60(a1)           ;4 Masks (*)
        move    #64,62(a1)          ;Volume (0-64)
        move    #22200,64(a1)       ;Sampling rate (5000-28000)

sayit:                          ;** Examine and say text **
        lea     intext,a0           ;Original text
        move.l  #outtext-intext,d0  ;Text length
        lea     outtext,a1          ;Buffer for translation
        move.l  #512,d1             ;Buffer length
        move.l  tranbase,a6
        jsr     Translate(a6)       ;Translate text

        lea     talkio,a1
        move    #3,28(a1)           ;Command: Write
        move.l  #512,36(a1)         ;Length
        move.l  #outtext,40(a1)     ;Buffer
        move.l  execbase,a6
        jsr     DoIo(a6)            ;Say it!!

qu:                             ;** End **
        lea writerep,a1
        jsr RemPort(a6)             ;Remove Port

        lea talkio,a1
        jsr closedev(a6)           ;Close Narrator
```

```
        move.l tranbase,a1
        jsr     closelib(a6)       ;Close Translator-Lib

        clr.l   d0
error:
        rts

transname:    dc.b "translator.library",0
nardevice:    dc.b 'narrator.device',0
amaps:        dc.b 3,5,10,12
intext:       dc.b 'this is from the abacus book amiga
system programming',0
 align                              ; even
outtext:      blk.l 128,0
tranbase:     blk.l 1,0
narread:      blk.l 20,0
talkio:       blk.l 120,0
writerep:     blk.l 8,0
 end
```

When preparing the I/O area with the various modes and rates, only the values which are marked with an asterisk in the listing above must absolutely be supplied. All others are automatically set to the default values. These values are shown in the program and can be varied in the range given in the parentheses.

The narrator device also possesses the ability to send data to the calling program during speech output. Naturally, this is possible only when the speech output was started with SendIO() and not DoIO(), so that the data can also be received during the speech output.

The data received represents a bit pattern, which when sent to the screen, represents a mouth moving in unison with the spoken sounds. We won't discuss this any further here, however, since it involves graphic output and really belongs in a graphics book. We'll only say that these graphics are relatively primitive since they represent the mouth only as a parallelogram of the corresponding height. The width and height of this form is received from the device in the extension of the read request I/O structure.

This extension has the following structure:

| Offset | Name | Contents |
| --- | --- | --- |
| 48 | MRB_WIDTH | Width of the "mouth form" |
| 49 | MRB_HEIGHT | Height |
| 50 | MRB_SHAPE | Internal data byte |
| 51 | MRB_PAD | Pad byte for even address |

The I/O function can also go wrong. The error messages which then result can have the following values:

| *Narrator error messages:* | Number | Description |
|---|---|---|
| | -2 | Not enough memory |
| | -3 | Audio device not present |
| | -4 | Library cannot be created |
| | -5 | Wrong unit number in the I/O structure (0 only) |
| | -6 | No audio channels available |
| | -7 | Unknown command |
| | -8 | Mouth data read but not written |
| | -9 | Open impossible |
| | -20 | Text cannot be spoken |
| | -21 | Invalid rate |
| | -22 | Invalid pitch |
| | -23 | Invalid sex |
| | -24 | Invalid mode |
| | -25 | Invalid sample rate |
| | -26 | Invalid volume |

# 4.4 Serial device: the RS-232 interface

This device is responsible for the serial communcations with the outside world. Input and output through the serial port can also be performed with DOS functions by specifying SER: as the filename. This method has a significant disadvantage, however.

The usual disadvantage of using DOS is, of course, that the I/O does not run in the background and the program must wait until it is done. This can be avoided by programming the device with the SendIO() function.

Another disadvantage which occurs is that the transmission parameters like the baud rate must be set prior to use with the Preferences program.

The serial device offers its own function for setting the parameters. An extended I/O structure is used for this and the other functions, and it contains the following entries (default values in parentheses):

| Offset | IO Name | Contents |
|---|---|---|
| 0 | CTLCHAR | Control character: xON, xOFF, free, free ($11130000) |
| 4 | RBUFLEN | Input buffer length ($200) |
| 8 | WBUFLEN | Output buffer length ($200) |
| 12 | BAUD | Baudrate (9600) |
| 16 | BRKTIME | Break length in microseconds (250000) |
| 20 | TERMARRAY | Termination character array (8 Bytes) |
| 28 | READLEN | Bits per character when reading (8) |
| 29 | WRITELEN | Bits per character when writing (8) |
| 30 | STOPBITS | Number of stop bits (1) |
| 31 | SERFLAGS | Serial flags (see below) ($20) |
| 32 | STATUS | Status word |

*Returned bits of status word*

| Bit | If | Then |
|---|---|---|
| 0 | 0 | busy, transfer in progress |
| 1 | 0 | paper out, receiver not ready |
| 2 | 0 | select |
| 3 | 0 | Data Set Ready (DSR) |
| 4 | 0 | Clear To Send (CTS) |
| 5 | 0 | Carrier Detect (CD) |
| 6 | 0 | Ready To Send (RTS) |
| 7 | 0 | Data Terminal Ready (DTR) |
| 8 | 1 | read overrun |
| 9 | 1 | break sent |
| 10 | 1 | break received |
| 11 | 1 | transmit x-OFF |
| 12 | 1 | receive x-OFF |
| 13-15 | | reserved |

*IO_SERFLAG*
*bits*

| Bit | Name | Meaning, if set |
|-----|------|-----------------|
| 0 | PARITY_ON | Parity on |
| 1 | PARITY_ODD | Odd parity |
| 2 | | Unused |
| 3 | QUEUEDBRK | Break in background |
| 4 | RAD_BOOGIE | High speed mode on |
| 5 | SHARED | General access allowed |
| 6 | EOFMODE | EOF recognition enabled |
| 7 | XDISABLED | xON/xOFF disabled |

In addition to the standard commands, the serial device has three others:

| Number | SDCMD Name | Function |
|--------|-----------|----------|
| 9 | QUERY | |
| 10 | BREAK | Send break |
| 11 | SETPARAMS | Set parameters |

To demonstrate these commands, especially the last one, SDCMD _SETPARAMS, another example program follows. In this program the baud rate is set to 1200 and the famous "Hello, world!" text is sent.

```
;*****  Serial-Device-Demonstration  6/87  S.D.   *****


ExecBase   = 4         ;EXEC base address
FindTask   = -294      ;Search for Task-Structure
AddPort    = -354      ;Add a port
RemPort    = -360      ;Remove a port
OpenLib    = -408      ;Open library
CloseLib   = -414      ;Close library
AddDev     = -432      ; add device
OpenDev    = -444      ;Open device
CloseDev   = -450      ;Close device
DoIo       = -456      ;Start I/O and wait

output     = -60       ;Send standard output
write      = -48       ;Display data


run:
       move.l  execbase,a6    ;Pointer to EXEC library
       sub.l   a1,a1          ;Your own task
       jsr     FindTask(a6)   ;Search for task

       move.l  d0,reply+$10   ;Set SigTask
       lea     reply,a1
       jsr     AddPort(a6)    ;Add Reply-Port

       lea     devio,a1       ;Pointer to I/O-Structure
       clr.l   d0
       clr.l   d1
       lea     devicename,a0
       jsr     openDev(a6)    ;Open serial device
       tst.l   d0             ;OK?
```

```
         bne      error              ;NO: End

         lea      devio,a1

         move.l   #reply,14(a1)      ;set Reply-Port

         move     #11,28(a1)         ;Command: SETPARAMS
         move.l   #1200,ioextd+12    ;1200 baud
         jsr      DoIo(a6)           ;Set parameters

         move     #3,28(a1)          ;Command: WRITE
         move.l   #ttext,40(a1)      ;Buffer
         move.l   #textl,36(a1)      ;length
         jsr      DoIo(a6)           ;Send text

error:
         lea      reply,a1
         jsr      RemPort(a6)        ;Remove Port

         lea      devio,a1
         jsr      CloseDev(a6)       ;Close Device


         rts                         ;End


devicename: dc.b "serial.device",0
ttext:      dc.b "hello, world!"
textl:      = 13
 align                       ; even
devio:
message: blk.w 10,0
io:      blk.w  6,0
ioreq:   blk.w  8,0
ioextd:  blk.w 17,0
reply:   blk.l  8,0

 end
```

# 4.5    Printer device

The printer can also be accessed in ways other than the PRT: channel. This is what the printer device is for, which has an additional interesting feature besides the normal printer operation. This is the ability to output the contents of a window or screen to the printer.

For normal printer operation, the following I/O structure extension, called IOPrtCmdReq, is required:

| Offset | Name | Contents |
| --- | --- | --- |
| 32 | io_PrtCommand | Printer command |
| 34 | io_Param0 | Command parameter |
| 35 | io_Param1 | Command parameter |
| 36 | io_Param2 | Command parameter |
| 37 | io_Param3 | Command parameter |

Here the control commands are passed to the printer to set the type style, etc. This is output in connection with the PRTCOMMAND command.

The commands which this device offers in addition to the standard commands are the following:

| Value | Name | Function |
| --- | --- | --- |
| 9 | PRD_RAWWRITE | Print without interpreting control char |
| 10 | PRD_PRTCOMMAND | Send printer command |
| 11 | PRD_DUMPRPORT | Print screen or window contents |

If WRITE is used to output the data instead of RAWWRITE, the standard Amiga control characters are converted to the printer-specific control characters according to the printer installed. Thus a program can send its output to any printer without having to know anything about the features or characteristics of this printer.

The DUMPRPORT command, as mentioned already, allows the contents of a window or screen to be sent to the printer. The I/O structure extension required for this is contructed as follows:

| Offset | Name | Contents |
| --- | --- | --- |
| 32 | RastPort | Pointer to the RastPort to be output |
| 36 | ColorMap | Pointer to the color table |
| 40 | Modes | Graphic mode of the ViewPort |
| 44 | SrcX | X position of the window/screen |
| 46 | SrcY | Y position |
| 48 | SrcWidth | Window/screen width |
| 50 | SrcHeight | Window/screen height |
| 52 | DestCols | Destination width |
| 56 | DestRows | Destination height |
| 60 | Special | Flags for special functions |

# 4.6 Parallel device: digital I/O

Other devices can be connected to the same connection to which the printer is usually connected, provided they have the appropriate electical characteristics. Digital data can then be both sent and received. It is also possible to program individual bits of the eight data lines as inputs and the rest as outputs. This is only possible with direct programming of the hardware register $BFE301.

Here we'll just look at using the entire port as input or output. There is also a device for this: the parallel device. An extension must be made to the normal I/O structure in order to use this device. This extension has the following construction:

| Offset | Name | Contents |
| --- | --- | --- |
| 48 | PWBufLen | Length of the output buffer |
| 52 | ParStatus | Status of the device |
| 53 | ParFlags | Parallel flags |
| 54-61 | PTermArray | Termination mask |

The status byte contains the following status bits:

| Bit | Name | Meaning, if set |
| --- | --- | --- |
| 0 | PSEL | Printer selected |
| 1 | PAPEROUT | No more paper |
| 2 | PBUSY | Printer busy |
| 3 | RWDIR | Data direction (0=read, 1=write) |

The following bits represent the parallel flags:

| Bit | Name | Meaning, if set |
| --- | --- | --- |
| 1 | EOFMODE | EOF mode enabled |
| 5 | SHARED | Access possible for other tasks |

If you want to read from the parallel port, the question arises as to how the receiver is to recognize the end of the transfer. It is possible to use a given byte sequence to stop the reception. This sequence is stored in the two long words of TermArray. This termination sequence is activated if bit 1 of the flag byte is set (EOFMODE) and the SETPARAMS command (10) is then called.

# 4.7    Gameport device: mouse and joystick

This device processes all the inputs from the two gameports. The I/O structure of this device doesn't need an extension, but two additional structures are used.

One of these structures is the event structure, which was present in the section on the RAW: window. This structure is called InputEvent and is constructed as follows:

*InputEvent structure*

| Offset | Name | Contents |
|--------|------|----------|
| 0 | NextEvent | Pointer to the next structure |
| 4 | Class | Even class |
| 5 | SubClass | Subclass of the event |
| 6 | Code | Event code |
| 8 | Qualifier | Event type |
| 10 | X | X position |
| 12 | Y | Y position, usually relative |
| 14 | TimeStamp | Seconds, microseconds |

The other structure is needed for setting the event which causes the parameters to be transferred in the even structure. This can be pressing or releasing a button or the horizontal or vertical movement of the mouse or joystick. The desired value is entered in the appropriate word of the following structure, called GamePortTrigger:

*GamePort Trigger structure*

| Offset | Name | Contents |
|--------|------|----------|
| 0 | Keys | Key modification: |
|  |  |    Bit 0: key pressed |
|  |  |    Bit 1: key released |
| 2 | Timeout | Terminate after this number of 1/60 seconds |
| 4 | XDelta | Horizontal movement |
| 6 | YDelta | Vertical movement |

For example, if you want to wait 10 seconds until the joystick is moved or its button is pressed, you would write a 1 in Keys (key pressed), a 600 in Timeout (600/10=10 seconds) and a 1 in XDelta.

Before this monitoring process can be started, some preparations must be made. First the Gameport device must be opened, the port in which the joystick is inserted must be configured as a joystick port, and then you can wait for the desired event. The commands available for this device are:

*GamePort*
*commands*

| Command | Name | Description |
|---------|------|-------------|
| 9 | READEVENT | Start monitoring |
| 10 | ASKCTYPE | Read port type |
| 11 | SETCTYPE | Set port type |
| 12 | ASKTRIGGER | Determine triggering event |
| 13 | SETTRIGGER | Set triggering event |

The possible port types which can be set with SETVTYPE are:

| Number | Name | Description |
|--------|------|-------------|
| 0 | NOCONTROLLER | Disable port |
| 1 | MOUSE | Mouse port |
| 2 | RELJOYSTICK | Port for relative joysticks |
| 3 | ABSJOYSTICK | Port for absolute joysticks and the type |
| -1 | ALLOCATED | |

which can result from ASKCTYPE; the port is then allocated by another task.

The difference between a relative joystick and an absolute joystick is that the X and Y values of a relative joystick are continually incremented or decremented if the joystick is held in one position, while with an absolute joystick there is only one position value change per movement.

To demonstrate the programming of the gameport device, here is an assembly language program which montiors a joystick in the right port (port 2):

```
;***** Gameport-Device-Demo: Joystick  6/87  S.D.  *****

ExecBase = 4
FindTask = -294
AddPort  = -354
RemPort  = -360
OpenLib  = -408
CloseLib = -414
OpenDev  = -444
CloseDev = -450
DoIo     = -456
SendIo   = -462

run:
      move.l  execbase,a6         ;Pointer to EXEC library
      sub.l   a1,a1              ;Your own task
      jsr     FindTask(a6)       ;Search task
      move.l  d0,readreply+$10   ;Set SigTask

      lea     readreply,a1
      jsr     AddPort(a6)        ;Add Reply-Port

      lea     devio,a1
```

```
        move.l  #1,d0              ;Unit 1: Right port
        clr.l   d1
        lea     devicename,a0
        jsr     OpenDev(a6)        ;Open Gameport-Device
        tst.l   d0
        bne     error

;*** Set Port type ***

        move    #11,28(a1)         ;Command: SETCTYPE
        move.l  #Event,40(a1)      ;Buffer
        move.l  #1,36(a1)          ;Length
        move.b  #3,NextEvent       ;ABSJOYSTICK
        lea     devio,a1
        move.l  #readreply,14(a1)  ;Set Reply Port
        move.l  execbase,a6
        jsr     DoIo(a6)           ;Read joystick

;*** Define solution ***

        move    #13,28(a1)         ;Command: SETTRIGGER
        move.l  #trigger,40(a1)    ;Buffer
        move.l  #8,36(a1)          ;length

        move    #3,Keys            ;DOWN & UP
        move    #0,Timeout         ;Timeout
        move    #1,XDelta          ;XDelta
        move    #1,YDelta          ;YDelta

        lea     devio,a1
        move.l  #readreply,14(a1)  ;set Reply-Port
        move.l  execbase,a6
        jsr     DoIo(a6)           ;Set code

;*** Start task ***

        move    #9,28(a1)          ;Command: READEVENT
        move.l  #Event,40(a1)      ;Puffer
        move.l  #22,36(a1)         ;Length of one event
        clr.b   30(a1)             ;Flags

        lea     devio,a1
        move.l  #readreply,14(a1)  ;set Reply-Port
        move.l  execbase,a6
        jsr     DoIo(a6)           ;Wait for an event

;*** Return port control ***

        move    #11,28(a1)         ;Command: SETCTYPE
        move.l  #Event,40(a1)      ;Buffer
        move.l  #1,36(a1)          ;Length
        move.b  #0,NextEvent       ;NOCONTROLLER
        lea     devio,a1
        move.l  #readreply,14(a1)  ;set Reply-Port
        move.l  execbase,a6
        jsr     DoIo(a6)           ;Read joystick
```

```
ende:
    lea     readreply,a1
    jsr     RemPort(a6)             ;Remove port

    lea     devio,a1
    jsr     closedev(a6)           ;Close device

error:
    rts                            ;* End *


devicename: dc.b 'gameport.device',0
 align                             ;some assemblers use even
devio:
message:    blk.b 20,0
io:         blk.b 1
```

Normally it makes more sense to start the monitoring with SendIO() so that the program does not have to wait for a joystick event and can go on processing. For this example it is better to wait, however, because otherwise the device would be disabled before the event, which can lead to problems. To see how this program performs in the AssemPro Debugger, set a breakpoint at error: when the program is started it will wait for a joystick event before reaching the breakpoint.

# Appendix

# An overview of library functions

The following table gives you an overview of all of the available libraries and their functions. The title of each library is given, followed by its functions.

These functions are listed with their negative offsets in hex and decimal, their names and their parameters. The parameter names are specified in parentheses behind the function name, and the second set of parentheses contains the registers in the same order as the parameters are passed. If no parameters are required, this is indicated by ().

### *clist.library*

```
-$001E  -30  InitCLPool (cLPool, size) (A0,D0)
-$0024  -36  AllocCList (cLPool) (A1)
-$002A  -42  FreeCList (cList) (A0)
-$0030  -48  FlushCList (cList) (A0)
-$0036  -54  SizeCList (cList) (A0)
-$003C  -60  PutCLChar (cList,byte) (A0,D0)
-$0042  -66  GetCLChar (cList) (A0)
-$0048  -72  UnGetCLChar (cList,byte) (A0,D0)
-$004E  -78  UnPutCLChar (cList) (A0)
-$0054  -84  PutCLWord (cList,word) (A0,D0)
-$005A  -90  GetCLWord (cList) (A0)
-$0060  -96  UnGetCLWord (cList,word) (A0,D0)
-$0066  -102 UnPutCLWord (cList) (A0)
-$006C  -108 PutCLBuf (cList,buffer,length) (A0,A1,D1)
-$0072  -114 GetCLBuf (cList,buffer,maxLength) (A0,A1,D1)
-$0078  -120 MarkCList (cList,offset) (A0,D0)
-$007E  -126 IncrCLMark (cList) (A0)
-$0084  -132 PeekCLMark (cList) (A0)
-$008A  -138 SplitCList (cList) (A0)
-$0090  -144 CopyCList (cList) (A0)
-$0096  -150 SubCList (cList,index,length)  (A0,D0,D1)
-$009C  -156 ConcatCList (sourceCList,destCList)  (A0,A1)
```

### *console.library*

```
-$002A  -42  CDInputHandler (events,device) (A0,A1)
-$0030  -48  RawKeyConvert (events,buffer,length, keyMap) (A0,A1,D1,A2)
```

## *diskfont.library*

```
-$001E  -30  OpenDiskFont (textAttr) (A0)
-$0024  -36  AvailFonts (buffer,bufBytes,flags)  (A0,D0,D1)
```

## *dos.library*

```
-$001E  -30   Open (name,accessMode) (D1,D2)
-$0024  -36   Close (file) (D1)
-$002A  -42   Read (file,buffer,length) (D1,D2,D3)
-$0030  -48   Write (file,buffer,length) (D1,D2,D3)
-$0036  -54   Input ()
-$003C  -60   Output ()
-$0042  -66   Seek (file,position,offset) (D1,D2,D3)
-$0048  -72   DeleteFile (name) (D1)
-$004E  -78   Rename (oldName,newName) (D1,D2)
-$0054  -84   Lock (name,type) (D1,D2)
-$005A  -90   UnLock (lock) (D1)
-$0060  -96   DupLock (lock) (D1)
-$0066  -102  Examine (lock,fileInfoBlock) (D1,D2)
-$006C  -108  ExNext (lock,fileInfoBlock) (D1,D2)
-$0072  -114  Info (lock,parameterBlock) (D1,D2)
-$0078  -120  CreateDir (name) (D1)
-$007E  -126  CurrentDir (lock) (D1)
-$0084  -132  IoErr ()
-$008A  -138  CreateProc (name,pri,segList,stackSize) (D1,D2,D3,D4)
-$0090  -144  Exit (returnCode) (D1)
-$0096  -150  LoadSeg (fileName) (D1)
-$009C  -156  UnLoadSeg (segment) (D1)
-$00A2  -162  GetPacket (wait) (D1)
-$00A8  -168  QueuePacket (packet) (D1)
-$00AE  -174  DeviceProc (name) (D1)
-$00B4  -180  SetComment (name,comment) (D1,D2)
-$00BA  -186  SetProtection (name,mask) (D1,D2)
-$00C0  -192  DateStamp (date) (D1)
-$00C6  -198  Delay (timeout) (D1)
-$00CC  -204  WaitForChar (file,timeout) (D1,D2)
-$00D2  -210  ParentDir (lock) (D1)
-$00D8  -216  IsInteractive (file) (D1)
-$00DE  -222  Execute (string,file,file) (D1,D2,D3)
```

## *exec.library*

```
-$001E  -30  Supervisor ()
-$0024  -36  ExitIntr ()
-$002A  -42  Schedule ()
-$0030  -48  Reschedule ()
-$0036  -54  Switch ()
-$003C  -60  Dispatch ()
-$0042  -66  Exception ()
-$0048  -72  InitCode (startClass,version) (D0,D1)
-$004E  -78  InitStruct (initTable,memory,size)  (A1,A2,D0)
-$0054  -84  MakeLibrary (funcInit,structInit,libInit,dataSize,
             nodeSize) (A0,A1,A2,D0,D1)
-$005A  -90  MakeFunctions (target,functionArray,funcDispBase)
```

```
          (A0,A1,A2)
-$0060  -96  FindResident (name)(A1)
-$0066 -102  InitResident (resident,segList)(A1,D1)
-$006C -108  Alert (alertNum,parameters)(D7,A5)
-$0072 -114  Debug ()
-$0078 -120  Disable ()
-$007E -126  Enable ()
-$0084 -132  Forbid ()
-$008A -138  Permit ()
-$0090 -144  SetSR (newSR,mask)(D0,D1)
-$0096 -150  SuperState ()
-$009C -156  UserState (sysStack)(D0)
-$00A2 -162  SetIntVector (intNumber,interrupt)(D0,A1)
-$00A8 -168  AddIntServer (intNumber,interrupt)(D0,A1)
-$00AE -174  RemIntServer (intNumber,interrupt)(D0,A1)
-$00B4 -180  Cause (interrupt)(A1)
-$00BA -186  Allocate (freeList,byteSize)(A0,D0)
-$00C0 -192  Deallocate (freeList,memoryBlock,byteSize)(A0,A1,D0)
-$00C6 -198  AllocMem (byteSize,requirements)(D0,D1)
-$00CC -204  AllocAbs (byteSize,location)(D0,A1)
-$00D2 -210  FreeMem (memoryBlock,byteSize)(A1,D0)
-$00D8 -216  AvailMem (requirements)(D1)
-$00DE -222  AllocEntry (entry)(A0)
-$00E4 -228  FreeEntry (entry)(A0)
-$00EA -234  Insert (list,node,pred)(A0,A1,A2)
-$00F0 -240  AddHead (list,node)(A0,A1)
-$00F6 -246  AddTail (list,node)(A0,A1)
-$00FC -252  Remove (node)(A1)
-$0102 -258  RemHead (list)(A0)
-$0108 -264  RemTail (list)(A0)
-$010E -270  Enqueue (list,node)(A0,A1)
-$0114 -276  FindName (list,name)(A0,A1)
-$011A -282  AddTask (task,initPC,finalPC)(A1,A2,A3)
-$0120 -288  RemTask (task)(A1)
-$0126 -294  FindTask (name)(A1)
-$012C -300  SetTaskPri (task,priority)(A1,D0)
-$0132 -306  SetSignal (newSignals,signalSet)(D0,D1)
-$0138 -312  SetExcept (newSignals,signalSet)(D0,D1)
-$013E -318  Wait (signalSet)(D0)
-$0144 -324  Signal (task,signalSet)(A1,D0)
-$014A -330  AllocSignal (signalNum)(D0)
-$0150 -336  FreeSignal (signalNum)(D0)
-$0156 -342  AllocTrap (trapNum)(D0)
-$015C -348  FreeTrap (trapNum)(D0)
-$0162 -354  AddPort (port)(A1)
-$0168 -360  RemPort (port)(A1)
-$016E -366  PutMsg (port,message)(A0,A1)
-$0174 -372  GetMsg (port)(A0)
-$017A -378  ReplyMsg (message)(A1)
-$0180 -384  WaitPort (port)(A0)
-$0186 -390  FindPort (name)(A1)
-$018C -396  AddLibrary (library)(A1)
-$0192 -402  RemLibrary (library)(A1)
-$0198 -408  OldOpenLibrary (libName)(A1)
-$019E -414  CloseLibrary (library)(A1)
-$01A4 -420  SetFunction (library,funcOffset,funcEntry)(A1,A0,D0)
```

```
-$01AA  -426  SumLibrary (library)(A1)
-$01B0  -432  AddDevice (device)(A1)
-$01B6  -438  RemDevice (device)(A1)
-$01BC  -444  OpenDevice (devName,unit,ioRequest,flags)(A0,D0,A1,D1)
-$01C2  -450  CloseDevice (ioRequest)(A1)
-$01C8  -456  DoIO (ioRequest)(A1)
-$01CE  -462  SendIO (ioRequest)(A1)
-$01D4  -468  CheckIO (ioRequest)(A1)
-$01DA  -474  WaitIO (ioRequest)(A1)
-$01E0  -480  AbortIO (ioRequest)(A1)
-$01E6  -486  AddRescource (rescource)(A1)
-$01EC  -492  RemRescource (rescource)(A1)
-$01F2  -498  OpenRescource (resName,version)(A1,D0)
-$01F8  -504  RawIOInit ()
-$01FE  -510  RawMayGetChar ()
-$0204  -516  RawPutChar (char)(D0)
-$020A  -522  RawDoFmt ()(A0,A1,A2,A3)
-$0210  -528  GetCC ()
-$0216  -534  TypeOfMem (address)(A1)
-$021C  -540  Procedure (semaport,bidMsg)(A0,A1)
-$0222  -546  Vacate (semaport)(A0)
-$0228  -552  OpenLibrary (libName,version)(A1,D0)
```

### *graphics.library*

```
-$001E   -30  BltBitMap (srcBitMap,srcX,srcY,destBitMap,destX,destY,
              sizeX,sizeY,minterm,mask,tempA)(A0,D0,D1,A1,D2,D3,D4,
              D5,D6,D7,A2)
-$0024   -36  BltTemplate (source,srcX,srcMod,destRastPort,destX,destY,
              sizeX,sizeY)(A0,D0,D1,A1,D2,D3,D4,D5)
-$002A   -42  ClearEOL (rastPort)(A1)
-$0030   -48  ClearScreen (rastPort)(A1)
-$0036   -54  TextLength (RastPort,string,count)(A1,A0,D0)
-$003C   -60  Text (RastPort,String,count)(A1,A0,D0)
-$0042   -66  SetFont (RAstPortID,textFont)(A1,A0)
-$0048   -72  OpenFont (textAttr)(A0)
-$004E   -78  CloseFont (textFont)(A1)
-$0054   -84  AskSoftStyle (rastPort)(A1)
-$005A   -90  SetSoftStyle (rastPort,style,enable)(A1,D0,D1)
-$0060   -96  AddBob (bob,rastPort)(A0,A1)
-$0066  -102  AddVSprite (vSprite,rastPort)(A0,A1)
-$006C  -108  DoCollision (rastPort)(A1)
-$0072  -114  DrawGList (rastPort,viewPort)(A1,A0)
-$0078  -120  InitGels (dummyHead,dummyTail,GelsInfo)(A0,A1,A2)
-$007E  -126  InitMasks (vSprite)(A0)
-$0084  -132  RemIBob (bob,rastPort,viewPort)(A0,A1,A2)
-$008A  -138  RemVSprite (vSprite)(A0)
-$0090  -144  SetCollision (type,routine,gelsInfo)(D0,A0,A1)
-$0096  -150  SortGList (rastPort)(A1)
-$009C  -156  AddAnimObj (obj,animationKey,rastPort)(A0,A1,A2)
-$00A2  -162  Animate (animationKey,rastPort)(A0,A1)
-$00A8  -168  GetGBuffers (animationObj,rastPort,doubleBuffer)
              (A0,A1,D0)
-$00AE  -174  InitGMasks (animationObj)(A0)
-$00B4  -180  GelsFuncE ()
-$00BA  -186  GelsFuncF ()
```

```
-$00C0 -192   LoadRGB4 (viewPort,colors,count) (A0,A1,D0)
-$00C6 -198   InitRastPort (rastPort) (A1)
-$00CC -204   InitVPort (viewPort) (A0)
-$00D2 -210   MrgCop (view) (A1)
-$00D8 -216   MakeVPort (view,viewPort) (A0,A1)
-$00DE -222   LoadView (view) (A1)
-$00E4 -228   WaitBlit ()
-$00EA -234   SetRast (rastPort,color) (A1,D0)
-$00F0 -240   Move (rastPort,x,y) (A1,D0,D1)
-$00F6 -246   Draw (rastPort,x,y) (A1,D0,D1)
-$00FC -252   AreaMove (rastPort,x,y) (A1,D0,D1)
-$0102 -258   AreaDraw (rastPort,x,y) (A1,D0,D1)
-$0108 -264   AreaEnd (rastPort) (A1)
-$010E -270   WaitTOF ()
-$0114 -276   QBlit (blit) (A1)
-$011A -282   InitArea (areaInfo,vectorTable,vectorTableSize) (A0,A1,D0)
-$0120 -288   SetRGB4 (viewPort,index,r,g,b) (A0,D0,D1,D2,D3)
-$0126 -294   QBSBlit (blit) (A1)
-$012C -300   BltClear (memory,size,flags) (A1,D0,D1)
-$0132 -306   RectFill (rastPort,xl,yl,xu,yu) (A1,D0,D1,D2,D3)
-$0138 -312   BltPattern (rastPort,ras,xl,yl,maxX,maxY,fillBytes)
              (A1,A0,D0,D1,D2,D3,D4)
-$013E -318   ReadPixel (rastPort,x,y) (A1,D0,D1)
-$0144 -324   WritePixel (rastPort,x,y) (A1,D0,D1)
-$014A -330   Flood (rastPort,mode,x,y) (A1,D2,D0,D1)
-$0150 -336   PolyDraw (rastPort,count,polyTable) (A1,D0,A0)
-$0156 -342   SetAPen (rastPort,pen) (A1,D0)
-$015C -348   SetBPen (rastPort,pen) (A1,D0)
-$0162 -354   SetDrMd (rastPort,drawMode) (A1,D0)
-$0168 -360   InitView (view) (A1)
-$016E -366   CBump (copperList) (A1)
-$0174 -372   CMove (copperList,destination,data) (A1,D0,D1)
-$017A -378   CWait (copperList,x,y) (A1,D0,D1)
-$0180 -384   VBeamPos ()
-$0186 -390   InitBitMap (bitMap,depth,width,heigth) (A0,D0,D1,D2)
-$018C -396   ScrollRaster (rastPort,dX,dY,minx,miny,maxx,maxy) (A1,D0,
              D1,D2,D3,D4,D5)
-$0192 -402   WaitBOVP (viewPort) (A0)
-$0198 -408   GetSprite (simpleSprite,num) (A0,D0)
-$019E -414   FreeSprite (num) (D0)
-$01A4 -420   ChangeSprite (vp,simpleSprite,data) (A0,A1,A2)
-$01AA -426   MoveSprite (viewPort,simpleSprite,x,y) (A0,A1,D0,D1)
-$01B0 -432   LockLayerRom (layer) (A5)
-$01B6 -438   UnlockLayerRom (layer) (A5)
-$01BC -444   SyncSBitMap (1) (A0)
-$01C2 -450   CopySBitMap (11,12) (A0,A1)
-$01C8 -456   OwnBlitter ()
-$01CE -462   DisownBlitter ()
-$01D4 -468   InitTmpRas (tmpras,buff,size) (A0,A1,D0)
-$01DA -474   AskFont (rastPort,textAttr) (A1,A0)
-$01E0 -480   AddFont (textFont) (A1)
-$01E6 -486   RemFont (textFont) (A1)
-$01EC -492   AllocRaster (width,heigth) (D0,D1)
-$01F2 -498   FreeRaster (planeptr,width,heigth) (A0,D0,D1)
-$01F8 -504   AndRectRegion (rgn,rect) (A0,A1)
-$01FE -510   OrRectRegion (rgn,rect) (A0,A1)
```

```
-$0204 -516  NewRegion ()
-$020A -522  ** reserved **
-$0210 -528  ClearRegion (rgn) (A0)
-$0216 -534  DisposeRegion (rgn) (A0)
-$021C -540  FreeVPortCopLists (viewPort) (A0)
-$0222 -546  FreeCopList (coplist) (A0)
-$0228 -552  ClipBlit (srcrp,srcX,srcY,destrp,destX,destY,sizeX,
             sizeY,minterm) (A0,D0,D1,A1,D2,D3,D4,D5,D6)
-$022E -558  XorRectRegion (rgn,rect) (A0,A1)
-$0234 -564  FreeCprList (cprlist) (A0)
-$023A -570  GetColorMap (entries) (D0)
-$0240 -576  FreeColorMap (colormap) (A0)
-$0246 -582  GetRGB4 (colormap,entry) (A0,D0)
-$024C -588  ScrollVPort (vp) (A0)
-$0252 -594  UCopperListInit (copperlist,num) (A0,D0)
-$0258 -600  FreeGBuffers (animationObj,rastPort,
             doubleBuffer) (A0,A1,D0)
-$025E -606  BltBitMapRastPort (srcbm,srcx,srcy,destrp,destX,destY,
             sizeX,sizeY,minter) (A0,D0,D1,A1,D2,D3,D4,D5,D6)
```

## icon.library

```
-$001E  -30  GetWBObject (name) (A0)
-$0024  -36  PutWBObject (name,object) (A0,A1)
-$002A  -42  GetIcon (name,icon,freelist) (A0,A1,A2)
-$0030  -48  PutIcon (name,icon) (A0,A1)
-$0036  -54  FreeFreeList (freelist) (A0)
-$003C  -60  FreeWBObject (WBObject) (A0)
-$0042  -66  AllocWBObject ()
-$0048  -72  AddFreeList (freelist,mem,size) (A0,A1,A2)
-$004E  -78  GetDiskObject (name) (A0)
-$0054  -84  PutDiskObject (name,diskobj) (A0,A1)
-$005A  -90  FreeDiskObj (diskobj) (A0)
-$0060  -96  FindToolType (toolTypeArray,typeName) (A0,A1)
-$0066 -102  MatchToolValue (typeString,value) (A0,A1)
-$006C -108  BumbRevision (newname,oldname) (A0,A1)
```

## intuition.library

```
-$001E  -30  OpenIntuition ()
-$0024  -36  Intuition (ievent) (A0)
-$002A  -42  AddGadget (AddPtr,Gadget,Position) (A0,A1,D0)
-$0030  -48  ClearDMRequest (Window) (A0)
-$0036  -54  ClearMenuStrip (Window) (A0)
-$003C  -60  ClearPointer (Window) (A0)
-$0042  -66  CloseScreen (Screen) (A0)
-$0048  -72  CloseWindow (Window) (A0)
-$004E  -78  CloseWorkBench ()
-$0054  -84  CurrentTime (Seconds,Micros) (A0,A1)
-$005A  -90  DisplayAlert (AlertNumber,String,Height) (D0,A0.D1)
-$0060  -96  DisplayBeep (Screen) (A0)
-$0066 -102  DoubleClick (sseconds,smicros,cseconds,cmicros)
             (D0,D1,D2,D3)
-$006C -108  DrawBorder (Rport,Border,LeftOffset,TopOffset)
             (A0,A1,D0,D1)
-$0072 -114  DrawImage (RPort,Image,LeftOffset,TopOffset) (A0,A1,D0,D1)
```

```
-$0078    -120    EndRequest (requester,window)(A0,A1)
-$007E    -126    GetDefPrefs (preferences,size)(A0,D0)
-$0084    -132    GetPrefs (preferences,size)(A0,D0)
-$008A    -138    InitRequester (req)(A0)
-$0090    -144    ItemAddress (MenuStrip,MenuNumber)(A0,D0)
-$0096    -150    ModifyIDCMP (Window,Flags)(A0,D0)
-$009C    -156    ModifyProp (Gadget,Ptr,Reg,Flags,HPos,VPos,HBody,VBody)
                     (A0,A1,A2,D0,D1,D2,D3,D4)
-$00A2    -162    MoveScreen (Screen,dx,dy)(A0,D0,D1)
-$00A8    -168    MoveWindow (Window,dx,dy)(A0,D0,D1)
-$00AE    -174    OffGadget (Gadget,Ptr,Req)(A0,A1,A2)
-$00B4    -180    OffMenu (Window,MenuNumber)(A0,D0)
-$00BA    -186    OnGadget (Gadget,Ptr,Req)(A0,A1,A2)
-$00C0    -192    OnMenu (Window,MenuNumber)(A0,D0)
-$00C6    -198    OpenScreen (OSArgs)(A0)
-$00CC    -204    OpenWindow (OWArgs)(A0)
-$00D2    -210    OpenWorkBench ()
-$00D8    -216    PrintIText (rp,itext,left,top)(A0,A1,D0,D1)
-$00DE    -222    RefreshGadgets (Gadgets,Ptr,Req)(A0,A1,A2)
-$00E4    -228    RemoveGadgets (RemPtr,Gadget)(A0,A1)
-$00EA    -234    ReportMouse (Window,Boolean)(A0,D0)
-$00F0    -240    Request (Requester,Window)(A0,A1)
-$00F6    -246    ScreenToBack (Screen)(A0)
-$00FC    -252    SCreenToFront (Screen)(A0)
-$0102    -258    SetDMRequest (Window,req)(A0,A1)
-$0108    -264    SetMenuStrip (Window,Menu)(A0,A1)
-$010E    -270    SetPointer (Window,Pointer,Height,Width,XOffset,YOffset)
                     (A0,A1,D0,D1,D2,D3)
-$0114    -276    SetWindowTitles (Window,windowTitle,screenTitle)
                     (A0,A1,A2)
-$011A    -282    ShowTitle (Screen,ShowIt)(A0,D0)
-$0120    -288    SizeWindow (Window,dx,dy)(A0,D0,D1)
-$0126    -294    ViewAddress ()
-$012C    -300    ViewPortAddress (Window)(A0)
-$0132    -306    WindowToBack (Window)(A0)
-$0138    -312    WindowToFront (Window)(A0)
-$013E    -318    WindowLimits (Window,minwidth,minheight,maxwidth,
                     maxheight)(A0,D0,D1,D2,D3)
-$0144    -324    SetPrefs (preferences,size,flag)(A0,D0,D1)
-$014A    -330    IntuiTextLength (itext)(A0)
-$0150    -336    WBenchToBack ()
-$0156    -342    WBenchToFront ()
-$015C    -348    AutoRequest (WIndow,Body,PText,NText,PFlag,NFlag,W,H)
                     (A0,A1,A2,A3,D0,D1,D2,D3)
-$0162    -354    BeginRefresh (Window)(A0)
-$0168    -360    BuildSysRequest (Window,Body,PosText,NegText,Flags,W,H)
                     (A0,A1,A2,A3,D0,D1,D2)
-$016E    -366    EndRefresh (Window,Complete)(A0,D0)
-$0174    -372    FreeSysRequest (Window)(A0)
-$017A    -378    MakeScreen (Screen)(A0)
-$0180    -384    RemakeDisplay ()
-$0186    -390    RethinkDisplay ()
-$018C    -396    AllocRemember (RememberKey,Size,Flags)(A0,D0,D1)
-$0192    -402    AlohaWorkbench (wbport)(A0)
-$0198    -408    FreeRemember (RememberKey,ReallyForget)(A0,D0)
-$019E    -414    LockIBase (dontknow)(D0)
```

```
        -$01A4   -420    UnlockIBase (IBLock) (A0)
```

## layers.library

```
        -$001E   -30     InitLayers (li) (A0)
        -$0024   -36     CreateUpfrontLayer  (li,bm,x0,y0,x1,y1,flags,bm2) (A0,A1,
                         D0,D1,D2,D3,D4,A2)
        -$002A   -42     CreateBehindLayer  (li,bm,x0,y0,x1,y1,flags,bm2) (A0,A1,D0,
                         D1,D2,D3,D4,A2)
        -$0030   -48     UpfrontLayer (li,layer) (A0,A1)
        -$0036   -54     BehindLayer (li,layer) (A0,A1)
        -$003C   -60     MoveLayer (li,layer,dx,dy) (A0,A1,D0,D1)
        -$0042   -66     SizeLayer (li,layer,dx,dy) (A0,A1,D0,D1)
        -$0048   -72     ScrollLayer (li,layer,dx,dy) (A0,A1,D0,D1)
        -$004E   -78     BeginUpdate (layer) (A0)
        -$0054   -84     EndUpdate (layer) (A0)
        -$005A   -90     DeleteLayer (li,layer) (A0,A1)
        -$0060   -96     LockLayer (li,layer) (A0,A1)
        -$0066   -102    UnlockLayer (li,layer) (A0,A1)
        -$006C   -108    LockLayers (li) (A0)
        -$0072   -114    UnlockLayers (li) (A0)
        -$0078   -120    LockLayerInfo (li) (A0)
        -$007E   -126    SwapBitsRastPortClipRect (rp,cr) (A0,A1)
        -$0084   -132    WhichLayer (li,x,y) (A0,D0,D1)
        -$008A   -138    UnlockLayerInfo (li) (A0)
        -$0090   -144    NewLayerInfo ()
        -$0096   -150    DisposeLayerInfo (li) (A0)
        -$009C   -156    FattenLayerInfo (li) (A0)
        -$00A2   -162    ThinLayerInfo (li) (A0)
        -$00A8   -168    MoveLayerInFrontOf (layer_to_move,layer_to_be_in_front_
                         of) (A0,A1)
```

## mathffp.library

```
        -$001E   -30     SPFix (float) (D0)
        -$0024   -36     SPFlt (integer) (D0)
        -$002A   -42     SPCmp (leftFloat,rightFloat) (D1,D0)
        -$0030   -48     SPTst (float) (D1)
        -$0036   -54     SPAbs (float) (D0)
        -$003C   -60     SPNeg (float) (D0)
        -$0042   -66     SPAdd (leftFloat,rightFloat) (D1,D0)
        -$0048   -72     SPSub (leftFloat,rightFloat) (D1,D0)
        -$004E   -78     SPMul (leftFloat,rightFloat) (D1,D0)
        -$0054   -84     SPDiv (leftFloat,rightFloat) (D1,D0)
```

## mathieeedoubbas.library

```
        -$001E  -30   IEEEDPFix (integer,integer) (D0,D1)
        -$0024  -36   IEEEDPFlt (integer) (D0)
        -$002A  -42   IEEEDPCmp (integer,integer,integer, integer) (D0,D1,D2,D3)
        -$0030  -48   IEEEDPTst (integer,integer) (D0,D1)
        -$0036  -54   IEEEDPAbs (integer,integer) (D0,D1)
        -$003C  -60   IEEEDPNeg (integer,integer) (D0,D1)
        -$0042  -66   IEEEDPAdd (integer,integer,integer, integer) (D0,D1,D2,D3)
        -$0048  -72   IEEEDPSub (integer,integer,integer, integer) (D0,D1,D2,D3)
```

```
    -$004E  -78  IEEEDPMul (integer,integer,integer, integer) (D0,D1,D2,D3)
    -$0054  -84  IEEEDPDiv (integer,integer,integer, integer) (D0,D1,D2,D3)
```

## mathtrans.library

```
    -$001E   -30  SPAtan (float) (D0)
    -$0024   -36  SPSin (float) (D0)
    -$002A   -42  SPCos (float) (D0)
    -$0030   -48  SPTan (float) (D0)
    -$0036   -54  SPSincos (leftFloat,rightFloat) (D1,D0)
    -$003C   -60  SPSinh (float) (D0)
    -$0042   -66  SPCosh (float) (D0)
    -$0048   -72  SPTanh (float) (D0)
    -$004E   -78  SPExp (float) (D0)
    -$0054   -84  SPLog (float) (D0)
    -$005A   -90  SPPow (leftFloat,rightFloat) (D1,D0)
    -$0060   -96  SPSqrt (float) (D0)
    -$0066  -102  SPTieee (float) (D0)
    -$006C  -108  SPFieee (float) (D0)
    -$0072  -114  SPAsin (float) (D0)
    -$0078  -120  SPAcos (float) (D0)
    -$007E  -126  SPLog10 (float) (D0)
```

## potgo.library

```
    -$0006   -6  AllocPotBits (bits) (D0)
    -$000C  -12  FreePotBits (bits) (D0)
    -$0012  -18  WritePotgo (word,mask) (D0,D1)
```

## timer.library

```
    -$002A  -42  AddTime (dest,src) (A0,A1)
    -$0030  -48  SubTime (dest,src) (A0,A1)
    -$0036  -54  CmpTime (dest,src) (A0,A1)
```

## translator.library

```
    -$001E  -30  Translate (inputString,inputLength, output Buffer,
         bufferSize) (A0,D0,A1,D1)
```

# Index

# Optional Diskette

For your convenience, the program listings contained in this book are available on an Amiga formatted floppy disk. You should order the diskette if you want to use the programs, but don't want to type them in from the listings in the book.

All programs on the diskette have been fully tested. You can change the programs for your particular needs. The diskette is available for $14.95 plus $2.00 ($5.00 foreign) for postage and handling.

When ordering, please give your name and shipping address. Enclose a check, money order or credit card information. Mail your order to:

5370 52nd Street SE
Grand Rapids, MI 49508

Or for fast service (credit card orders only)
call **616/698-0330** (orders within Michigan)
or **800-451-4319** (orders outside Michigan)

# New Software

The *Ideal* AMIGA wordprocessor

# TextPro
## AMIGA

TextPro AMIGA upholds the true spirit of the AMIGA: it's powerful, it has a surprising number of "extra" features, but it's also very easy to use. **TextPro** AMIGA—the Ideal AMIGA word processor that proves just how easy word processing can be. You can write your first documents immediately, with a minimum of learning—without even reading the manual. But **TextPro** AMIGA is much more than a beginner's package. Ultra-fast onscreen formatting, graphic merge capabilities, automatic hyphenation and many more features make **TextPro** AMIGA ideal for the professional user as well. **TextPro** AMIGA features:

- High-speed text input and editing
- Functions accessible through menus or shortcut keys
- Fast onscreen formatting
- Automatic hyphenation
- Versatile function key assignment
- Save any section of an AMIGA screen & print as text
- Loading and saving through the RS-232 interface
- Multiple tab settings
- Accepts IFF format graphics in texts
- Extremely flexible printer adaptations. Printer drivers for most popular dot-matrix printers included
- Includes thorough manual
- Not copy protected

**TextPro** AMIGA sets a new standard for word processing packages in its price range. So easy to use and modestly priced that any AMIGA owner can use it—so packed with advanced features, you can't pass it up.

**Suggested retail price:** **$79.95**

More than word processing...

# BeckerText
## AMIGA

This is one program for <u>serious</u> AMIGA owners. **BeckerText Amiga** is more than a word processor. It has all the features of **TextPro** AMIGA, but it also has features that you might not expect:

- Fast WYSIWYG formatting
- Calculations within a text—like having a spreadsheet program anytime you want it
- Templates for calculations in columns
- Line spacing options
- Auto-hyphenation and Auto-indexing
- Multiple-column printing, up to 5 columns on a single page
- Online dictionary checks spelling in text as it's written
- Spell checker for interactive proofing of documents
- Up to 999 characters per line (with scrolling)
- Many more features for the professional

**BeckerText** AMIGA is a vital addition for C programmers—it's an extremely flexible C editor. Whether you're deleting, adding or duplicating a block of C source-code, **BeckerText** AMIGA does it all, automatically. And the online dictionary acts as a C syntax checker and finds syntax errors in a flash.

**BeckerText** AMIGA. When you need more from your word processor than just word processing.

Suggested retail price: **$150.00**

Imagine the <u>perfect</u> database

# DataRetrieve
## AMIGA

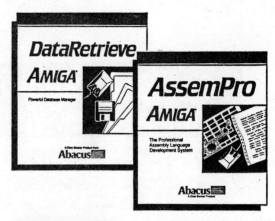

Imagine, for a moment, what the perfect database for your AMIGA would have. You'd want power and speed, for quick access to your information. An unlimited amount of storage space. And you'd want it easy to use—no baffling commands or file structures—with a graphic interface that does your AMIGA justice.

Enter **DataRetrieve** AMIGA. It's unlike any other database you can buy. Powerful, feature-packed, with the capacity for any business or personal application—mailing lists, inventory, billing, etc. Yet it's so simple to use, it's startling. **DataRetrieve** AMIGA's drop-down menus help you to define files quickly. Then you conveniently enter information using on-screen templates. **DataRetrieve** AMIGA takes advantage of the Amiga's multi-tasking capability for *optimum* processing speed.

**DataRetrieve** AMIGA features:

- Open eight files simultaneously
- Password protection
- Edit files in memory
- Maximum of 80 index fields with variable precision (1-999 characters)
- Convenient search/select criteria (range, AND / OR comparisons)
- Text, date, time, numeric and selection fields, IFF file reading capability
- Exchange data with other software packages (for form letters, mailing lists, etc.)
- Control operations with keyboard or mouse
- Adjustable screen masks, up to 5000 x 5000 pixels
- Insert graphic elements into screen masks (e.g., rectangles, circles, lines, patterns, etc.)
- Screen masks support different text styles and sizes
- Multiple text fields with word make-up and formatting capabilities
- Integrated printer masks and list editor.
- Maximum filesize 2 billion characters
- Maximum data record size 64,000 characters
- Maximum data set 2 billion characters
- Unlimited number of data fields
- Maximum field size 32,000 characters

**DataRetrieve** AMIGA —it'll handle your data with the speed and easy operation that you've come to expect from Abacus products for the AMIGA.

Suggested retail price: **$79.95**

Not just for the experts

# AssemPro
## AMIGA

AssemPro AMIGA lets every Amiga owner enjoy the benefits of fast machine language programming.

Because machine language programming isn't just for 68000 experts. **AssemPro** AMIGA is easily learned and user-friendly—it uses Amiga menus for simplicity. But **AssemPro** AMIGA boasts a long list of professional features that eliminate the tedium and repetition of M/L programming. **AssemPro** AMIGA is the complete developer's package for writing of 68000 machine language on the Amiga, complete with editor, debugger, disassembler and reassembler. **AssemPro** AMIGA is the perfect introduction to machine langage development and programming. And it's even got what you 68000 experts need.

**AssemPro** AMIGA features:

- Written completely in machine language, for ultra-fast operation
- Integrated editor, debugger, disassembler, reassembler
- Large operating system library
- Runs under CLI and Workbench
- Produces either PC-relocatable or absolute code
- Macros possible for nearly any parameter (of different types)
- Error search function
- Cross-reference list
- Menu-controlled conditional and repeated assembly
- Full 32-bit arithmetic
- Debugger with 68020 single-step emulation
- Runs on any AMIGA with 512K and Kickstart 1.2.

Suggested retail price: **$99.95**

# How to Order

**Abacus** 5370 52nd Street SE Grand Rapids, MI 49508

All of our Amiga products–application and language software, and our Amiga Reference Library–are available at more than 2000 dealers in the U.S. and Canada. To find out the location of the Abacus dealer nearest you, call:

## Toll Free 1-800-451-4319

8:30 am-8:00 pm Eastern Standard Time

Or order from Abacus directly by phone with your credit card. We accept Mastercard, Visa and American Express.

Every one of our software packages is backed by the **Abacus 30-Day Guarantee**—if for any reason you're not satisfied by the software purchased directly from us, simply return the product for a full refund of the purchase price.

### Order Blank

Name:

Address:

City    State    Zip    Country

Phone: /

| Qty | Name of product | Price |
|-----|-----------------|-------|
|     |                 |       |
|     |                 |       |
|     | Mich. residents add 4% sales tax | |
|     | Shipping/Handling charge (Foreign Orders $12 per item) | |
|     | Check/Money order  TOTAL enclosed | |

Credit Card#

Expiration date

**Send your completed order blank to:**

Abacus Software, Inc.
5370 52nd St. S.E.
Grand Rapids, MI 49508

**Your order will be shipped within 24 hours of our receiving it**

VISA

MasterCard

AMERICAN EXPRESS Card

**For extra-fast 24-hour shipment service, order by phone with your credit card**